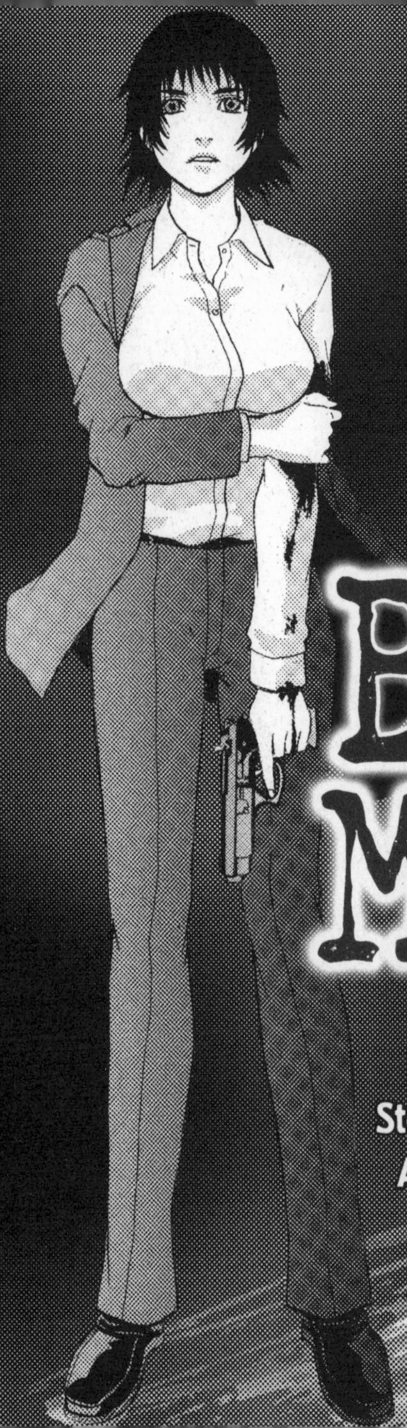

BLOODY MONDAY

VOLUME 4

Story by Ryou Ryumon
Art by Kouji Megumi

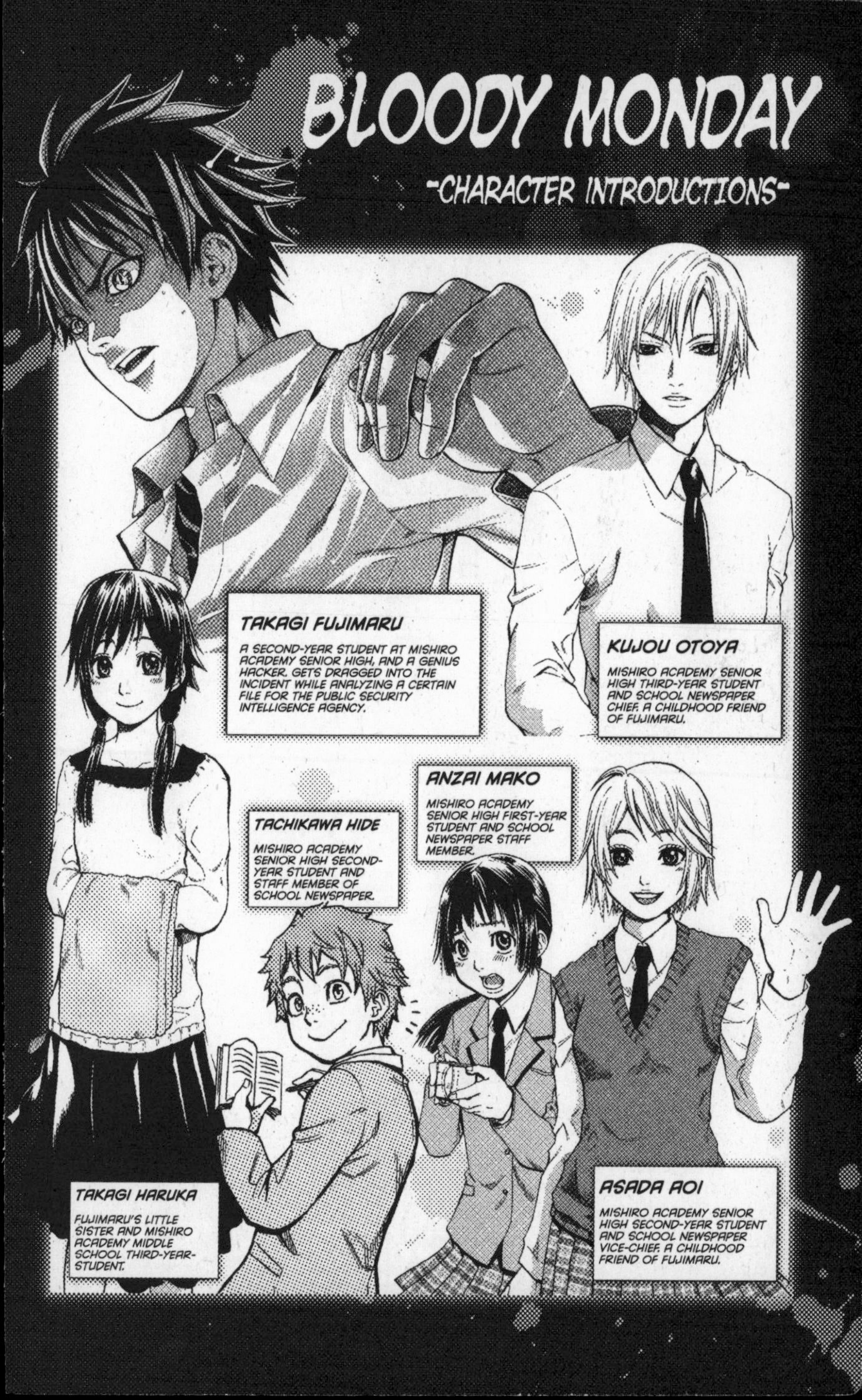
BLOODY MONDAY
-CHARACTER INTRODUCTIONS-
KUJOU OTOYA
MISHIRO ACADEMY SENIOR HIGH THIRD-YEAR STUDENT AND SCHOOL NEWSPAPER CHIEF. A CHILDHOOD FRIEND OF FUJIMARU.
TAKAGI FUJIMARU
A SECOND-YEAR STUDENT AT MISHIRO ACADEMY SENIOR HIGH, AND A GENIUS HACKER. GETS DRAGGED INTO THE INCIDENT WHILE ANALYZING A CERTAIN FILE FOR THE PUBLIC SECURITY INTELLIGENCE AGENCY.
ANZAI MAKO
MISHIRO ACADEMY SENIOR HIGH FIRST-YEAR STUDENT AND SCHOOL NEWSPAPER STAFF MEMBER.
TACHIKAWA HIDE
MISHIRO ACADEMY SENIOR HIGH SECOND-YEAR STUDENT AND STAFF MEMBER OF SCHOOL NEWSPAPER.
ASADA AOI
MISHIRO ACADEMY SENIOR HIGH SECOND-YEAR STUDENT AND SCHOOL NEWSPAPER VICE-CHIEF. A CHILDHOOD FRIEND OF FUJIMARU.
TAKAGI HARUKA
FUJIMARU'S LITTLE SISTER AND MISHIRO ACADEMY MIDDLE SCHOOL THIRD-YEAR-STUDENT.

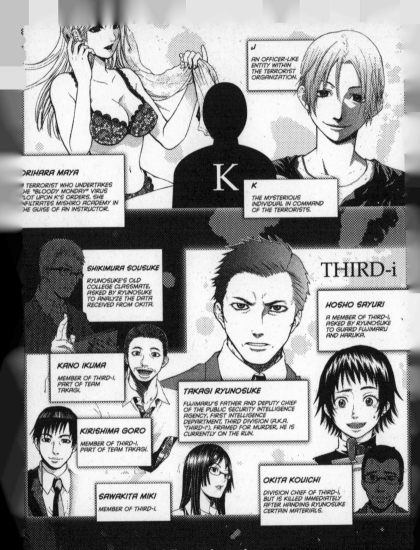

J
AN OFFICER-LIKE ENTITY WITHIN THE TERRORIST ORGANIZATION.
K
K
THE MYSTERIOUS INDIVIDUAL IN COMMAND OF THE TERRORISTS.
RIHARA MAYA
TERRORIST WHO UNDERTAKES HE "BLOODY MONDAY" VIRUS LOT UPON K'S ORDERS. SHE NFILTRATES MISHIRO ACADEMY IN HE GUISE OF AN INSTRUCTOR.
THIRD-i
HOSHO SAYURI
A MEMBER OF THIRD-I, ASKED BY RYUNOSUKE TO GUARD FUJIMARU AND HARUKA.
SHIKIMURA SOUSUKE
RYUNOSUKE'S OLD COLLEGE CLASSMATE, ASKED BY RYUNOSUKE TO ANALYZE THE DATA RECEIVED FROM OKITA.
TAKAGI RYUNOSUKE
FUJIMARU'S FATHER AND DEPUTY CHIEF OF THE PUBLIC SECURITY INTELLIGENCE AGENCY, FIRST INTELLIGENCE DEPARTMENT, THIRD DIVISION (A.K.A. 'THIRD-I'). FRAMED FOR MURDER, HE IS CURRENTLY ON THE RUN.
KANO IKUMA
MEMBER OF THIRD-I. PART OF TEAM TAKAGI.
KIRISHIMA GORO
MEMBER OF THIRD-I. PART OF TEAM TAKAGI.
OKITA KOUICHI
DIVISION CHIEF OF THIRD-I, BUT IS KILLED IMMEDIATELY AFTER HANDING RYUNOSUKE CERTAIN MATERIALS.
SAWAKITA MIKI
MEMBER OF THIRD-I.

Summary of the story through the previous volume:

Fujimaru finds himself caught up in a virus-based bio-terrorist plot called "Bloody Monday" that is being orchestrated by the mysterious individual 'K.' Thanks to Otoya's advice, Fujimaru is alerted to Maya's true identity, confronts her in a face-to-face showdown, and manages to detain her. THIRD-i takes Maya into custody and interrogates her in order to obtain intel on the terror plot. Meanwhile, Fujimaru, upon decoding the two files Ryunosuke had handed to him to elucidate the full picture of the plot, notices a commonality between the current plot and "a certain incident from two years ago"...!!

Contents

File 24 Springing the Prophet

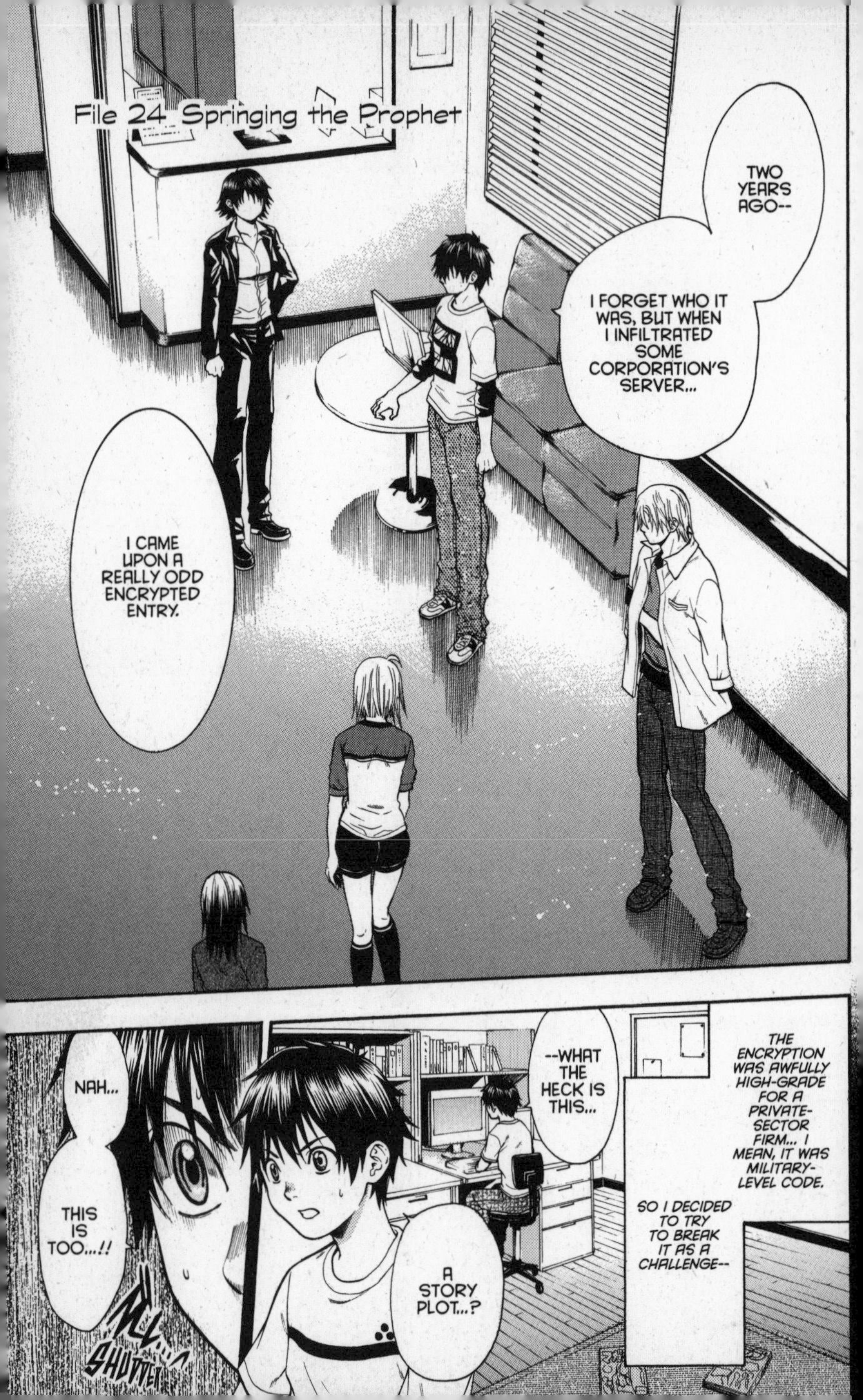
TWO YEARS AGO--
I FORGET WHO IT WAS, BUT WHEN I INFILTRATED SOME CORPORATION'S SERVER...
I CAME UPON A REALLY ODD ENCRYPTED ENTRY.
THE ENCRYPTION WAS AWFULLY HIGH-GRADE FOR A PRIVATE-SECTOR FIRM... I MEAN, IT WAS MILITARY-LEVEL CODE.
SO I DECIDED TO TRY TO BREAK IT AS A CHALLENGE--
--WHAT THE HECK IS THIS...
A STORY PLOT...?
NAH...
THIS IS TOO...!!

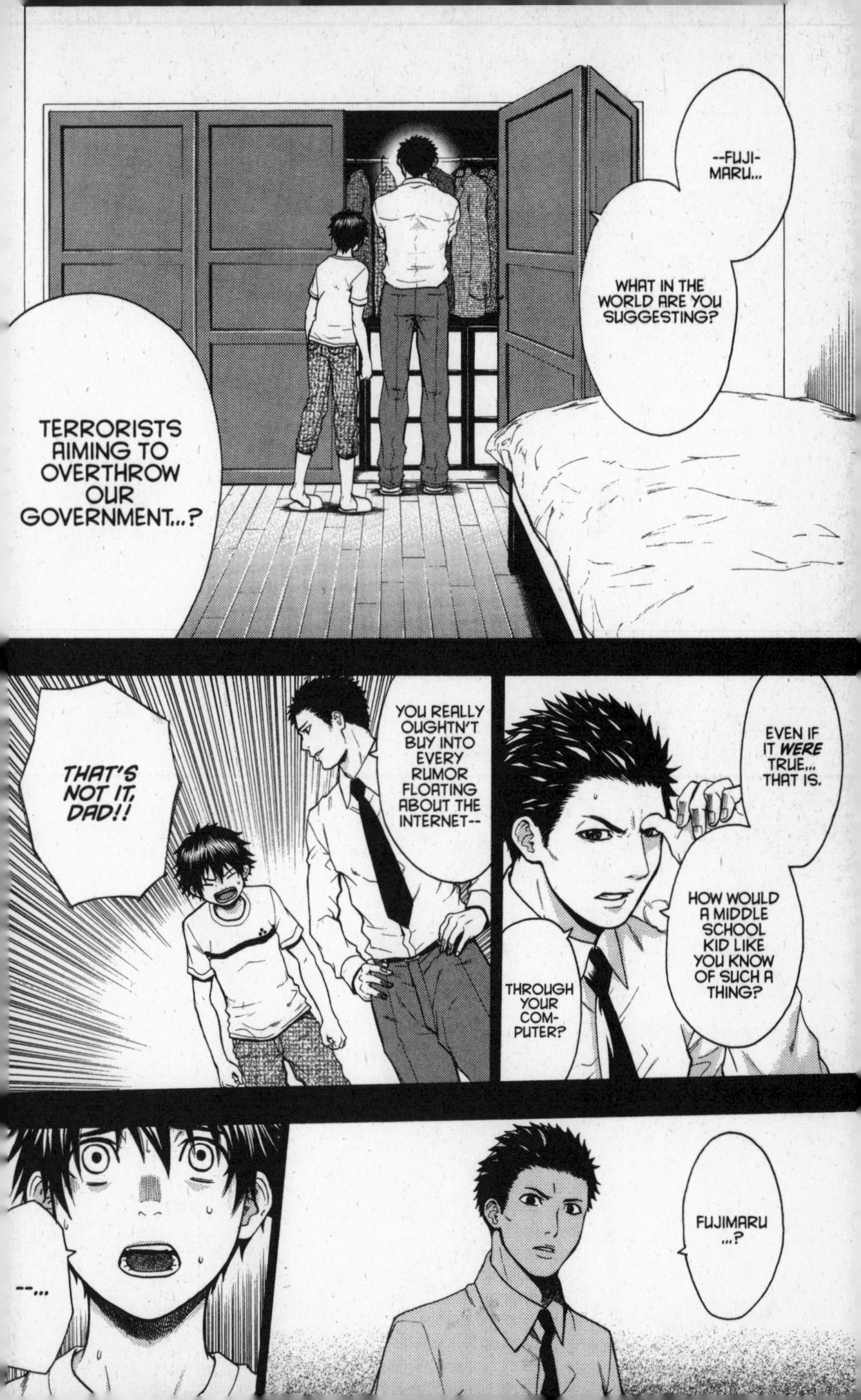
--FUJI-MARU...
WHAT IN THE WORLD ARE YOU SUGGESTING?
TERRORISTS AIMING TO OVERTHROW OUR GOVERNMENT...?
EVEN IF IT *WERE* TRUE... THAT IS.
HOW WOULD A MIDDLE SCHOOL KID LIKE YOU KNOW OF SUCH A THING?
THROUGH YOUR COM-PUTER?
YOU REALLY OUGHTN'T BUY INTO EVERY RUMOR FLOATING ABOUT THE INTERNET--
THAT'S NOT IT, DAD!!
FUJIMARU ...?
--...

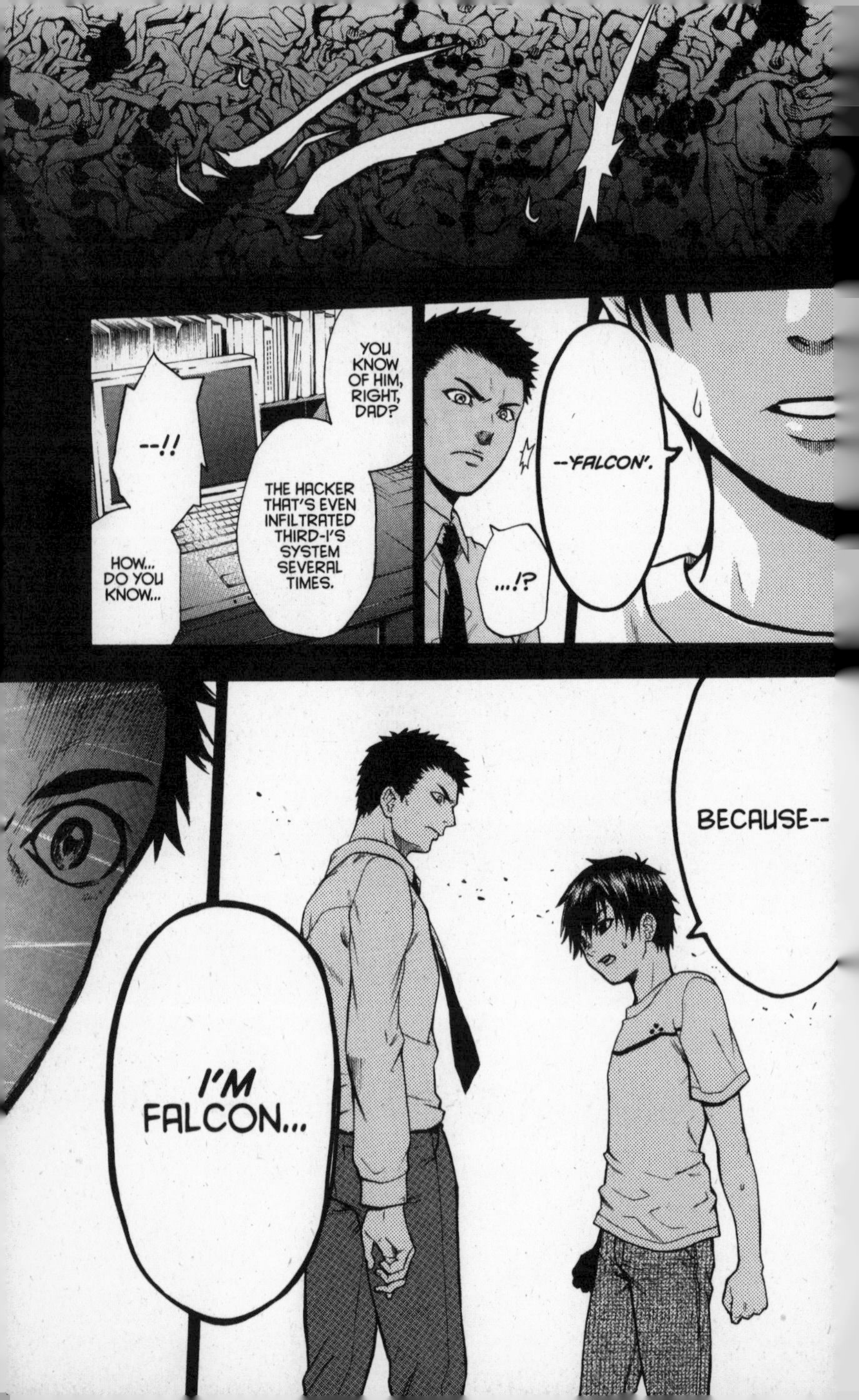
--'FALCON'.
...!?
YOU KNOW OF HIM, RIGHT, DAD?
THE HACKER THAT'S EVEN INFILTRATED THIRD-I'S SYSTEM SEVERAL TIMES.
--!!
HOW... DO YOU KNOW...
BECAUSE--
I'M FALCON...

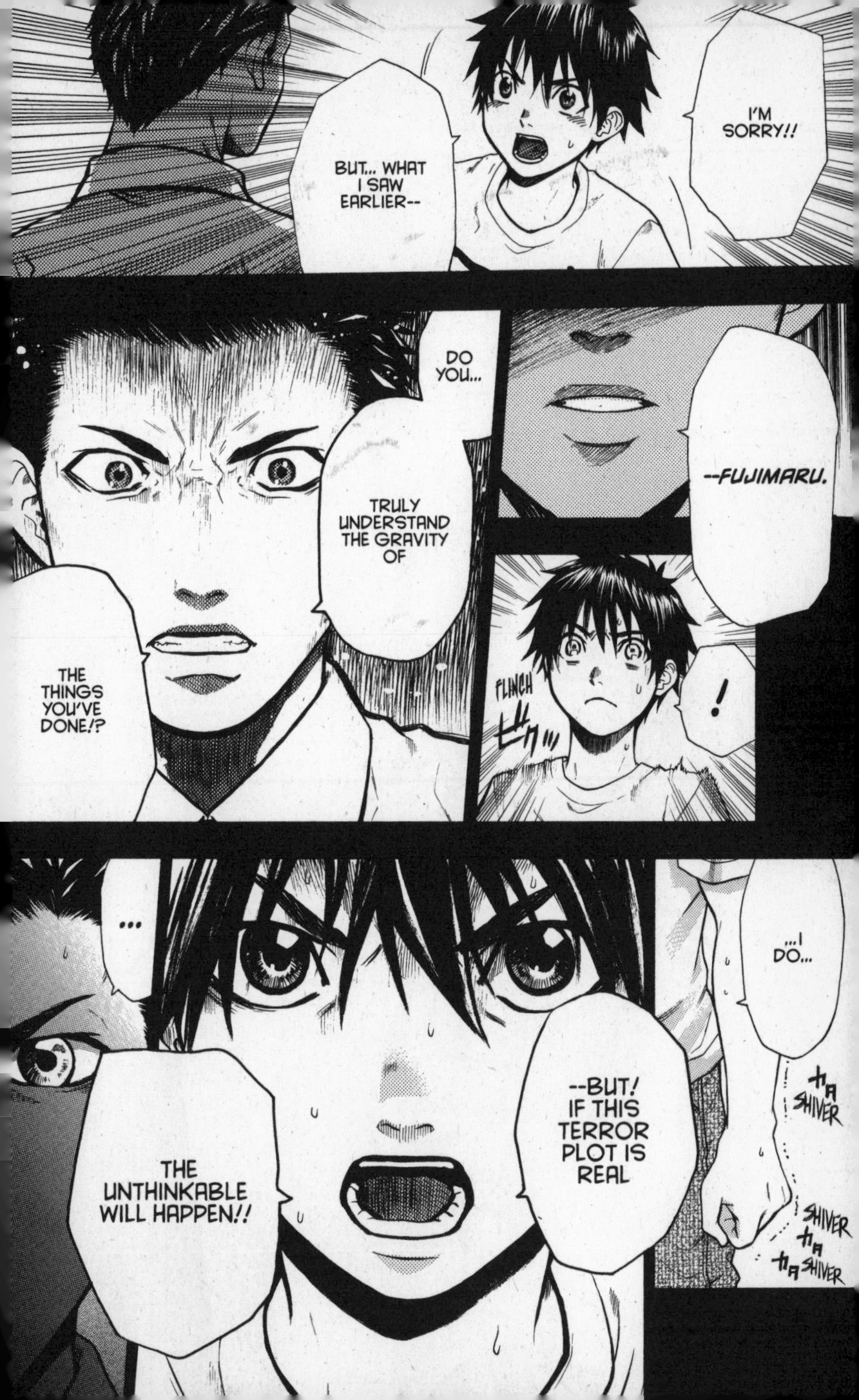
I'M SORRY!!
BUT... WHAT I SAW EARLIER--
DO YOU...
TRULY UNDERSTAND THE GRAVITY OF
THE THINGS YOU'VE DONE!?
--FUJIMARU.
!
FLINCH
...I DO...
SHIVER
SHIVER
SHIVER
--BUT! IF THIS TERROR PLOT IS REAL
...
THE UNTHINKABLE WILL HAPPEN!!

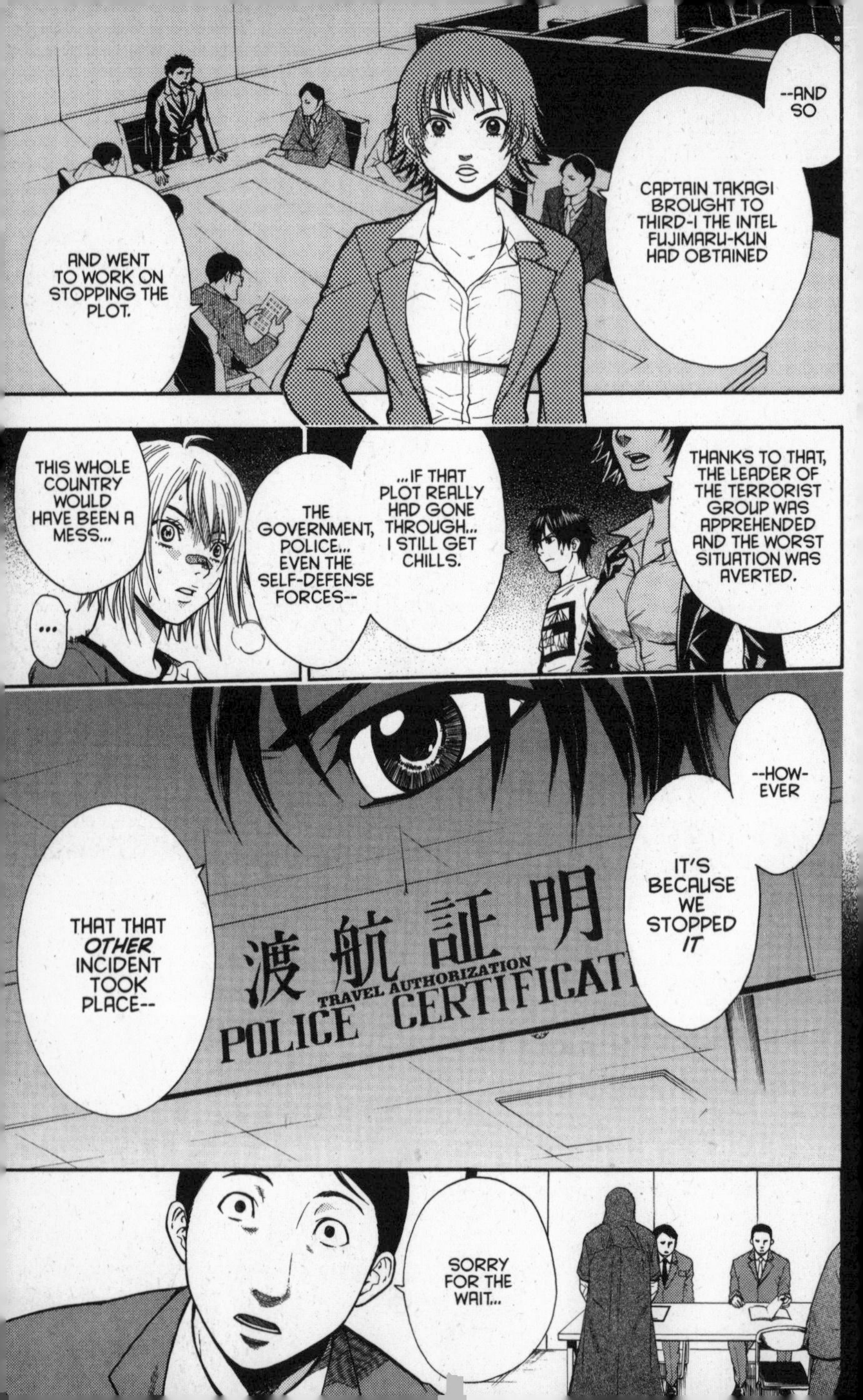
--AND SO
CAPTAIN TAKAGI BROUGHT TO THIRD-I THE INTEL FUJIMARU-KUN HAD OBTAINED
AND WENT TO WORK ON STOPPING THE PLOT.
THANKS TO THAT, THE LEADER OF THE TERRORIST GROUP WAS APPREHENDED AND THE WORST SITUATION WAS AVERTED.
...IF THAT PLOT REALLY HAD GONE THROUGH... I STILL GET CHILLS.
THE GOVERNMENT, POLICE... EVEN THE SELF-DEFENSE FORCES--
THIS WHOLE COUNTRY WOULD HAVE BEEN A MESS...
...
--HOW-EVER
IT'S BECAUSE WE STOPPED *IT*
THAT THAT *OTHER* INCIDENT TOOK PLACE--
渡航証明
TRAVEL AUTHORIZATION
POLICE CERTIFICAT
SORRY FOR THE WAIT...

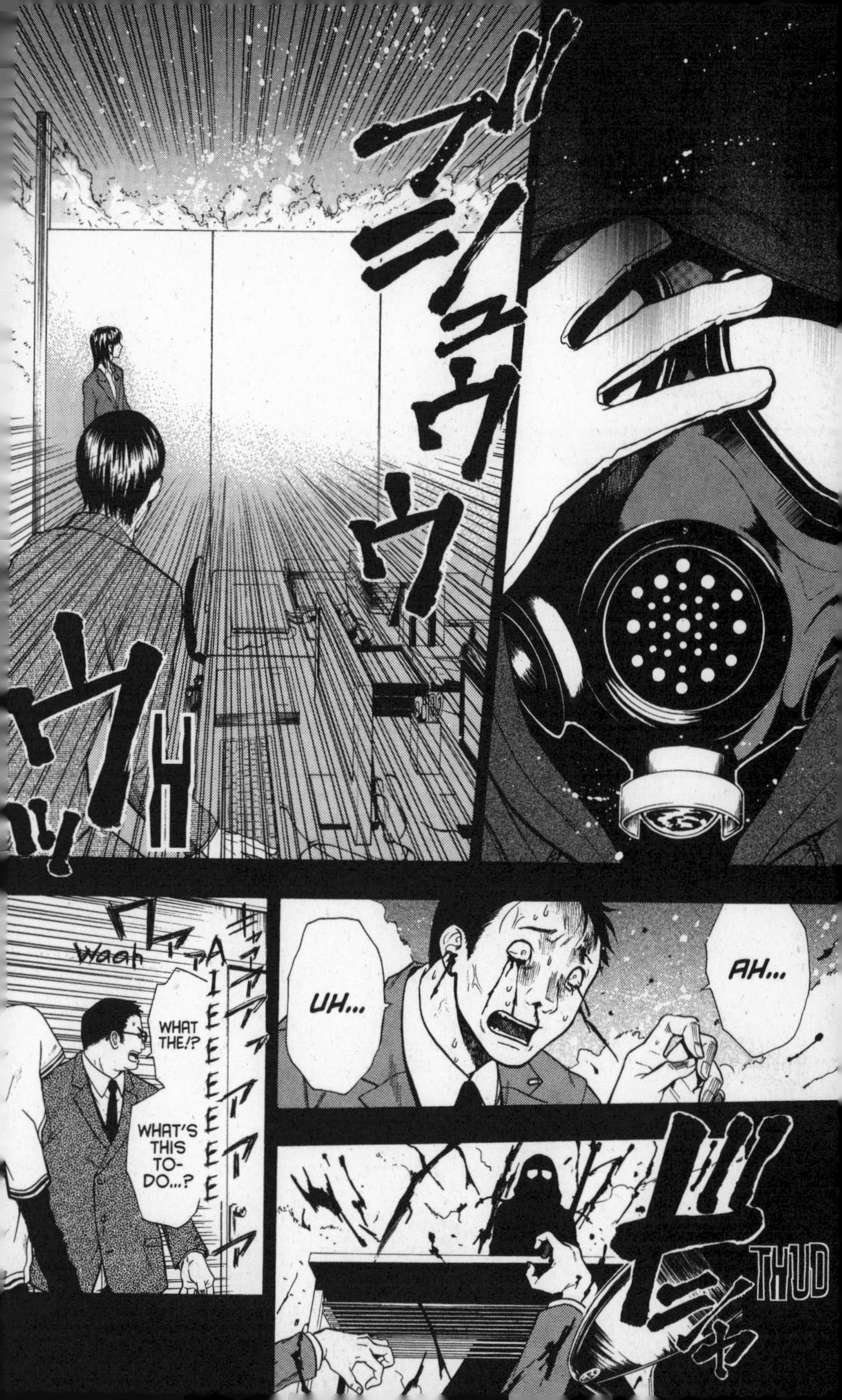
H
AH...
UH...
THUD
Waah
AIEEEEEE
WHAT THE!?
WHAT'S THIS TO-DO...?

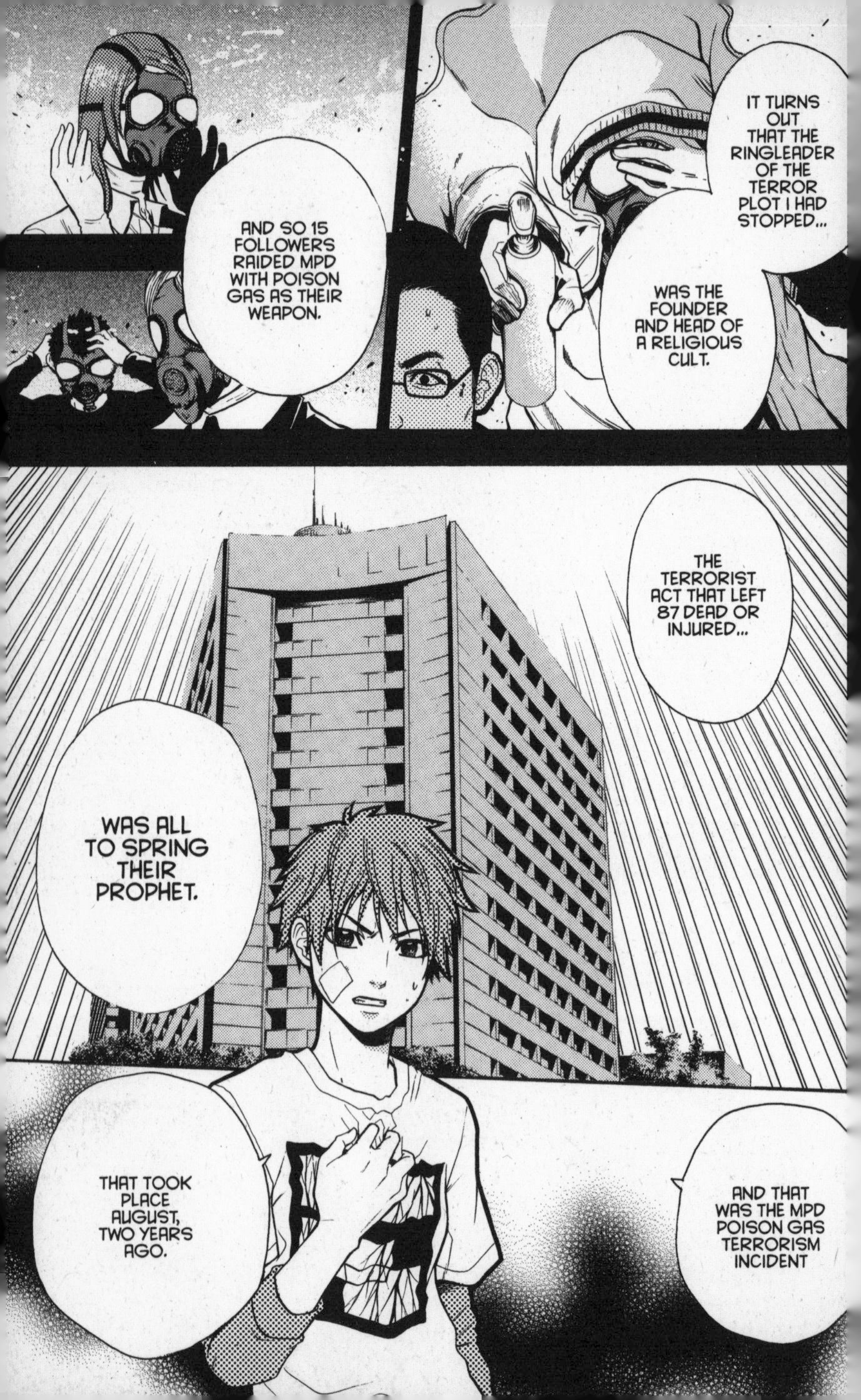

IT TURNS OUT THAT THE RINGLEADER OF THE TERROR PLOT I HAD STOPPED...
WAS THE FOUNDER AND HEAD OF A RELIGIOUS CULT.
AND SO 15 FOLLOWERS RAIDED MPD WITH POISON GAS AS THEIR WEAPON.
THE TERRORIST ACT THAT LEFT 87 DEAD OR INJURED...
WAS ALL TO SPRING THEIR PROPHET.
AND THAT WAS THE MPD POISON GAS TERRORISM INCIDENT
THAT TOOK PLACE AUGUST, TWO YEARS AGO.

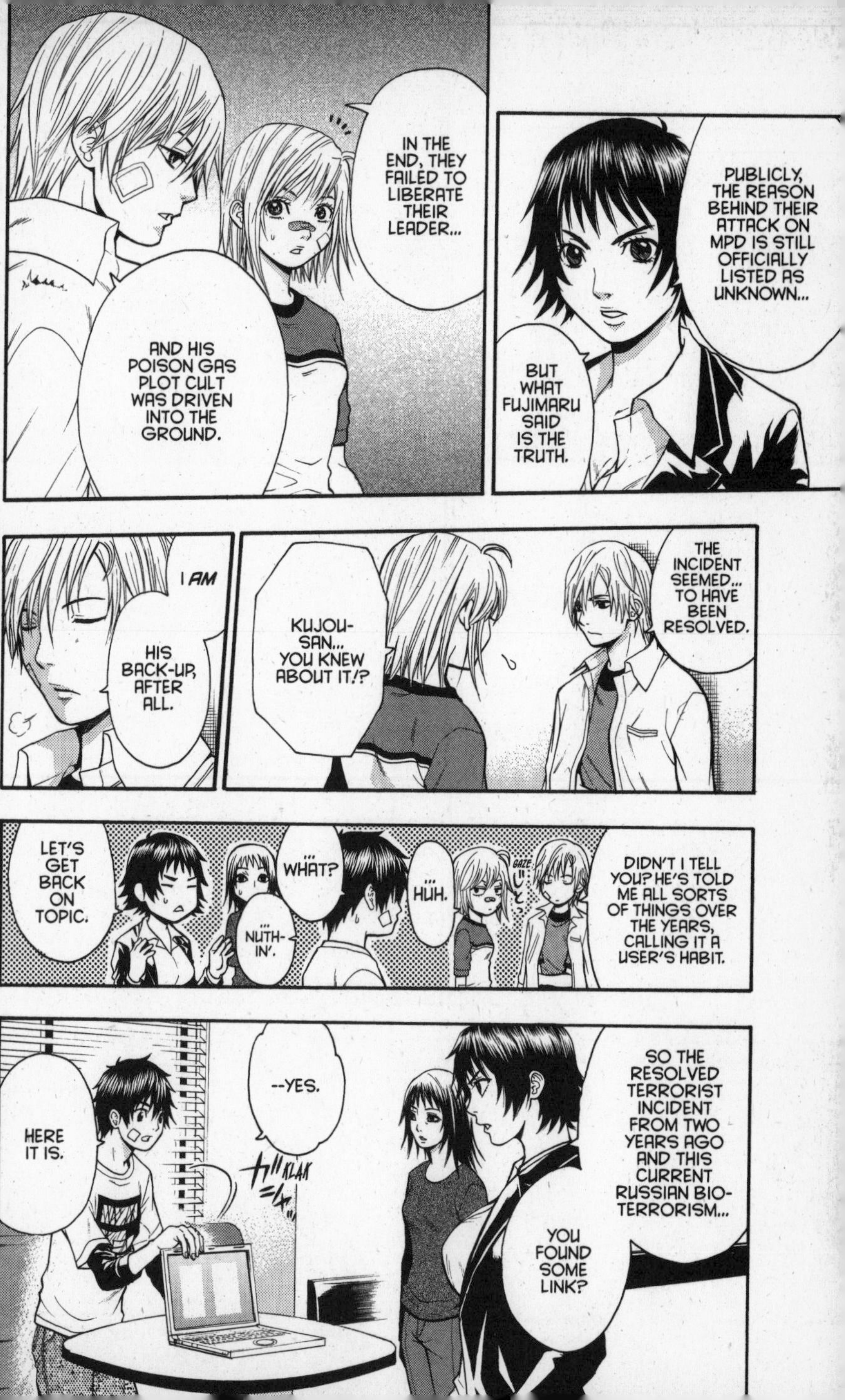
PUBLICLY, THE REASON BEHIND THEIR ATTACK ON MPD IS STILL OFFICIALLY LISTED AS UNKNOWN...
BUT WHAT FUJIMARU SAID IS THE TRUTH.
IN THE END, THEY FAILED TO LIBERATE THEIR LEADER...
AND HIS POISON GAS PLOT CULT WAS DRIVEN INTO THE GROUND.
THE INCIDENT SEEMED... TO HAVE BEEN RESOLVED.
KUJOU-SAN... YOU KNEW ABOUT IT!?
I AM HIS BACK-UP, AFTER ALL.
DIDN'T I TELL YOU? HE'S TOLD ME ALL SORTS OF THINGS OVER THE YEARS, CALLING IT A USER'S HABIT.
GAZE
...HUH.
...WHAT?
...NUTH-IN'.
LET'S GET BACK ON TOPIC.
SO THE RESOLVED TERRORIST INCIDENT FROM TWO YEARS AGO AND THIS CURRENT RUSSIAN BIO-TERRORISM...
YOU FOUND SOME LINK?
--YES.
KLAK
HERE IT IS.

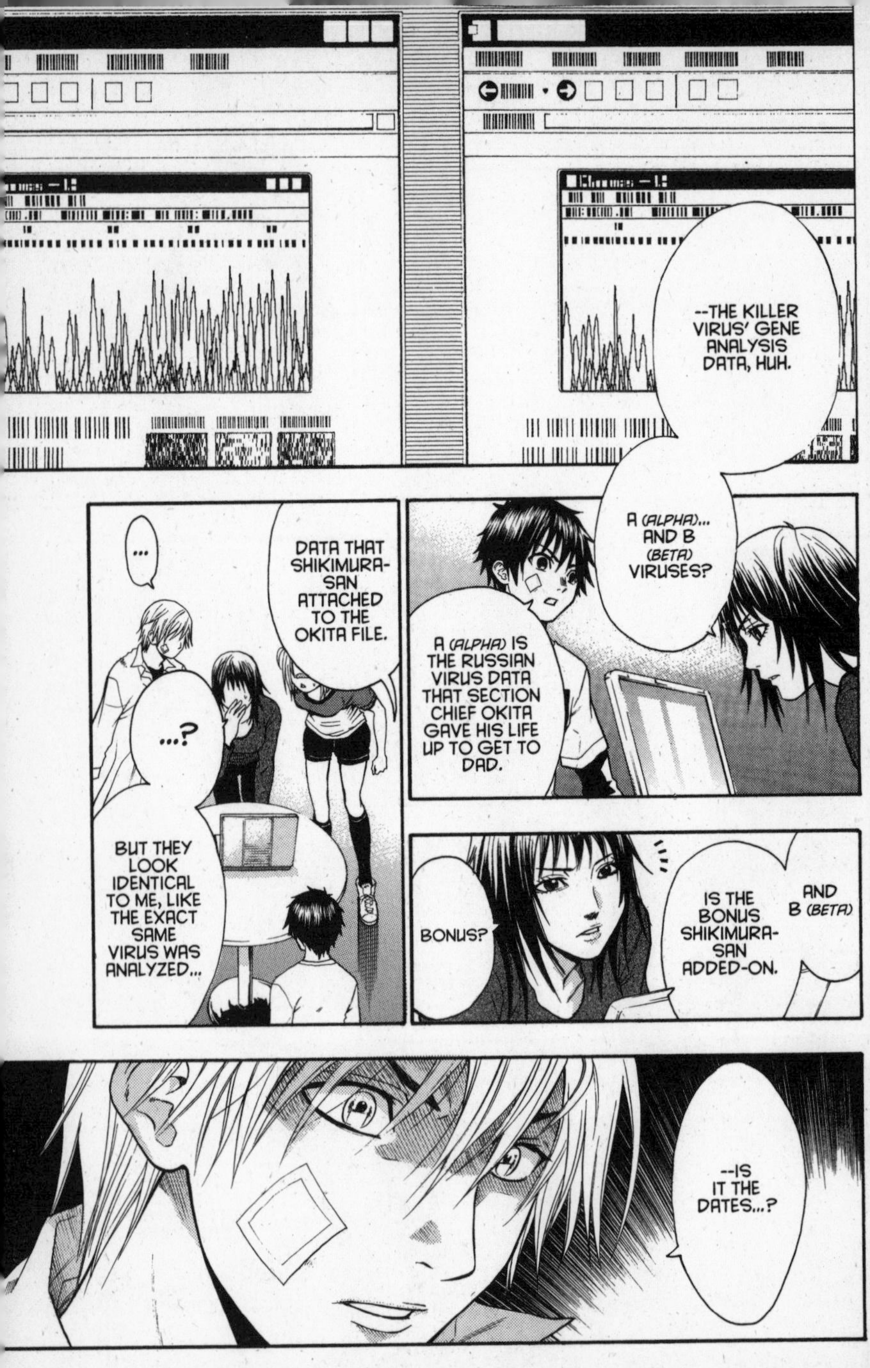
--THE KILLER VIRUS' GENE ANALYSIS DATA, HUH.
A (ALPHA)... AND B (BETA) VIRUSES?
A (ALPHA) IS THE RUSSIAN VIRUS DATA THAT SECTION CHIEF OKITA GAVE HIS LIFE UP TO GET TO DAD.
AND B (BETA)
IS THE BONUS SHIKIMURA-SAN ADDED-ON.
BONUS?
DATA THAT SHIKIMURA-SAN ATTACHED TO THE OKITA FILE.
...
...?
BUT THEY LOOK IDENTICAL TO ME, LIKE THE EXACT SAME VIRUS WAS ANALYZED...
--IS IT THE DATES...?

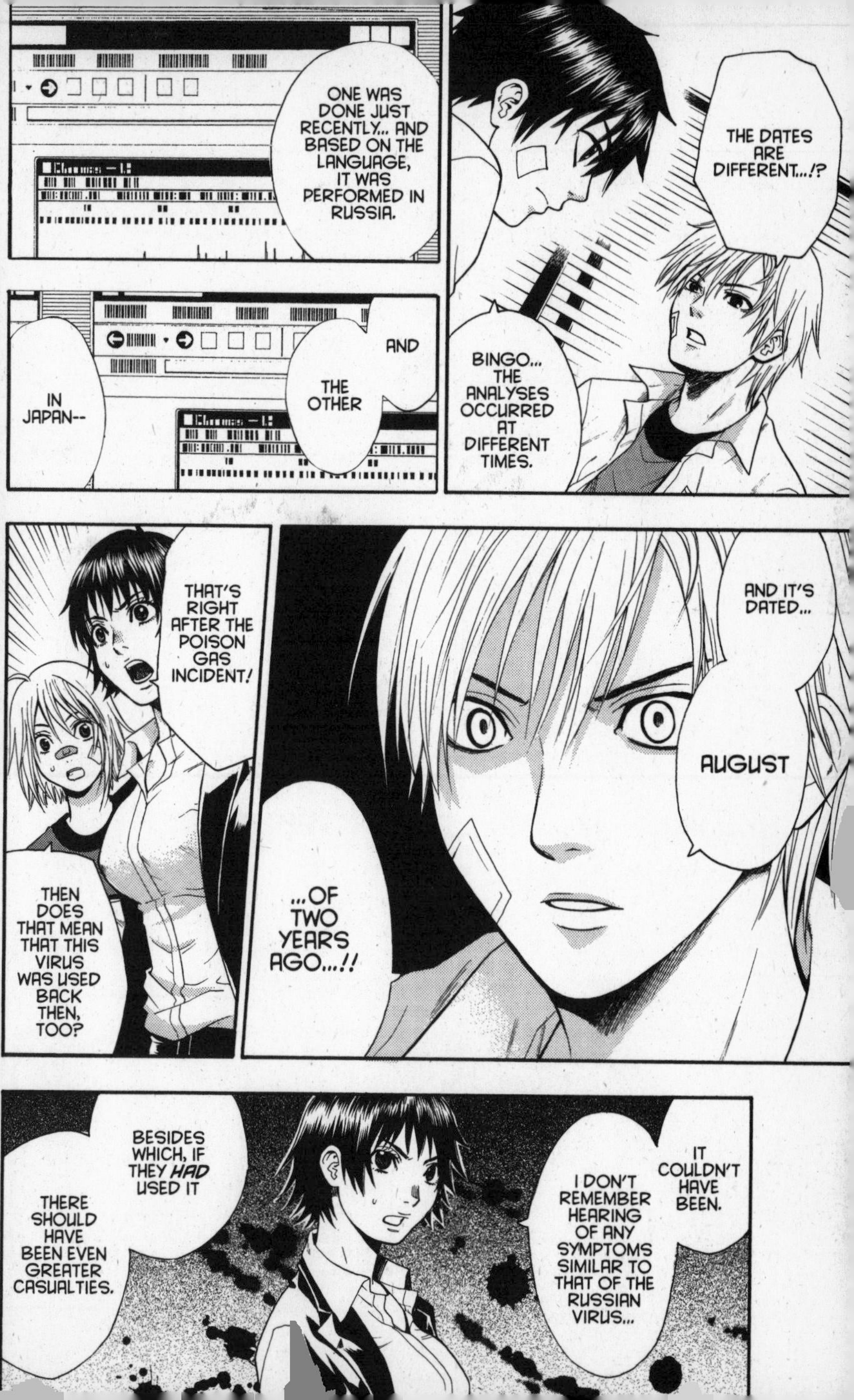
THE DATES ARE DIFFERENT...!?
BINGO... THE ANALYSES OCCURRED AT DIFFERENT TIMES.
ONE WAS DONE JUST RECENTLY... AND BASED ON THE LANGUAGE, IT WAS PERFORMED IN RUSSIA.
AND
THE OTHER
IN JAPAN--
AND IT'S DATED...
AUGUST
...OF TWO YEARS AGO...!!
THAT'S RIGHT AFTER THE POISON GAS INCIDENT!
THEN DOES THAT MEAN THAT THIS VIRUS WAS USED BACK THEN, TOO?
IT COULDN'T HAVE BEEN.
I DON'T REMEMBER HEARING OF ANY SYMPTOMS SIMILAR TO THAT OF THE RUSSIAN VIRUS...
BESIDES WHICH, IF THEY *HAD* USED IT
THERE SHOULD HAVE BEEN EVEN GREATER CASUALTIES.

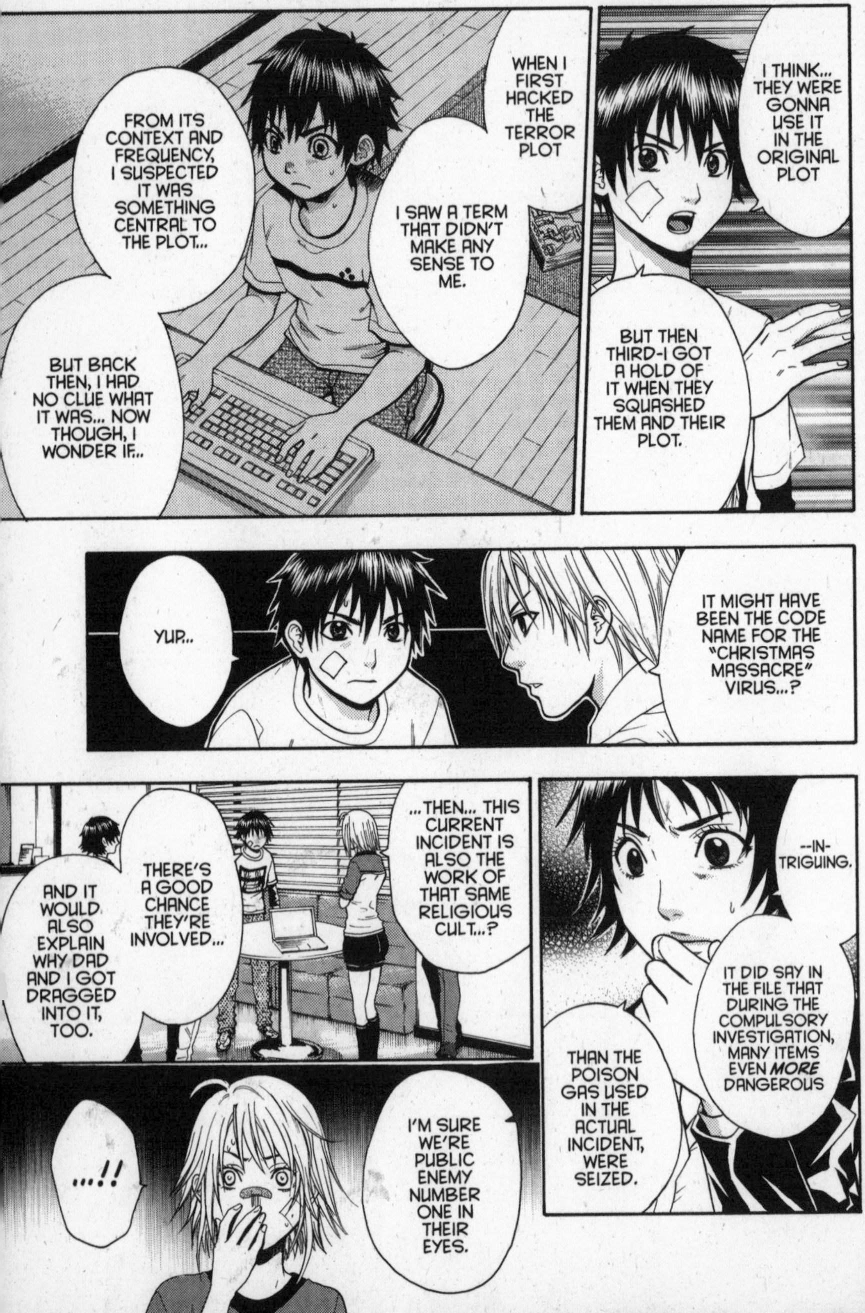
I THINK... THEY WERE GONNA USE IT IN THE ORIGINAL PLOT
BUT THEN THIRD-I GOT A HOLD OF IT WHEN THEY SQUASHED THEM AND THEIR PLOT.
WHEN I FIRST HACKED THE TERROR PLOT
I SAW A TERM THAT DIDN'T MAKE ANY SENSE TO ME.
FROM ITS CONTEXT AND FREQUENCY, I SUSPECTED IT WAS SOMETHING CENTRAL TO THE PLOT...
BUT BACK THEN, I HAD NO CLUE WHAT IT WAS... NOW THOUGH, I WONDER IF...
IT MIGHT HAVE BEEN THE CODE NAME FOR THE "CHRISTMAS MASSACRE" VIRUS...?
YUP...
--IN-TRIGUING.
IT DID SAY IN THE FILE THAT DURING THE COMPULSORY INVESTIGATION, MANY ITEMS EVEN *MORE* DANGEROUS
THAN THE POISON GAS USED IN THE ACTUAL INCIDENT, WERE SEIZED.
...THEN... THIS CURRENT INCIDENT IS ALSO THE WORK OF THAT SAME RELIGIOUS CULT...?
THERE'S A GOOD CHANCE THEY'RE INVOLVED...
AND IT WOULD ALSO EXPLAIN WHY DAD AND I GOT DRAGGED INTO IT, TOO.
I'M SURE WE'RE PUBLIC ENEMY NUMBER ONE IN THEIR EYES.
...!!

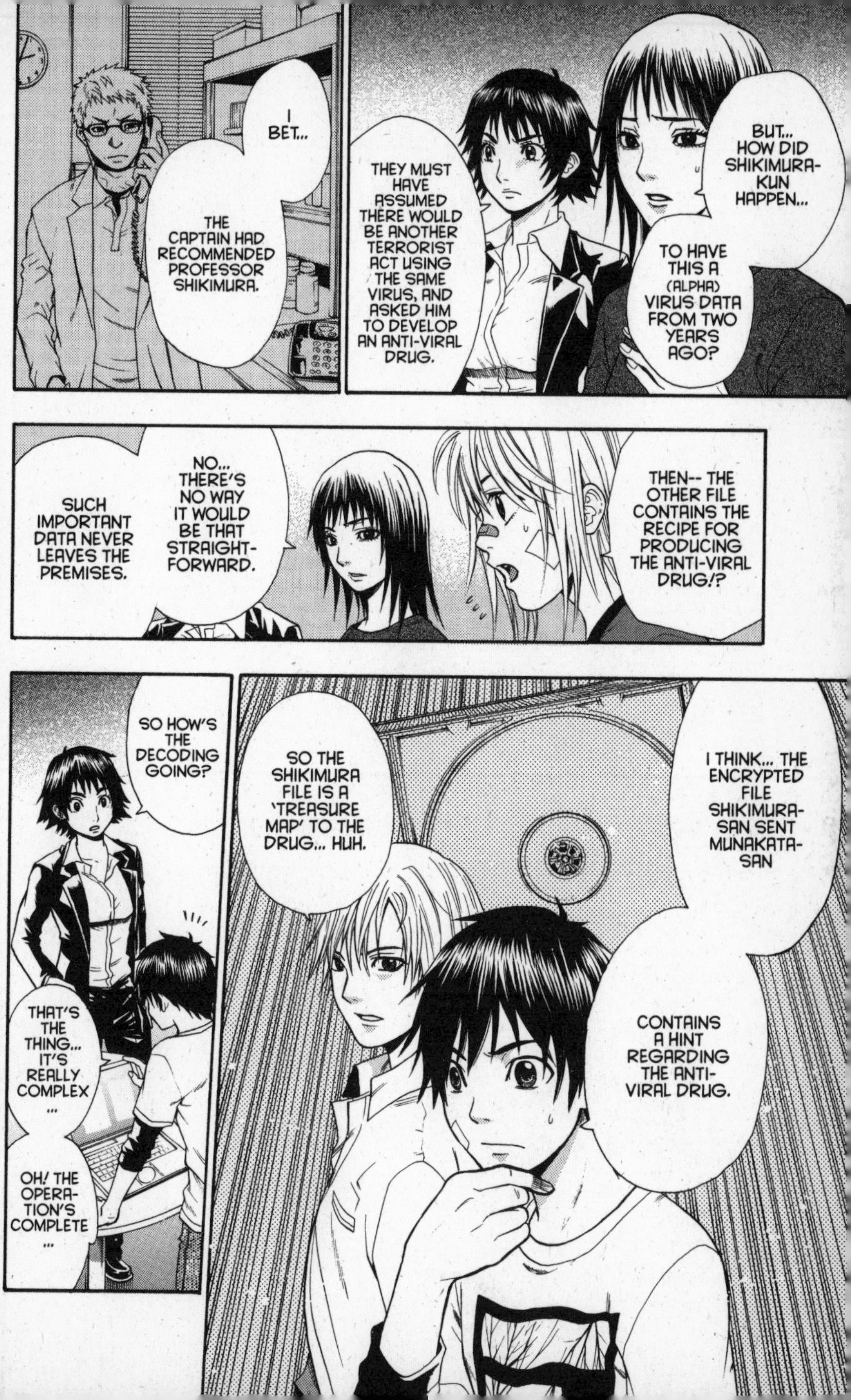
BUT... HOW DID SHIKIMURA-KUN HAPPEN...
TO HAVE THIS A (ALPHA) VIRUS DATA FROM TWO YEARS AGO?
THEY MUST HAVE ASSUMED THERE WOULD BE ANOTHER TERRORIST ACT USING THE SAME VIRUS, AND ASKED HIM TO DEVELOP AN ANTI-VIRAL DRUG.
I BET...
THE CAPTAIN HAD RECOMMENDED PROFESSOR SHIKIMURA.
THEN-- THE OTHER FILE CONTAINS THE RECIPE FOR PRODUCING THE ANTI-VIRAL DRUG!?
NO... THERE'S NO WAY IT WOULD BE THAT STRAIGHT-FORWARD.
SUCH IMPORTANT DATA NEVER LEAVES THE PREMISES.
I THINK... THE ENCRYPTED FILE SHIKIMURA-SAN SENT MUNAKATA-SAN
CONTAINS A HINT REGARDING THE ANTI-VIRAL DRUG.
SO THE SHIKIMURA FILE IS A 'TREASURE MAP' TO THE DRUG... HUH.
SO HOW'S THE DECODING GOING?
THAT'S THE THING... IT'S REALLY COMPLEX ...
OH! THE OPERA-TION'S COMPLETE ...

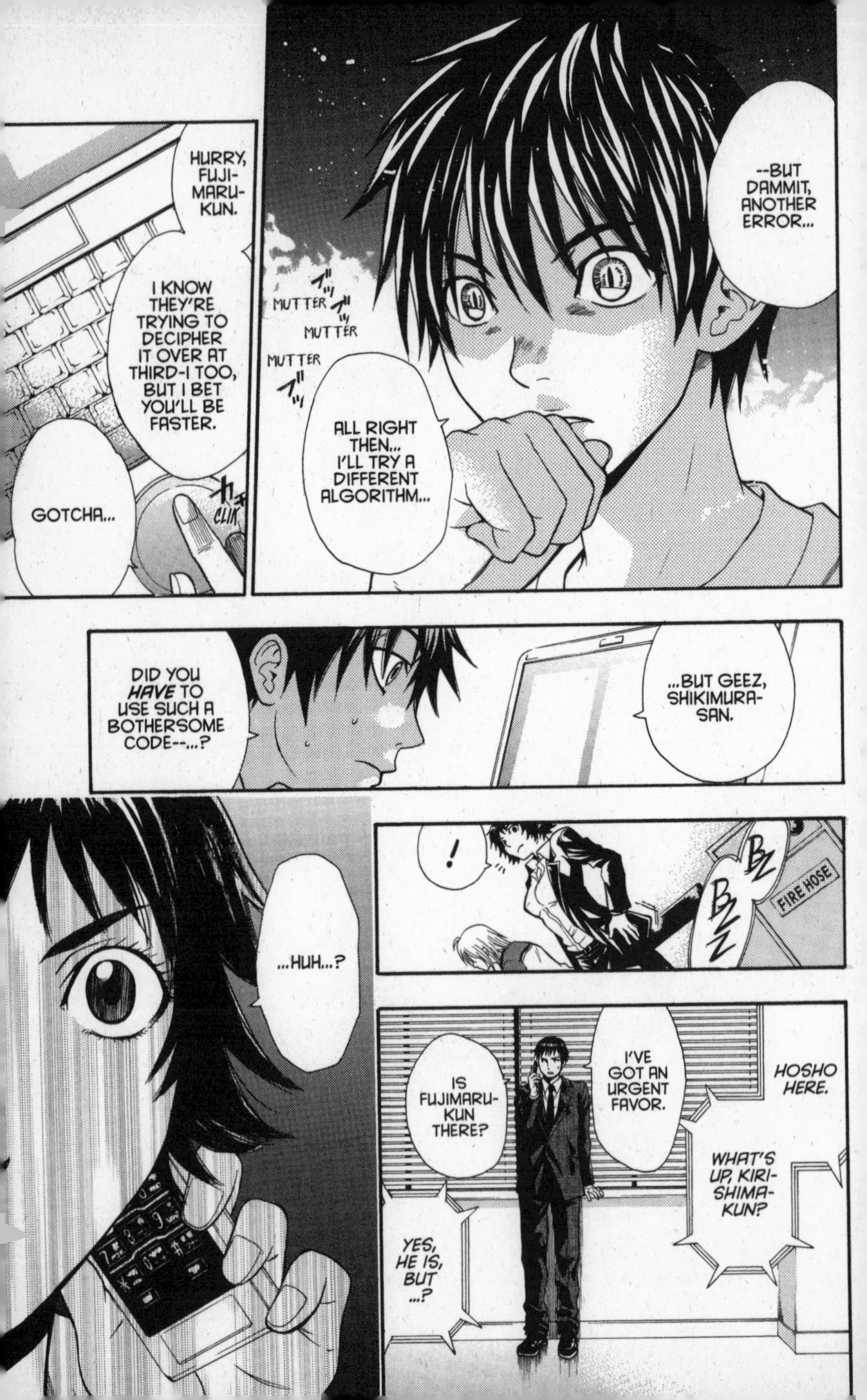
--BUT DAMMIT, ANOTHER ERROR...
MUTTER
MUTTER
MUTTER
ALL RIGHT THEN... I'LL TRY A DIFFERENT ALGORITHM...
HURRY, FUJI-MARU-KUN.
I KNOW THEY'RE TRYING TO DECIPHER IT OVER AT THIRD-I TOO, BUT I BET YOU'LL BE FASTER.
CLIK
GOTCHA...
...BUT GEEZ, SHIKIMURA-SAN.
DID YOU *HAVE* TO USE SUCH A BOTHERSOME CODE--...?
BZZ
BZZ
FIRE HOSE
!
HOSHO HERE.
WHAT'S UP, KIRI-SHIMA-KUN?
I'VE GOT AN URGENT FAVOR.
IS FUJIMARU-KUN THERE?
YES, HE IS, BUT ...?
...HUH...?

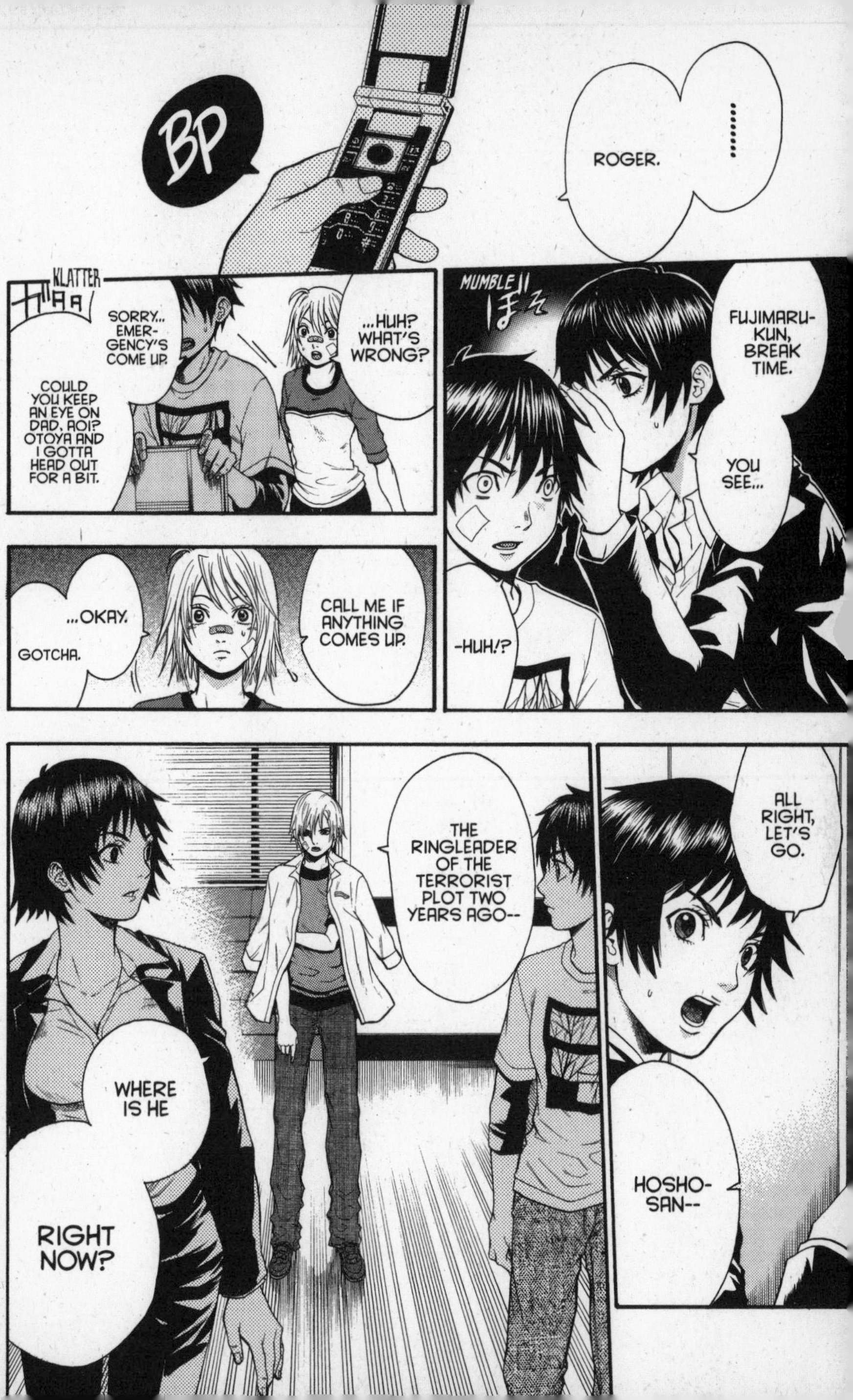
……
ROGER.
BP
MUMBLE
FUJIMARU-KUN, BREAK TIME.
YOU SEE...
-HUH!?
...HUH? WHAT'S WRONG?
SORRY... EMERGENCY'S COME UP.
COULD YOU KEEP AN EYE ON DAD, AOI? OTOYA AND I GOTTA HEAD OUT FOR A BIT.
KLATTER
CALL ME IF ANYTHING COMES UP.
...OKAY.
GOTCHA.
ALL RIGHT, LET'S GO.
HOSHO-SAN--
THE RINGLEADER OF THE TERRORIST PLOT TWO YEARS AGO--
WHERE IS HE
RIGHT NOW?

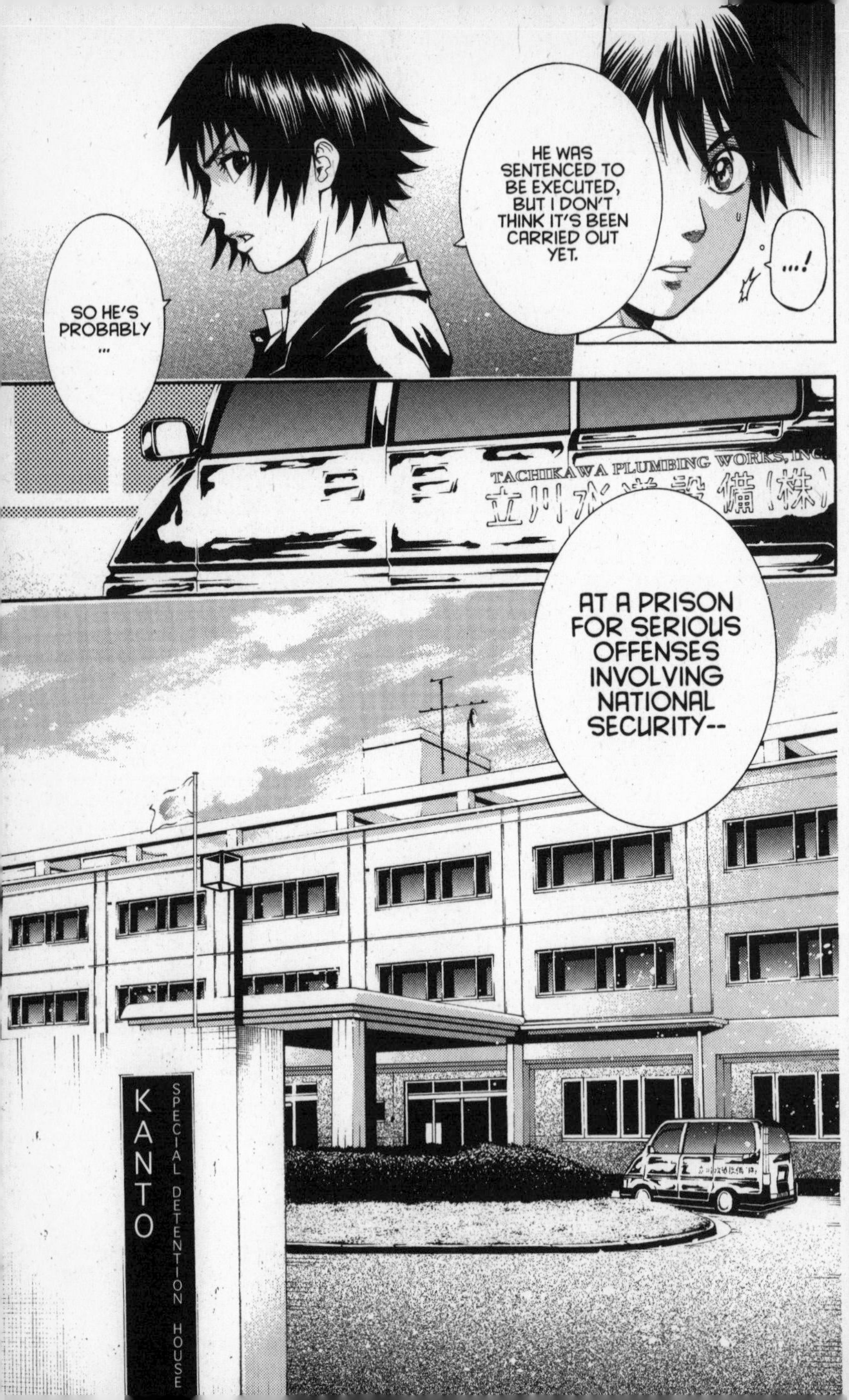
HE WAS SENTENCED TO BE EXECUTED, BUT I DON'T THINK IT'S BEEN CARRIED OUT YET.
...!
SO HE'S PROBABLY ...
TACHIKAWA PLUMBING WORKS, INC.
AT A PRISON FOR SERIOUS OFFENSES INVOLVING NATIONAL SECURITY--
KANTO
SPECIAL DETENTION HOUSE

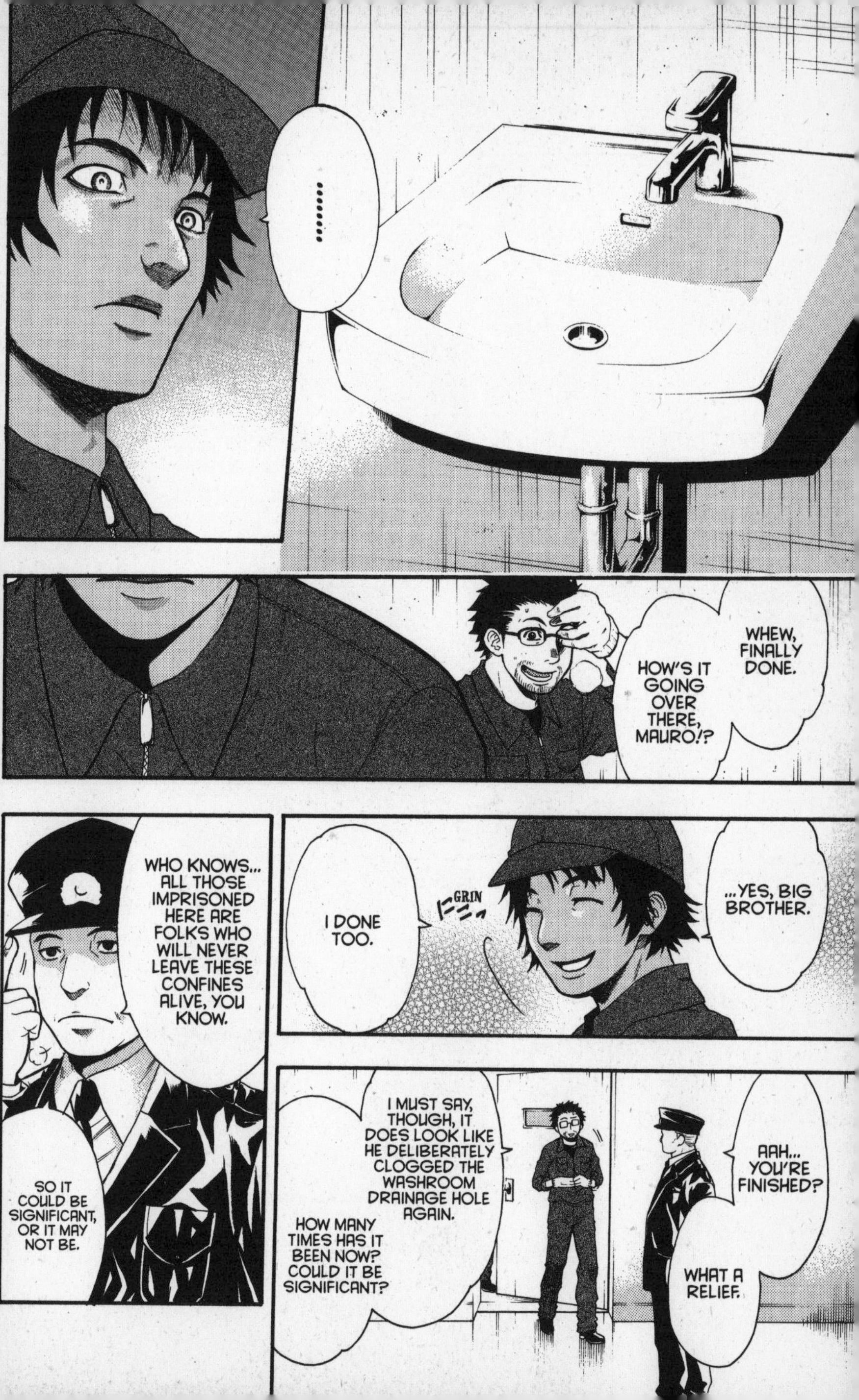
......
WHEW, FINALLY DONE.
HOW'S IT GOING OVER THERE, MAURO!?
...YES, BIG BROTHER.
GRIN
I DONE TOO.
AAH... YOU'RE FINISHED?
WHAT A RELIEF.
I MUST SAY, THOUGH, IT DOES LOOK LIKE HE DELIBERATELY CLOGGED THE WASHROOM DRAINAGE HOLE AGAIN.
HOW MANY TIMES HAS IT BEEN NOW? COULD IT BE SIGNIFICANT?
WHO KNOWS... ALL THOSE IMPRISONED HERE ARE FOLKS WHO WILL NEVER LEAVE THESE CONFINES ALIVE, YOU KNOW.
SO IT COULD BE SIGNIFICANT, OR IT MAY NOT BE.

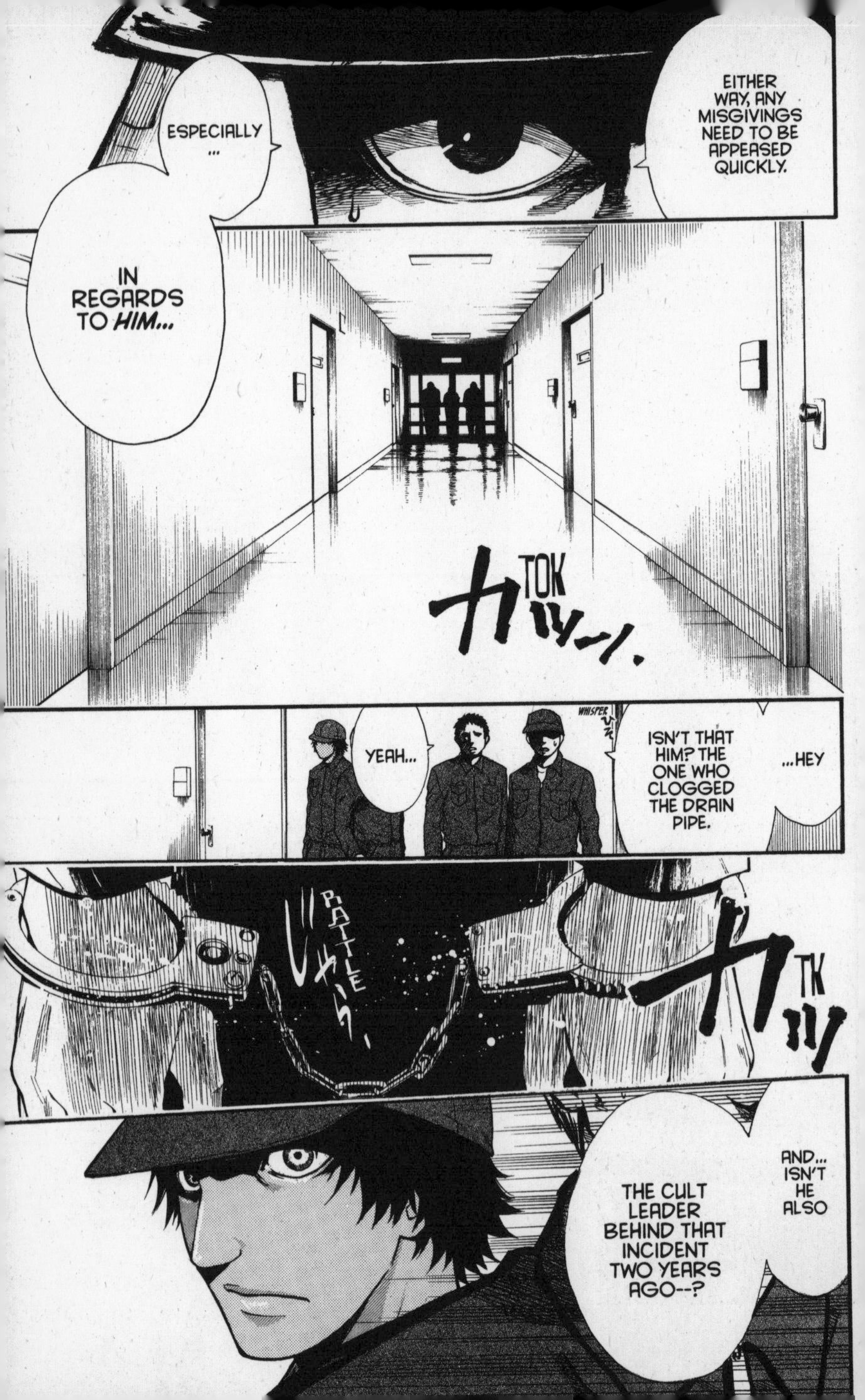
EITHER WAY, ANY MISGIVINGS NEED TO BE APPEASED QUICKLY.
ESPECIALLY ...
IN REGARDS TO *HIM*...
TOK
...HEY
WHISPER
ISN'T THAT HIM? THE ONE WHO CLOGGED THE DRAIN PIPE.
YEAH...
TK
RATTLE
AND... ISN'T HE ALSO
THE CULT LEADER BEHIND THAT INCIDENT TWO YEARS AGO--?

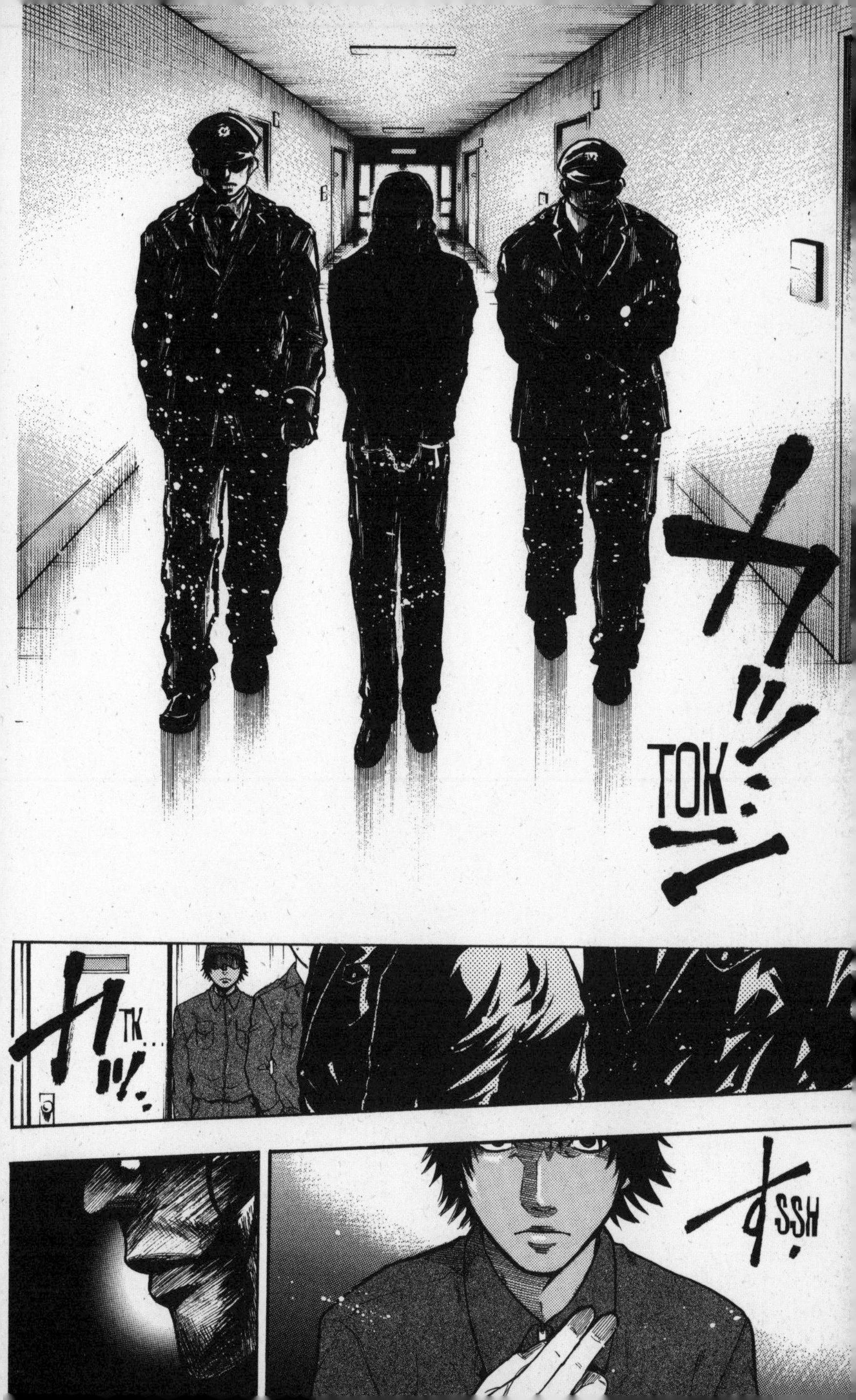
TOK
TK...
SSH

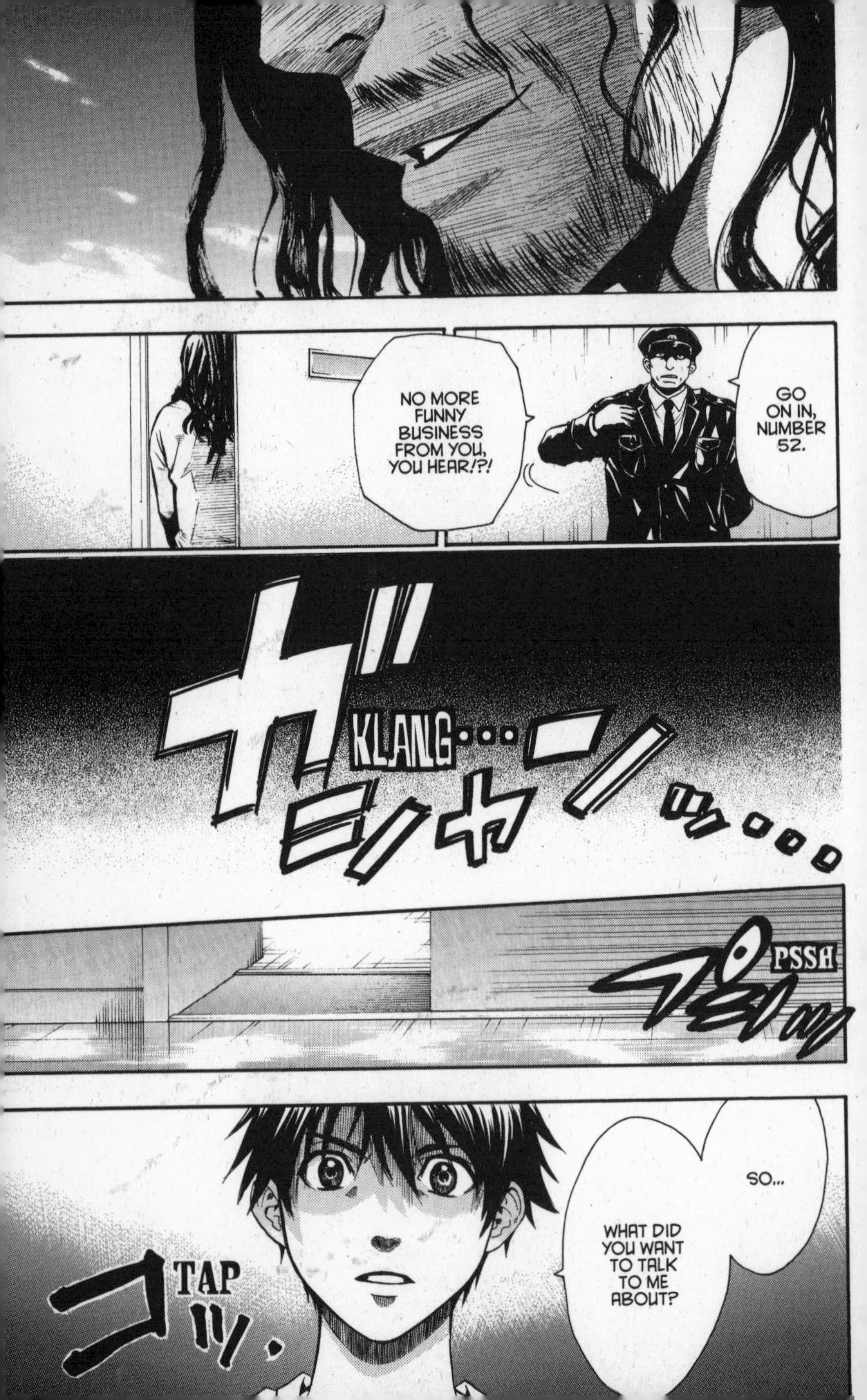
GO ON IN, NUMBER 52.
NO MORE FUNNY BUSINESS FROM YOU, YOU HEAR!?!
KLANG...
PSSH
SO...
WHAT DID YOU WANT TO TALK TO ME ABOUT?
TAP

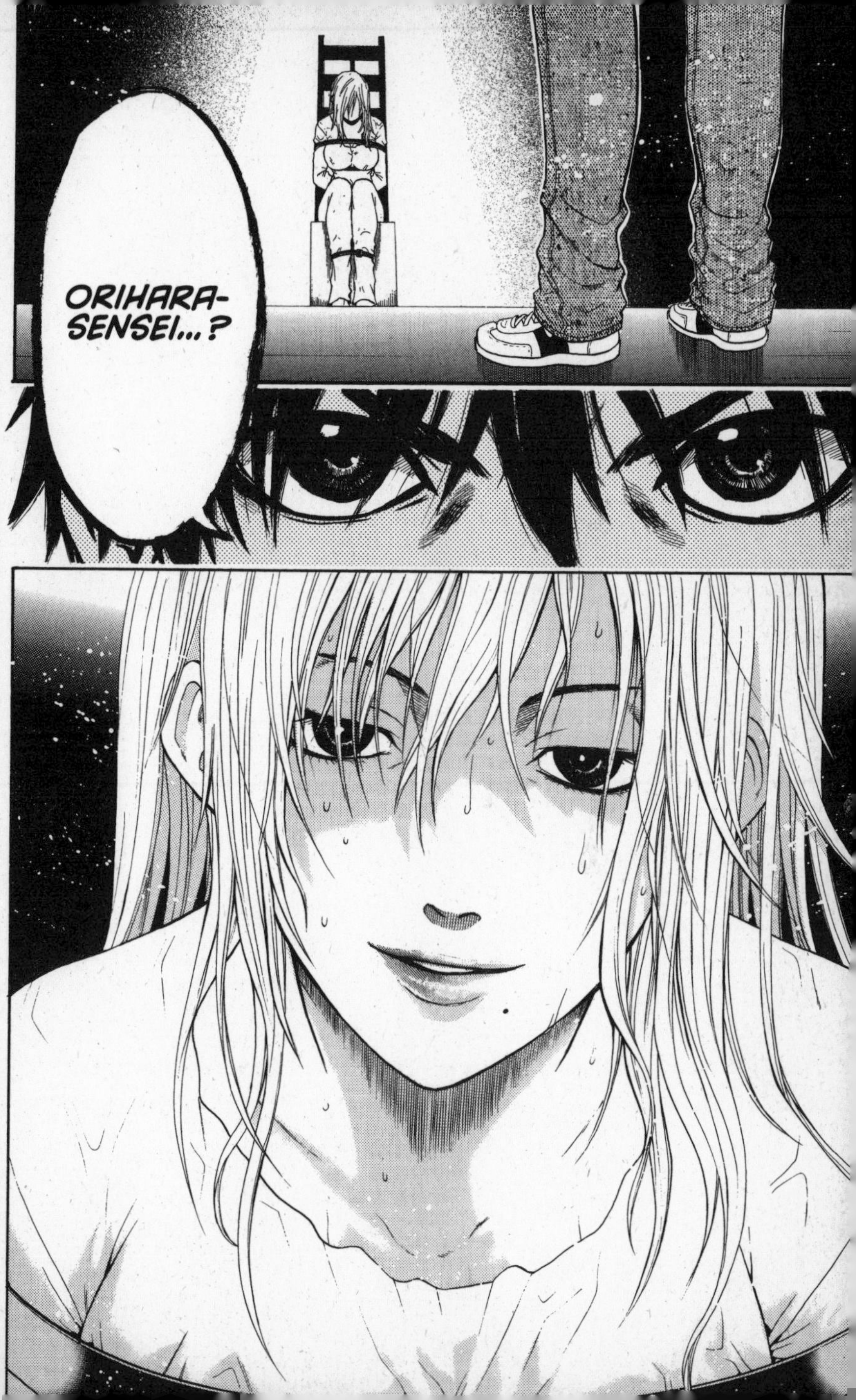
ORIHARA-SENSEI...?

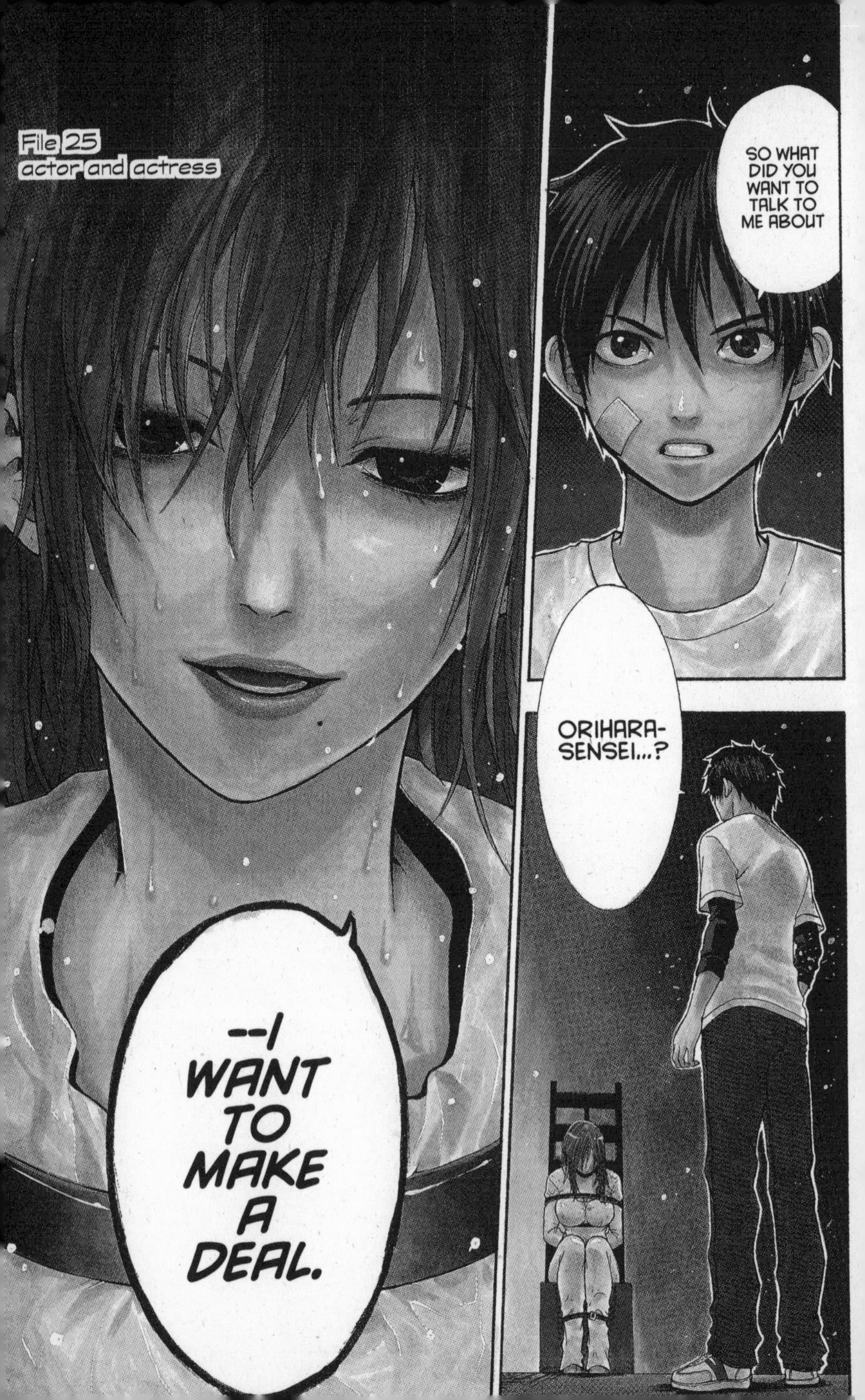
SO WHAT DID YOU WANT TO TALK TO ME ABOUT
ORIHARA-SENSEI...?
File 25
actor and actress
--I WANT TO MAKE A DEAL.

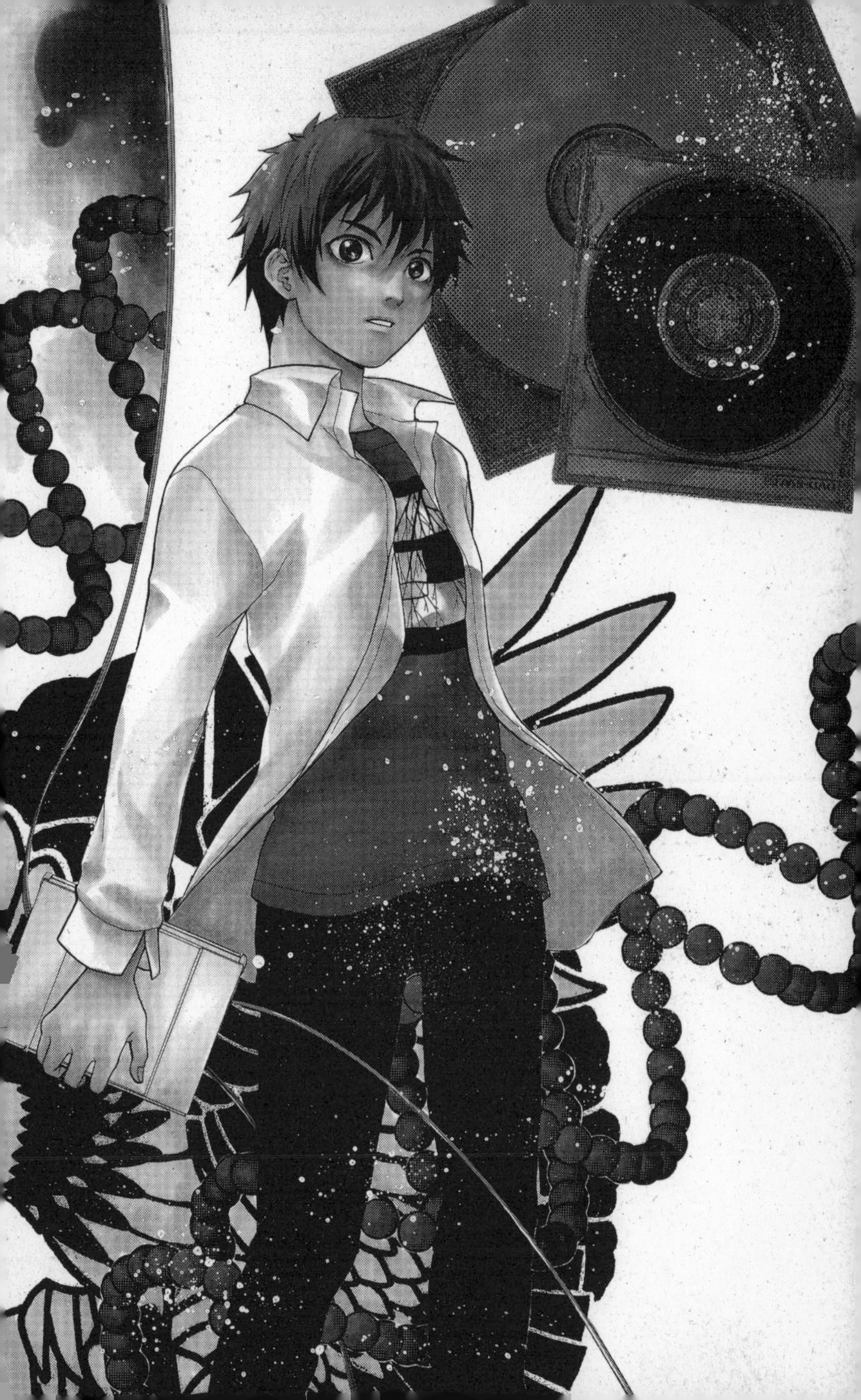

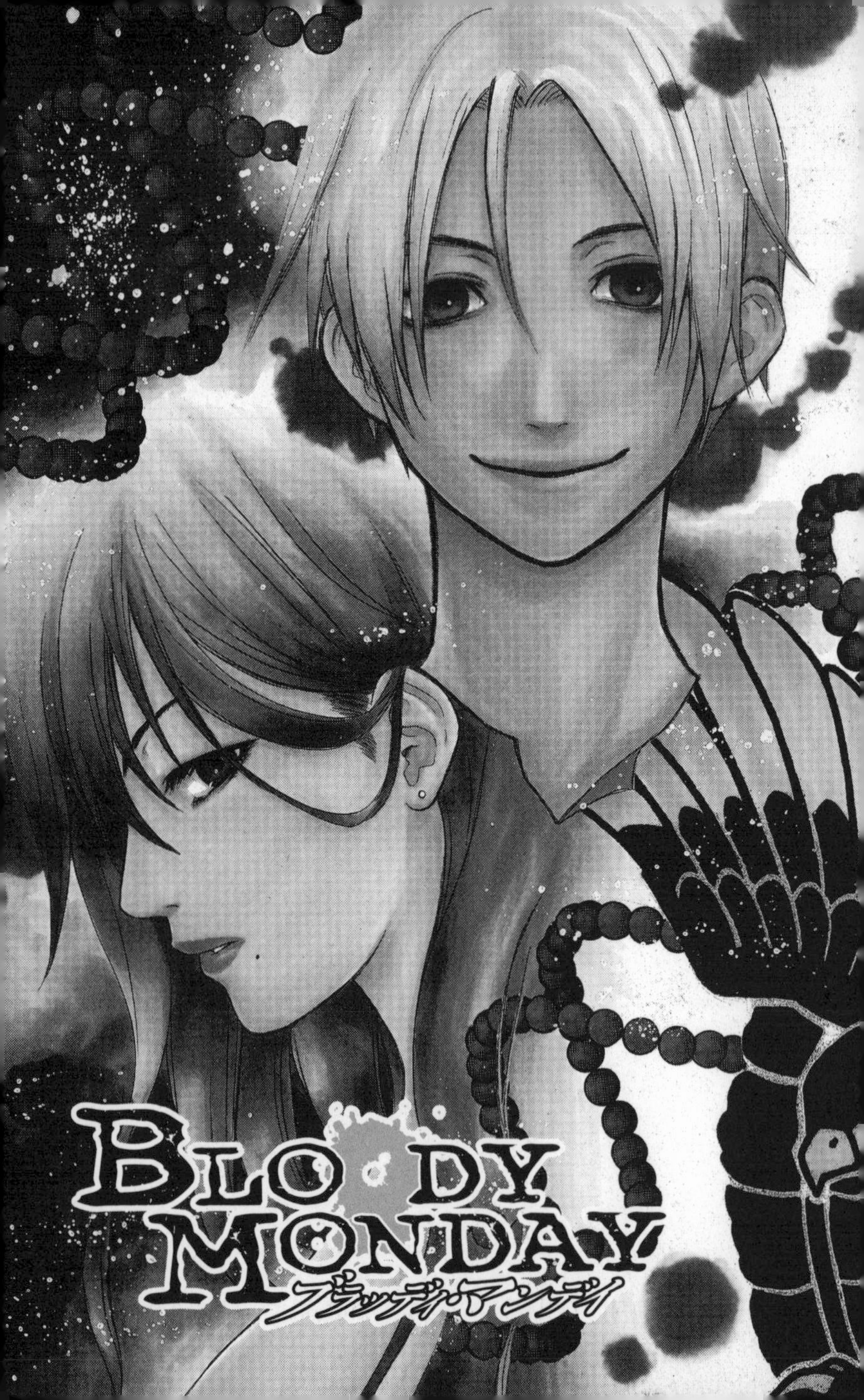
BLOODY MONDAY
ブラッディ・マンデイ

BLOODY MONDAY

- GLOSSARY OF TERMS • LIST 9 -

Server p5
A computer that provides services in response to requests from clients, over a network. Or, a computer program that provides services in response to client software. Examples of services provided include mail handling and webpage hosting.

Algorithm p17
A processing method that uses computers to achieve a particular objective. Most widely used as an accurate process to resolve mathematical problems.

PDF p39
Abbreviation for Portable Document Format. A standard for electronic documents that allows documents to be displayed with the same layout regardless of what hardware or operating system is being used. It preserves not just the actual text, but font size and type, and images as well.

Bone conduction p42
Hearing activated via the conduction of sound waves to the inner ear through the bones of the skull as opposed to the (external) ear. Sound transmitted through bone conduction is known as bone-conducted sound, and sound transmitted via sound waves that enter the ear and travel through air to hit and vibrate the tympanic membrane is called air-conducted sound.

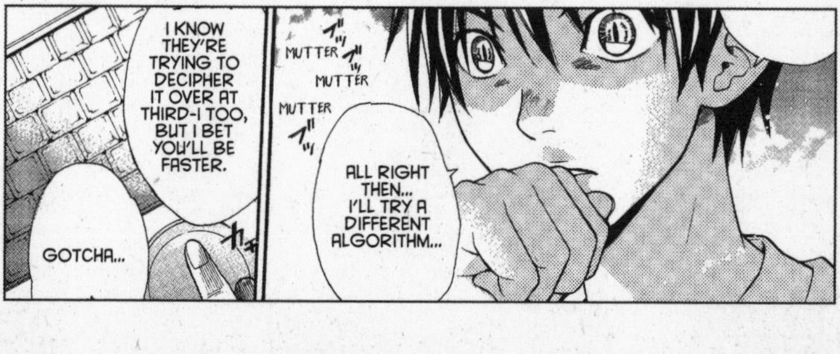
MUTTER
MUTTER
MUTTER
ALL RIGHT THEN... I'LL TRY A DIFFERENT ALGORITHM...
I KNOW THEY'RE TRYING TO DECIPHER IT OVER AT THIRD-I TOO, BUT I BET YOU'LL BE FASTER.
GOTCHA...

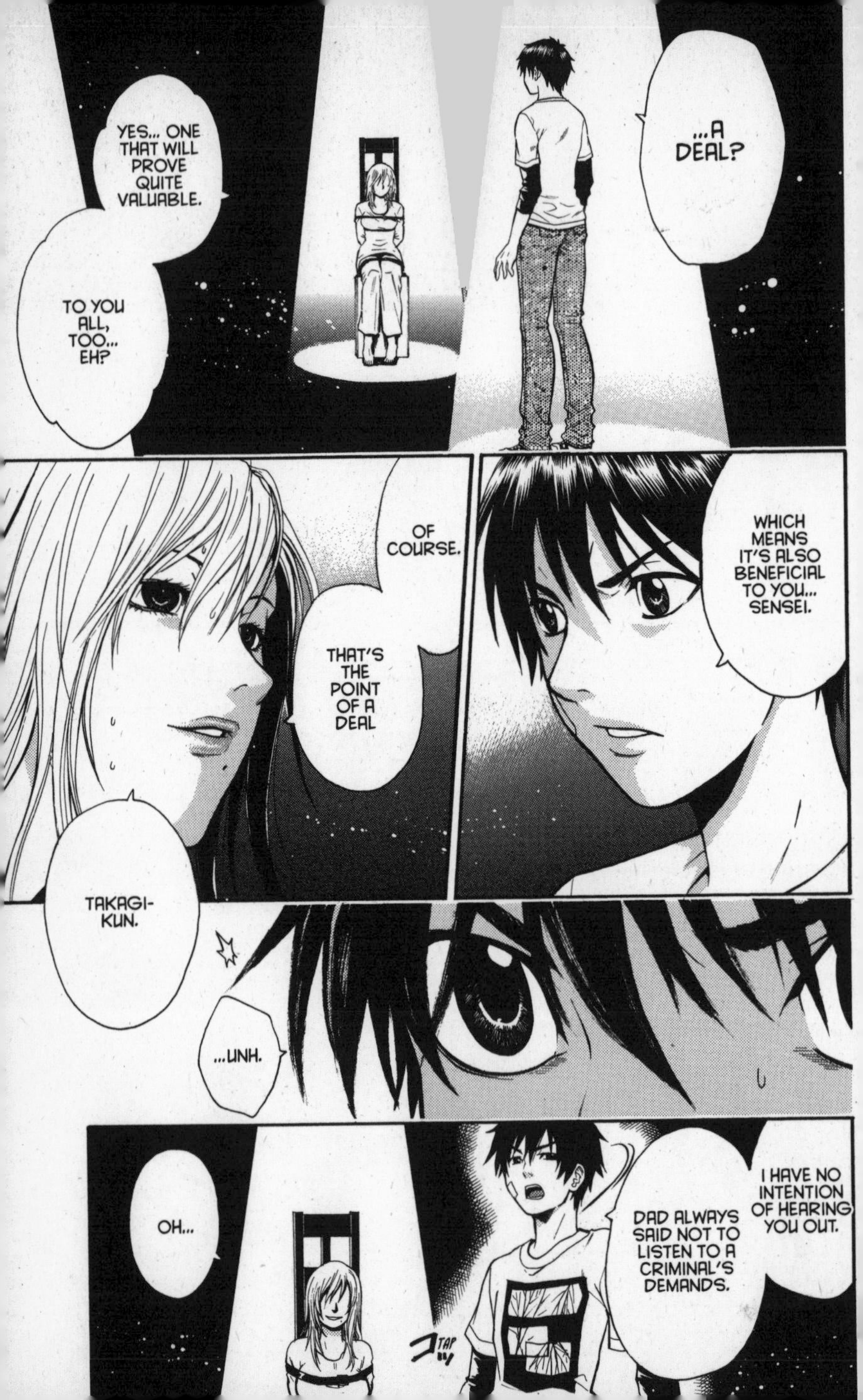
...A DEAL?
YES... ONE THAT WILL PROVE QUITE VALUABLE.
TO YOU ALL, TOO... EH?
WHICH MEANS IT'S ALSO BENEFICIAL TO YOU... SENSEI.
OF COURSE.
THAT'S THE POINT OF A DEAL
TAKAGI-KUN.
...UNH.
I HAVE NO INTENTION OF HEARING YOU OUT.
DAD ALWAYS SAID NOT TO LISTEN TO A CRIMINAL'S DEMANDS.
TAP
OH...

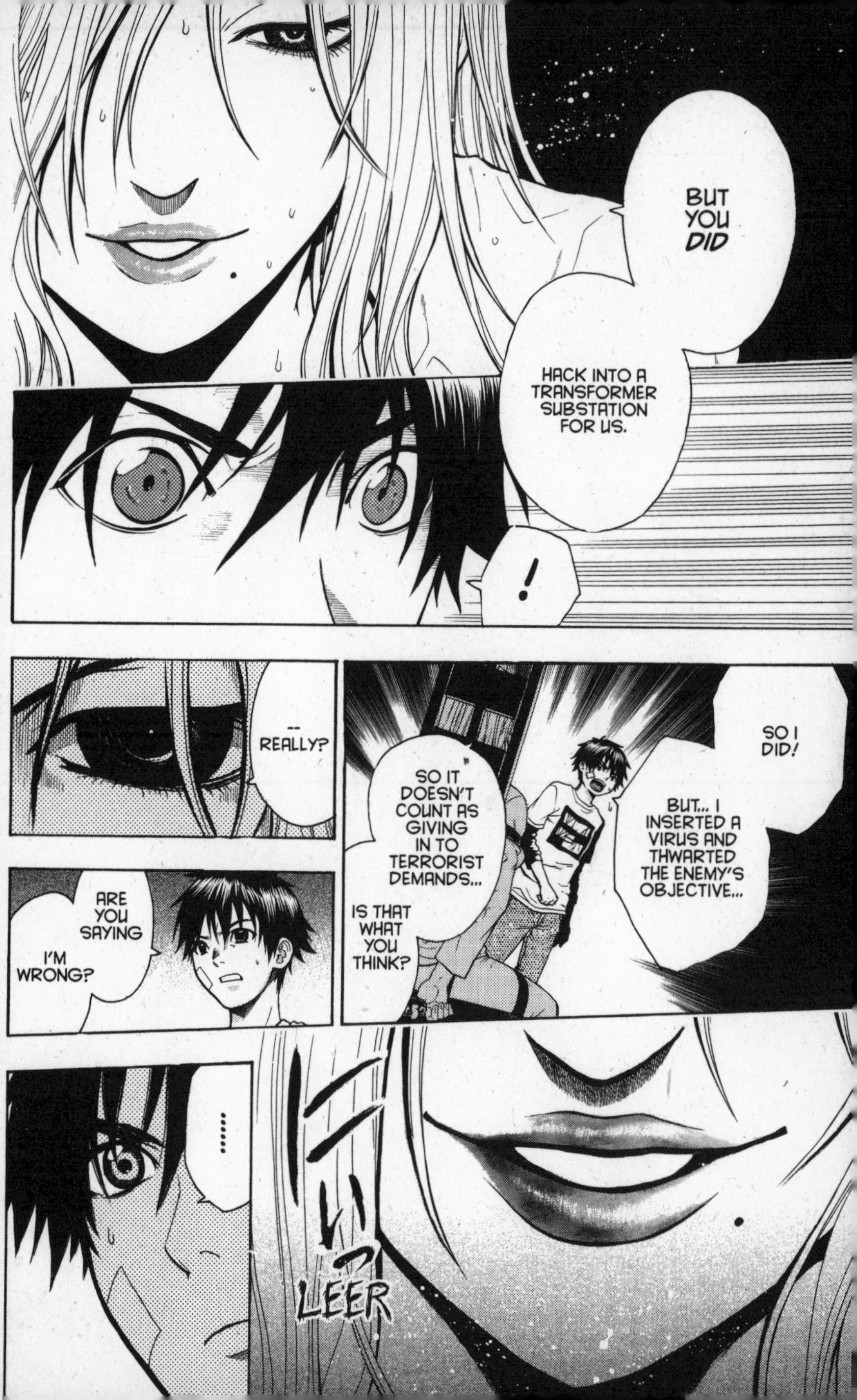
BUT YOU *DID*
HACK INTO A TRANSFORMER SUBSTATION FOR US.
!
SO I DID!
BUT... I INSERTED A VIRUS AND THWARTED THE ENEMY'S OBJECTIVE...
SO IT DOESN'T COUNT AS GIVING IN TO TERRORIST DEMANDS...
IS THAT WHAT YOU THINK?
--REALLY?
ARE YOU SAYING I'M WRONG?
LEER
......

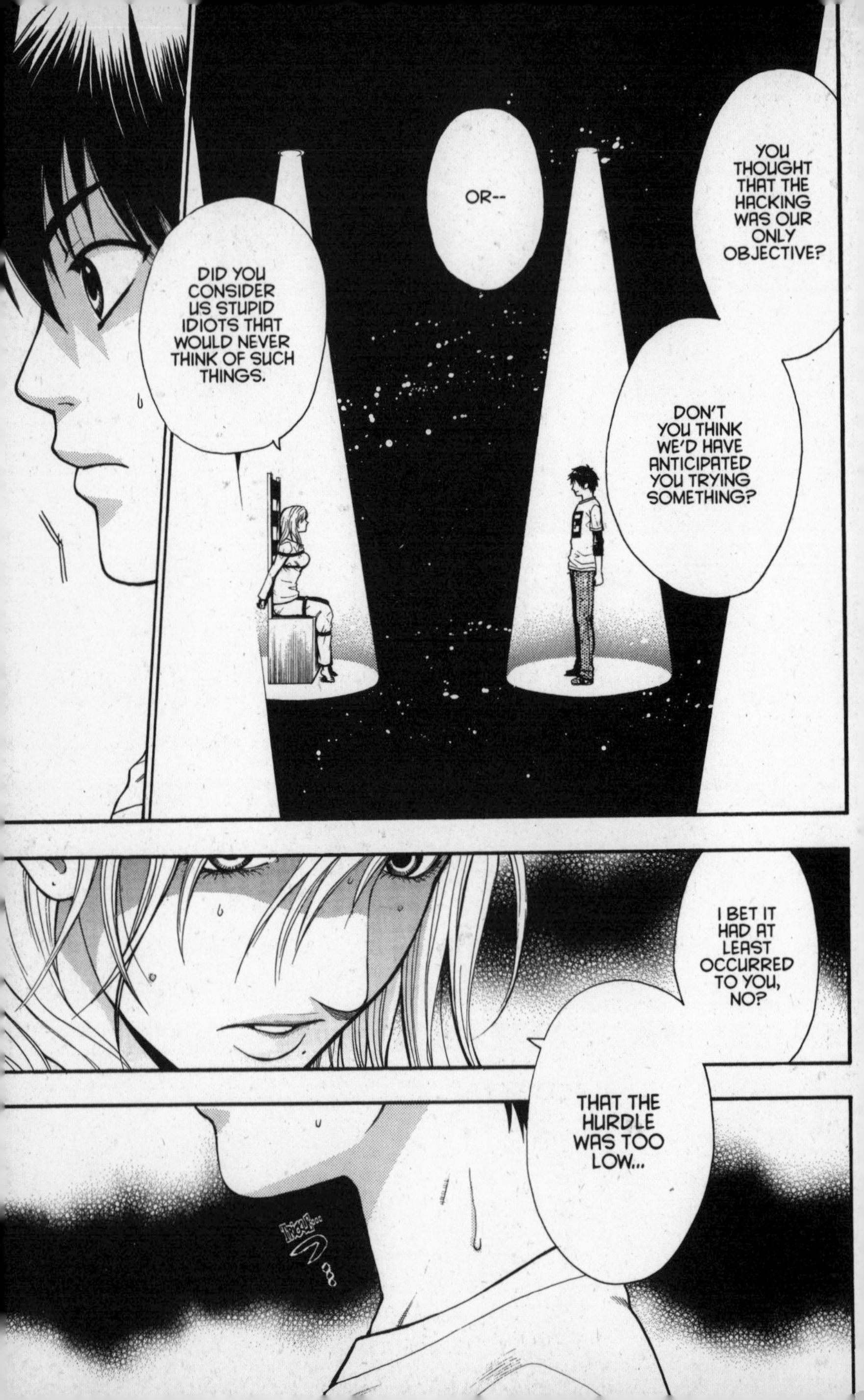
YOU THOUGHT THAT THE HACKING WAS OUR ONLY OBJECTIVE?
DON'T YOU THINK WE'D HAVE ANTICIPATED YOU TRYING SOMETHING?
OR--
DID YOU CONSIDER US STUPID IDIOTS THAT WOULD NEVER THINK OF SUCH THINGS.
I BET IT HAD AT LEAST OCCURRED TO YOU, NO?
THAT THE HURDLE WAS TOO LOW...

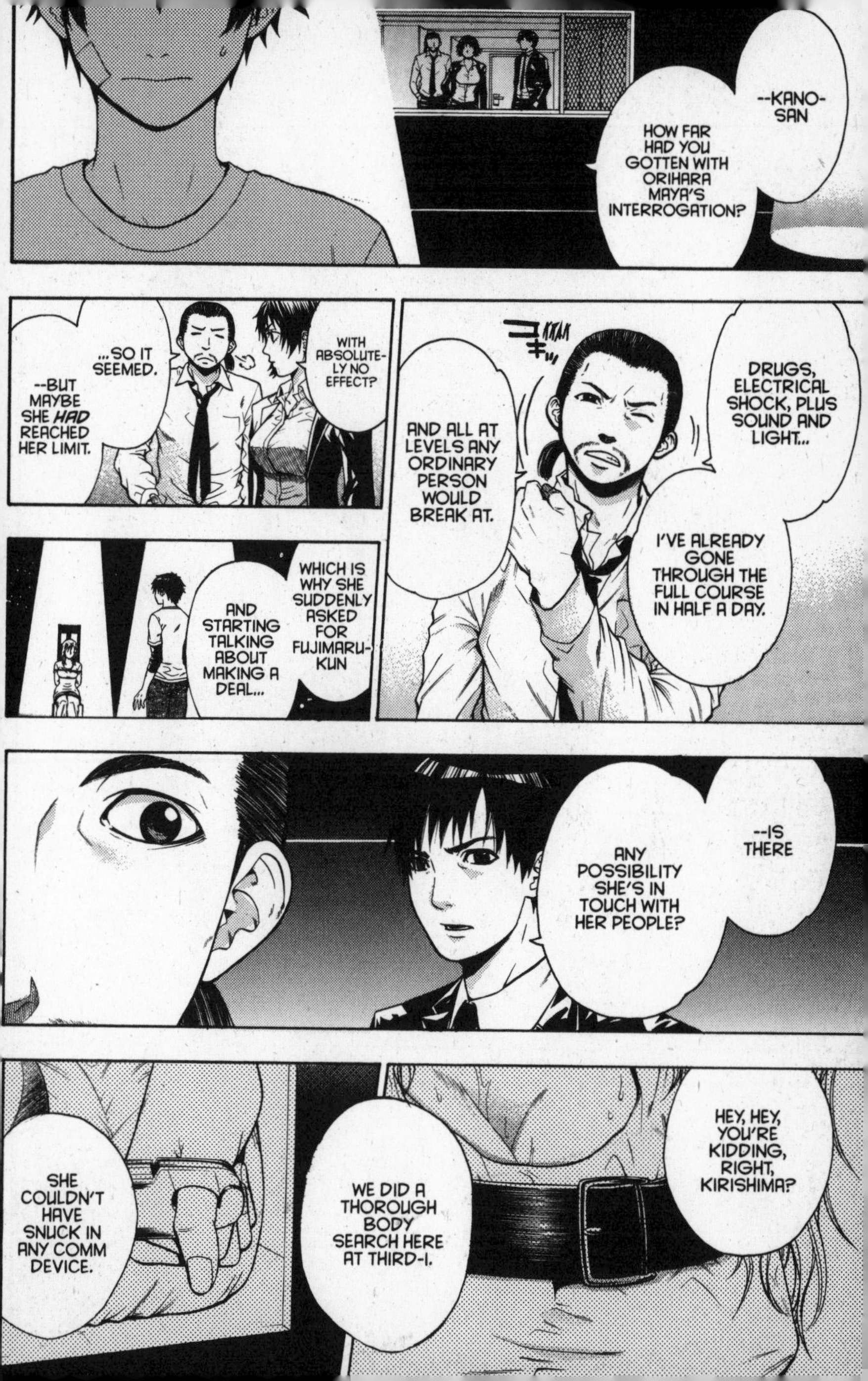
--KANO-SAN
HOW FAR HAD YOU GOTTEN WITH ORIHARA MAYA'S INTERROGATION?
DRUGS, ELECTRICAL SHOCK, PLUS SOUND AND LIGHT...
I'VE ALREADY GONE THROUGH THE FULL COURSE IN HALF A DAY.
AND ALL AT LEVELS ANY ORDINARY PERSON WOULD BREAK AT.
WITH ABSOLUTELY NO EFFECT?
...SO IT SEEMED.
--BUT MAYBE SHE *HAD* REACHED HER LIMIT.
WHICH IS WHY SHE SUDDENLY ASKED FOR FUJIMARU-KUN
AND STARTING TALKING ABOUT MAKING A DEAL...
--IS THERE
ANY POSSIBILITY SHE'S IN TOUCH WITH HER PEOPLE?
HEY, HEY, YOU'RE KIDDING, RIGHT, KIRISHIMA?
WE DID A THOROUGH BODY SEARCH HERE AT THIRD-I.
SHE COULDN'T HAVE SNUCK IN ANY COMM DEVICE.

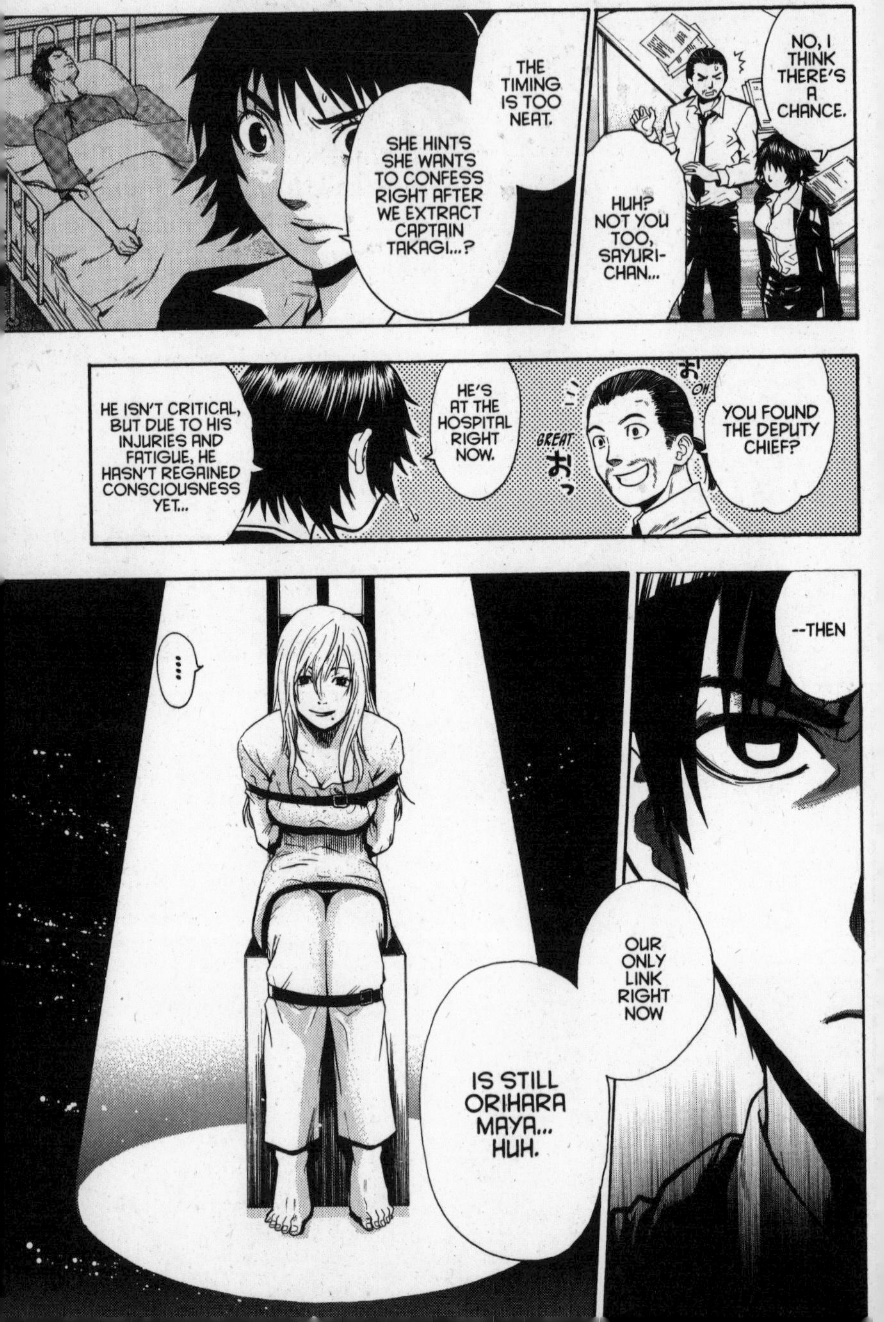
NO, I THINK THERE'S A CHANCE.
HUH? NOT YOU TOO, SAYURI-CHAN...
THE TIMING IS TOO NEAT.
SHE HINTS SHE WANTS TO CONFESS RIGHT AFTER WE EXTRACT CAPTAIN TAKAGI...?
YOU FOUND THE DEPUTY CHIEF?
OH
GREAT
HE'S AT THE HOSPITAL RIGHT NOW.
HE ISN'T CRITICAL, BUT DUE TO HIS INJURIES AND FATIGUE, HE HASN'T REGAINED CONSCIOUSNESS YET...
--THEN
OUR ONLY LINK RIGHT NOW
IS STILL ORIHARA MAYA... HUH.
....

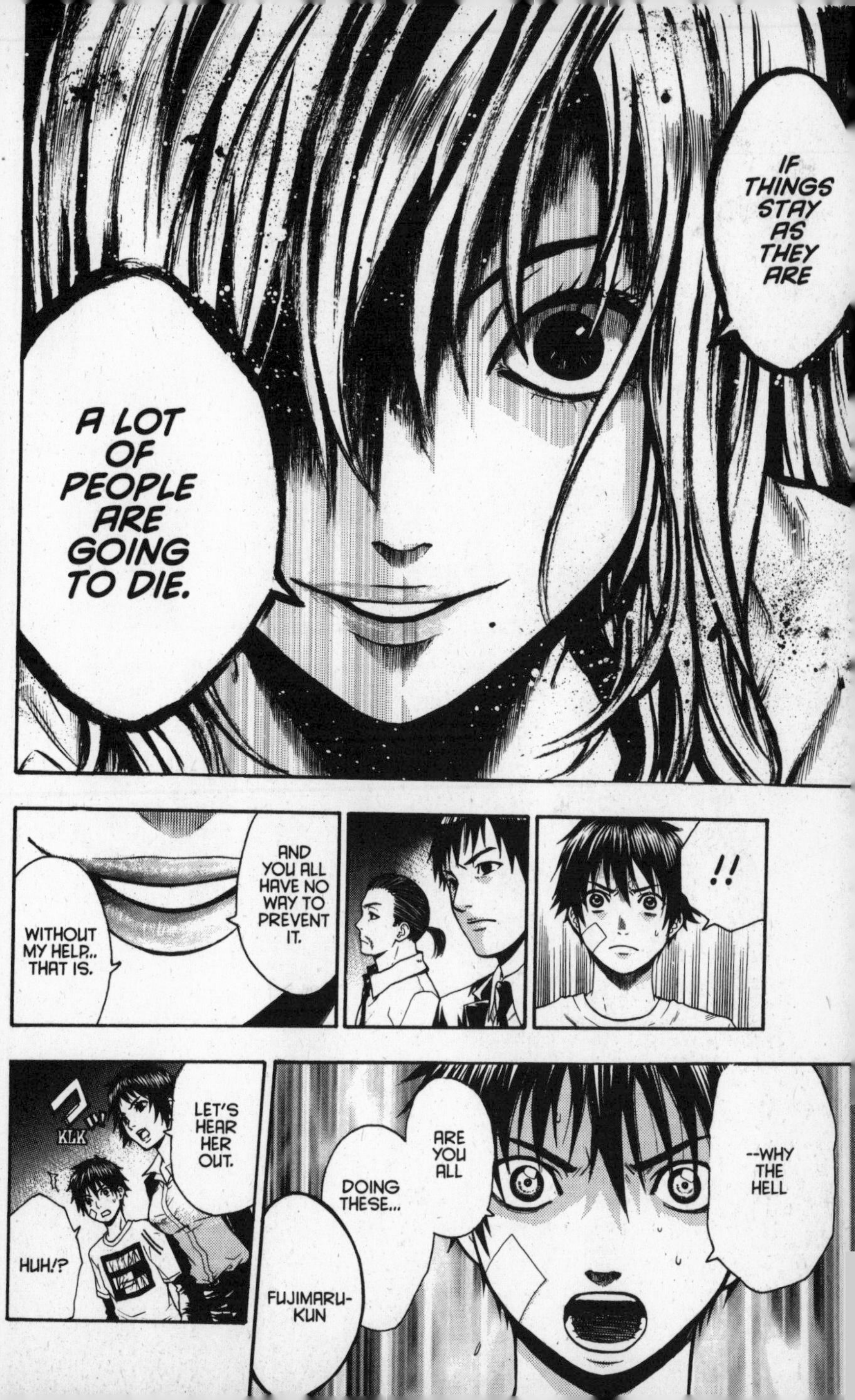
IF THINGS STAY AS THEY ARE
A LOT OF PEOPLE ARE GOING TO DIE.
!!
AND YOU ALL HAVE NO WAY TO PREVENT IT.
WITHOUT MY HELP... THAT IS.
--WHY THE HELL
ARE YOU ALL
DOING THESE...
FUJIMARU-KUN
LET'S HEAR HER OUT.
KLK
HUH!?

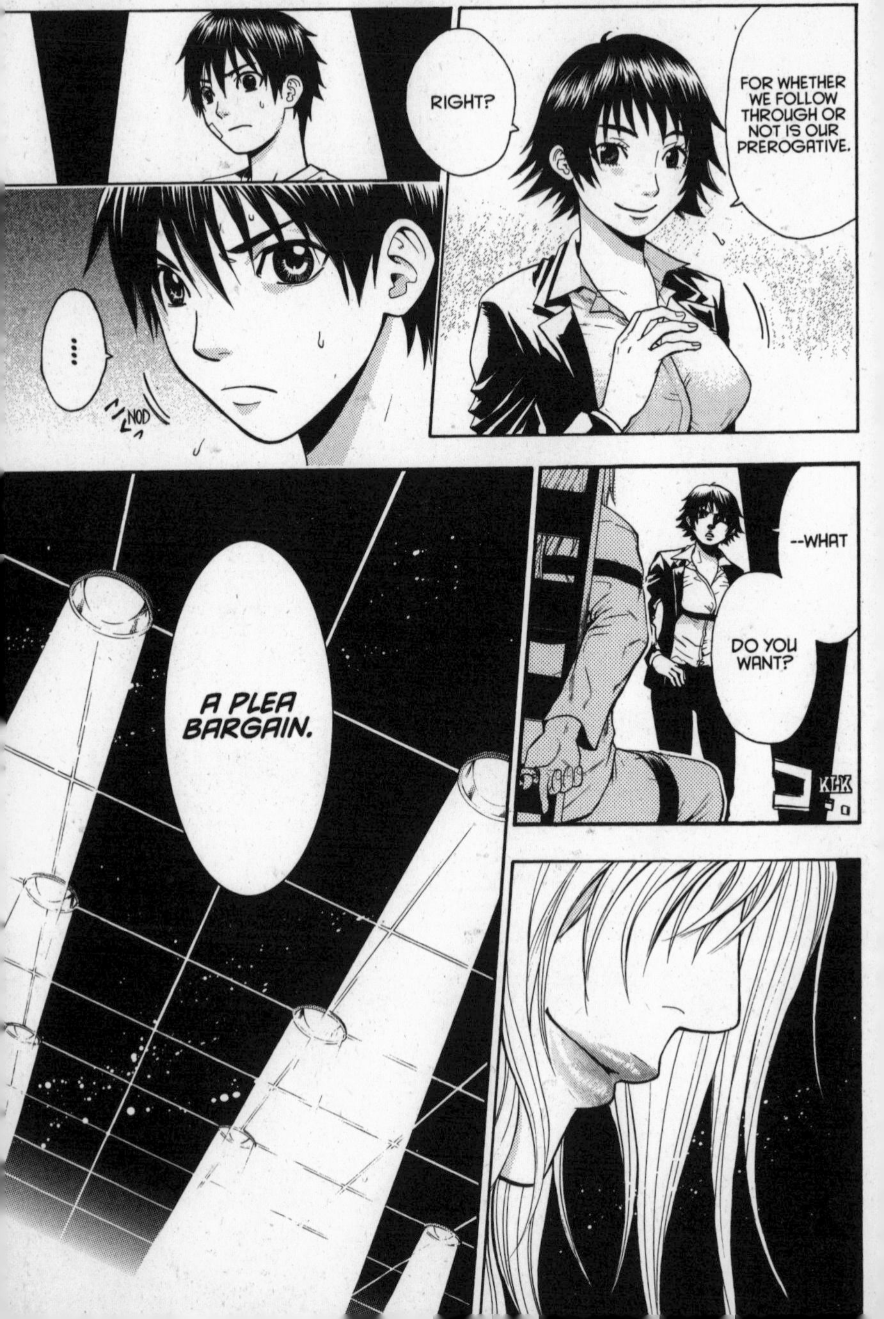
FOR WHETHER WE FOLLOW THROUGH OR NOT IS OUR PREROGATIVE.
RIGHT?
....
NOD
--WHAT
DO YOU WANT?
KLIK
A PLEA BARGAIN.

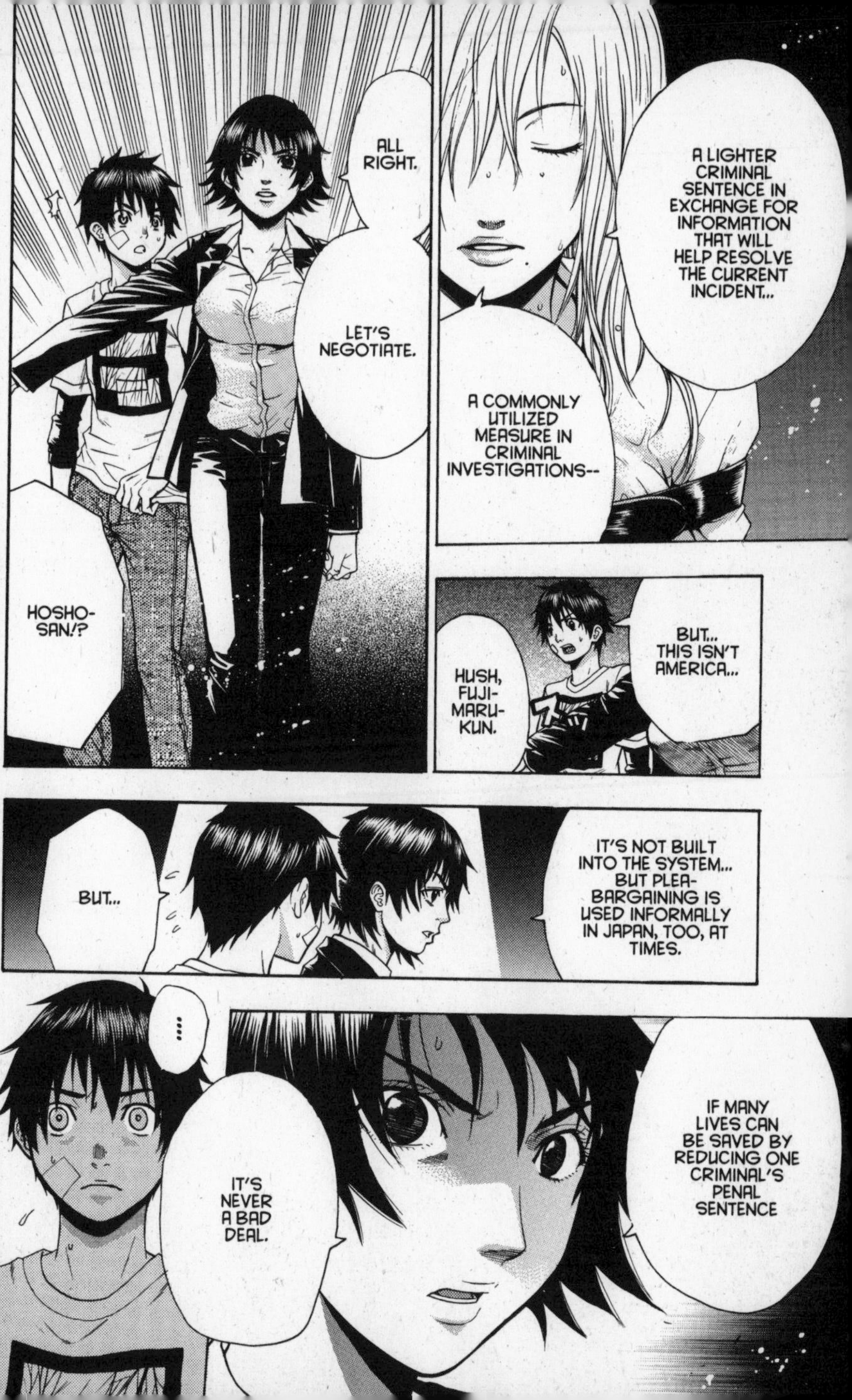
A LIGHTER CRIMINAL SENTENCE IN EXCHANGE FOR INFORMATION THAT WILL HELP RESOLVE THE CURRENT INCIDENT...
A COMMONLY UTILIZED MEASURE IN CRIMINAL INVESTIGATIONS--
BUT... THIS ISN'T AMERICA...
HUSH, FUJI-MARU-KUN.
ALL RIGHT.
LET'S NEGOTIATE.
HOSHO-SAN!?
IT'S NOT BUILT INTO THE SYSTEM... BUT PLEA-BARGAINING IS USED INFORMALLY IN JAPAN, TOO, AT TIMES.
BUT...
IF MANY LIVES CAN BE SAVED BY REDUCING ONE CRIMINAL'S PENAL SENTENCE
IT'S NEVER A BAD DEAL.
....

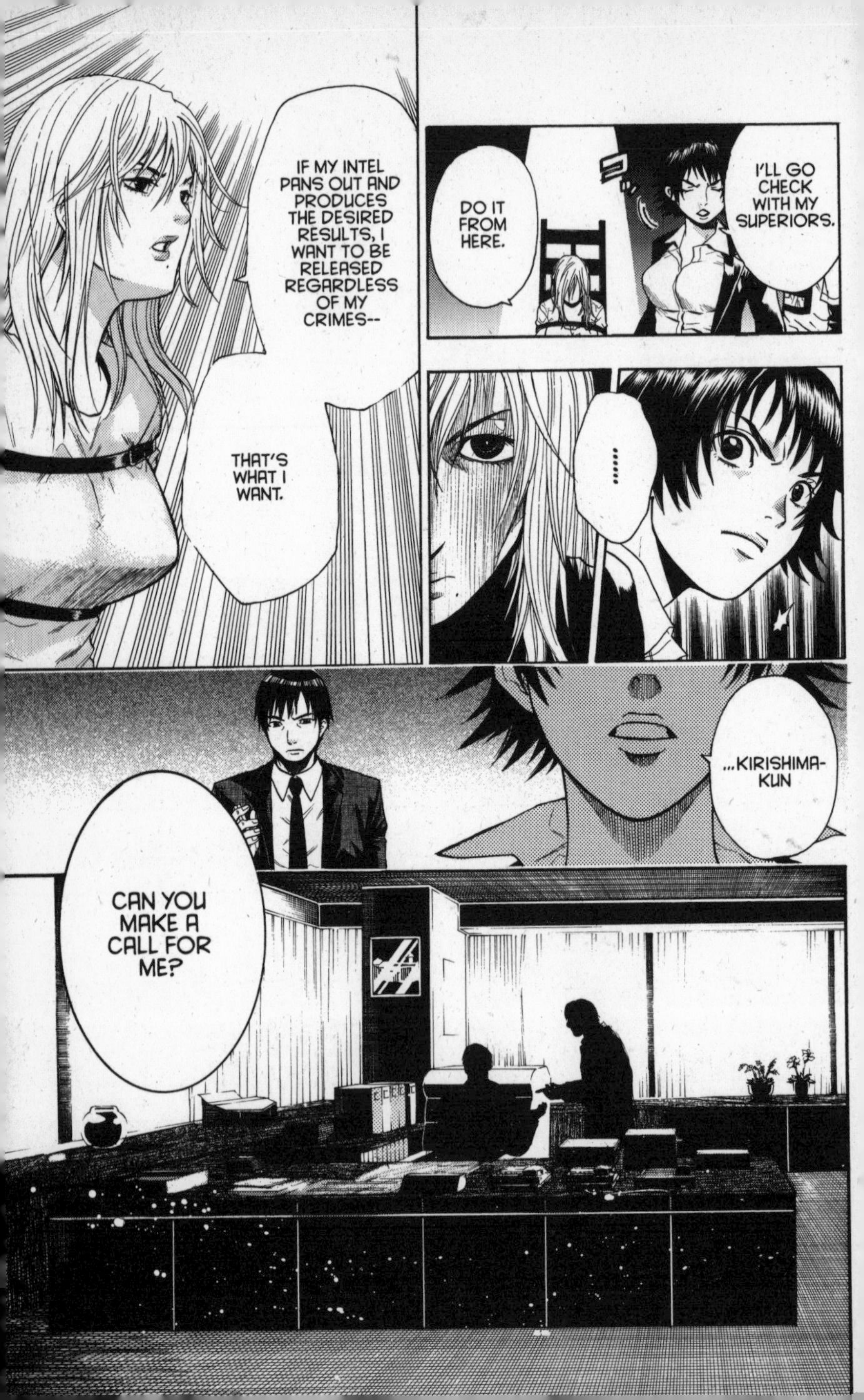
I'LL GO CHECK WITH MY SUPERIORS.
DO IT FROM HERE.
......
IF MY INTEL PANS OUT AND PRODUCES THE DESIRED RESULTS, I WANT TO BE RELEASED REGARDLESS OF MY CRIMES--
THAT'S WHAT I WANT.
...KIRISHIMA-KUN
CAN YOU MAKE A CALL FOR ME?

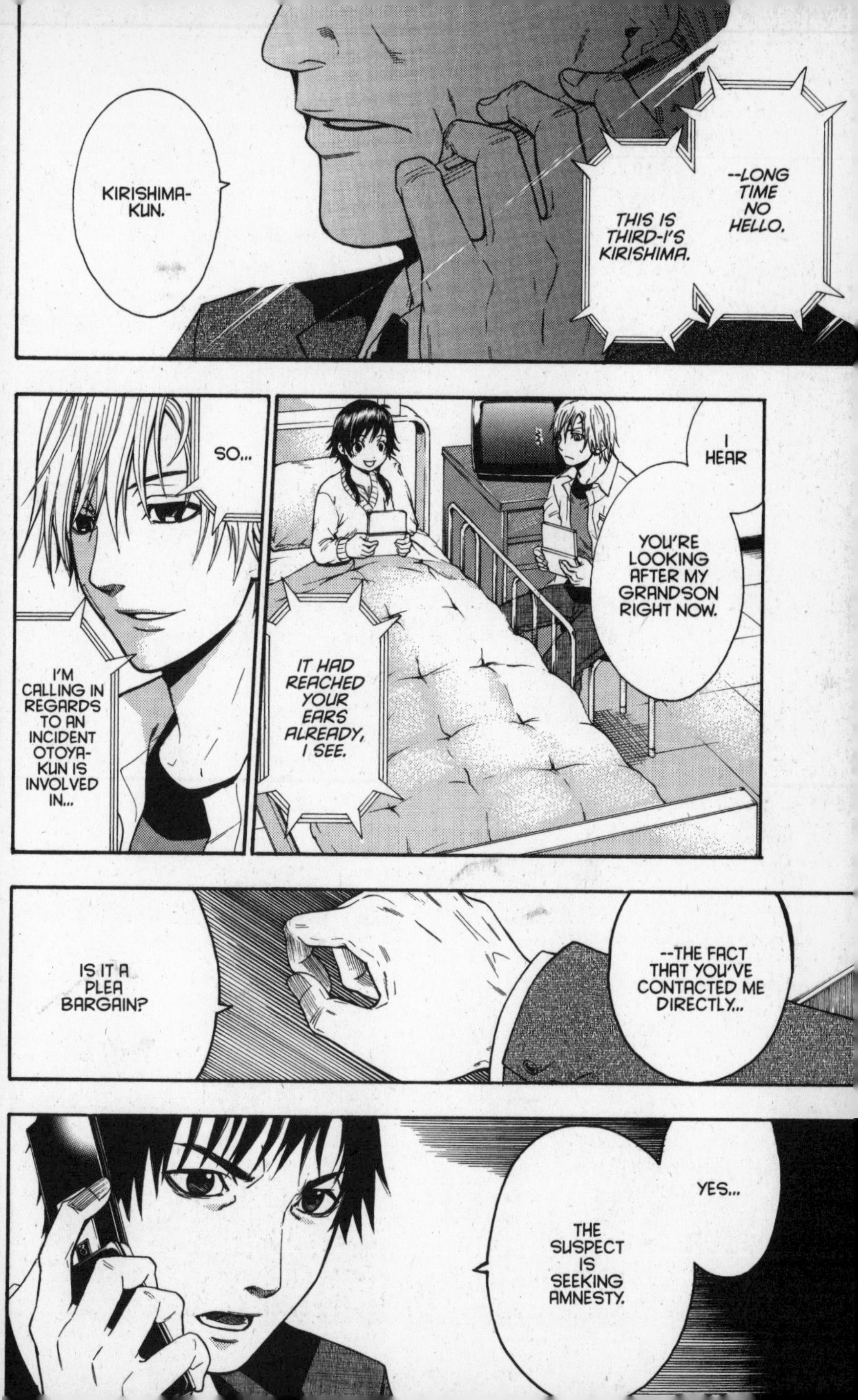
--LONG TIME NO HELLO.
THIS IS THIRD-I'S KIRISHIMA.
KIRISHIMA-KUN.
I HEAR
YOU'RE LOOKING AFTER MY GRANDSON RIGHT NOW.
IT HAD REACHED YOUR EARS ALREADY, I SEE.
SO...
I'M CALLING IN REGARDS TO AN INCIDENT OTOYA-KUN IS INVOLVED IN...
--THE FACT THAT YOU'VE CONTACTED ME DIRECTLY...
IS IT A PLEA BARGAIN?
YES...
THE SUSPECT IS SEEKING AMNESTY.

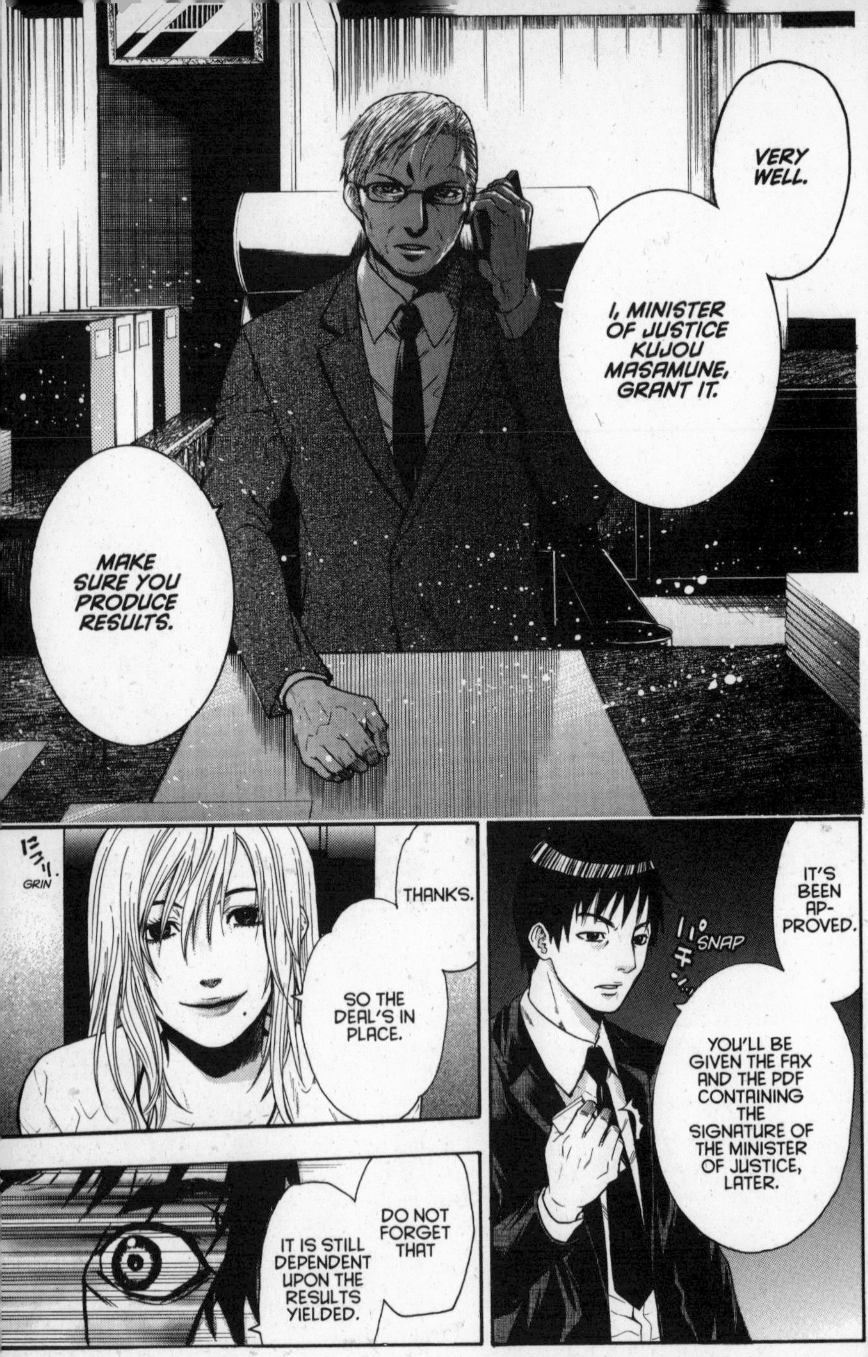
VERY WELL.
I, MINISTER OF JUSTICE KUJOU MASAMUNE, GRANT IT.
MAKE SURE YOU PRODUCE RESULTS.
IT'S BEEN AP-PROVED.
SNAP
YOU'LL BE GIVEN THE FAX AND THE PDF CONTAINING THE SIGNATURE OF THE MINISTER OF JUSTICE, LATER.
THANKS.
SO THE DEAL'S IN PLACE.
GRIN
DO NOT FORGET THAT
IT IS STILL DEPENDENT UPON THE RESULTS YIELDED.

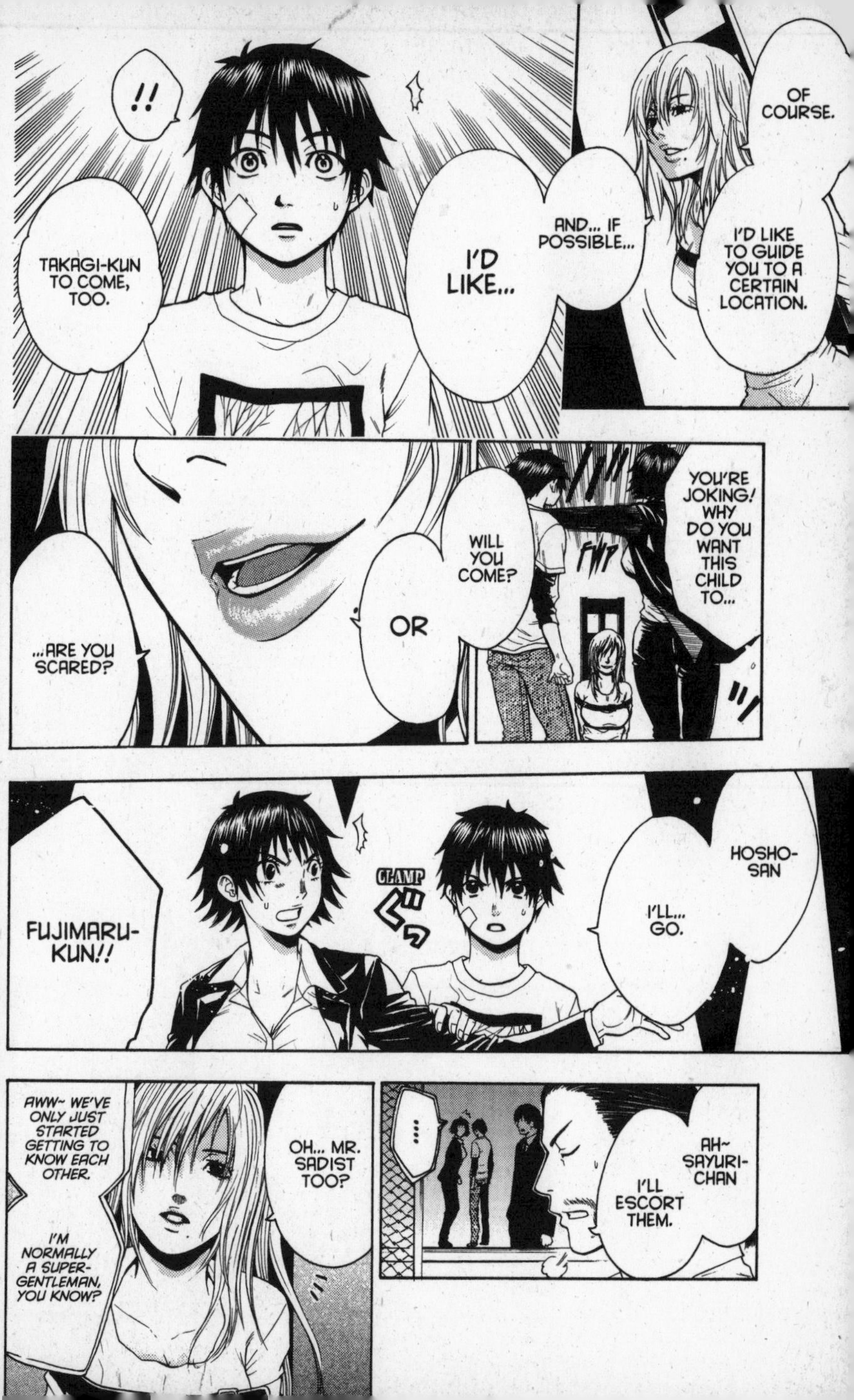
OF COURSE.
I'D LIKE TO GUIDE YOU TO A CERTAIN LOCATION.
AND... IF POSSIBLE...
I'D LIKE...
TAKAGI-KUN TO COME, TOO.
!!
YOU'RE JOKING! WHY DO YOU WANT THIS CHILD TO...
FWP
WILL YOU COME?
OR
...ARE YOU SCARED?
HOSHO-SAN
I'LL... GO.
CLAMP
FUJIMARU-KUN!!
AH~ SAYURI-CHAN
I'LL ESCORT THEM.
....
OH... MR. SADIST TOO?
AWW~ WE'VE ONLY JUST STARTED GETTING TO KNOW EACH OTHER.
I'M NORMALLY A SUPER-GENTLEMAN, YOU KNOW?

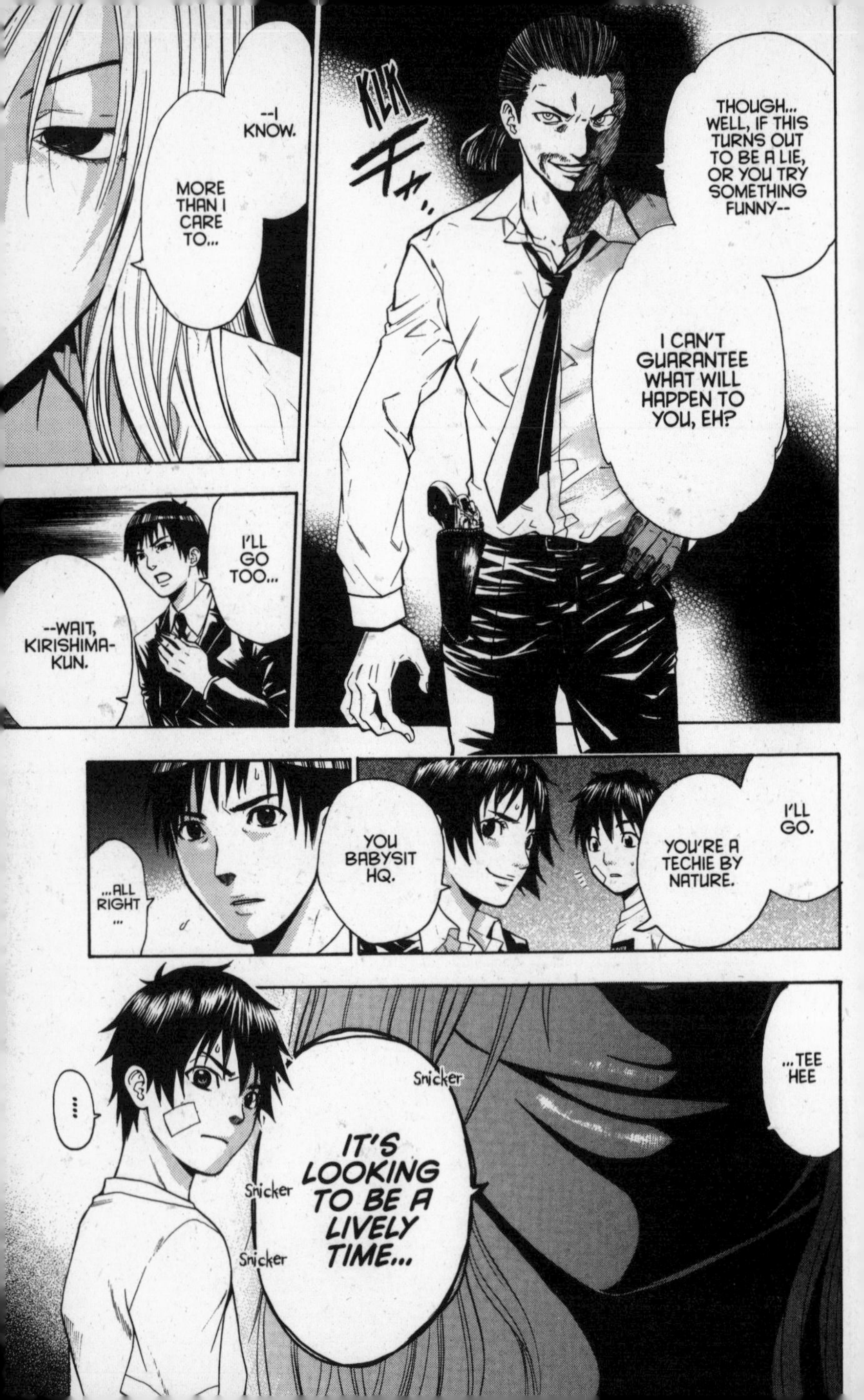
KLK
THOUGH... WELL, IF THIS TURNS OUT TO BE A LIE, OR YOU TRY SOMETHING FUNNY--
I CAN'T GUARANTEE WHAT WILL HAPPEN TO YOU, EH?
--I KNOW.
MORE THAN I CARE TO...
I'LL GO TOO...
--WAIT, KIRISHIMA-KUN.
I'LL GO.
YOU'RE A TECHIE BY NATURE.
YOU BABYSIT HQ.
...ALL RIGHT ...
...TEE HEE
Snicker
IT'S LOOKING TO BE A LIVELY TIME...
Snicker
Snicker
....

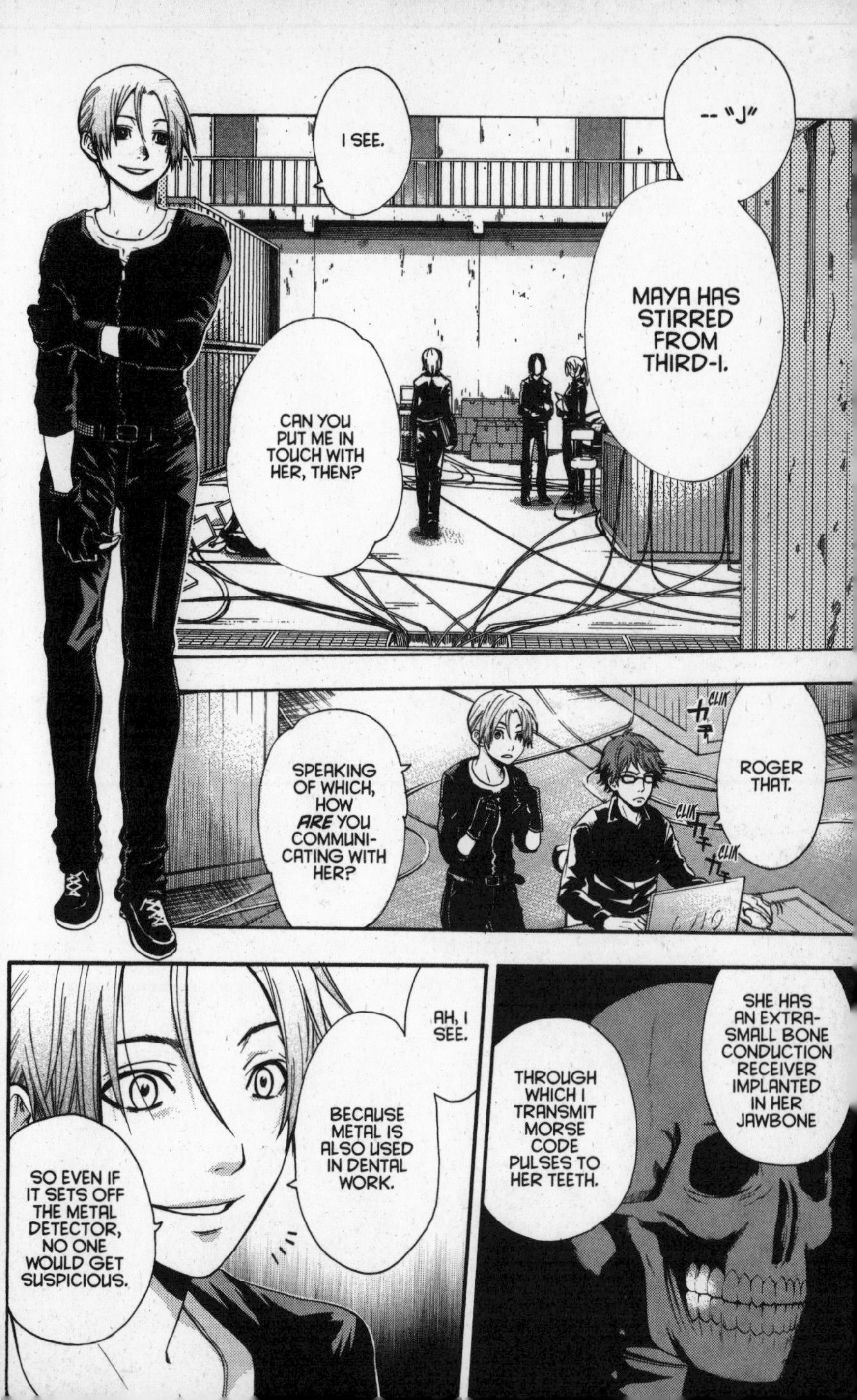
-- "J"
MAYA HAS STIRRED FROM THIRD-I.
I SEE.
CAN YOU PUT ME IN TOUCH WITH HER, THEN?
CLIK
ROGER THAT.
CLIK
CLIK
SPEAKING OF WHICH, HOW *ARE* YOU COMMUNICATING WITH HER?
SHE HAS AN EXTRA-SMALL BONE CONDUCTION RECEIVER IMPLANTED IN HER JAWBONE
THROUGH WHICH I TRANSMIT MORSE CODE PULSES TO HER TEETH.
AH, I SEE.
BECAUSE METAL IS ALSO USED IN DENTAL WORK.
SO EVEN IF IT SETS OFF THE METAL DETECTOR, NO ONE WOULD GET SUSPICIOUS.

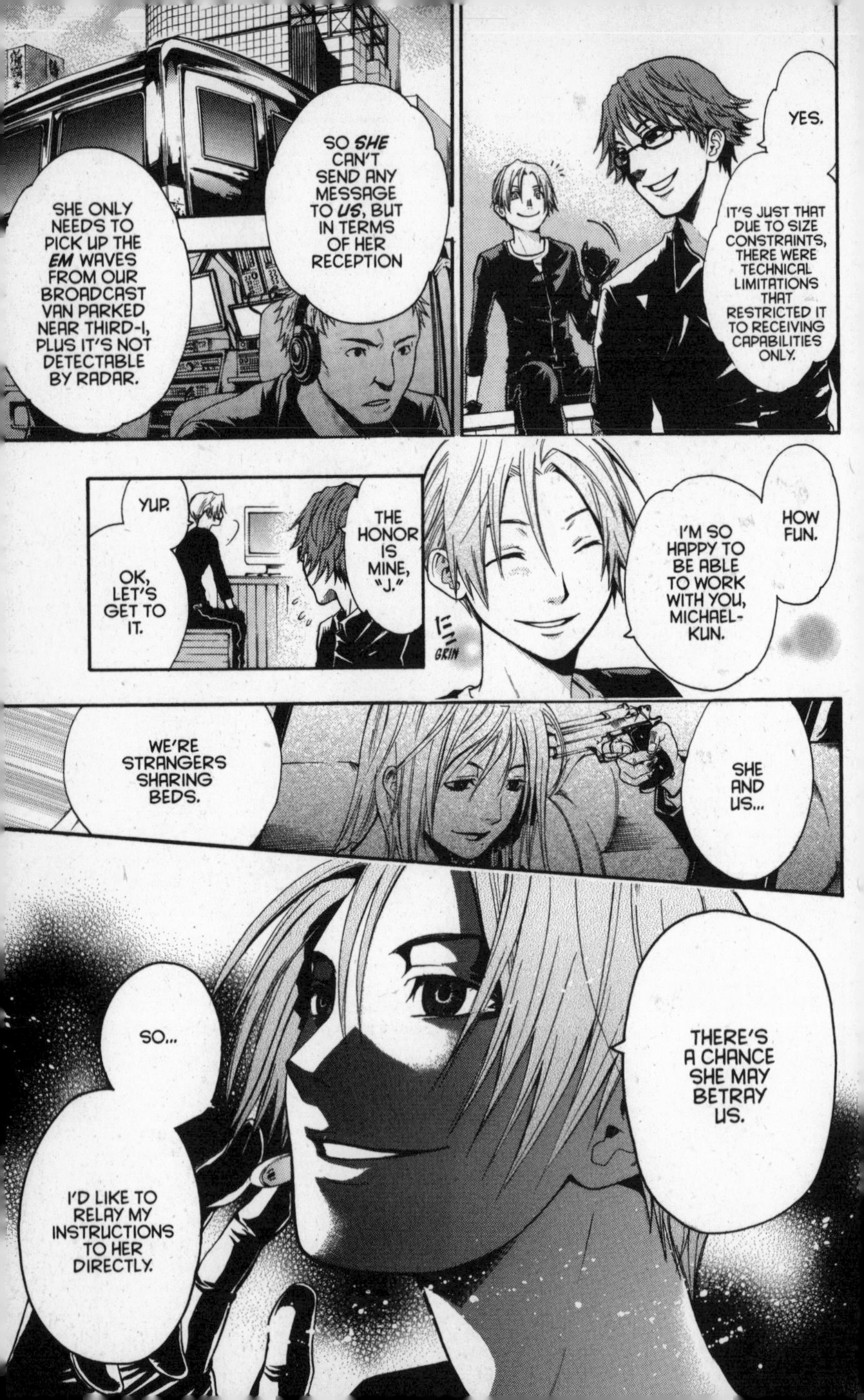
YES.
IT'S JUST THAT DUE TO SIZE CONSTRAINTS, THERE WERE TECHNICAL LIMITATIONS THAT RESTRICTED IT TO RECEIVING CAPABILITIES ONLY.
SO *SHE* CAN'T SEND ANY MESSAGE TO *US*, BUT IN TERMS OF HER RECEPTION
SHE ONLY NEEDS TO PICK UP THE *EM* WAVES FROM OUR BROADCAST VAN PARKED NEAR THIRD-I, PLUS IT'S NOT DETECTABLE BY RADAR.
HOW FUN.
I'M SO HAPPY TO BE ABLE TO WORK WITH YOU, MICHAEL-KUN.
GRIN
THE HONOR IS MINE, "J."
YUP.
OK, LET'S GET TO IT.
SHE AND US...
WE'RE STRANGERS SHARING BEDS.
THERE'S A CHANCE SHE MAY BETRAY US.
SO...
I'D LIKE TO RELAY MY INSTRUCTIONS TO HER DIRECTLY.

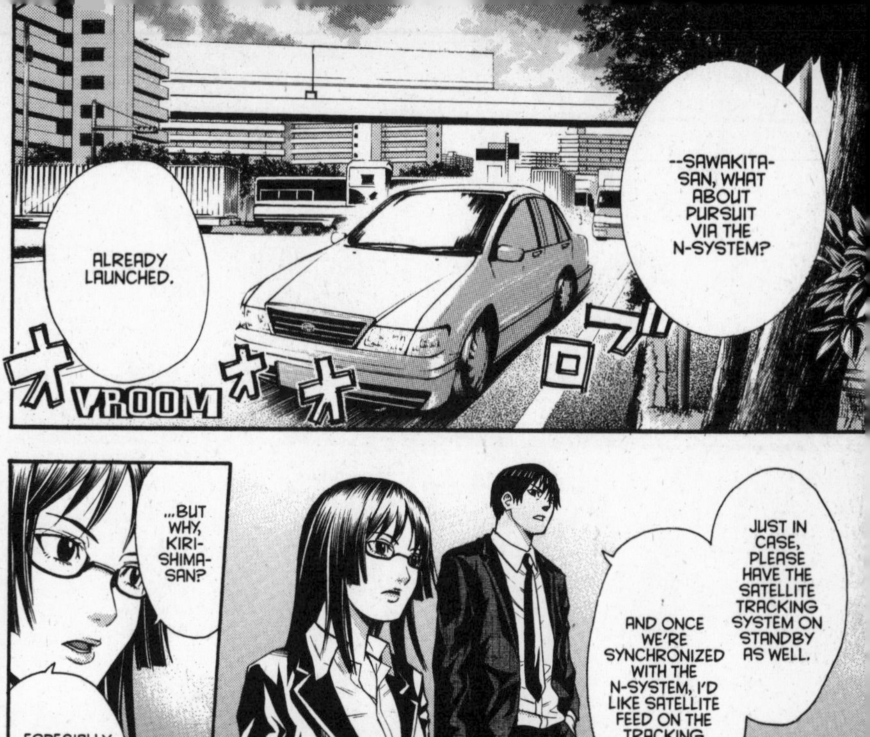
--SAWAKITA-SAN, WHAT ABOUT PURSUIT VIA THE N-SYSTEM?
ALREADY LAUNCHED.
VROOM
JUST IN CASE, PLEASE HAVE THE SATELLITE TRACKING SYSTEM ON STANDBY AS WELL.
AND ONCE WE'RE SYNCHRONIZED WITH THE N-SYSTEM, I'D LIKE SATELLITE FEED ON THE TRACKING VEHICLE TOO.
...BUT WHY, KIRI-SHIMA-SAN?
ESPECIALLY WHEN THERE ARE *TWO* THIRD-I INVESTI-GATORS RIDING ALONG.
...SAWAKITA-SAN
WHAT WAS YOUR OPINION OF ORIHARA MAYA'S INTERROGATION?
HONESTLY, I COULDN'T REALLY WATCH.
I ALMOST WANTED HER TO CONFESS QUICKLY.

N-SYSTEM: A MACHINE THAT TAKES AND RECORDS IMAGES OF LICENSE PLATES (CALLED NUMBER PLATES IN JAPANESE) OF PASSING VEHICLES.

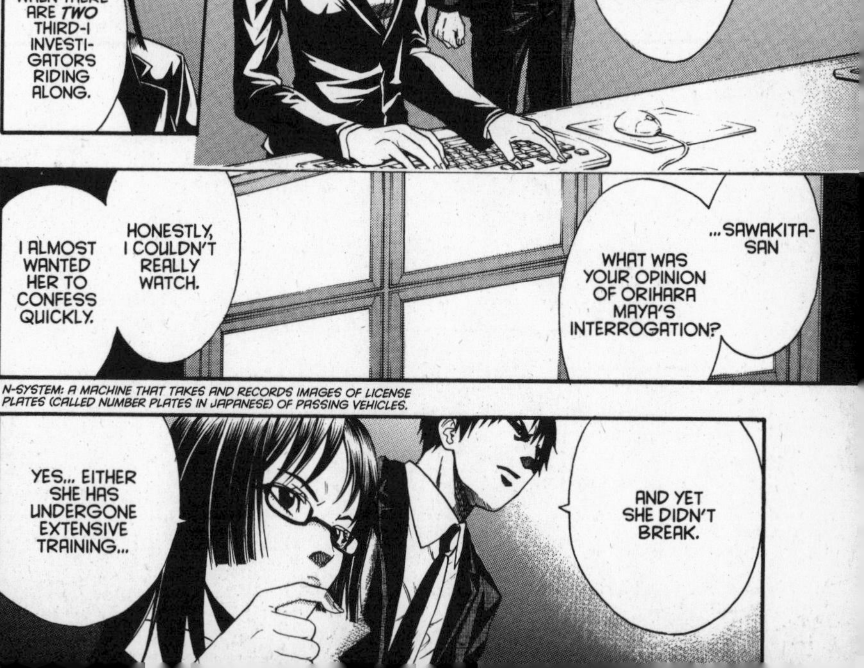
AND YET SHE DIDN'T BREAK.
YES... EITHER SHE HAS UNDERGONE EXTENSIVE TRAINING...

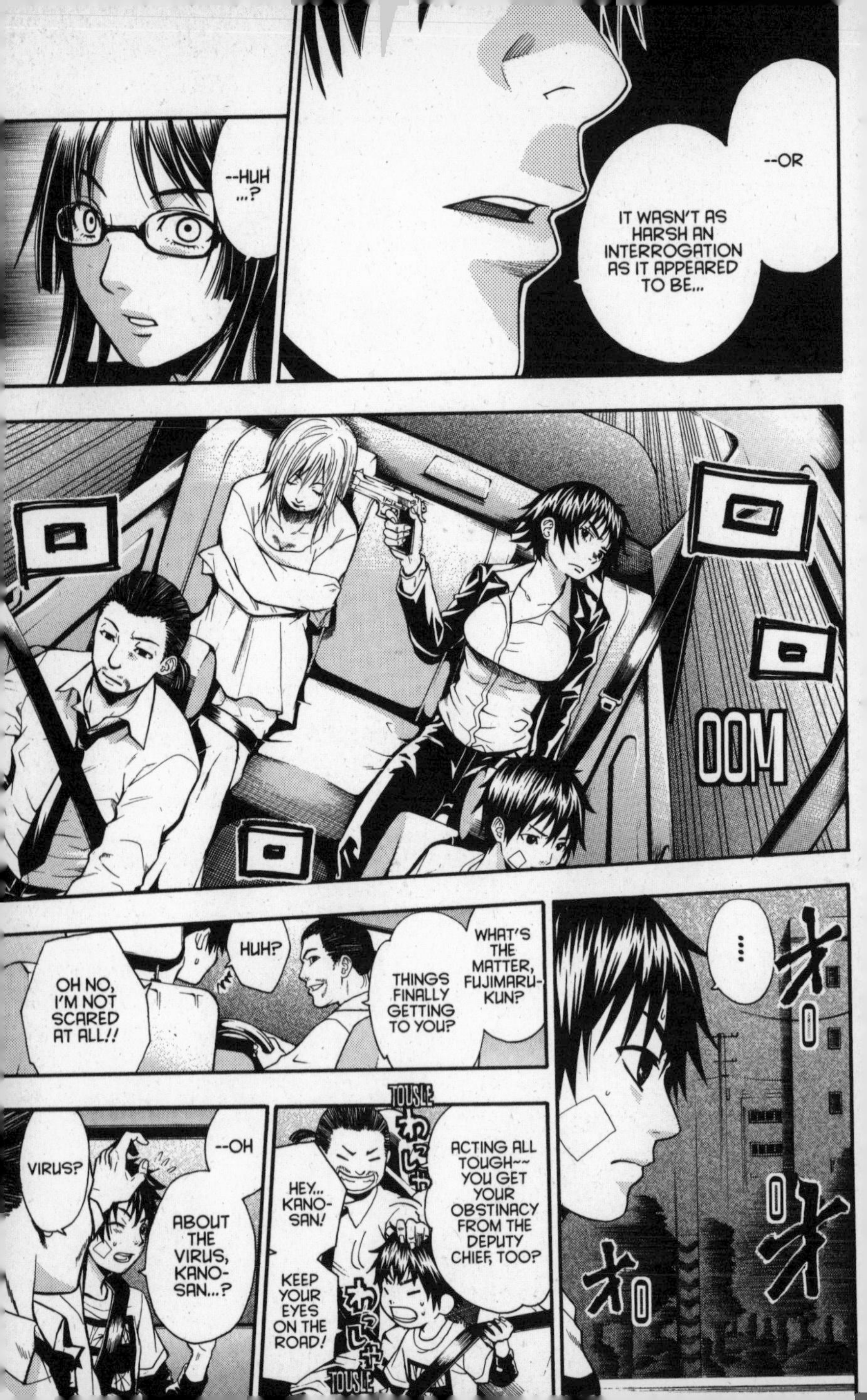
--OR
IT WASN'T AS HARSH AN INTERROGATION AS IT APPEARED TO BE...
--HUH ...?
OOM
....
WHAT'S THE MATTER, FUJIMARU-KUN?
THINGS FINALLY GETTING TO YOU?
HUH?
OH NO, I'M NOT SCARED AT ALL!!
ACTING ALL TOUGH~~ YOU GET YOUR OBSTINACY FROM THE DEPUTY CHIEF, TOO?
TOUSLE わっしゃ
HEY... KANO-SAN!
KEEP YOUR EYES ON THE ROAD!
わっしゃ TOUSLE
--OH
ABOUT THE VIRUS, KANO-SAN...?
VIRUS?

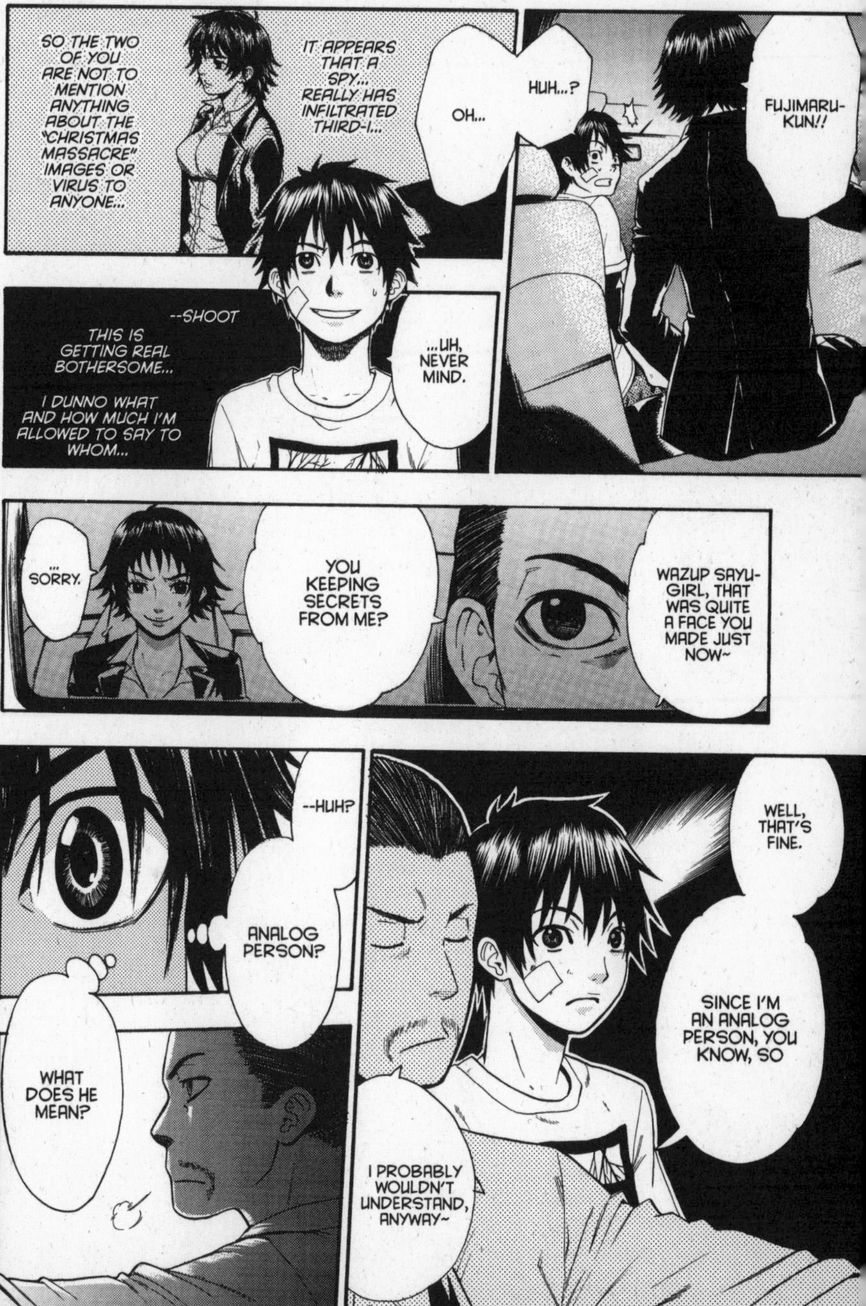
FUJIMARU-KUN!!
HUH...?
OH...
IT APPEARS THAT A SPY... REALLY HAS INFILTRATED THIRD-I...
SO THE TWO OF YOU ARE NOT TO MENTION ANYTHING ABOUT THE "CHRISTMAS MASSACRE" IMAGES OR VIRUS TO ANYONE...
...UH, NEVER MIND.
--SHOOT
THIS IS GETTING REAL BOTHERSOME...
I DUNNO WHAT AND HOW MUCH I'M ALLOWED TO SAY TO WHOM...
WAZUP SAYU-GIRL, THAT WAS QUITE A FACE YOU MADE JUST NOW~
YOU KEEPING SECRETS FROM ME?
... SORRY.
WELL, THAT'S FINE.
SINCE I'M AN ANALOG PERSON, YOU KNOW, SO
I PROBABLY WOULDN'T UNDERSTAND, ANYWAY~
--HUH?
ANALOG PERSON?
WHAT DOES HE MEAN?

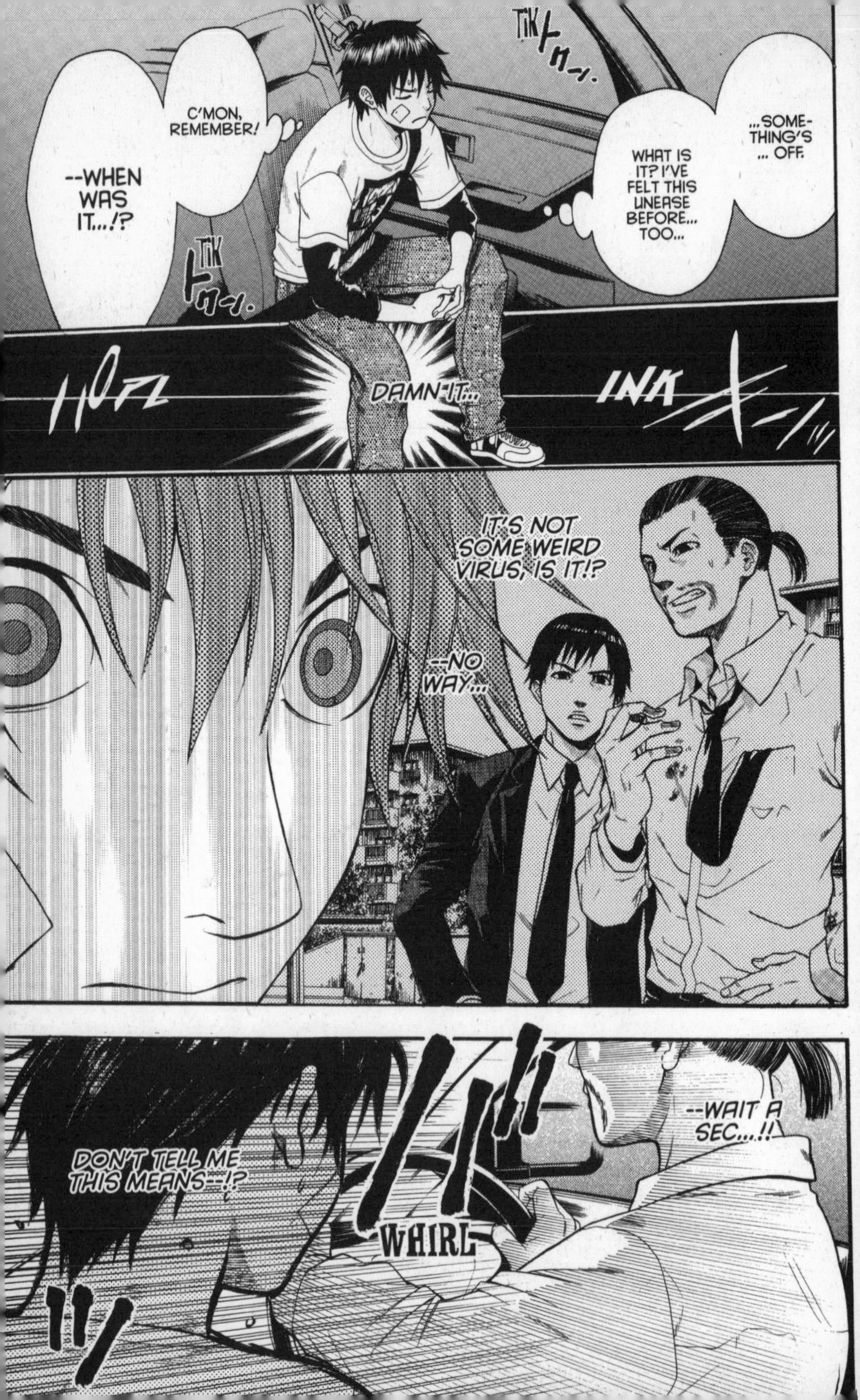
...SOME-THING'S ... OFF.
WHAT IS IT? I'VE FELT THIS UNEASE BEFORE... TOO...
TIK
C'MON, REMEMBER!
--WHEN WAS IT...!?
TIK
INK
DAMN IT...
IT'S NOT SOME WEIRD VIRUS, IS IT!?
--NO WAY...
--WAIT A SEC...!!
WHIRL
DON'T TELL ME THIS MEANS--!?

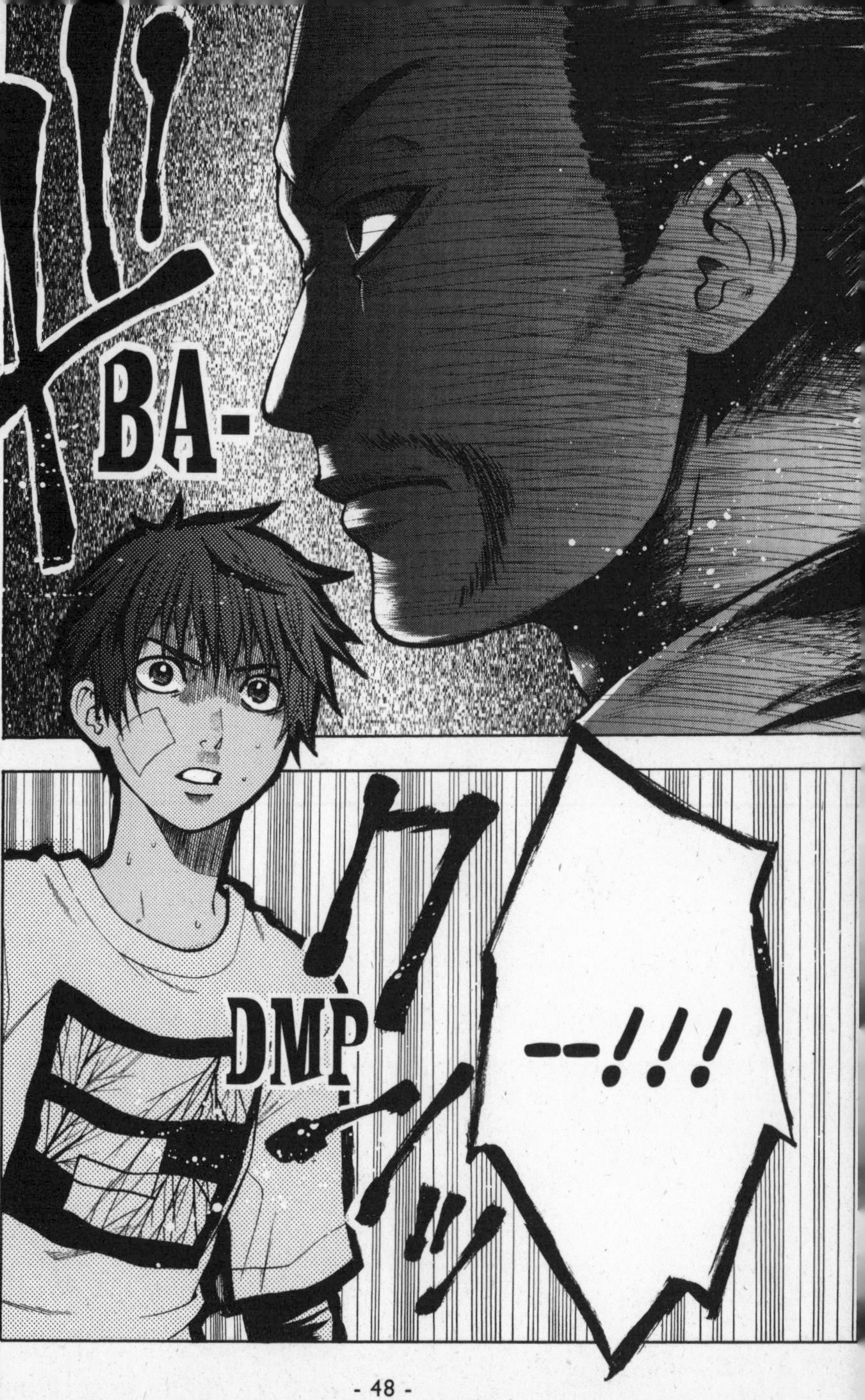
BA-
DMP
--!!!

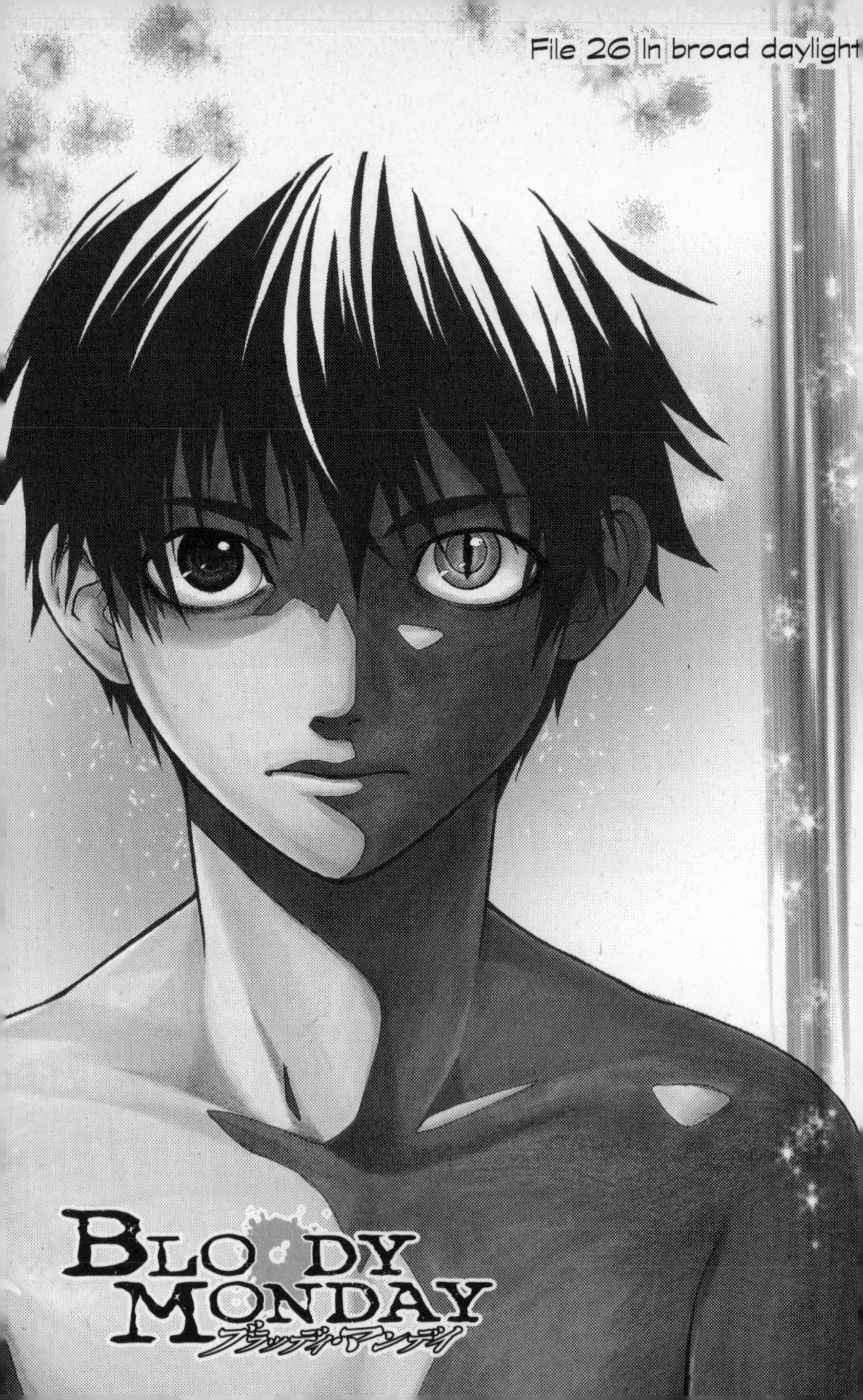
File 26 In broad daylight
BLOODY MONDAY
ブラッディ・マンデイ

BLOODY MONDAY

- GLOSSARY OF TERMS • LIST 10 -

Multichannel p71
Refers to multiplex communication (*multi*plex communication *channel*). A method of communication where a single signal is used to transmit multiple digitized data streams. Types of multiplexing include frequency-division multiplexing, where the signal is partitioned into (non-overlapping) bandwidths and assigned to different data streams, and time-division multiplexing where the signal's time domain is split into (non-overlapping) fixed timeslots and data streams take turns being transmitted.

Archive p152
The act of collecting multiple files together into one single file. Also refers to said single file. Archiving is performed to make data storage or transmission easier by gathering related files together (compressing them) and enabling them to be transferred to high-capacity storage devices. Software used to create archives are known as archivers.

DoS Attack p163
DoS is an abbreviation for denial-of-service. Also called "service rejection" and "service obstruction" in Japanese, it is a type of attack that occurs over a network. Such attacks include overloading the target computer or router with a large volume of illegitimate data and rendering it unavailable or unable to effectively provide services.

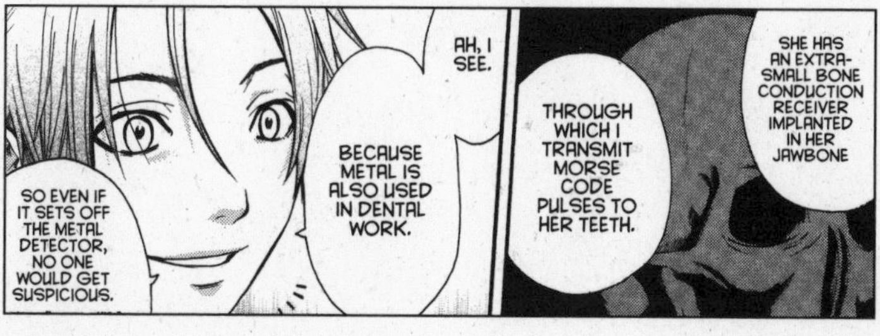
SHE HAS AN EXTRA-SMALL BONE CONDUCTION RECEIVER IMPLANTED IN HER JAWBONE
THROUGH WHICH I TRANSMIT MORSE CODE PULSES TO HER TEETH.
AH, I SEE.
BECAUSE METAL IS ALSO USED IN DENTAL WORK.
SO EVEN IF IT SETS OFF THE METAL DETECTOR, NO ONE WOULD GET SUSPICIOUS.

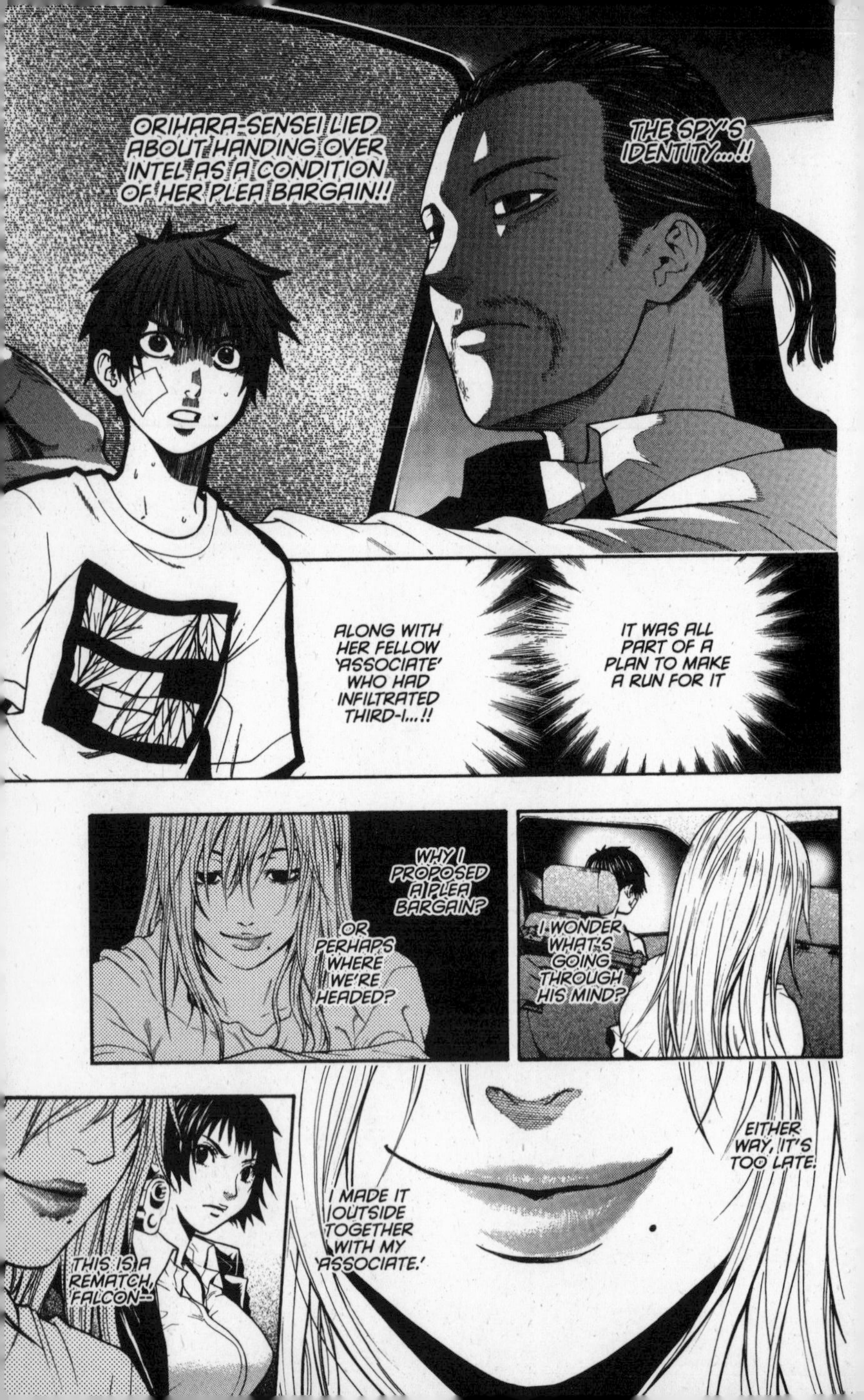
THE SPY'S IDENTITY...!!
ORIHARA-SENSEI LIED ABOUT HANDING OVER INTEL AS A CONDITION OF HER PLEA BARGAIN!!
IT WAS ALL PART OF A PLAN TO MAKE A RUN FOR IT
ALONG WITH HER FELLOW 'ASSOCIATE' WHO HAD INFILTRATED THIRD-I...!!
I WONDER WHAT'S GOING THROUGH HIS MIND?
WHY I PROPOSED A PLEA BARGAIN?
OR PERHAPS WHERE WE'RE HEADED?
EITHER WAY, IT'S TOO LATE.
I MADE IT OUTSIDE TOGETHER WITH MY 'ASSOCIATE.'
THIS IS A REMATCH, FALCON--

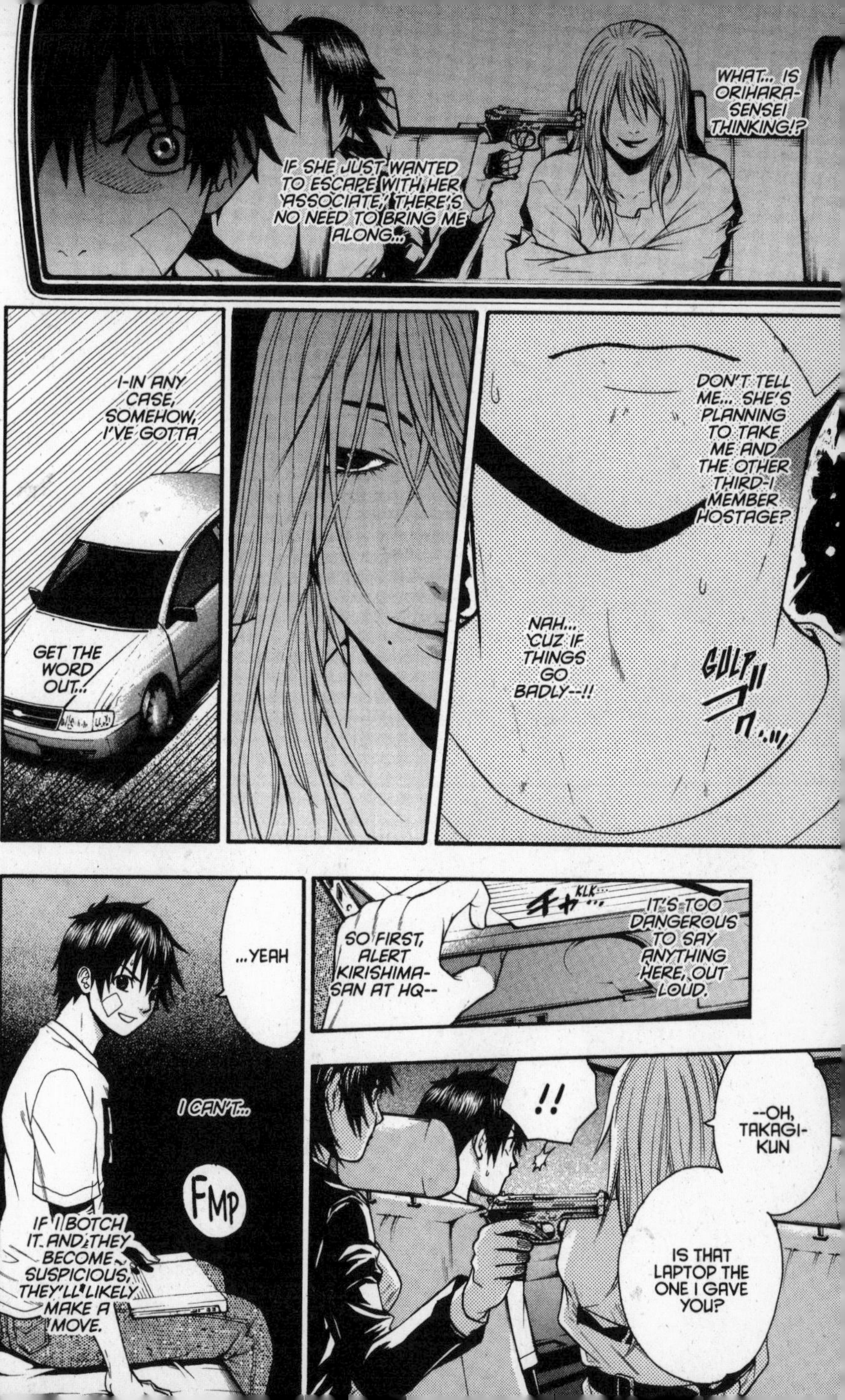
WHAT... IS ORIHARA-SENSEI THINKING!?
IF SHE JUST WANTED TO ESCAPE WITH HER 'ASSOCIATE,' THERE'S NO NEED TO BRING ME ALONG...
DON'T TELL ME... SHE'S PLANNING TO TAKE ME AND THE OTHER THIRD-I MEMBER HOSTAGE?
NAH... 'CUZ IF THINGS GO BADLY--!!
GULP
ゴク...
I-IN ANY CASE, SOMEHOW, I'VE GOTTA
GET THE WORD OUT...
チャ KLK...
IT'S TOO DANGEROUS TO SAY ANYTHING HERE, OUT LOUD.
SO FIRST, ALERT KIRISHIMA-SAN AT HQ--
--OH, TAKAGI-KUN
!!
IS THAT LAPTOP THE ONE I GAVE YOU?
...YEAH
I CAN'T...
FMP
IF I BOTCH IT AND THEY BECOME SUSPICIOUS, THEY'LL LIKELY MAKE A MOVE.

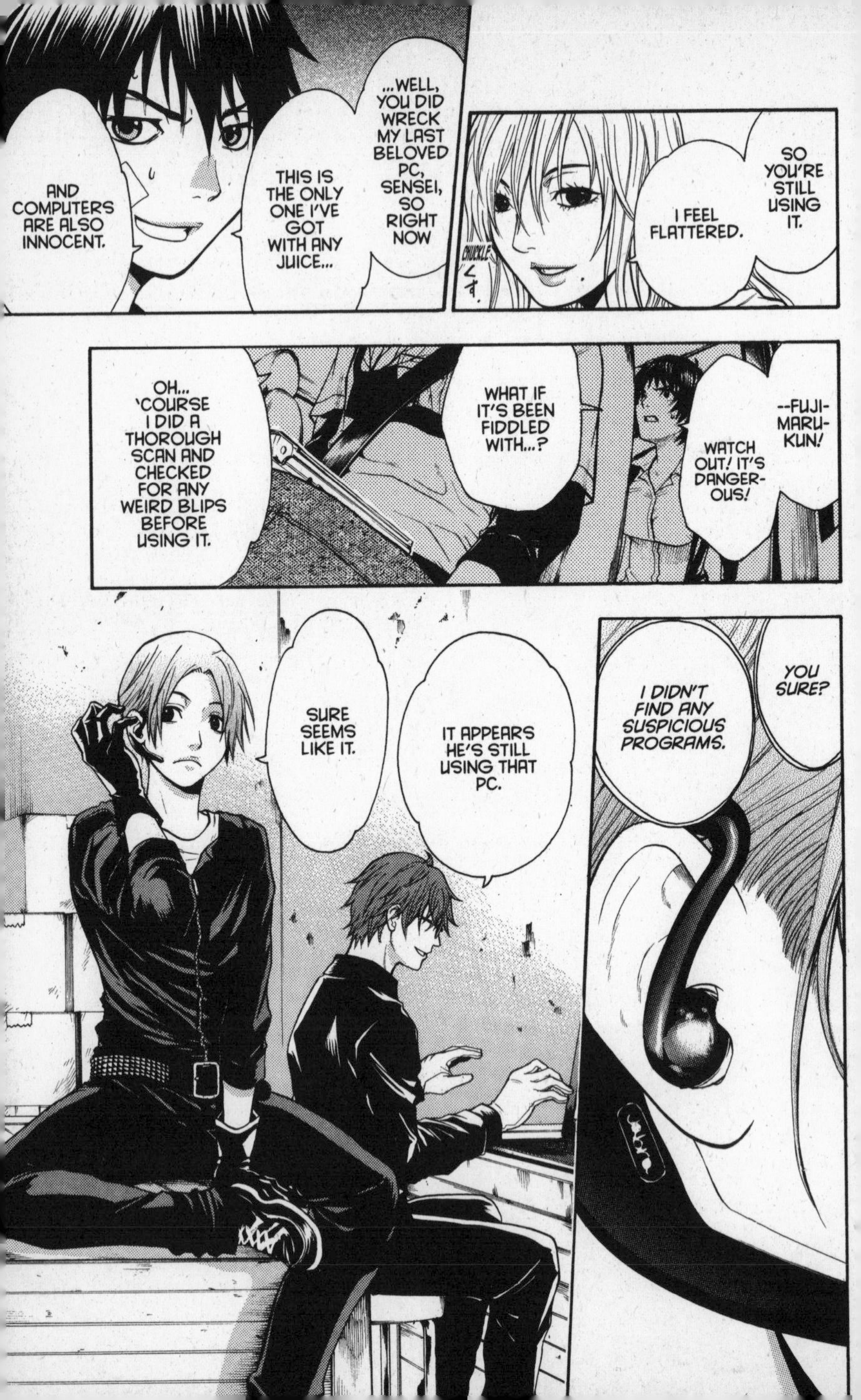
SO YOU'RE STILL USING IT.
I FEEL FLATTERED.
CHUCKLE
くす
...WELL, YOU DID WRECK MY LAST BELOVED PC, SENSEI, SO RIGHT NOW
THIS IS THE ONLY ONE I'VE GOT WITH ANY JUICE...
AND COMPUTERS ARE ALSO INNOCENT.
--FUJI-MARU-KUN!
WATCH OUT! IT'S DANGER-OUS!
WHAT IF IT'S BEEN FIDDLED WITH...?
OH... 'COURSE I DID A THOROUGH SCAN AND CHECKED FOR ANY WEIRD BLIPS BEFORE USING IT.
YOU SURE?
I DIDN'T FIND ANY SUSPICIOUS PROGRAMS.
IT APPEARS HE'S STILL USING THAT PC.
SURE SEEMS LIKE IT.

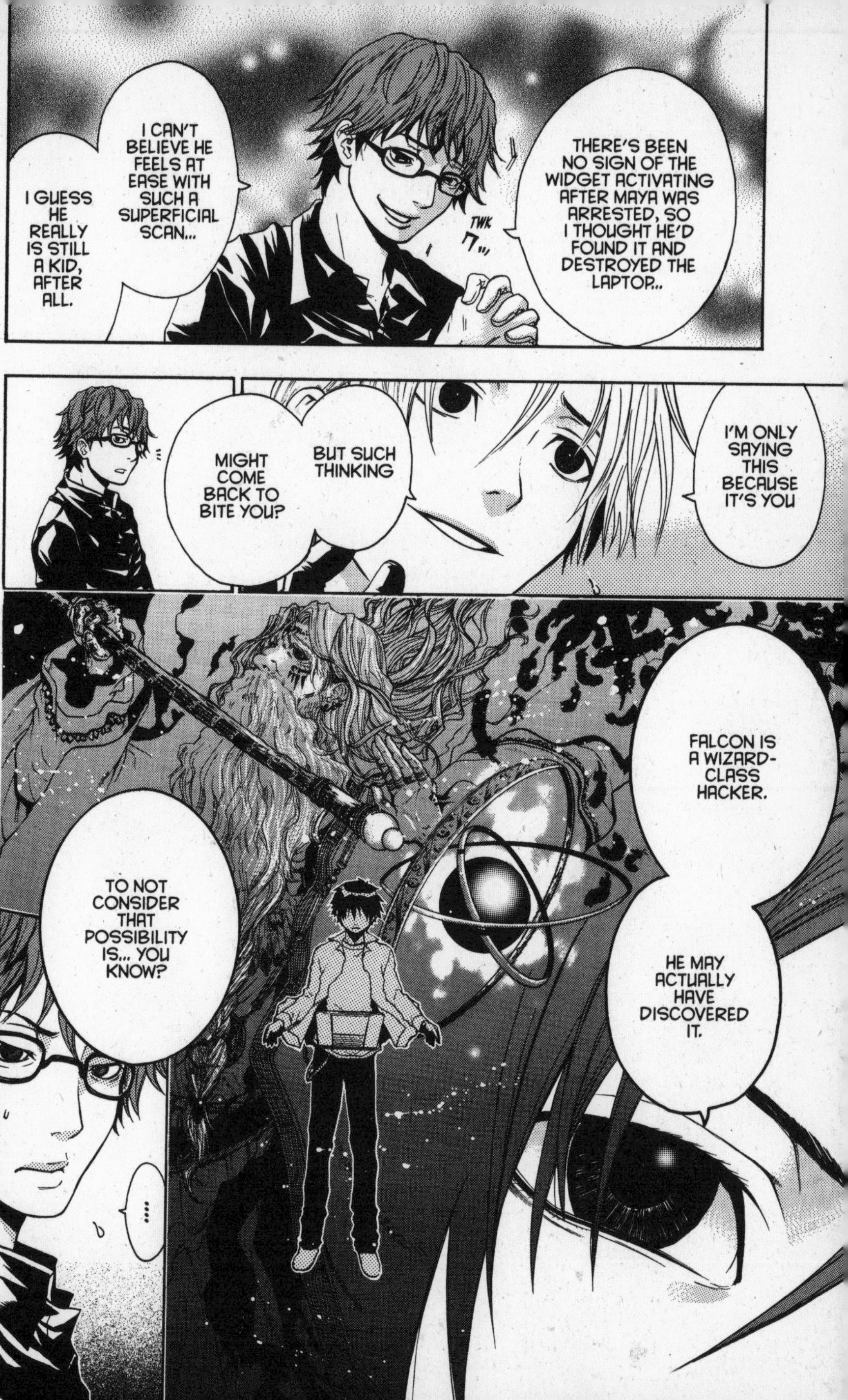
THERE'S BEEN NO SIGN OF THE WIDGET ACTIVATING AFTER MAYA WAS ARRESTED, SO I THOUGHT HE'D FOUND IT AND DESTROYED THE LAPTOP...
TWK
I CAN'T BELIEVE HE FEELS AT EASE WITH SUCH A SUPERFICIAL SCAN...
I GUESS HE REALLY IS STILL A KID, AFTER ALL.
I'M ONLY SAYING THIS BECAUSE IT'S YOU
BUT SUCH THINKING
MIGHT COME BACK TO BITE YOU?
FALCON IS A WIZARD-CLASS HACKER.
HE MAY ACTUALLY HAVE DISCOVERED IT.
TO NOT CONSIDER THAT POSSIBILITY IS... YOU KNOW?
....

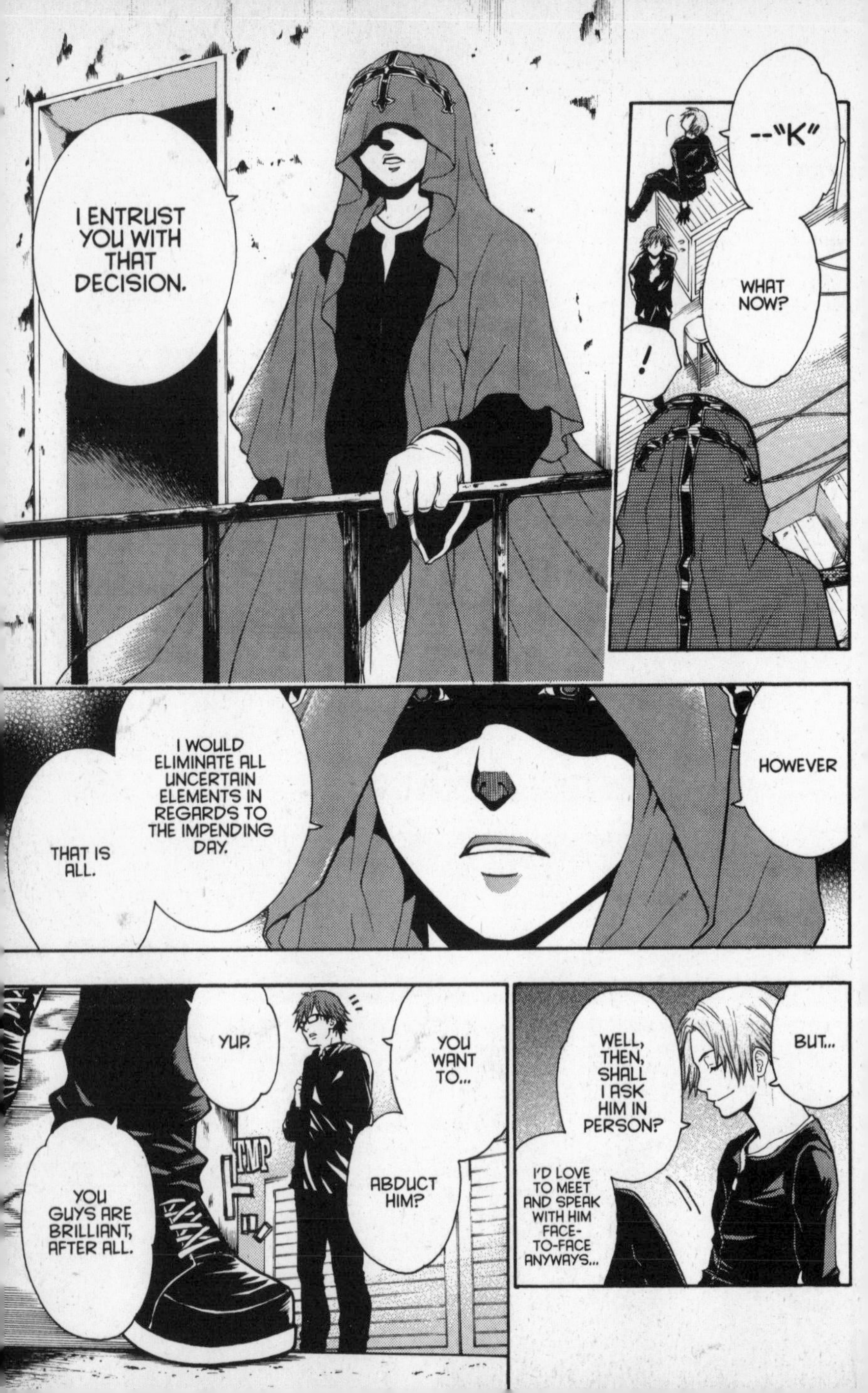
--"K"
WHAT NOW?
!
I ENTRUST YOU WITH THAT DECISION.
HOWEVER
I WOULD ELIMINATE ALL UNCERTAIN ELEMENTS IN REGARDS TO THE IMPENDING DAY.
THAT IS ALL.
BUT...
WELL, THEN, SHALL I ASK HIM IN PERSON?
I'D LOVE TO MEET AND SPEAK WITH HIM FACE-TO-FACE ANYWAYS...
YOU WANT TO...
YUP.
ABDUCT HIM?
TMP
YOU GUYS ARE BRILLIANT, AFTER ALL.

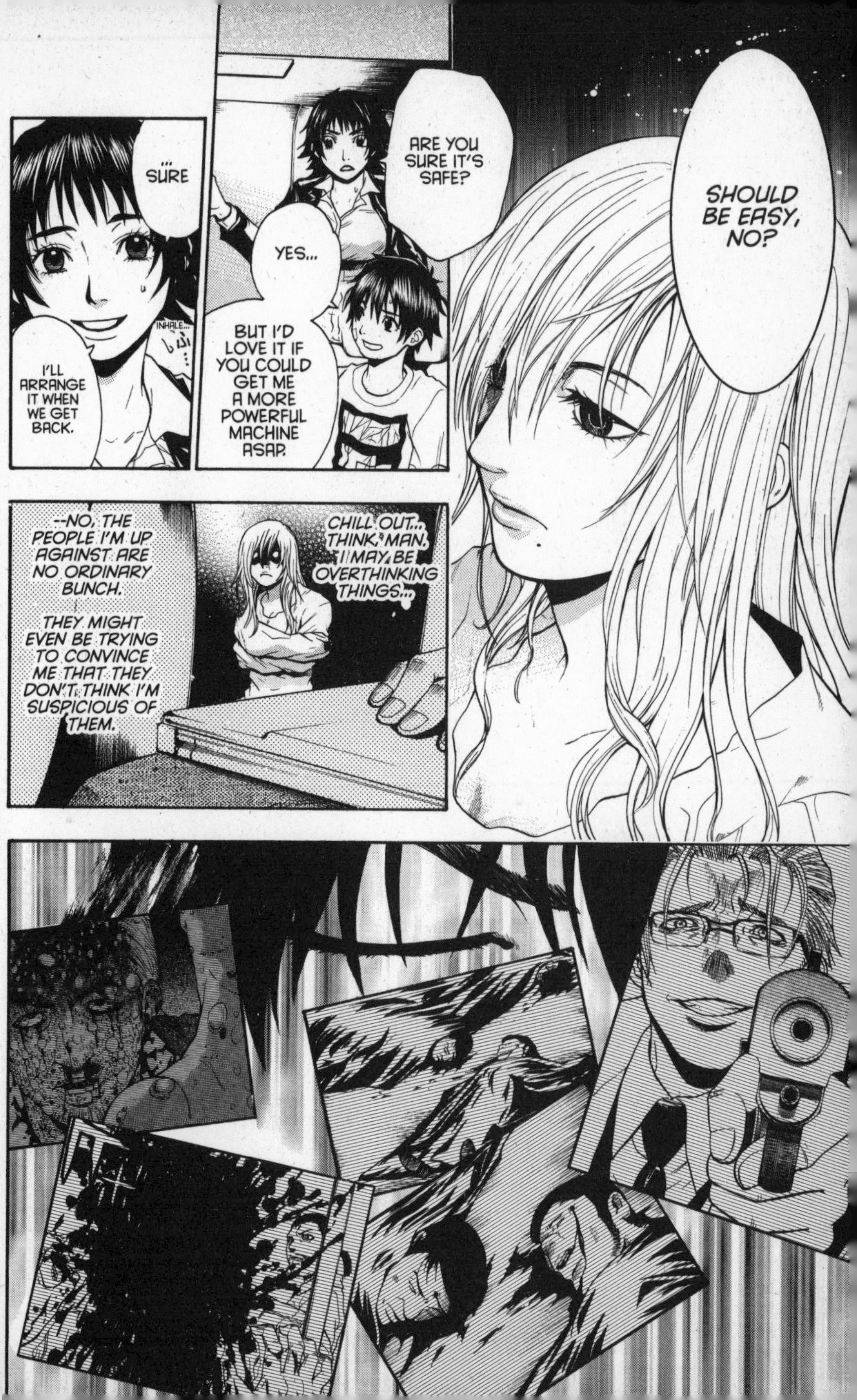
SHOULD BE EASY, NO?
ARE YOU SURE IT'S SAFE?
YES...
BUT I'D LOVE IT IF YOU COULD GET ME A MORE POWERFUL MACHINE ASAP.
...SURE
INHALE...
I'LL ARRANGE IT WHEN WE GET BACK.
CHILL OUT... THINK, MAN. I MAY BE OVERTHINKING THINGS...
--NO, THE PEOPLE I'M UP AGAINST ARE NO ORDINARY BUNCH.
THEY MIGHT EVEN BE TRYING TO CONVINCE ME THAT THEY DON'T THINK I'M SUSPICIOUS OF THEM.

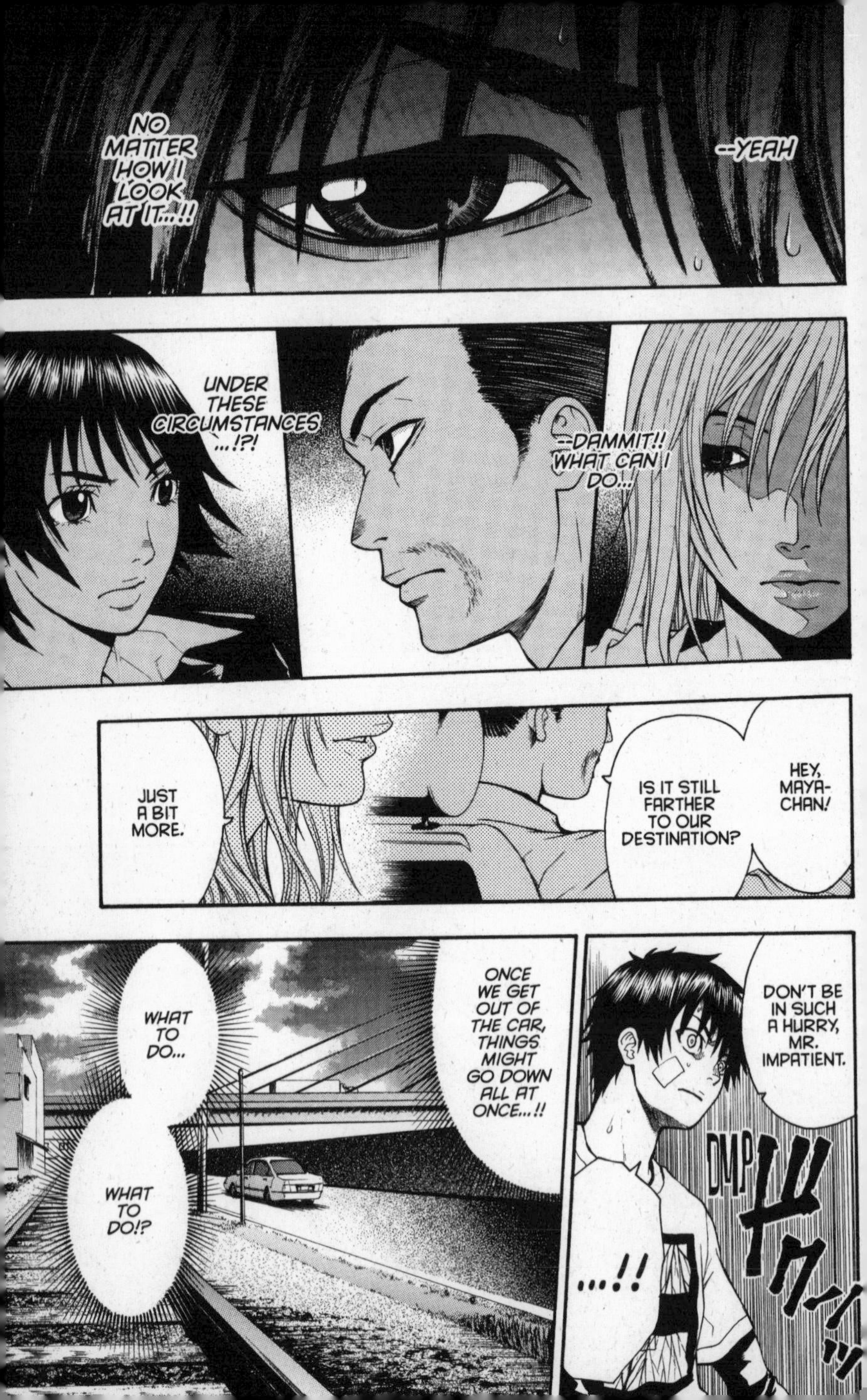
--YEAH
NO MATTER HOW I LOOK AT IT...!!
--DAMMIT!! WHAT CAN I DO...
UNDER THESE CIRCUMSTANCES ...!?!
HEY, MAYA-CHAN!
IS IT STILL FARTHER TO OUR DESTINATION?
JUST A BIT MORE.
DON'T BE IN SUCH A HURRY, MR. IMPATIENT.
DMP
...!!
ONCE WE GET OUT OF THE CAR, THINGS MIGHT GO DOWN ALL AT ONCE...!!
WHAT TO DO...
WHAT TO DO!?

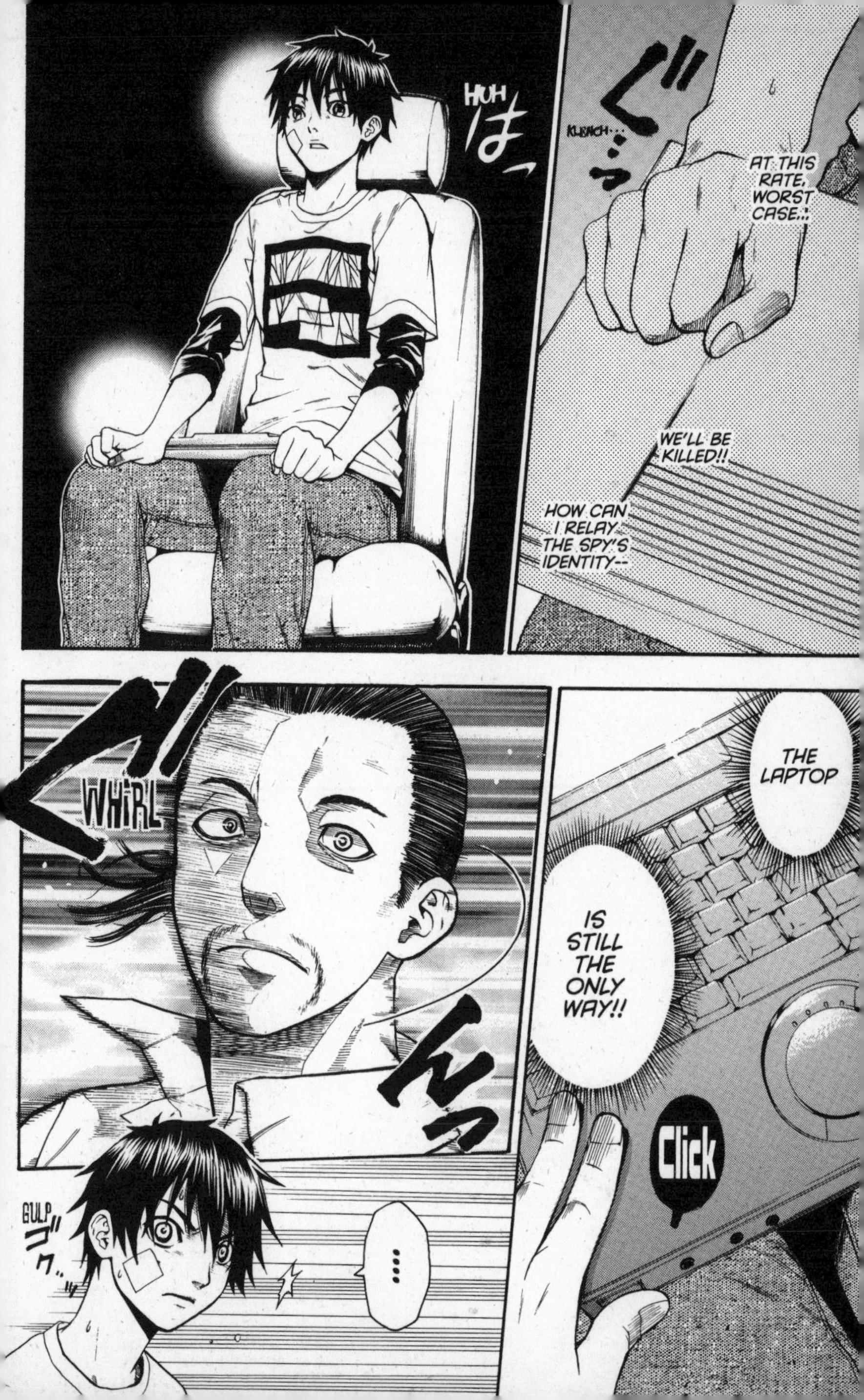
KLENCH...
AT THIS RATE, WORST CASE...
WE'LL BE KILLED!!
HOW CAN I RELAY THE SPY'S IDENTITY--
HUH
はっ
THE LAPTOP
IS STILL THE ONLY WAY!!
Click
WHIRL
GULP
....

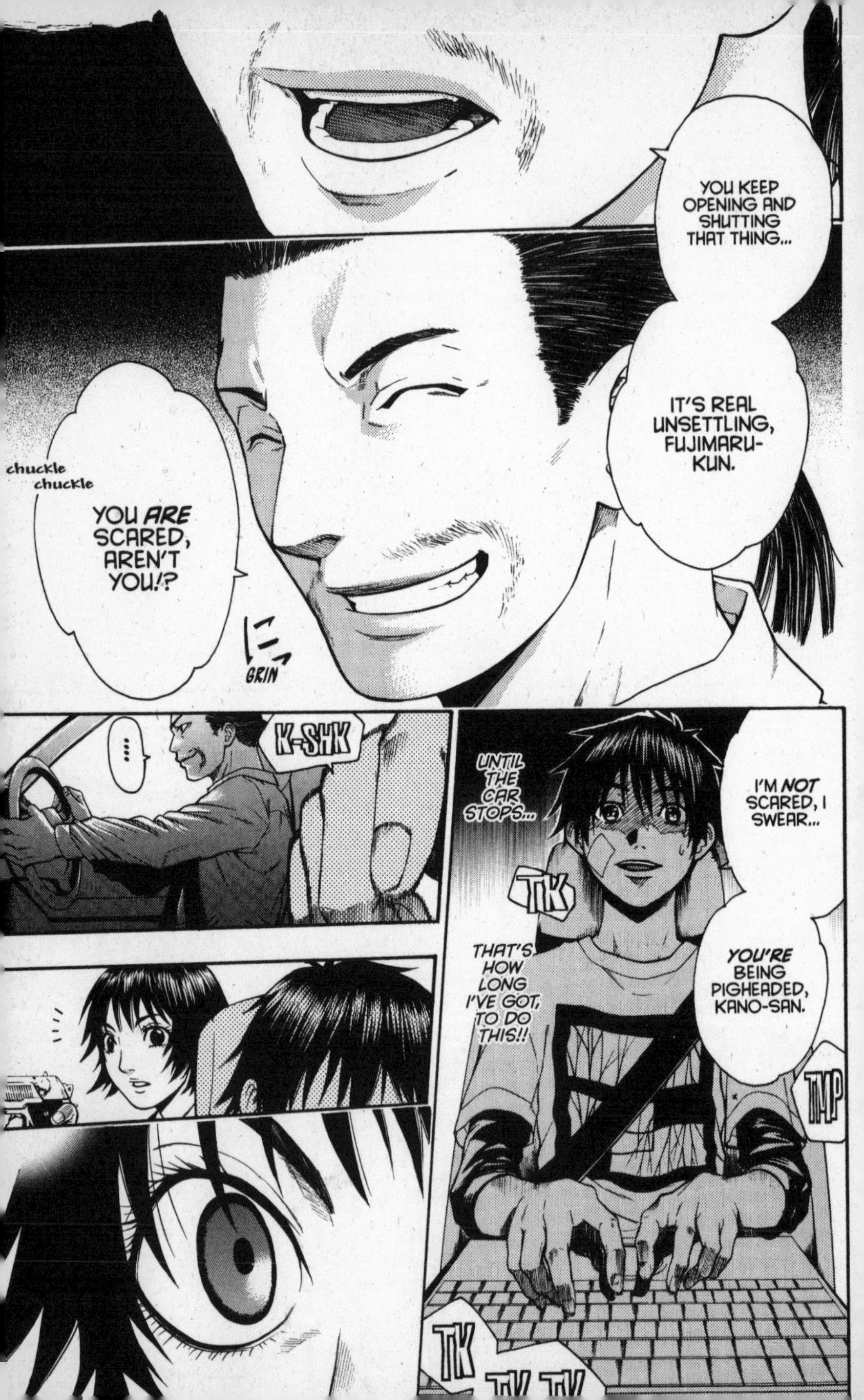
YOU KEEP OPENING AND SHUTTING THAT THING...
IT'S REAL UNSETTLING, FUJIMARU-KUN.
chuckle chuckle
YOU *ARE* SCARED, AREN'T YOU!?
GRIN
UNTIL THE CAR STOPS...
I'M *NOT* SCARED, I SWEAR...
TK
THAT'S HOW LONG I'VE GOT, TO DO THIS!!
YOU'RE BEING PIGHEADED, KANO-SAN.
TMP
TK
TK TK
....
K-SHK

Kirishima-san   g-kirishima@bocomne.jp

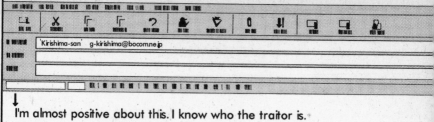

I'm almost positive about this. I know who the traitor is.
Had hoped to nail down some more positive proof, however,
I've now run out of time and so I can't wait. So here goes.
Kano is the in-house spy. Please help us to overtake him.

nod

KIRI-
SHIMA-
SAN

PLEASE
SEE
THIS...!!

TMP

....!!

VROO

Enter

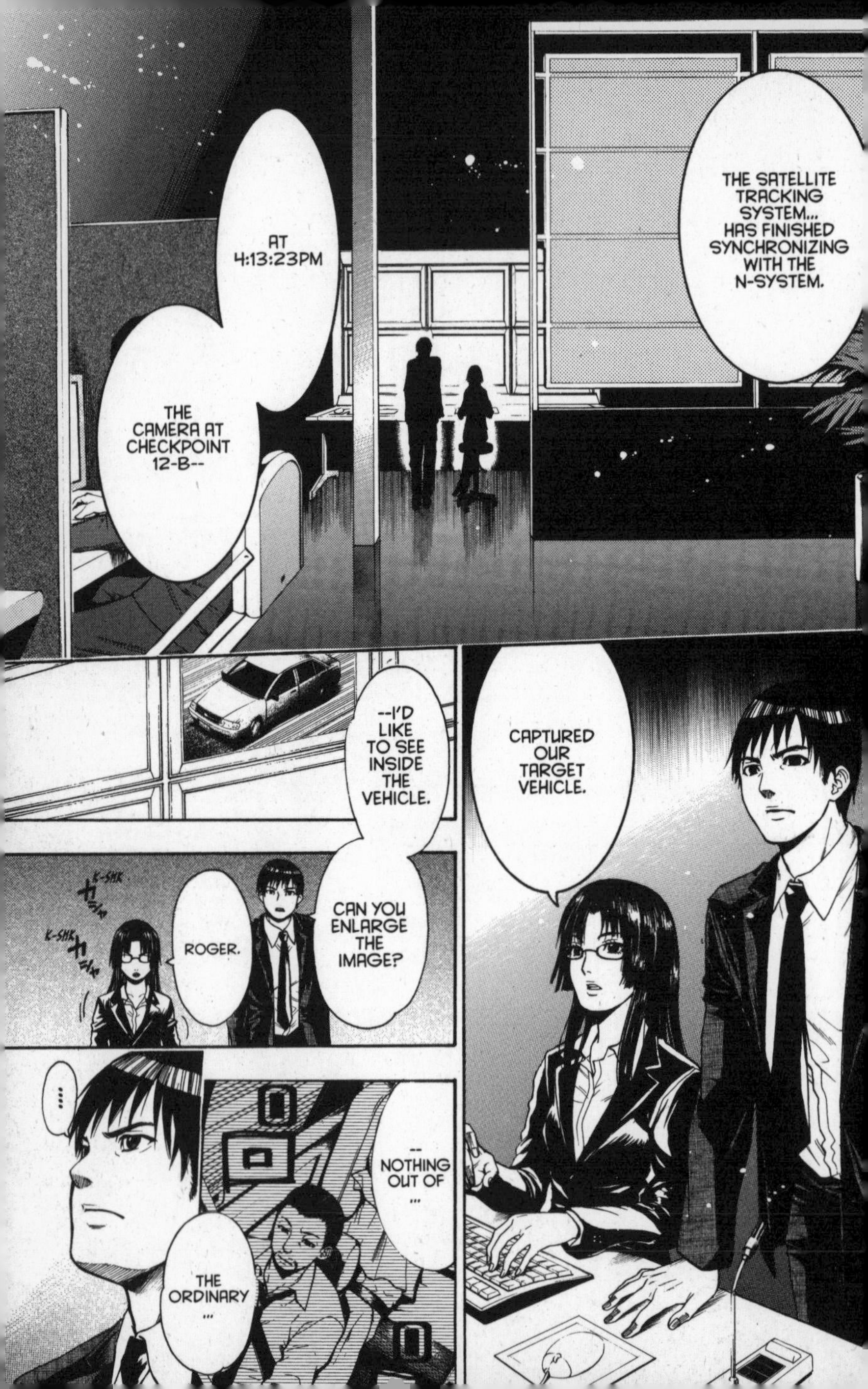
THE SATELLITE TRACKING SYSTEM... HAS FINISHED SYNCHRONIZING WITH THE N-SYSTEM.
AT 4:13:23PM
THE CAMERA AT CHECKPOINT 12-B--
CAPTURED OUR TARGET VEHICLE.
--I'D LIKE TO SEE INSIDE THE VEHICLE.
CAN YOU ENLARGE THE IMAGE?
K-SHK
K-SHK
ROGER.
--NOTHING OUT OF ...
THE ORDINARY ...
....

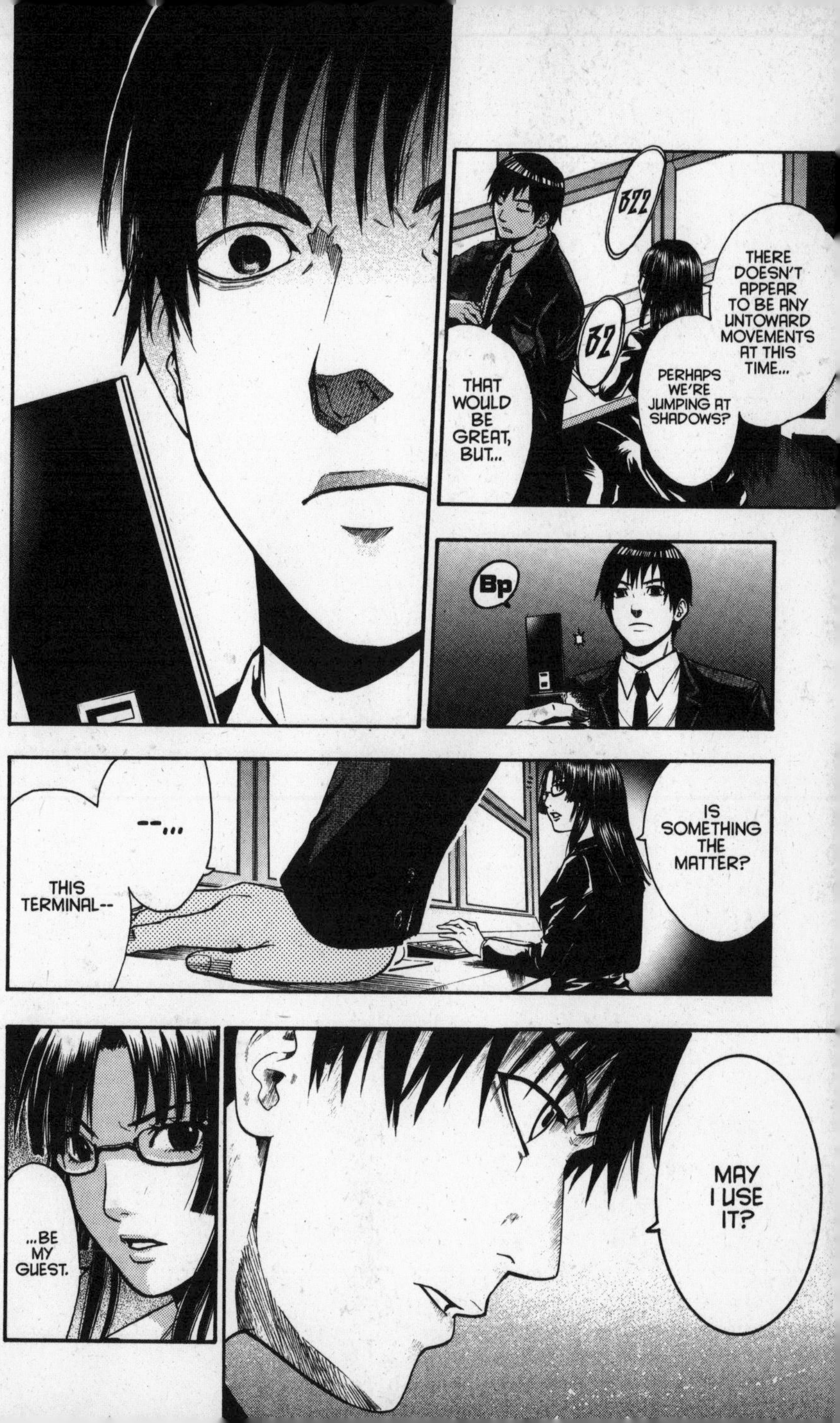
BZZ
THERE DOESN'T APPEAR TO BE ANY UNTOWARD MOVEMENTS AT THIS TIME...
BZ
PERHAPS WE'RE JUMPING AT SHADOWS?
THAT WOULD BE GREAT, BUT...
Bp
IS SOMETHING THE MATTER?
--...
THIS TERMINAL--
MAY I USE IT?
...BE MY GUEST.

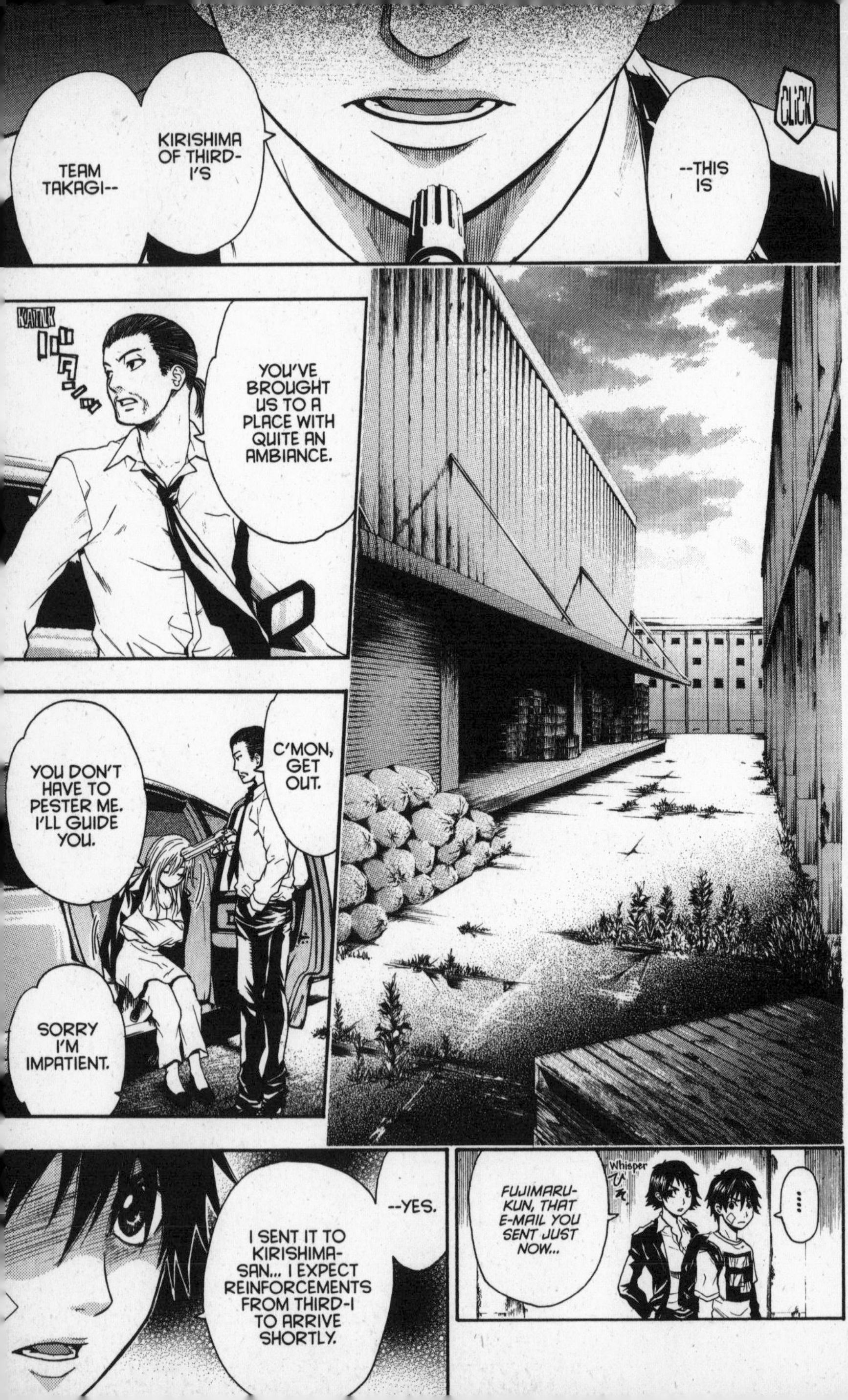
CLICK
--THIS IS
KIRISHIMA OF THIRD-I'S
TEAM TAKAGI--
KATNK
YOU'VE BROUGHT US TO A PLACE WITH QUITE AN AMBIANCE.
C'MON, GET OUT.
YOU DON'T HAVE TO PESTER ME. I'LL GUIDE YOU.
SORRY I'M IMPATIENT.
Whisper
FUJIMARU-KUN, THAT E-MAIL YOU SENT JUST NOW...
....
--YES.
I SENT IT TO KIRISHIMA-SAN... I EXPECT REINFORCEMENTS FROM THIRD-I TO ARRIVE SHORTLY.

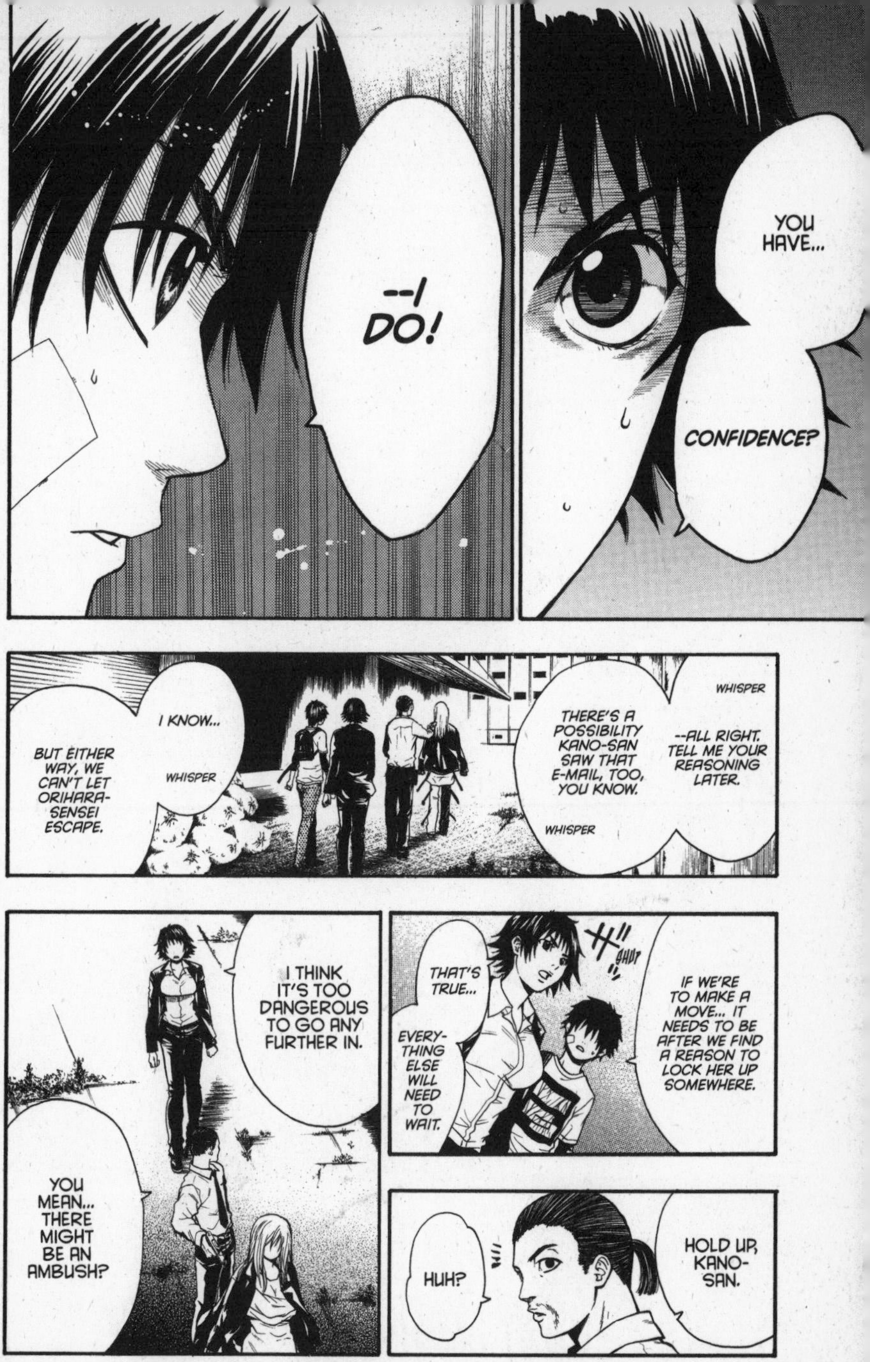
YOU HAVE... CONFIDENCE?
--I DO!
WHISPER
--ALL RIGHT. TELL ME YOUR REASONING LATER.
THERE'S A POSSIBILITY KANO-SAN SAW THAT E-MAIL, TOO, YOU KNOW.
WHISPER
I KNOW...
WHISPER
BUT EITHER WAY, WE CAN'T LET ORIHARA-SENSEI ESCAPE.
IF WE'RE TO MAKE A MOVE... IT NEEDS TO BE AFTER WE FIND A REASON TO LOCK HER UP SOMEWHERE.
THAT'S TRUE...
EVERYTHING ELSE WILL NEED TO WAIT.
HOLD UP, KANO-SAN.
HUH?
I THINK IT'S TOO DANGEROUS TO GO ANY FURTHER IN.
YOU MEAN... THERE MIGHT BE AN AMBUSH?

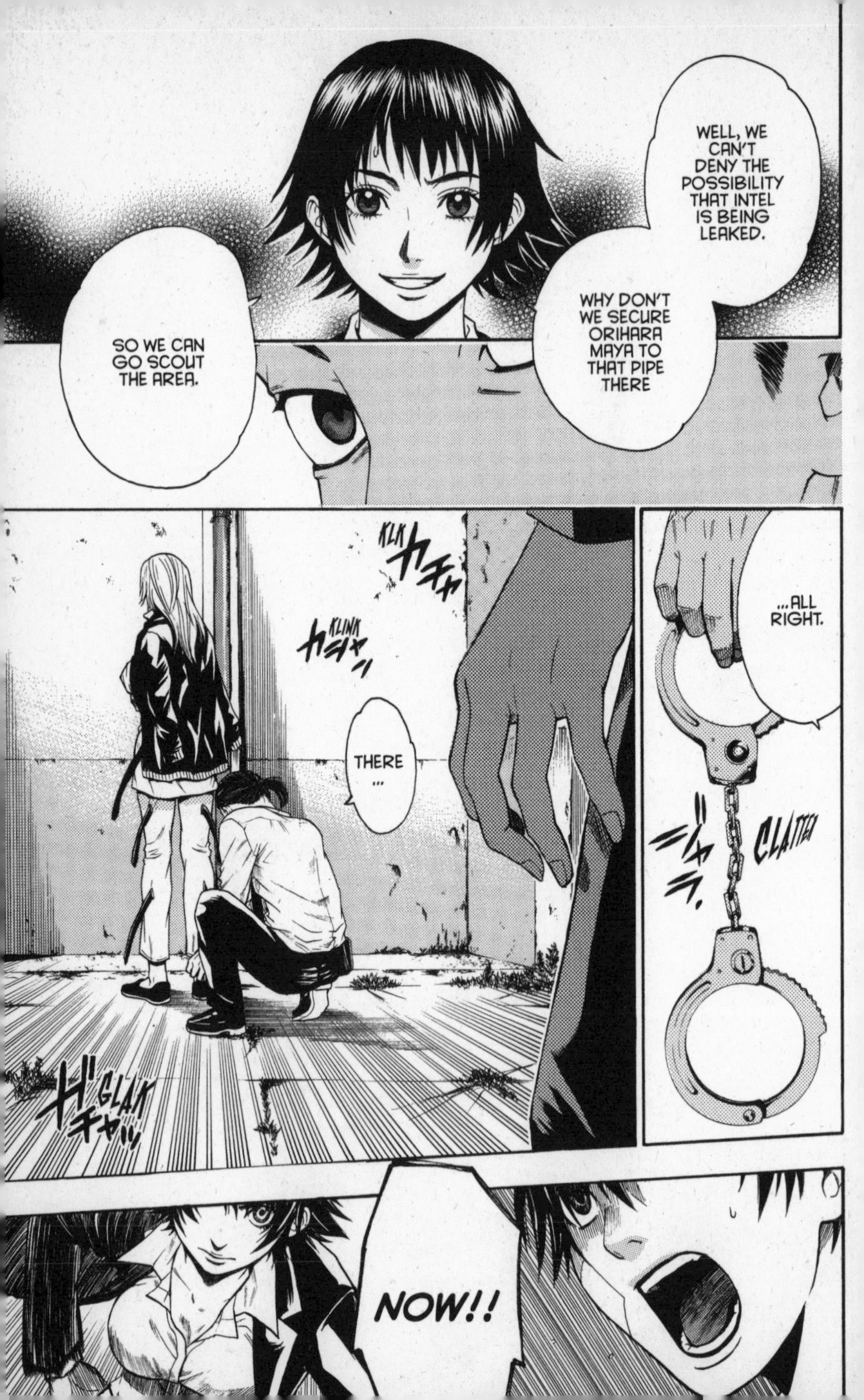
WELL, WE CAN'T DENY THE POSSIBILITY THAT INTEL IS BEING LEAKED.
WHY DON'T WE SECURE ORIHARA MAYA TO THAT PIPE THERE
SO WE CAN GO SCOUT THE AREA.
...ALL RIGHT.
CLATTER
KLK
KLINK
THERE ...
GLAK
NOW!!

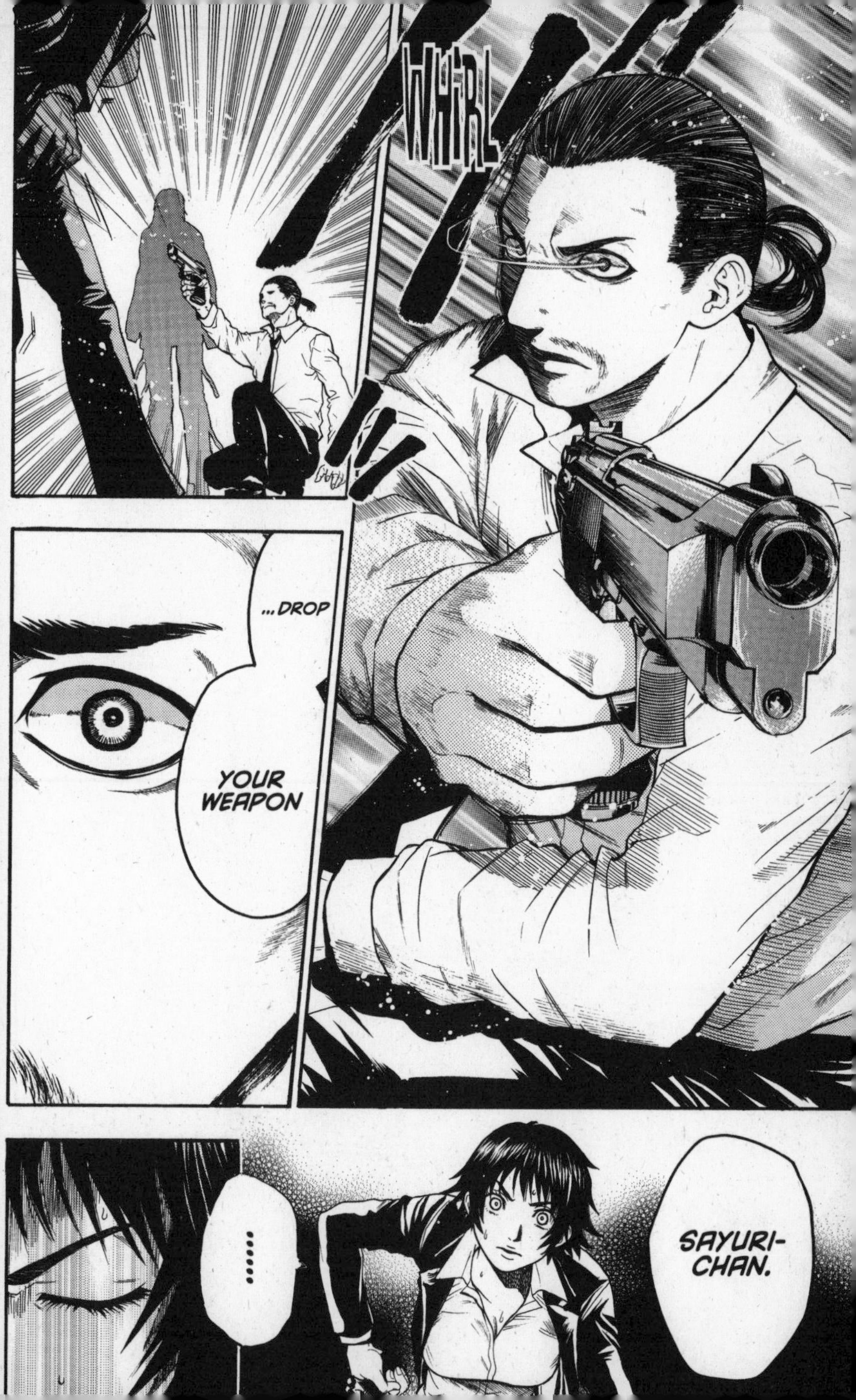
WHIRL
...DROP
YOUR WEAPON
SAYURI-CHAN.
......

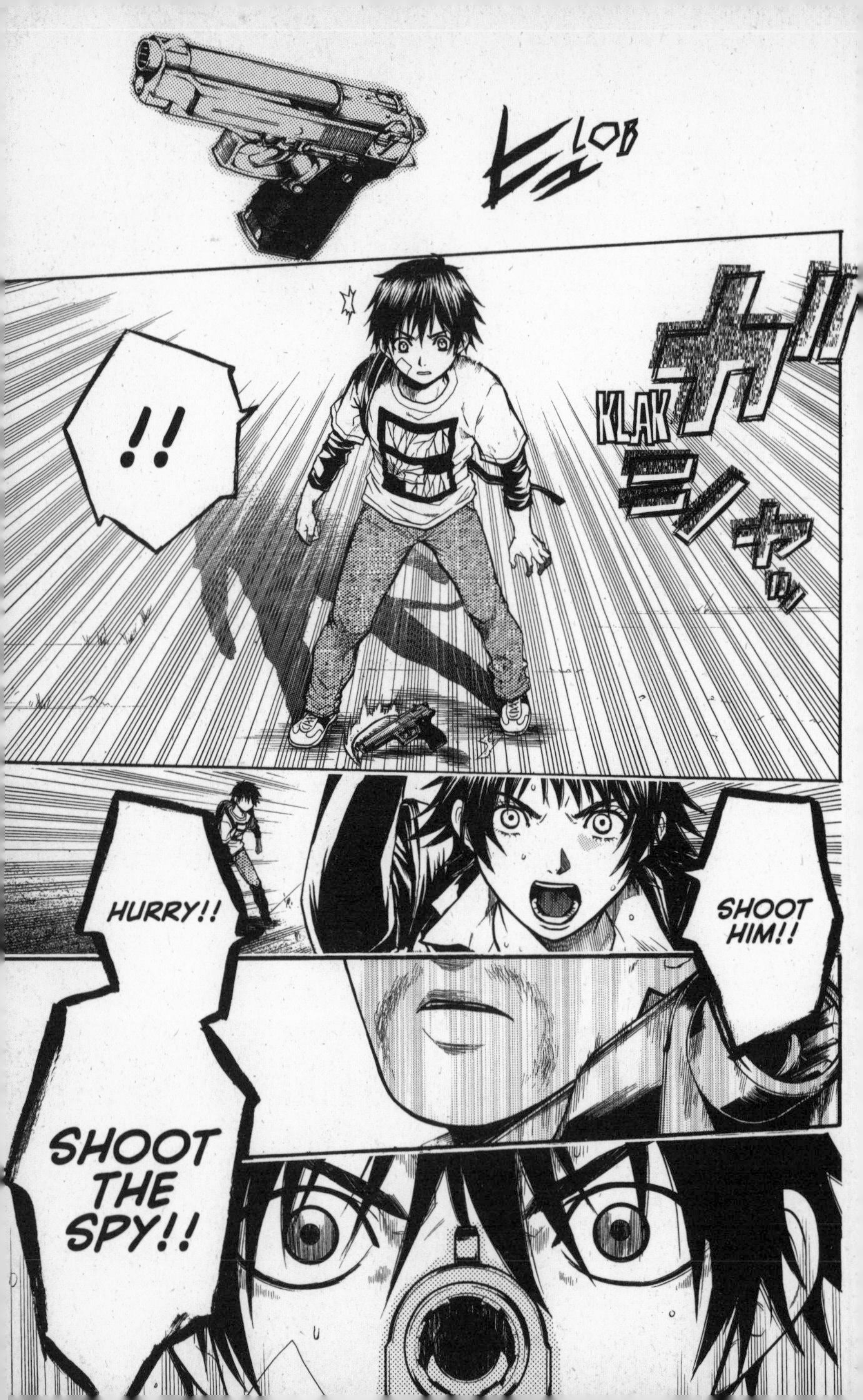
LOB
KLAK
!!
SHOOT HIM!!
HURRY!!
SHOOT THE SPY!!

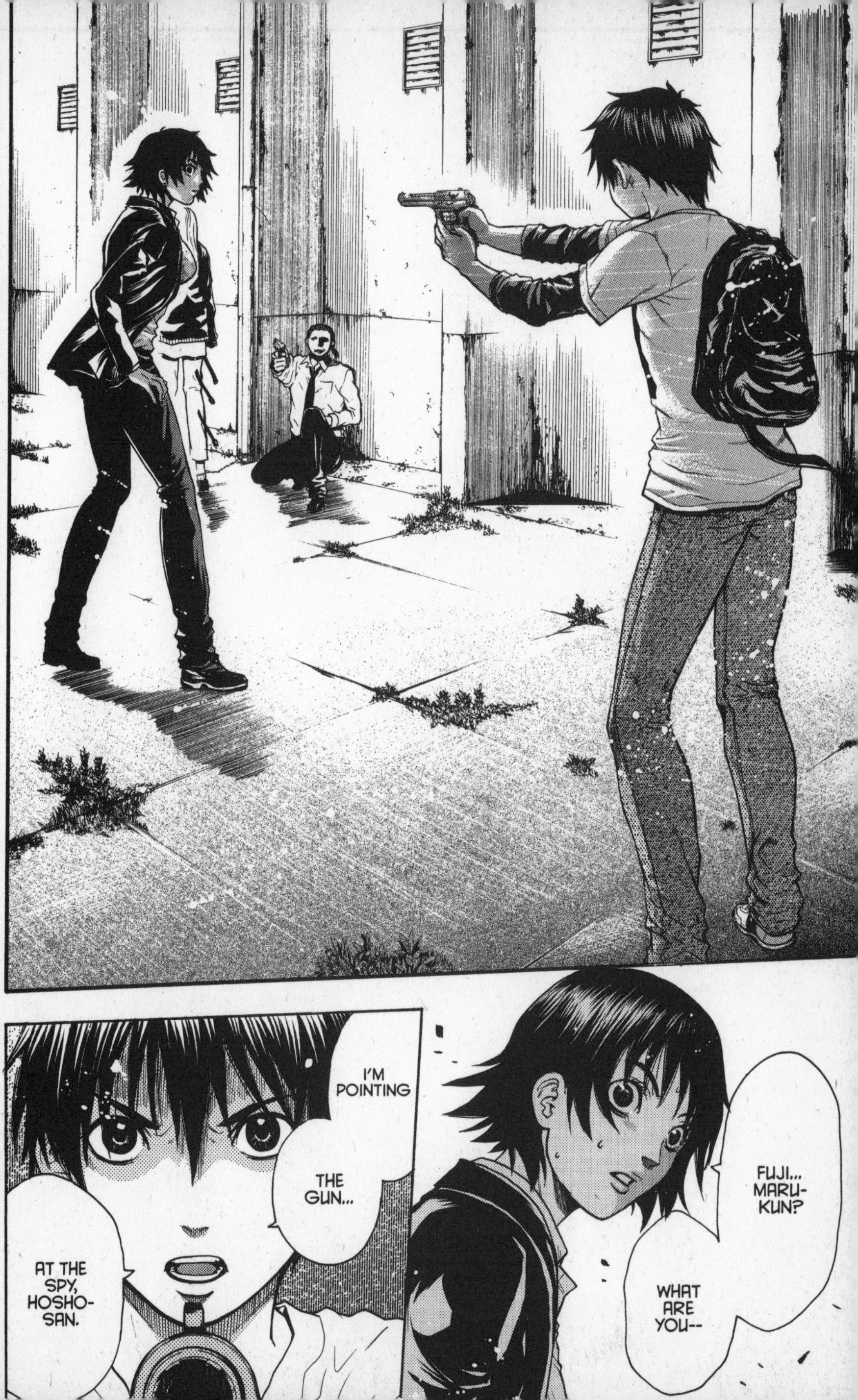
FUJI... MARU-KUN?
WHAT ARE YOU--
I'M POINTING
THE GUN...
AT THE SPY, HOSHO-SAN.

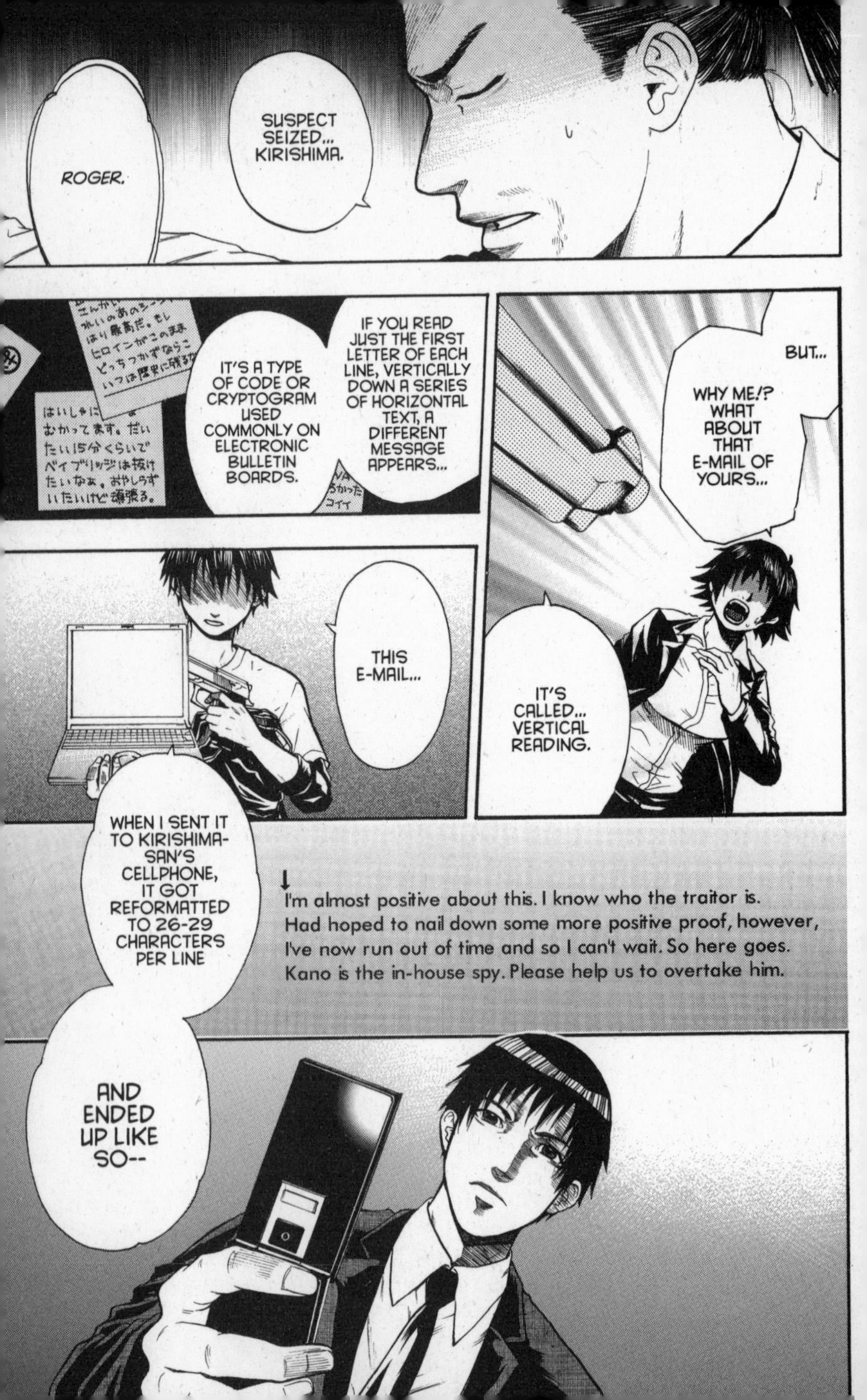
SUSPECT SEIZED... KIRISHIMA.
ROGER.
BUT...
WHY ME!? WHAT ABOUT THAT E-MAIL OF YOURS...
IT'S CALLED... VERTICAL READING.
IF YOU READ JUST THE FIRST LETTER OF EACH LINE, VERTICALLY DOWN A SERIES OF HORIZONTAL TEXT, A DIFFERENT MESSAGE APPEARS...
IT'S A TYPE OF CODE OR CRYPTOGRAM USED COMMONLY ON ELECTRONIC BULLETIN BOARDS.
はり最高だ。もし
ヒロインがこのまま
どっちつかずならこ
はいしゃに
むかってます。だい
たい15分くらいで
ベイブリッジは抜け
たいなぁ。おやしらず
いたいけど頑張る。
THIS E-MAIL...
WHEN I SENT IT TO KIRISHIMA-SAN'S CELLPHONE, IT GOT REFORMATTED TO 26-29 CHARACTERS PER LINE
I'm almost positive about this. I know who the traitor is.
Had hoped to nail down some more positive proof, however,
I've now run out of time and so I can't wait. So here goes.
Kano is the in-house spy. Please help us to overtake him.
AND ENDED UP LIKE SO--

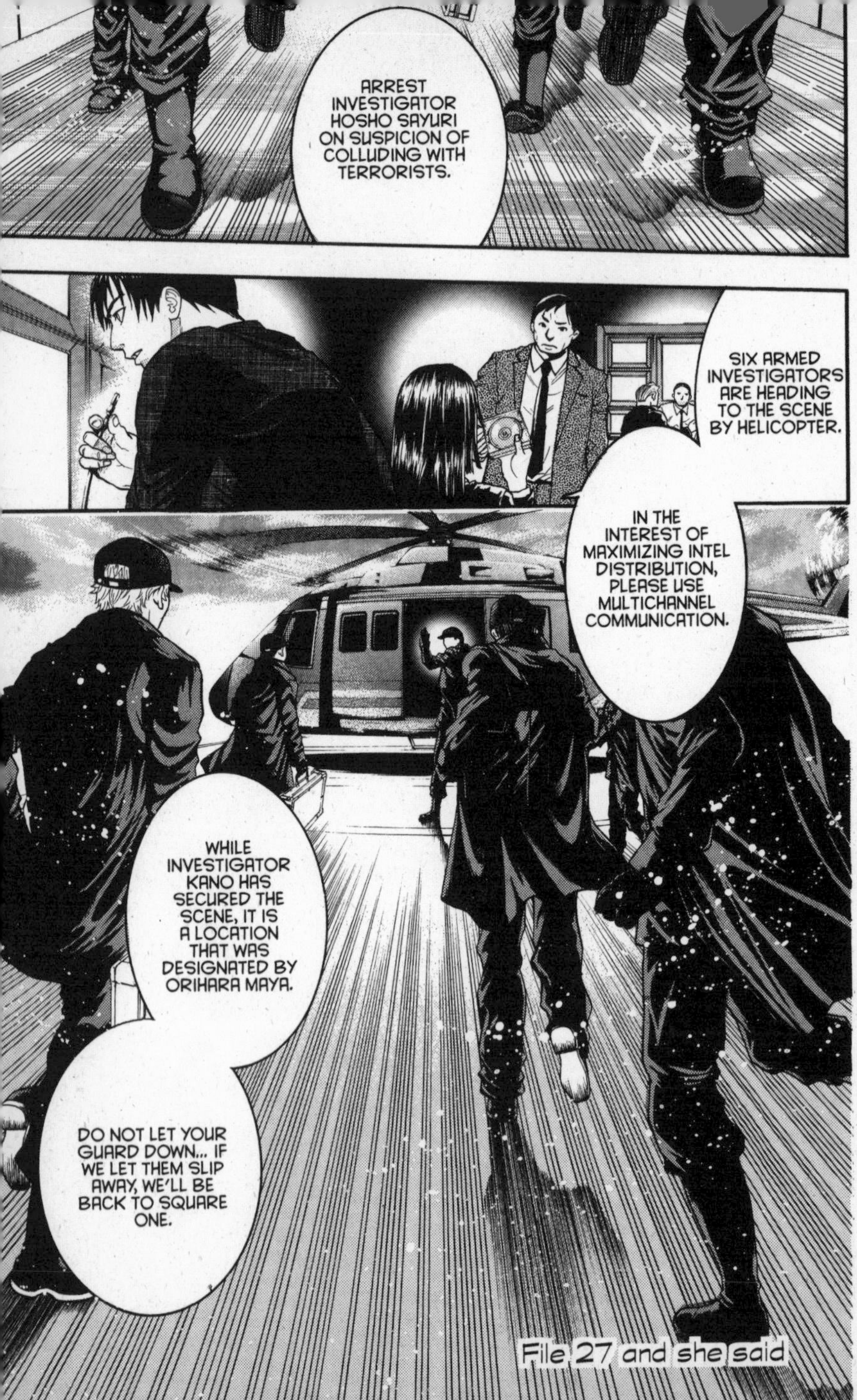
ARREST INVESTIGATOR HOSHO SAYURI ON SUSPICION OF COLLUDING WITH TERRORISTS.
SIX ARMED INVESTIGATORS ARE HEADING TO THE SCENE BY HELICOPTER.
IN THE INTEREST OF MAXIMIZING INTEL DISTRIBUTION, PLEASE USE MULTICHANNEL COMMUNICATION.
WHILE INVESTIGATOR KANO HAS SECURED THE SCENE, IT IS A LOCATION THAT WAS DESIGNATED BY ORIHARA MAYA.
DO NOT LET YOUR GUARD DOWN... IF WE LET THEM SLIP AWAY, WE'LL BE BACK TO SQUARE ONE.
File 27 and she said

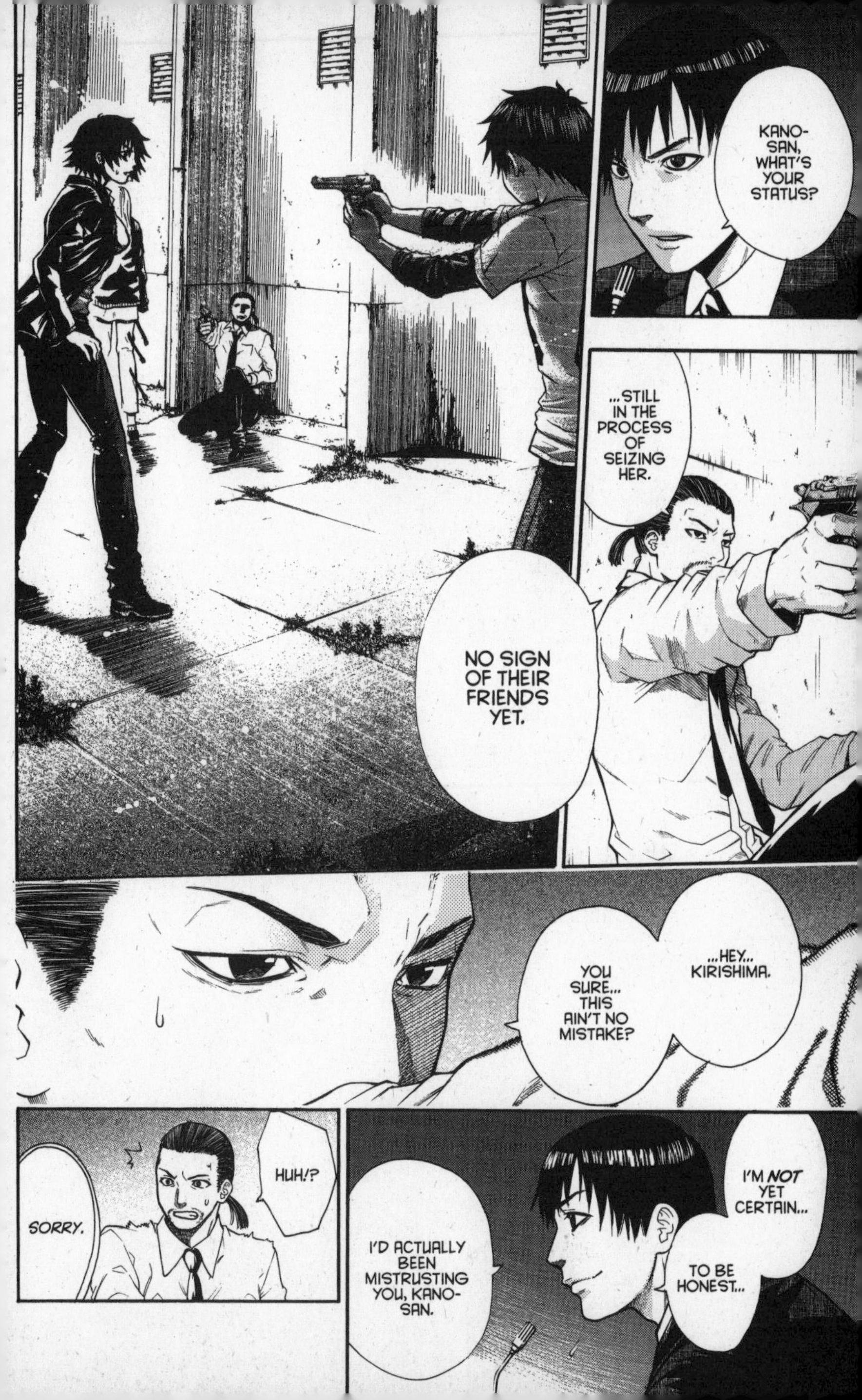
KANO-SAN, WHAT'S YOUR STATUS?
...STILL IN THE PROCESS OF SEIZING HER.
NO SIGN OF THEIR FRIENDS YET.
...HEY... KIRISHIMA.
YOU SURE... THIS AIN'T NO MISTAKE?
I'M *NOT* YET CERTAIN...
TO BE HONEST...
I'D ACTUALLY BEEN MISTRUSTING YOU, KANO-SAN.
HUH!?
SORRY.

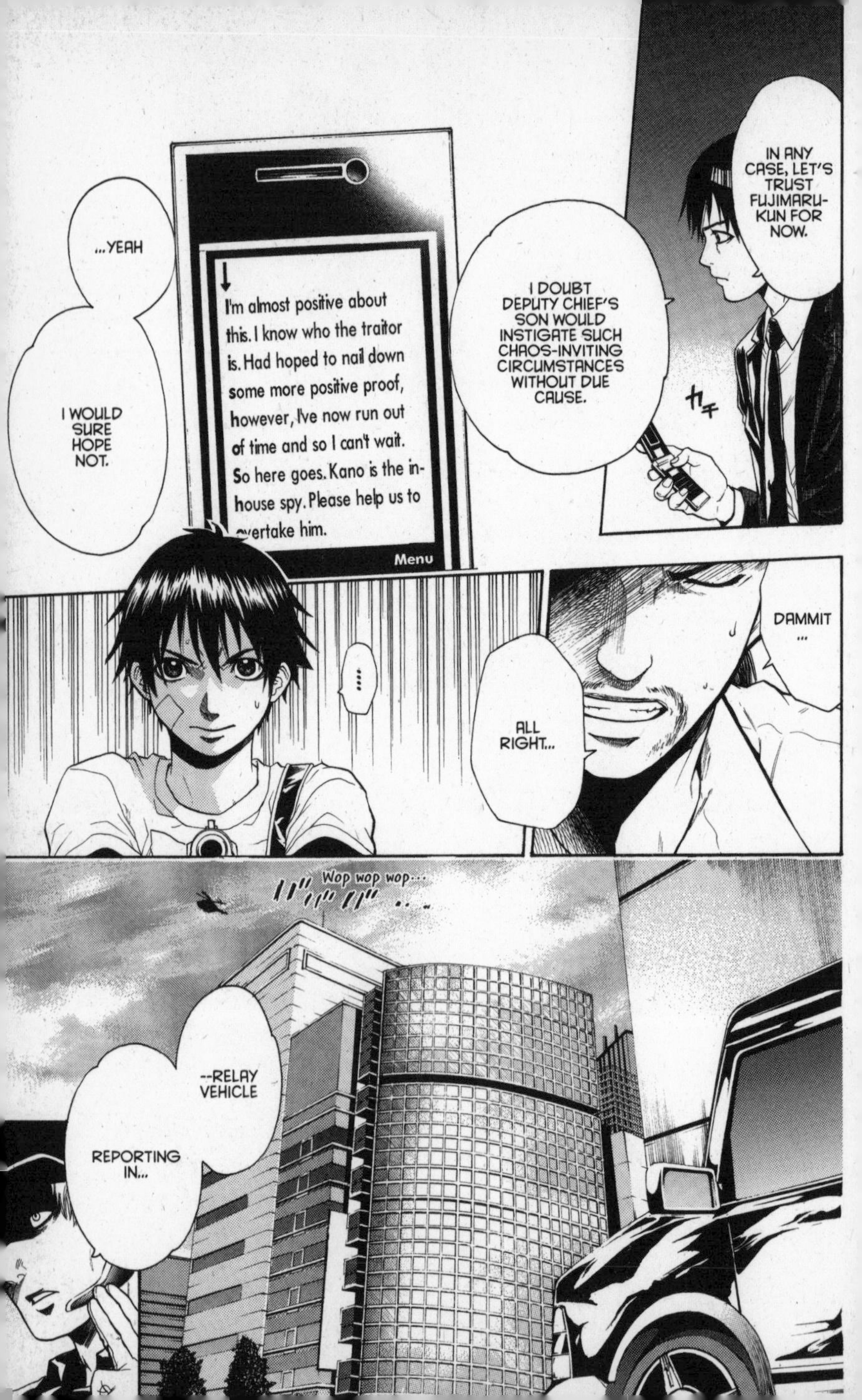
IN ANY CASE, LET'S TRUST FUJIMARU-KUN FOR NOW.
I DOUBT DEPUTY CHIEF'S SON WOULD INSTIGATE SUCH CHAOS-INVITING CIRCUMSTANCES WITHOUT DUE CAUSE.
カチ
I'm almost positive about this. I know who the traitor is. Had hoped to nail down some more positive proof, however, I've now run out of time and so I can't wait. So here goes. Kano is the in-house spy. Please help us to overtake him.
Menu
...YEAH
I WOULD SURE HOPE NOT.
DAMMIT ...
ALL RIGHT...
....
Wop wop wop...
--RELAY VEHICLE
REPORTING IN...

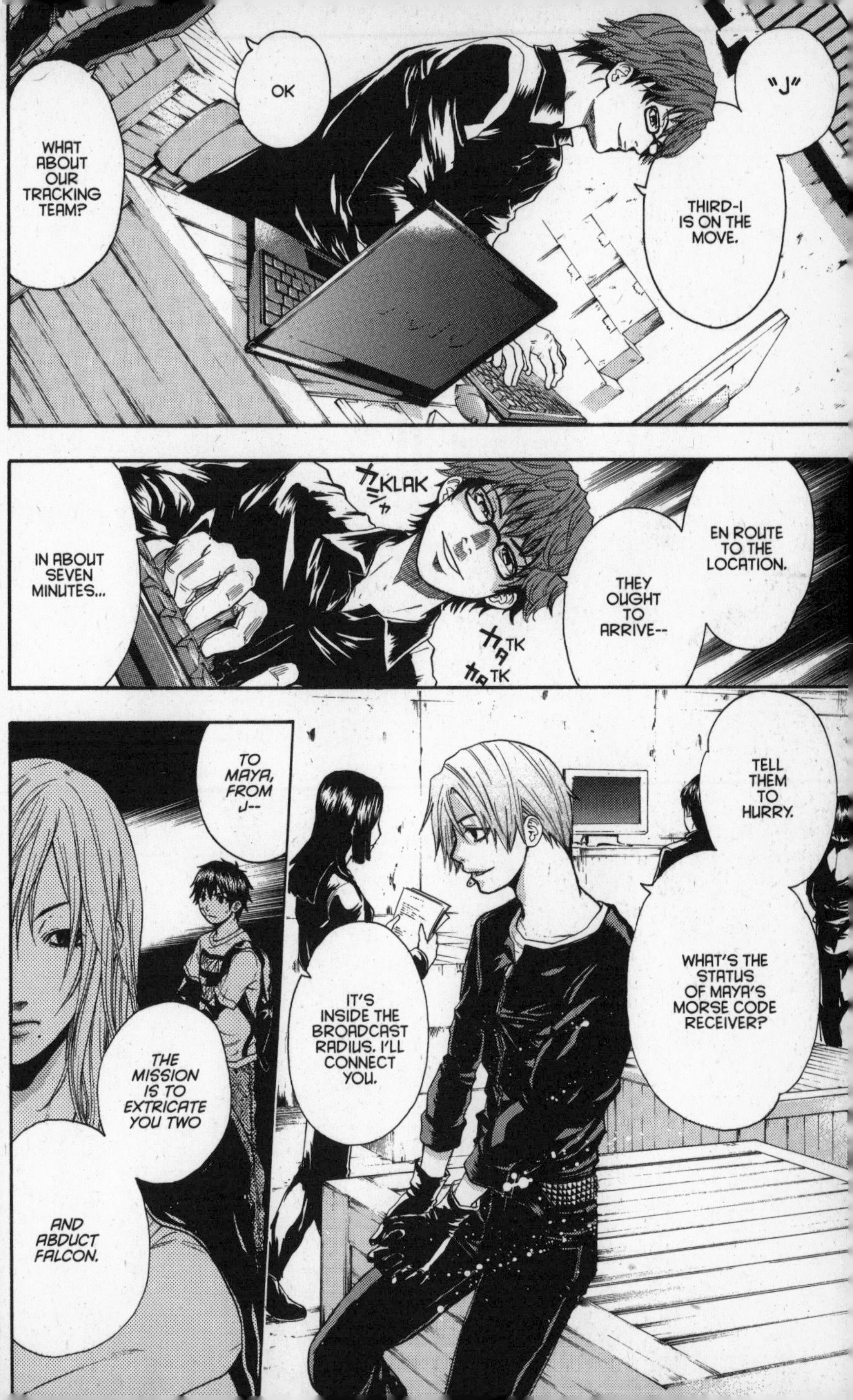
"J"
THIRD-I IS ON THE MOVE.
OK
WHAT ABOUT OUR TRACKING TEAM?
EN ROUTE TO THE LOCATION.
THEY OUGHT TO ARRIVE--
KLAK
TK
TK
IN ABOUT SEVEN MINUTES...
TELL THEM TO HURRY.
WHAT'S THE STATUS OF MAYA'S MORSE CODE RECEIVER?
IT'S INSIDE THE BROADCAST RADIUS. I'LL CONNECT YOU.
TO MAYA, FROM J--
THE MISSION IS TO EXTRICATE YOU TWO
AND ABDUCT FALCON.

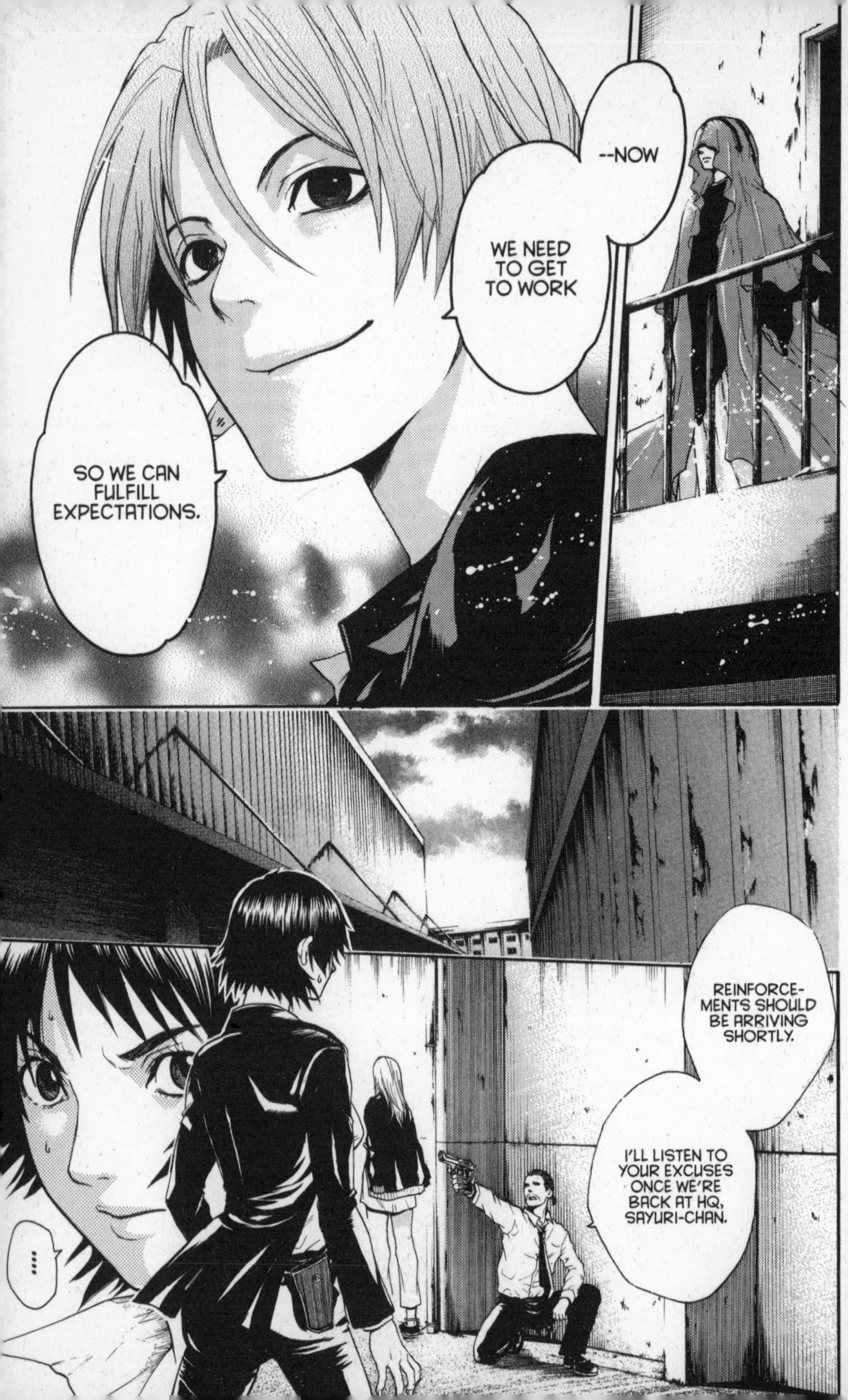
--NOW
WE NEED TO GET TO WORK
SO WE CAN FULFILL EXPECTATIONS.
REINFORCE-MENTS SHOULD BE ARRIVING SHORTLY.
I'LL LISTEN TO YOUR EXCUSES ONCE WE'RE BACK AT HQ, SAYURI-CHAN.
....

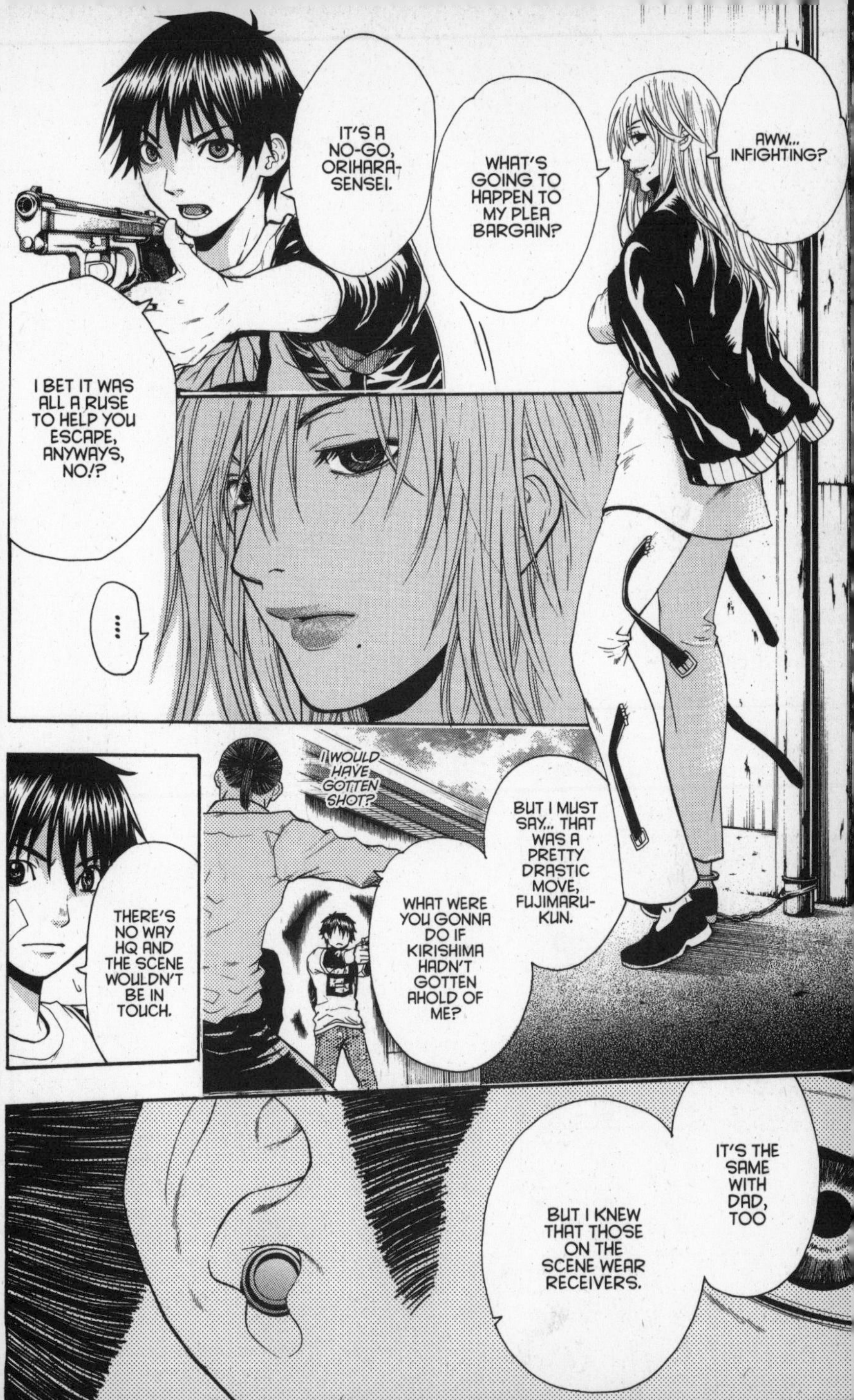
AWW... INFIGHTING?
WHAT'S GOING TO HAPPEN TO MY PLEA BARGAIN?
IT'S A NO-GO, ORIHARA-SENSEI.
I BET IT WAS ALL A RUSE TO HELP YOU ESCAPE, ANYWAYS, NO!?
....
BUT I MUST SAY... THAT WAS A PRETTY DRASTIC MOVE, FUJIMARU-KUN.
WHAT WERE YOU GONNA DO IF KIRISHIMA HADN'T GOTTEN AHOLD OF ME?
I WOULD HAVE GOTTEN SHOT?
THERE'S NO WAY HQ AND THE SCENE WOULDN'T BE IN TOUCH.
IT'S THE SAME WITH DAD, TOO
BUT I KNEW THAT THOSE ON THE SCENE WEAR RECEIVERS.

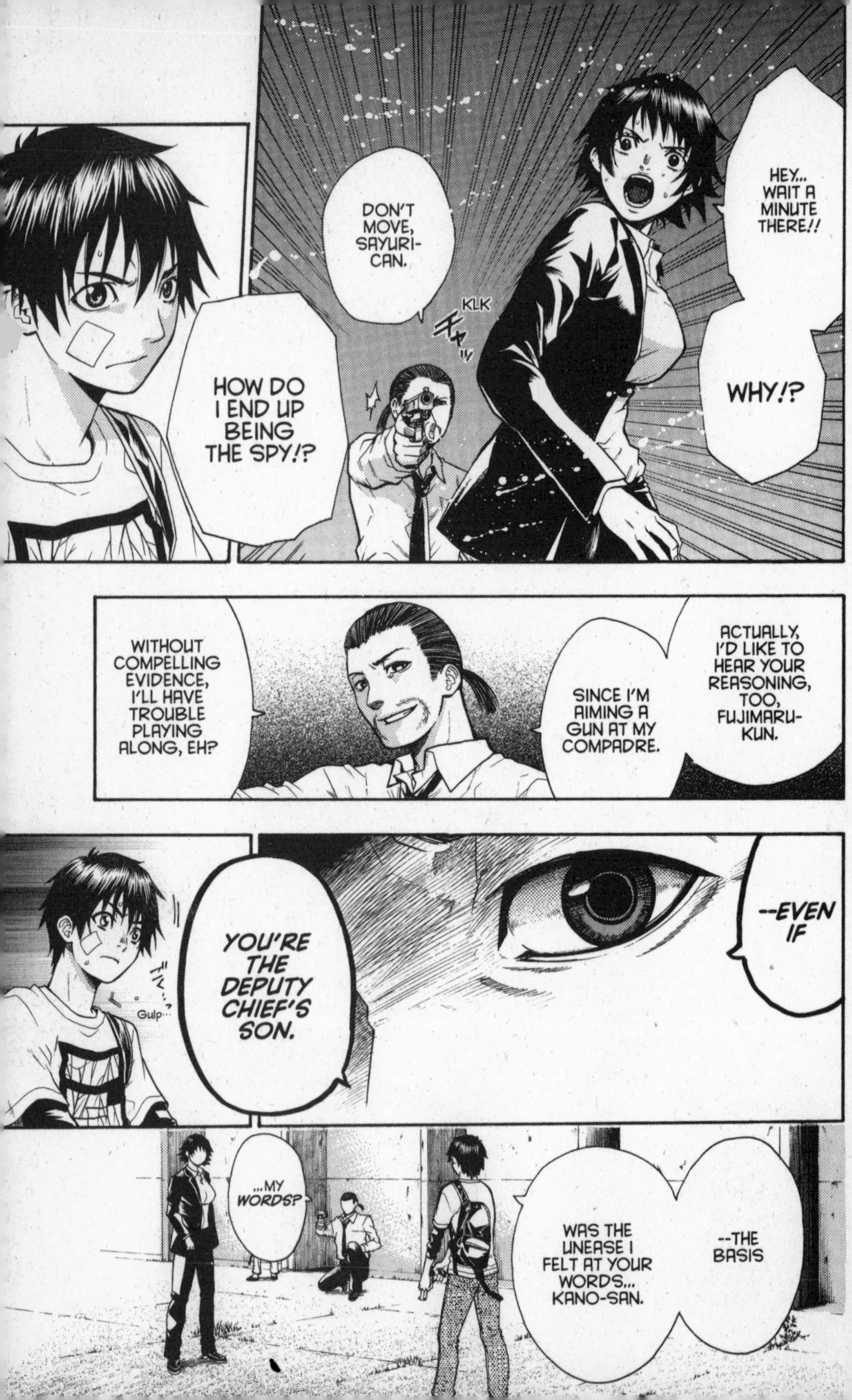
HEY... WAIT A MINUTE THERE!!
DON'T MOVE, SAYURI-CAN.
KLK
WHY!?
HOW DO I END UP BEING THE SPY!?
ACTUALLY, I'D LIKE TO HEAR YOUR REASONING, TOO, FUJIMARU-KUN.
SINCE I'M AIMING A GUN AT MY COMPADRE.
WITHOUT COMPELLING EVIDENCE, I'LL HAVE TROUBLE PLAYING ALONG, EH?
--EVEN IF
YOU'RE THE DEPUTY CHIEF'S SON.
Gulp...
--THE BASIS
WAS THE UNEASE I FELT AT YOUR WORDS... KANO-SAN.
...MY WORDS?

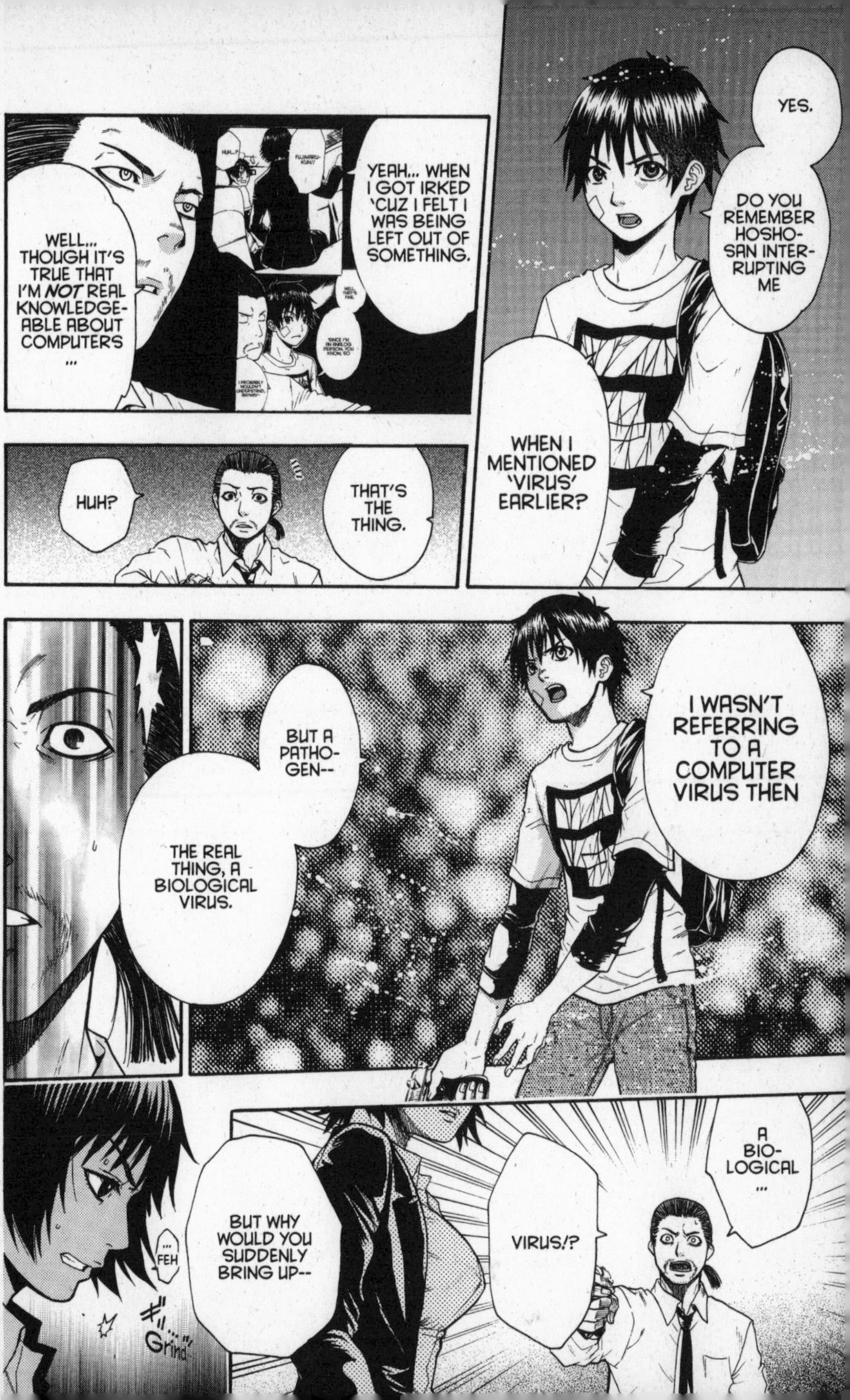
YES.
DO YOU REMEMBER HOSHO-SAN INTERRUPTING ME
WHEN I MENTIONED 'VIRUS' EARLIER?
YEAH... WHEN I GOT IRKED 'CUZ I FELT I WAS BEING LEFT OUT OF SOMETHING.
FUJIMARU-KUN!/
HUH...?
WELL, THAT'S FINE.
SINCE I'M AN ANALOG PERSON, YOU KNOW, SO
I PROBABLY WOULDN'T UNDERSTAND, ANYWAY-
WELL... THOUGH IT'S TRUE THAT I'M ***NOT*** REAL KNOWLEDGE-ABLE ABOUT COMPUTERS ...
THAT'S THE THING.
HUH?
I WASN'T REFERRING TO A COMPUTER VIRUS THEN
BUT A PATHO-GEN--
THE REAL THING, A BIOLOGICAL VIRUS.
A BIO-LOGICAL ...
VIRUS!?
BUT WHY WOULD YOU SUDDENLY BRING UP--
...FEH
Grind

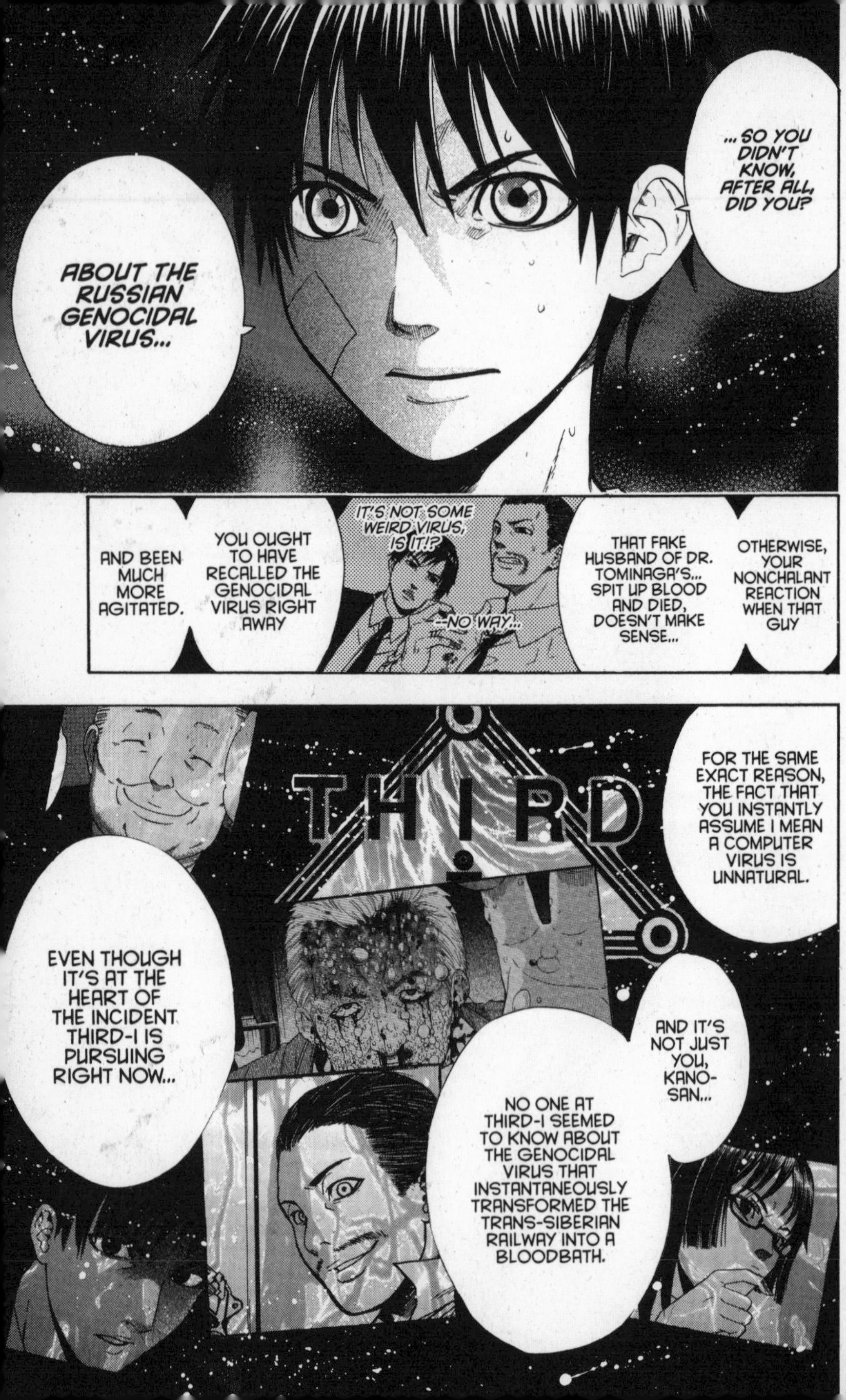
...SO YOU DIDN'T KNOW, AFTER ALL, DID YOU?
ABOUT THE RUSSIAN GENOCIDAL VIRUS...
OTHERWISE, YOUR NONCHALANT REACTION WHEN THAT GUY
THAT FAKE HUSBAND OF DR. TOMINAGA'S... SPIT UP BLOOD AND DIED, DOESN'T MAKE SENSE...
IT'S NOT SOME WEIRD VIRUS, IS IT!?
--NO WAY...
YOU OUGHT TO HAVE RECALLED THE GENOCIDAL VIRUS RIGHT AWAY
AND BEEN MUCH MORE AGITATED.
FOR THE SAME EXACT REASON, THE FACT THAT YOU INSTANTLY ASSUME I MEAN A COMPUTER VIRUS IS UNNATURAL.
THIRD
EVEN THOUGH IT'S AT THE HEART OF THE INCIDENT THIRD-I IS PURSUING RIGHT NOW...
AND IT'S NOT JUST YOU, KANO-SAN...
NO ONE AT THIRD-I SEEMED TO KNOW ABOUT THE GENOCIDAL VIRUS THAT INSTANTANEOUSLY TRANSFORMED THE TRANS-SIBERIAN RAILWAY INTO A BLOODBATH.

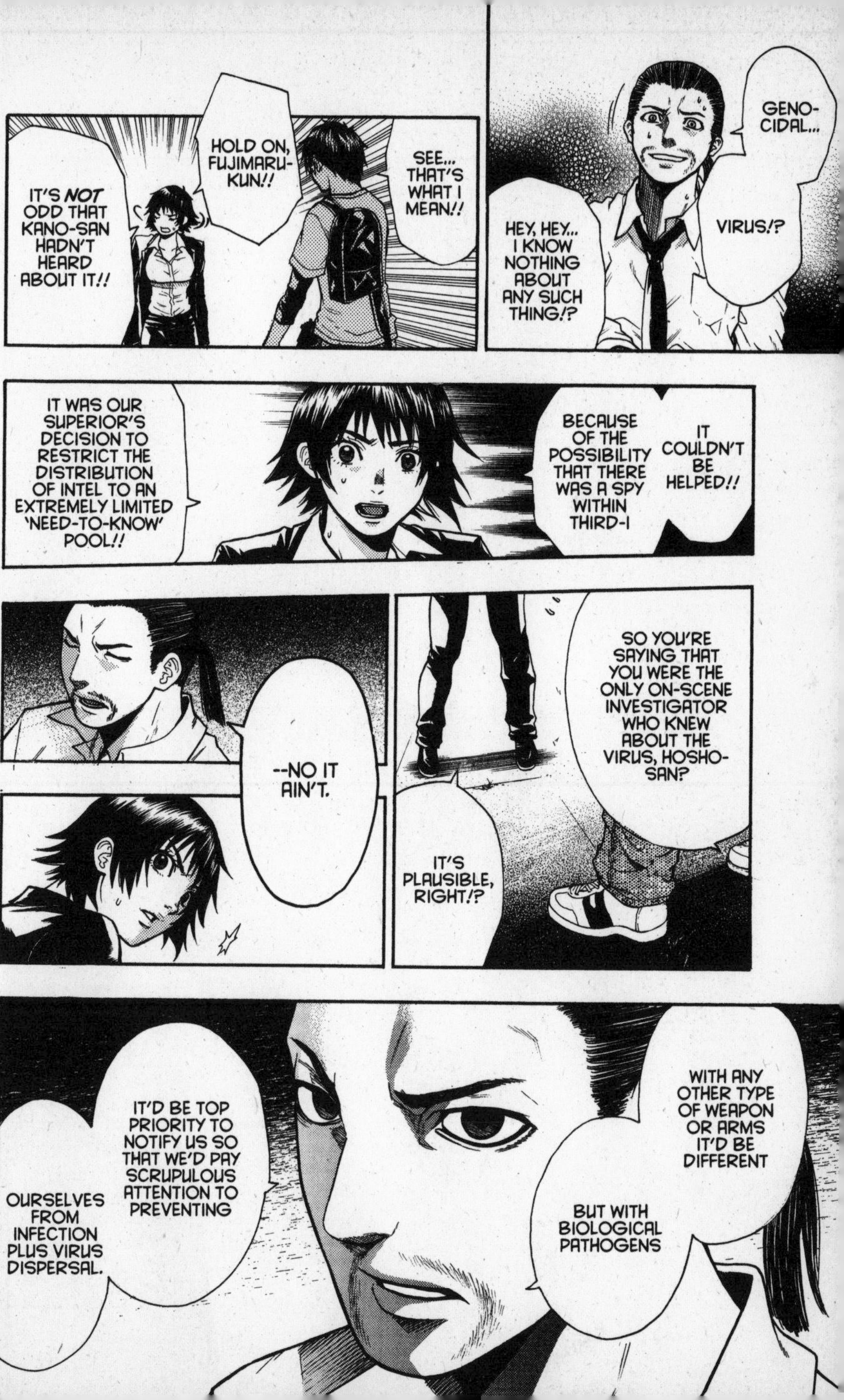
GENO-CIDAL...
VIRUS!?
HEY, HEY... I KNOW NOTHING ABOUT ANY SUCH THING!?
SEE... THAT'S WHAT I MEAN!!
HOLD ON, FUJIMARU-KUN!!
IT'S *NOT* ODD THAT KANO-SAN HADN'T HEARD ABOUT IT!!
IT COULDN'T BE HELPED!!
BECAUSE OF THE POSSIBILITY THAT THERE WAS A SPY WITHIN THIRD-I
IT WAS OUR SUPERIOR'S DECISION TO RESTRICT THE DISTRIBUTION OF INTEL TO AN EXTREMELY LIMITED 'NEED-TO-KNOW' POOL!!
SO YOU'RE SAYING THAT YOU WERE THE ONLY ON-SCENE INVESTIGATOR WHO KNEW ABOUT THE VIRUS, HOSHO-SAN?
IT'S PLAUSIBLE, RIGHT!?
--NO IT AIN'T.
WITH ANY OTHER TYPE OF WEAPON OR ARMS IT'D BE DIFFERENT
BUT WITH BIOLOGICAL PATHOGENS
IT'D BE TOP PRIORITY TO NOTIFY US SO THAT WE'D PAY SCRUPULOUS ATTENTION TO PREVENTING
OURSELVES FROM INFECTION PLUS VIRUS DISPERSAL.

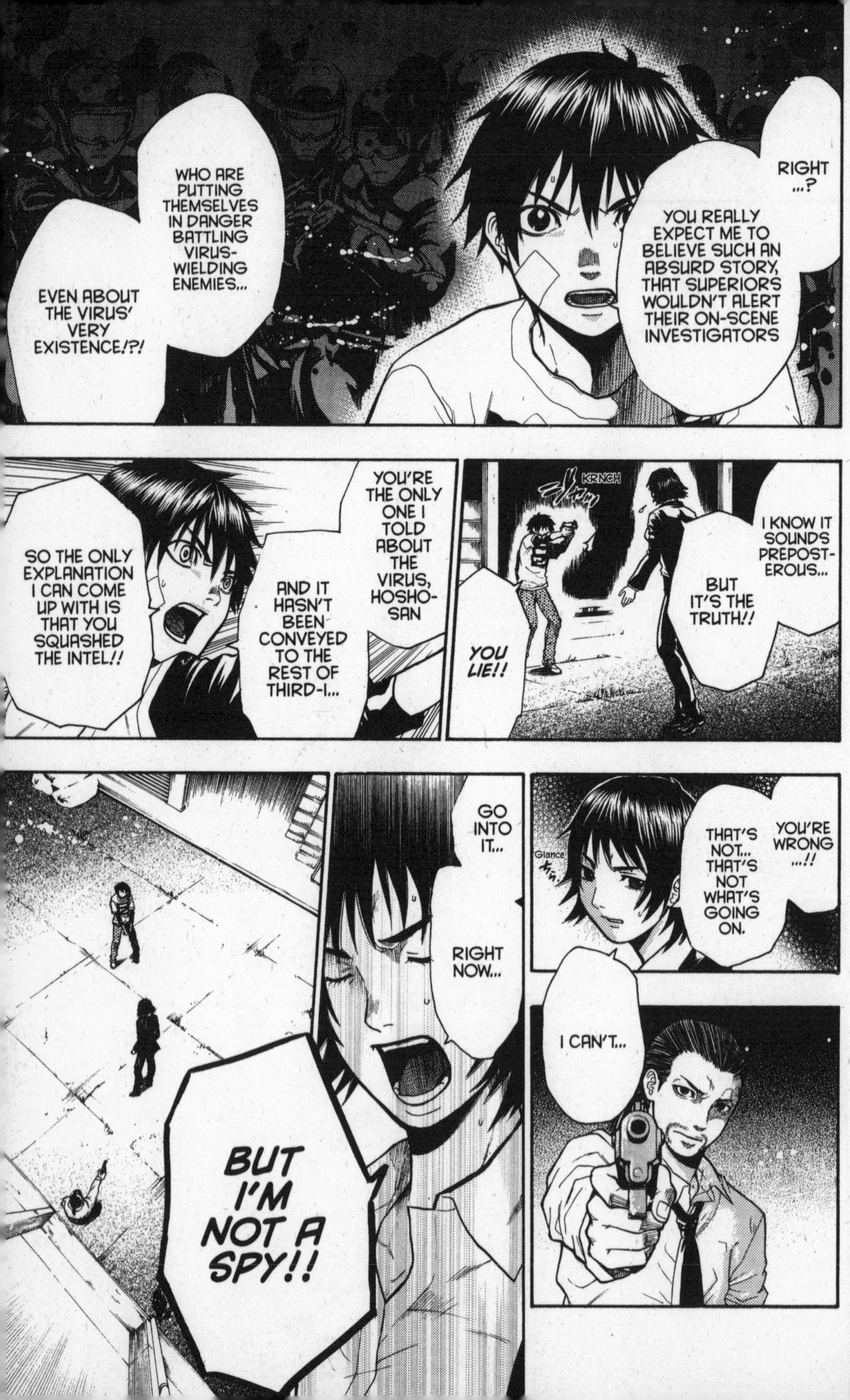
RIGHT ...?
YOU REALLY EXPECT ME TO BELIEVE SUCH AN ABSURD STORY, THAT SUPERIORS WOULDN'T ALERT THEIR ON-SCENE INVESTIGATORS
WHO ARE PUTTING THEMSELVES IN DANGER BATTLING VIRUS-WIELDING ENEMIES...
EVEN ABOUT THE VIRUS' VERY EXISTENCE!?!
KRNCH
I KNOW IT SOUNDS PREPOST-EROUS...
BUT IT'S THE TRUTH!!
YOU LIE!!
YOU'RE THE ONLY ONE I TOLD ABOUT THE VIRUS, HOSHO-SAN
AND IT HASN'T BEEN CONVEYED TO THE REST OF THIRD-I...
SO THE ONLY EXPLANATION I CAN COME UP WITH IS THAT YOU SQUASHED THE INTEL!!
YOU'RE WRONG ...!!
THAT'S NOT... THAT'S NOT WHAT'S GOING ON.
Glance
I CAN'T...
GO INTO IT...
RIGHT NOW...
BUT I'M NOT A SPY!!

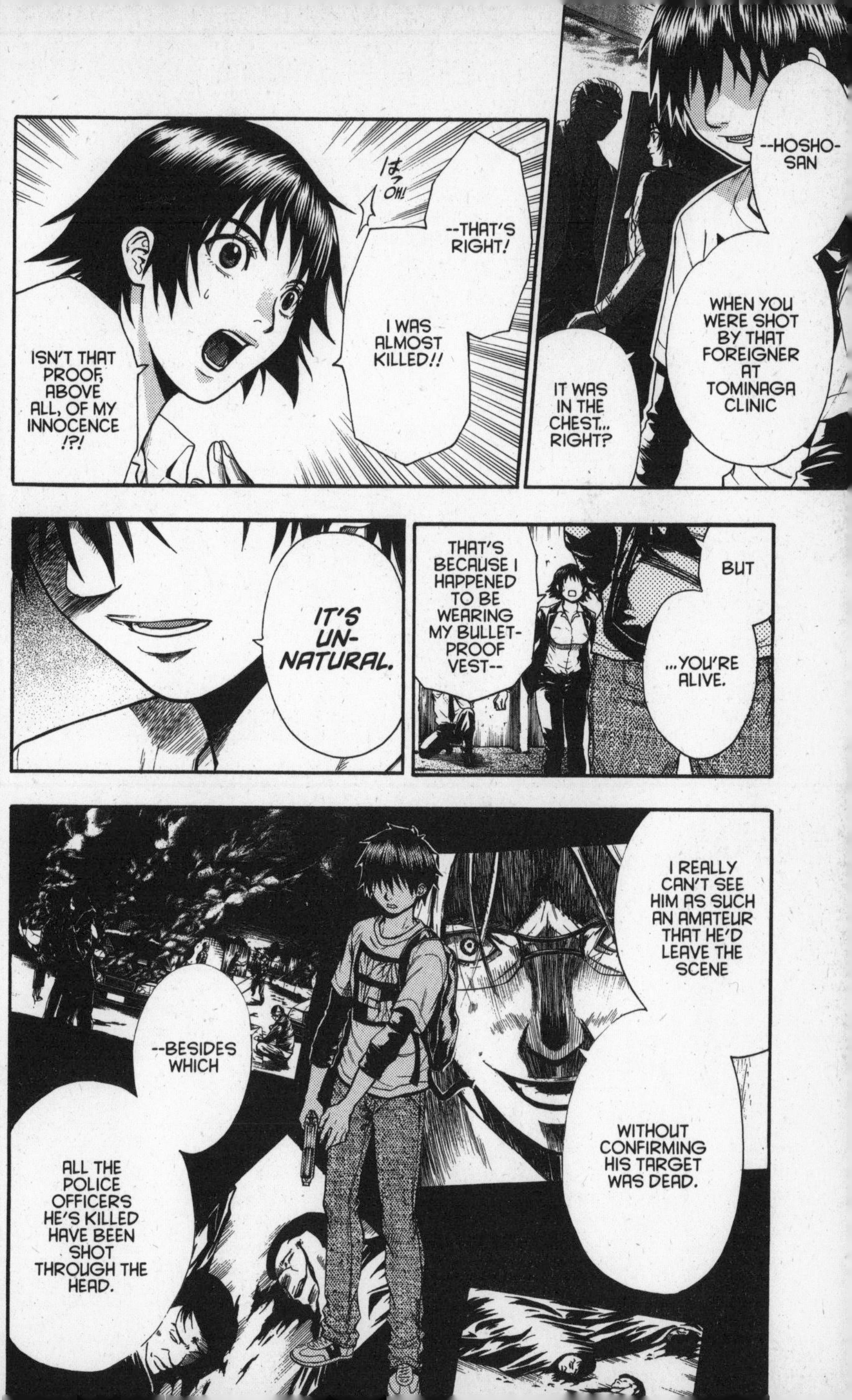
--HOSHO-SAN
WHEN YOU WERE SHOT BY THAT FOREIGNER AT TOMINAGA CLINIC
IT WAS IN THE CHEST... RIGHT?
はっ OH!
--THAT'S RIGHT!
I WAS ALMOST KILLED!!
ISN'T THAT PROOF, ABOVE ALL, OF MY INNOCENCE !?!
BUT
...YOU'RE ALIVE.
THAT'S BECAUSE I HAPPENED TO BE WEARING MY BULLET-PROOF VEST--
IT'S UN-NATURAL.
I REALLY CAN'T SEE HIM AS SUCH AN AMATEUR THAT HE'D LEAVE THE SCENE
WITHOUT CONFIRMING HIS TARGET WAS DEAD.
--BESIDES WHICH
ALL THE POLICE OFFICERS HE'S KILLED HAVE BEEN SHOT THROUGH THE HEAD.

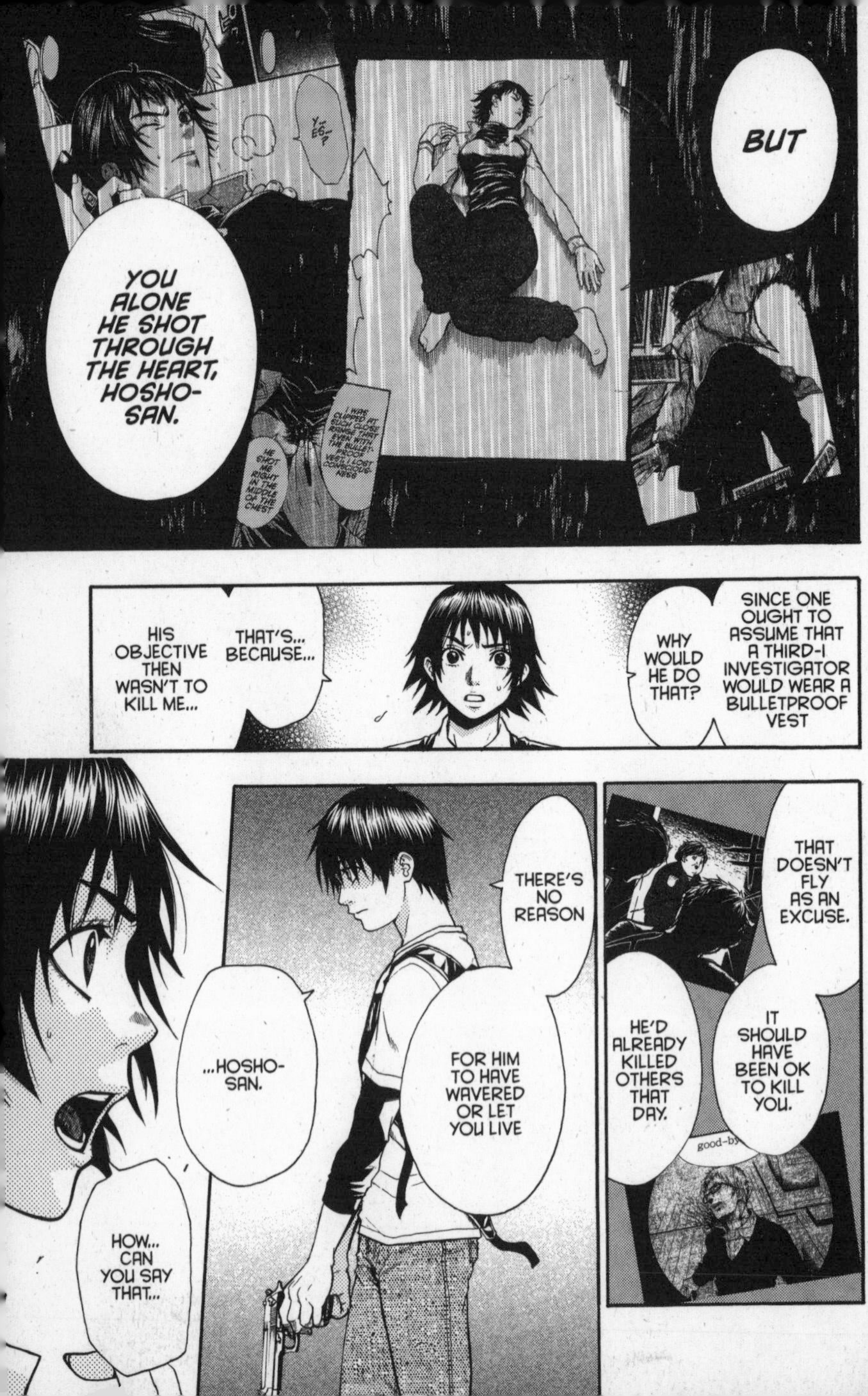

BUT
Y-ES-?
YOU ALONE HE SHOT THROUGH THE HEART, HOSHO-SAN.
I WAS CLIPPED AT SUCH CLOSE RANGE THAT EVEN WITH THE BULLET-PROOF VEST, I LOST CONSCIOUS-NESS
HE SHOT ME RIGHT IN THE MIDDLE OF THE CHEST
SINCE ONE OUGHT TO ASSUME THAT A THIRD-I INVESTIGATOR WOULD WEAR A BULLETPROOF VEST
WHY WOULD HE DO THAT?
THAT'S... BECAUSE...
HIS OBJECTIVE THEN WASN'T TO KILL ME...
THAT DOESN'T FLY AS AN EXCUSE.
IT SHOULD HAVE BEEN OK TO KILL YOU.
HE'D ALREADY KILLED OTHERS THAT DAY.
good-by
THERE'S NO REASON
FOR HIM TO HAVE WAVERED OR LET YOU LIVE
...HOSHO-SAN.
HOW... CAN YOU SAY THAT...

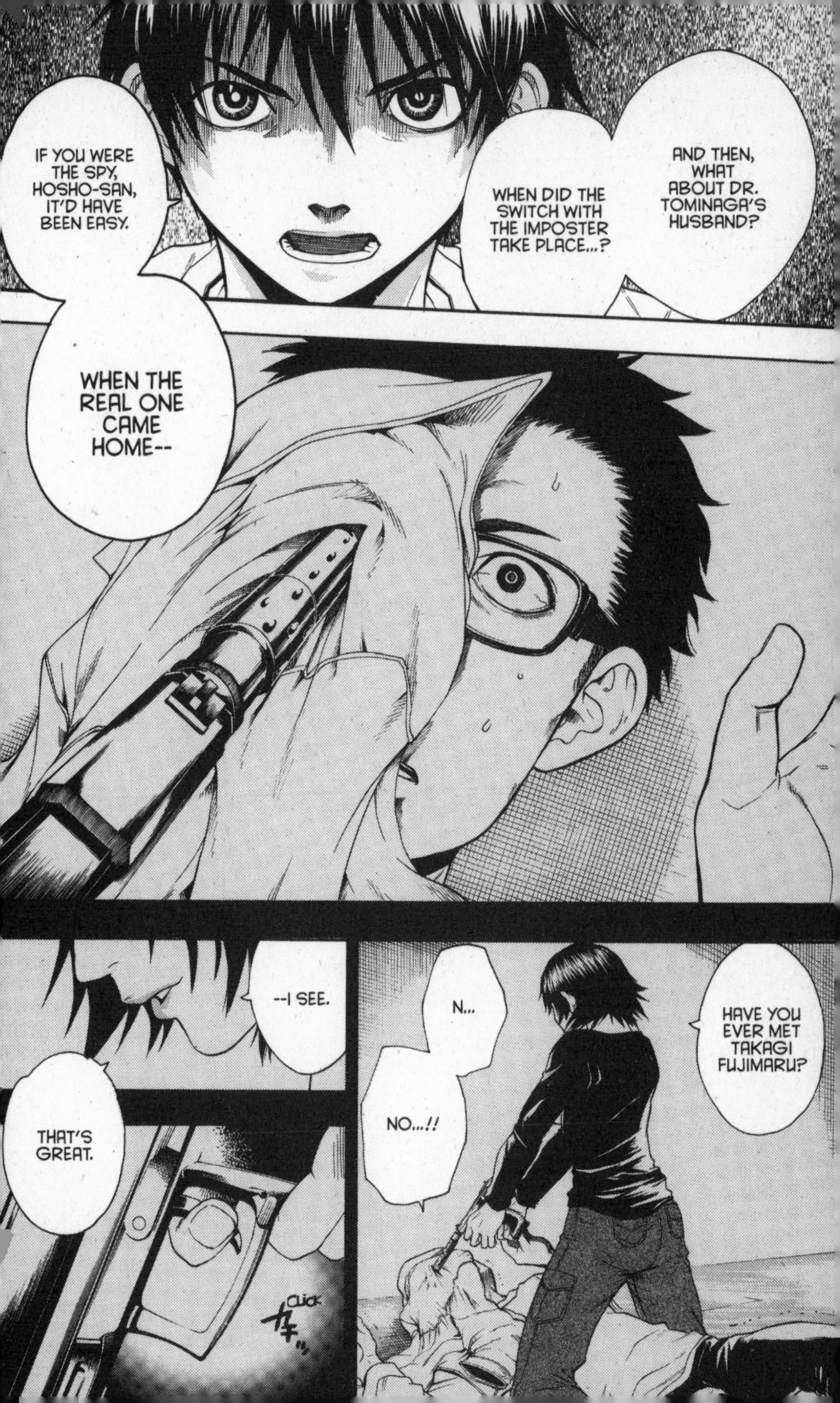
AND THEN, WHAT ABOUT DR. TOMINAGA'S HUSBAND?
WHEN DID THE SWITCH WITH THE IMPOSTER TAKE PLACE...?
IF YOU WERE THE SPY, HOSHO-SAN, IT'D HAVE BEEN EASY.
WHEN THE REAL ONE CAME HOME--
HAVE YOU EVER MET TAKAGI FUJIMARU?
N...
NO...!!
--I SEE.
THAT'S GREAT.
CLICK

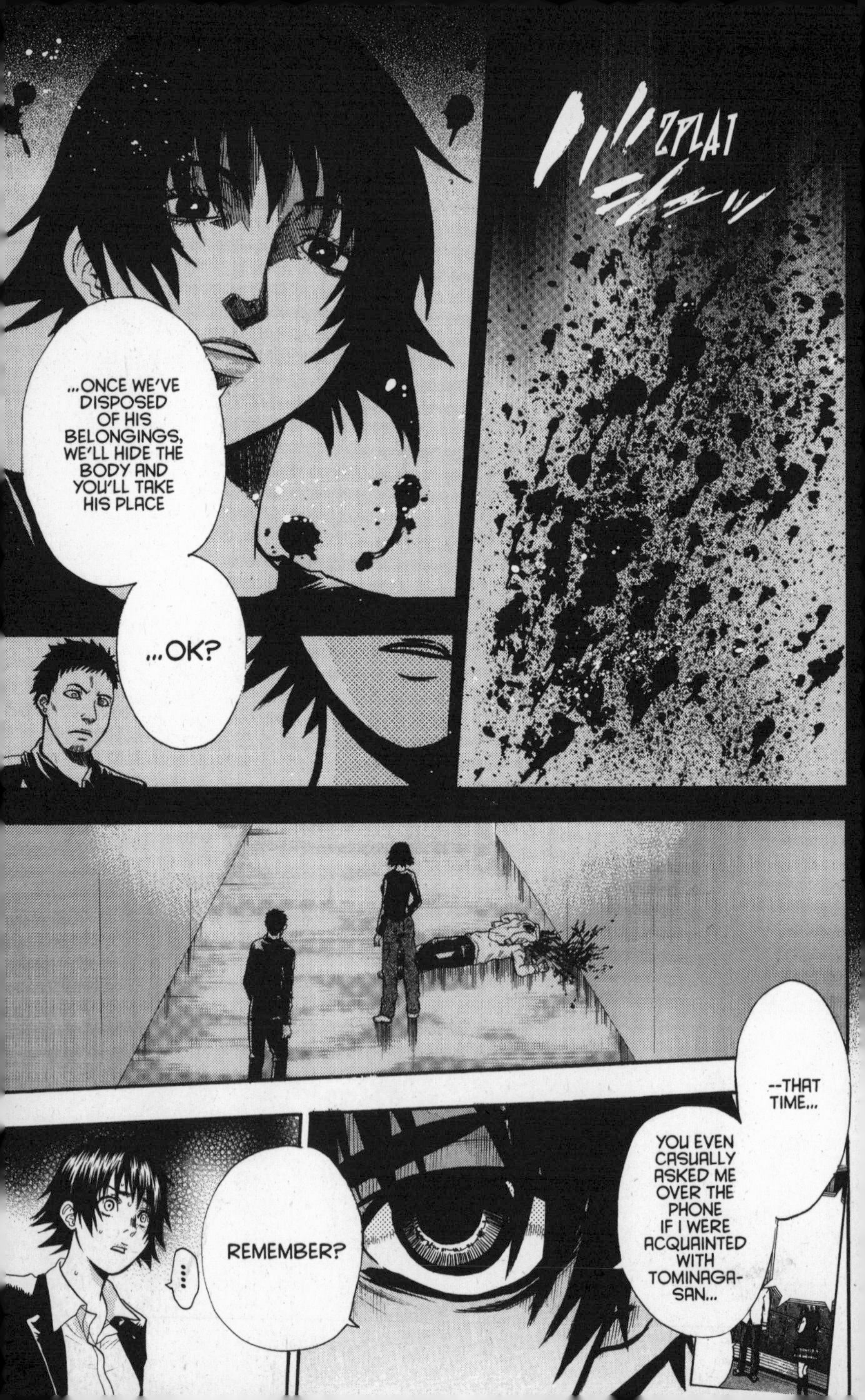
ZPLAT
...ONCE WE'VE DISPOSED OF HIS BELONGINGS, WE'LL HIDE THE BODY AND YOU'LL TAKE HIS PLACE
...OK?
--THAT TIME...
YOU EVEN CASUALLY ASKED ME OVER THE PHONE IF I WERE ACQUAINTED WITH TOMINAGA-SAN...
REMEMBER?
....

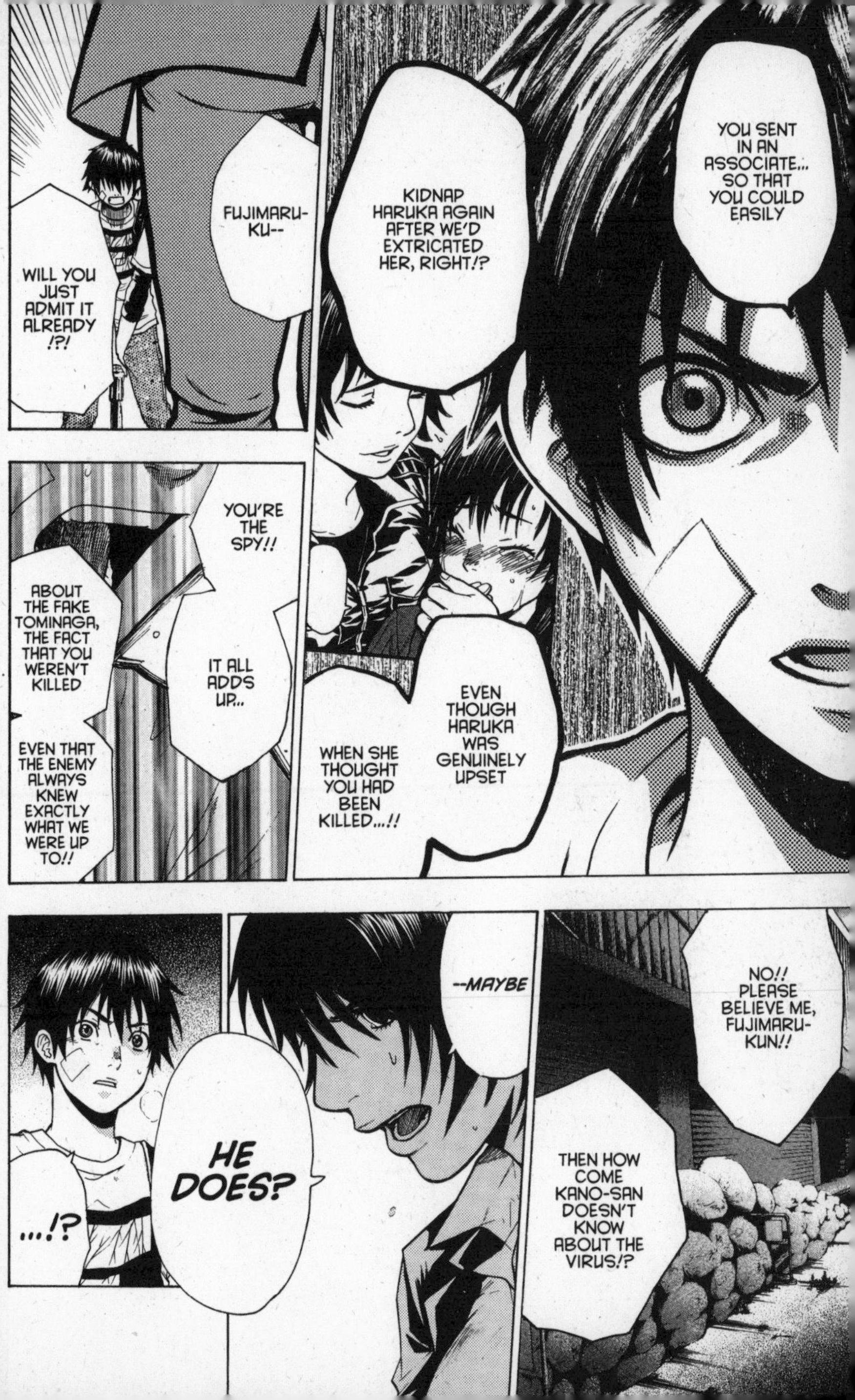
YOU SENT IN AN ASSOCIATE... SO THAT YOU COULD EASILY
KIDNAP HARUKA AGAIN AFTER WE'D EXTRICATED HER, RIGHT!?
EVEN THOUGH HARUKA WAS GENUINELY UPSET
WHEN SHE THOUGHT YOU HAD BEEN KILLED...!!
FUJIMARU-KU--
WILL YOU JUST ADMIT IT ALREADY !?!
YOU'RE THE SPY!!
IT ALL ADDS UP...
ABOUT THE FAKE TOMINAGA, THE FACT THAT YOU WEREN'T KILLED
EVEN THAT THE ENEMY ALWAYS KNEW EXACTLY WHAT WE WERE UP TO!!
NO!! PLEASE BELIEVE ME, FUJIMARU-KUN!!
THEN HOW COME KANO-SAN DOESN'T KNOW ABOUT THE VIRUS!?
--MAYBE
HE DOES?
...!?

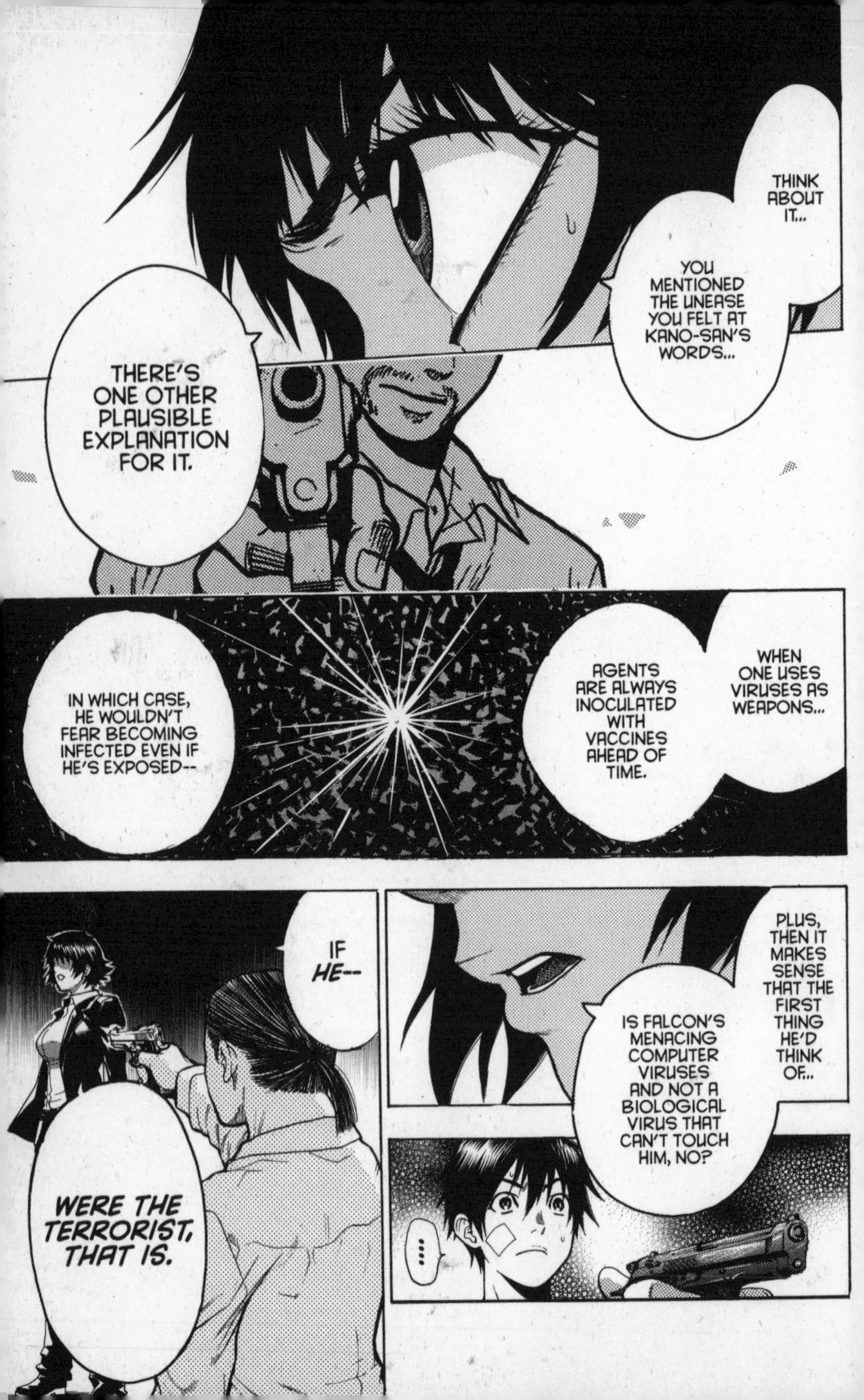
THINK ABOUT IT...
YOU MENTIONED THE UNEASE YOU FELT AT KANO-SAN'S WORDS...
THERE'S ONE OTHER PLAUSIBLE EXPLANATION FOR IT.
WHEN ONE USES VIRUSES AS WEAPONS...
AGENTS ARE ALWAYS INOCULATED WITH VACCINES AHEAD OF TIME.
IN WHICH CASE, HE WOULDN'T FEAR BECOMING INFECTED EVEN IF HE'S EXPOSED--
PLUS, THEN IT MAKES SENSE THAT THE FIRST THING HE'D THINK OF...
IS FALCON'S MENACING COMPUTER VIRUSES AND NOT A BIOLOGICAL VIRUS THAT CAN'T TOUCH HIM, NO?
....
IF *HE*--
WERE THE TERRORIST, THAT IS.

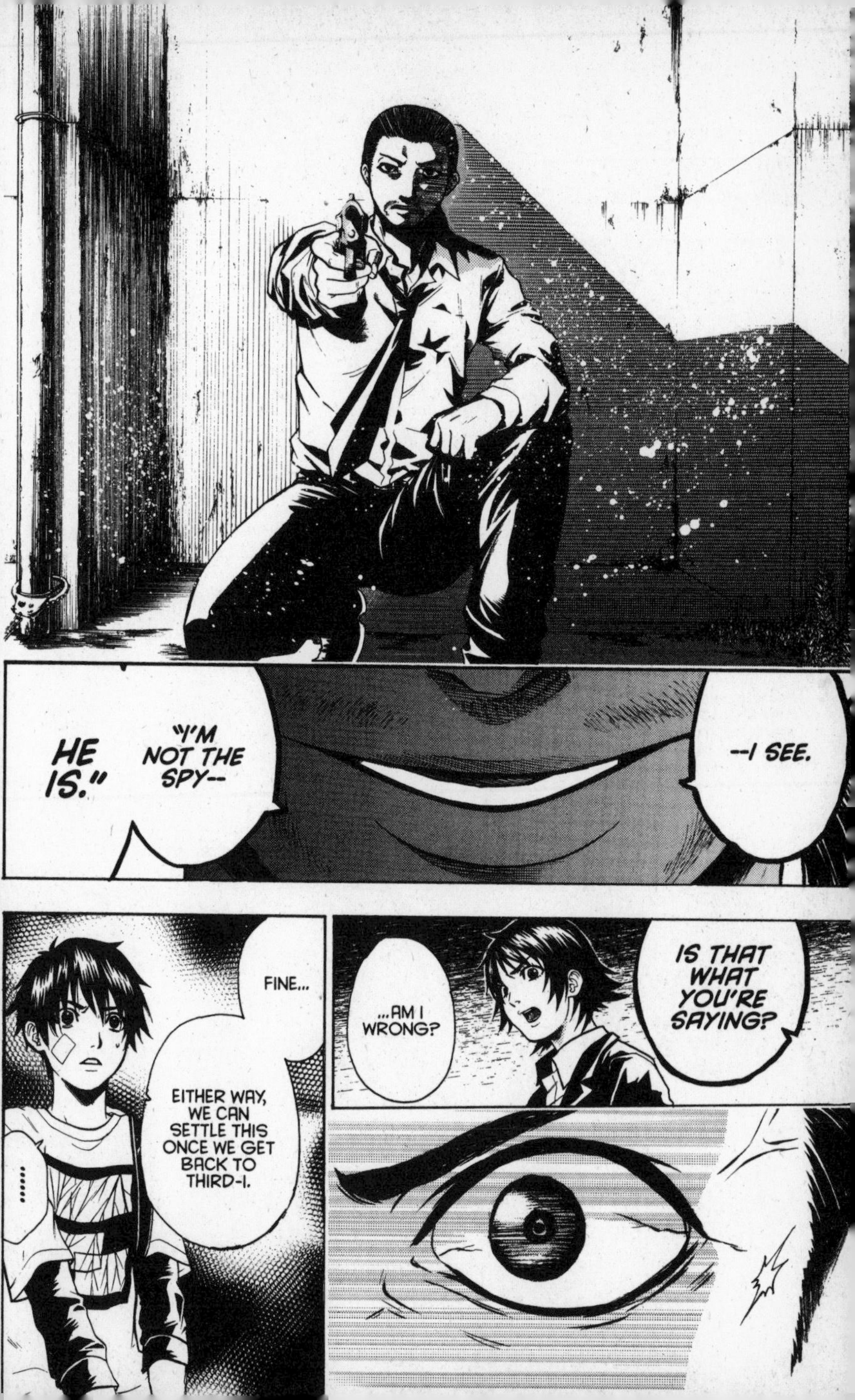
--I SEE.
"I'M NOT THE SPY--
HE IS."
IS THAT WHAT YOU'RE SAYING?
...AM I WRONG?
FINE...
EITHER WAY, WE CAN SETTLE THIS ONCE WE GET BACK TO THIRD-I.
......

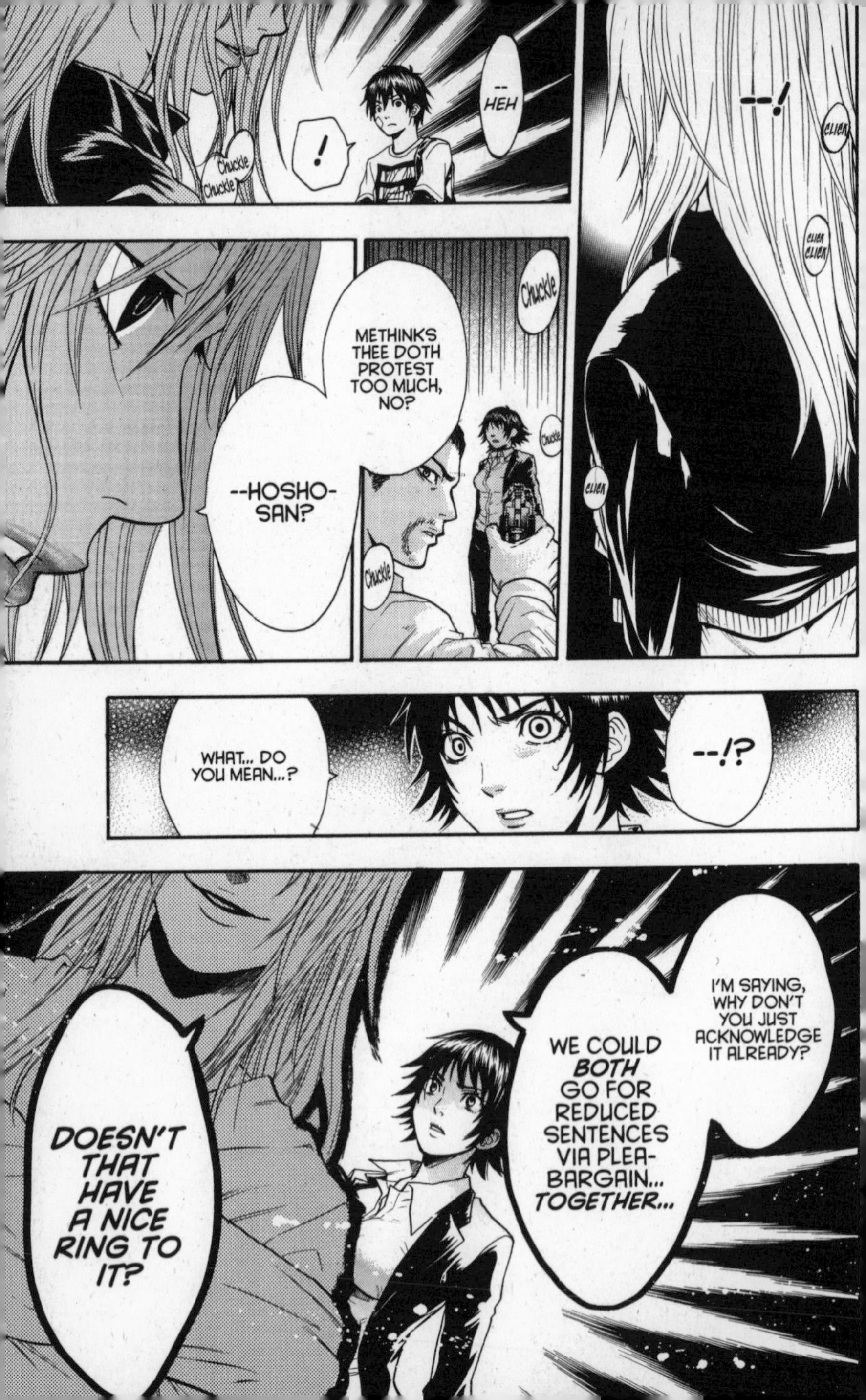
--!
CLICK
CLICK CLICK
CLICK
--HEH
!
Chuckle Chuckle
Chuckle
METHINKS THEE DOTH PROTEST TOO MUCH, NO?
Chuckle
Chuckle
--HOSHO-SAN?
--!?
WHAT... DO YOU MEAN...?
I'M SAYING, WHY DON'T YOU JUST ACKNOWLEDGE IT ALREADY?
WE COULD *BOTH* GO FOR REDUCED SENTENCES VIA PLEA-BARGAIN... *TOGETHER*...
DOESN'T THAT HAVE A NICE RING TO IT?

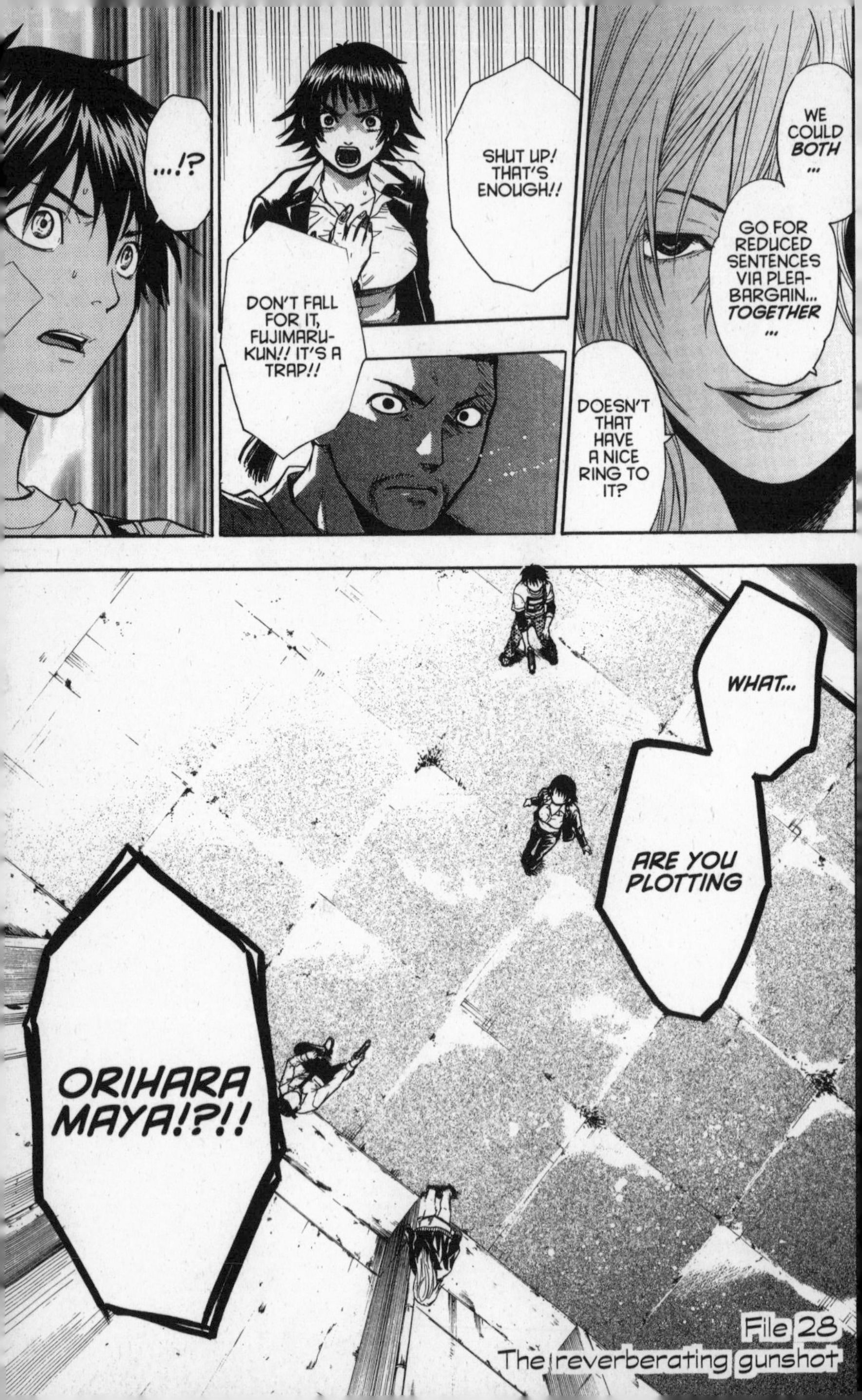
WE COULD BOTH ...
GO FOR REDUCED SENTENCES VIA PLEA-BARGAIN... TOGETHER ...
DOESN'T THAT HAVE A NICE RING TO IT?
SHUT UP! THAT'S ENOUGH!!
DON'T FALL FOR IT, FUJIMARU-KUN!! IT'S A TRAP!!
...!?
WHAT...
ARE YOU PLOTTING
ORIHARA MAYA!?!!

File 28
The reverberating gunshot

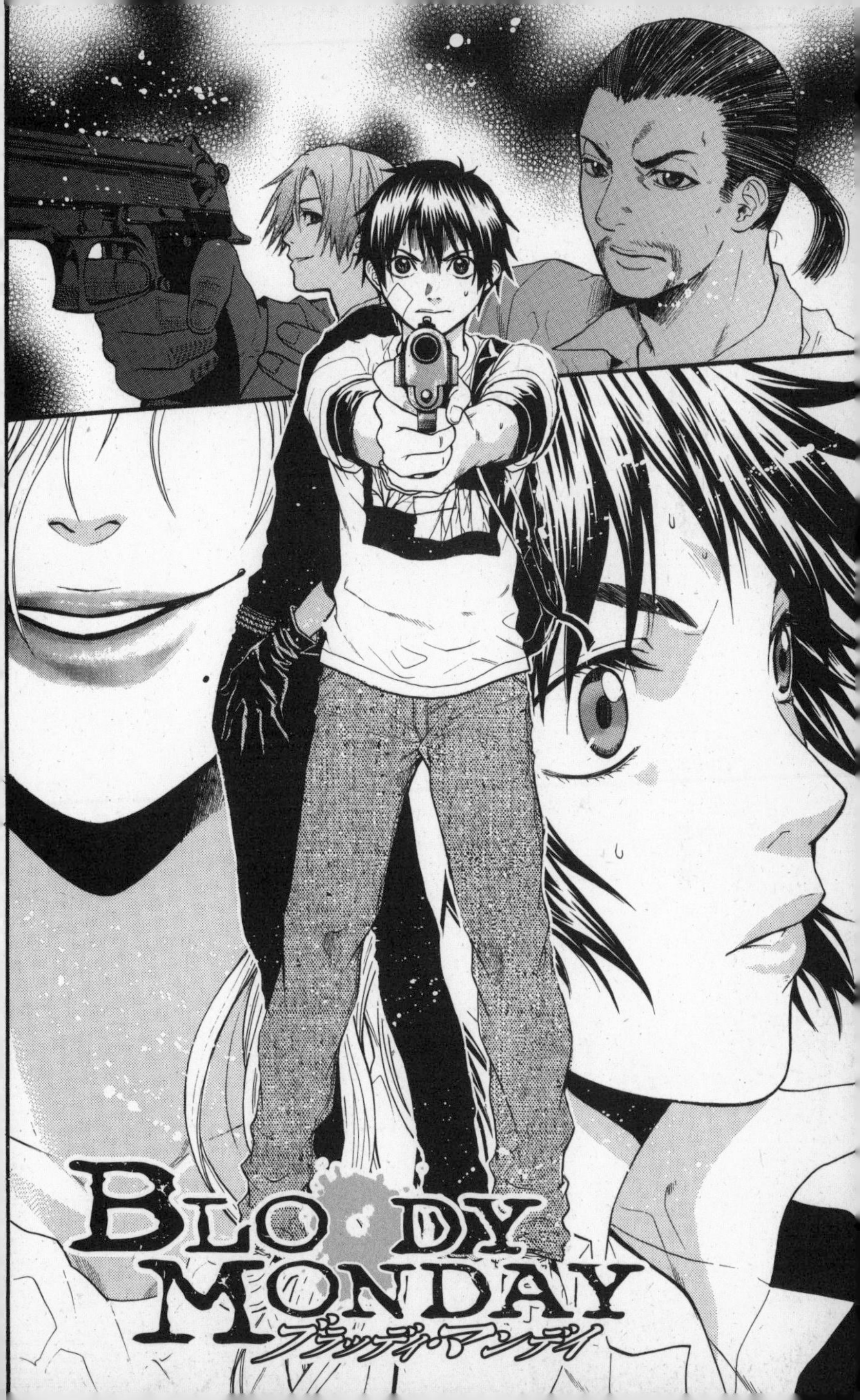
BLOODY MONDAY
ブラッディ・マンデイ

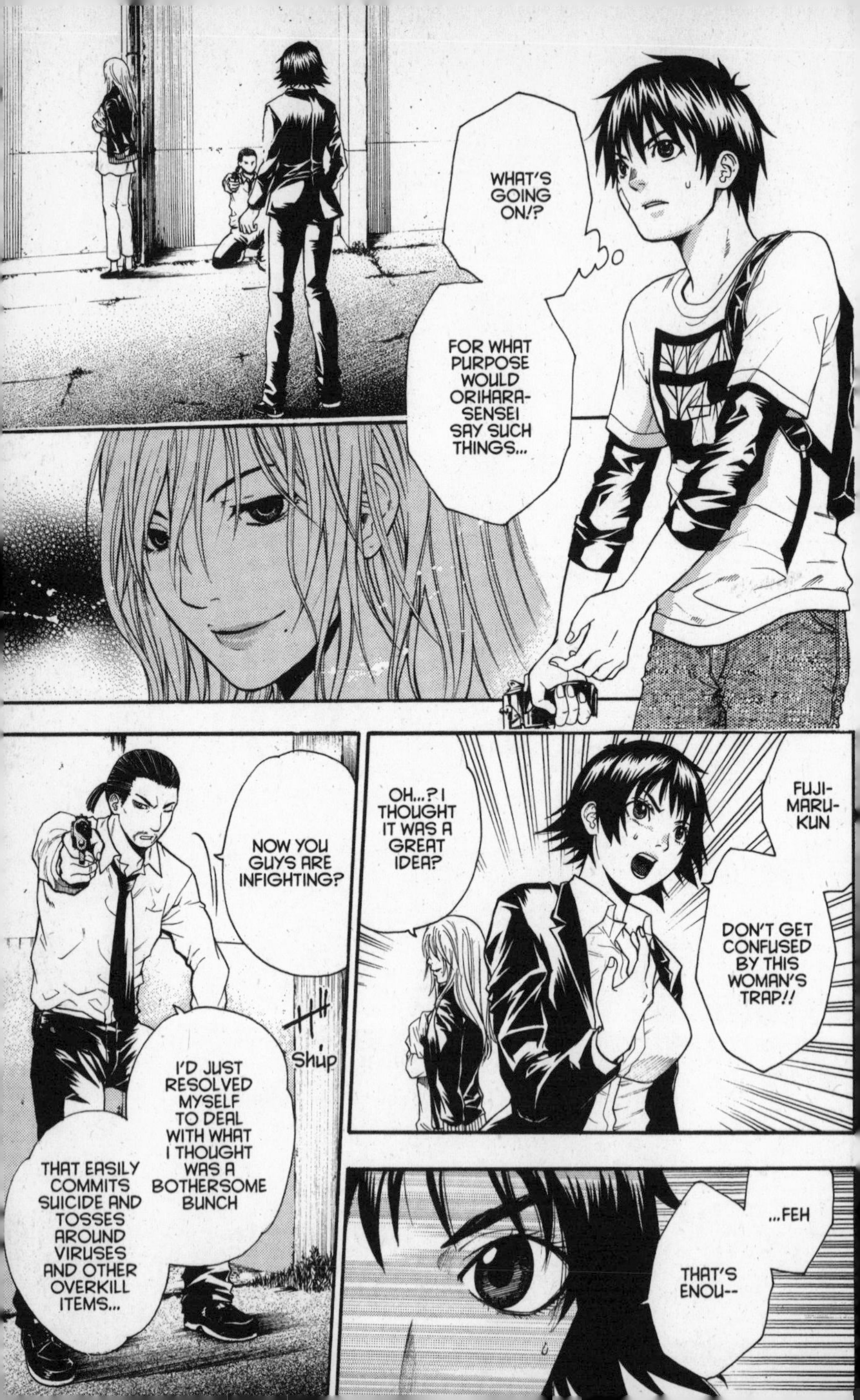
WHAT'S GOING ON!?
FOR WHAT PURPOSE WOULD ORIHARA-SENSEI SAY SUCH THINGS...
FUJI-MARU-KUN
DON'T GET CONFUSED BY THIS WOMAN'S TRAP!!
OH...? I THOUGHT IT WAS A GREAT IDEA?
...FEH
THAT'S ENOU--
NOW YOU GUYS ARE INFIGHTING?
Shup
I'D JUST RESOLVED MYSELF TO DEAL WITH WHAT I THOUGHT WAS A BOTHERSOME BUNCH
THAT EASILY COMMITS SUICIDE AND TOSSES AROUND VIRUSES AND OTHER OVERKILL ITEMS...

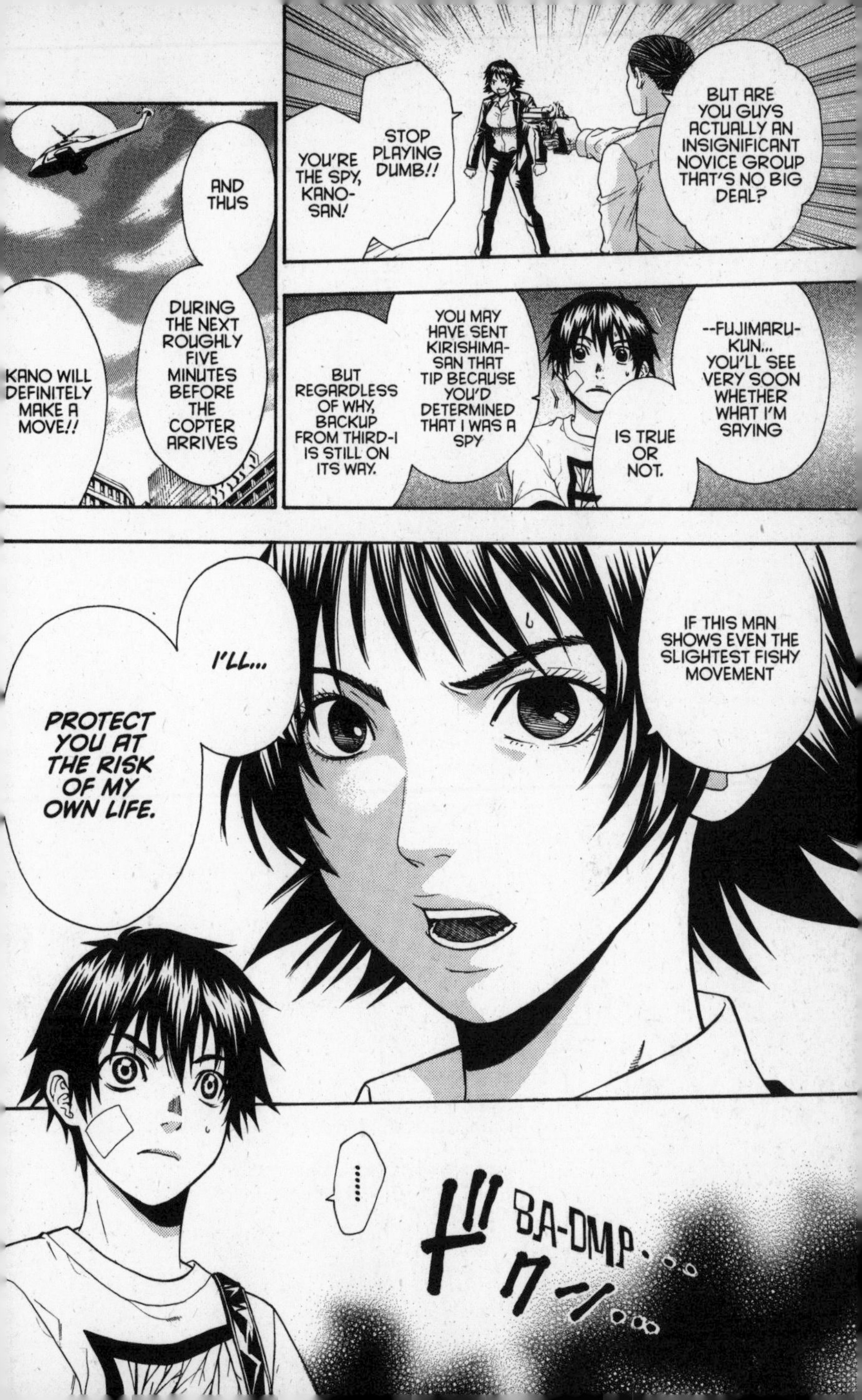
BUT ARE YOU GUYS ACTUALLY AN INSIGNIFICANT NOVICE GROUP THAT'S NO BIG DEAL?
STOP PLAYING DUMB!!
YOU'RE THE SPY, KANO-SAN!
--FUJIMARU-KUN... YOU'LL SEE VERY SOON WHETHER WHAT I'M SAYING
IS TRUE OR NOT.
YOU MAY HAVE SENT KIRISHIMA-SAN THAT TIP BECAUSE YOU'D DETERMINED THAT I WAS A SPY
BUT REGARDLESS OF WHY, BACKUP FROM THIRD-I IS STILL ON ITS WAY.
AND THUS
DURING THE NEXT ROUGHLY FIVE MINUTES BEFORE THE COPTER ARRIVES
KANO WILL DEFINITELY MAKE A MOVE!!
IF THIS MAN SHOWS EVEN THE SLIGHTEST FISHY MOVEMENT
I'LL...
PROTECT YOU AT THE RISK OF MY OWN LIFE.
......
ドクン
BA-DMP...

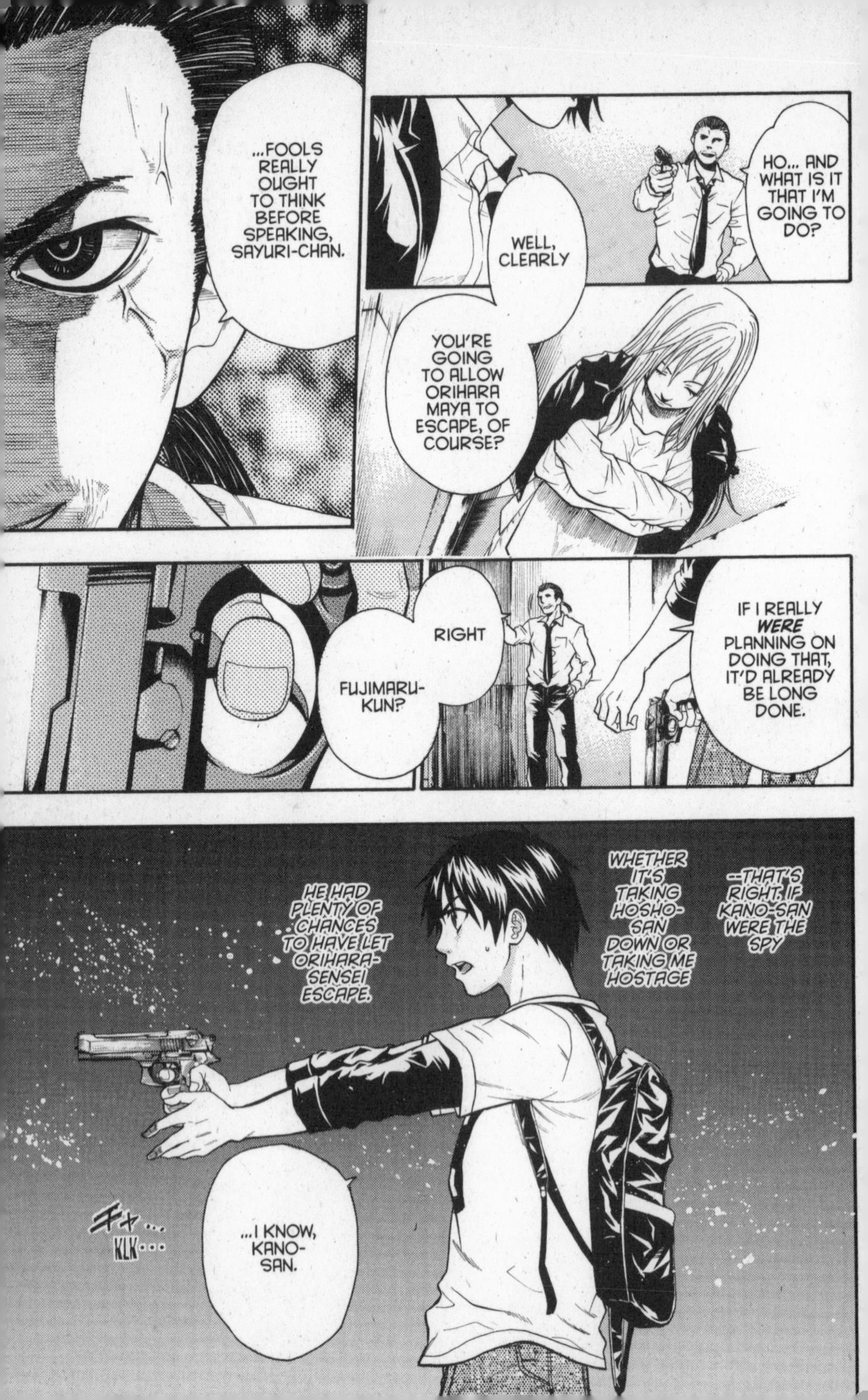
HO... AND WHAT IS IT THAT I'M GOING TO DO?
WELL, CLEARLY
YOU'RE GOING TO ALLOW ORIHARA MAYA TO ESCAPE, OF COURSE?
...FOOLS REALLY OUGHT TO THINK BEFORE SPEAKING, SAYURI-CHAN.
IF I REALLY *WERE* PLANNING ON DOING THAT, IT'D ALREADY BE LONG DONE.
RIGHT
FUJIMARU-KUN?
--THAT'S RIGHT. IF KANO-SAN WERE THE SPY
WHETHER IT'S TAKING HOSHO-SAN DOWN OR TAKING ME HOSTAGE
HE HAD PLENTY OF CHANCES TO HAVE LET ORIHARA-SENSEI ESCAPE.
KLK...
...I KNOW, KANO-SAN.

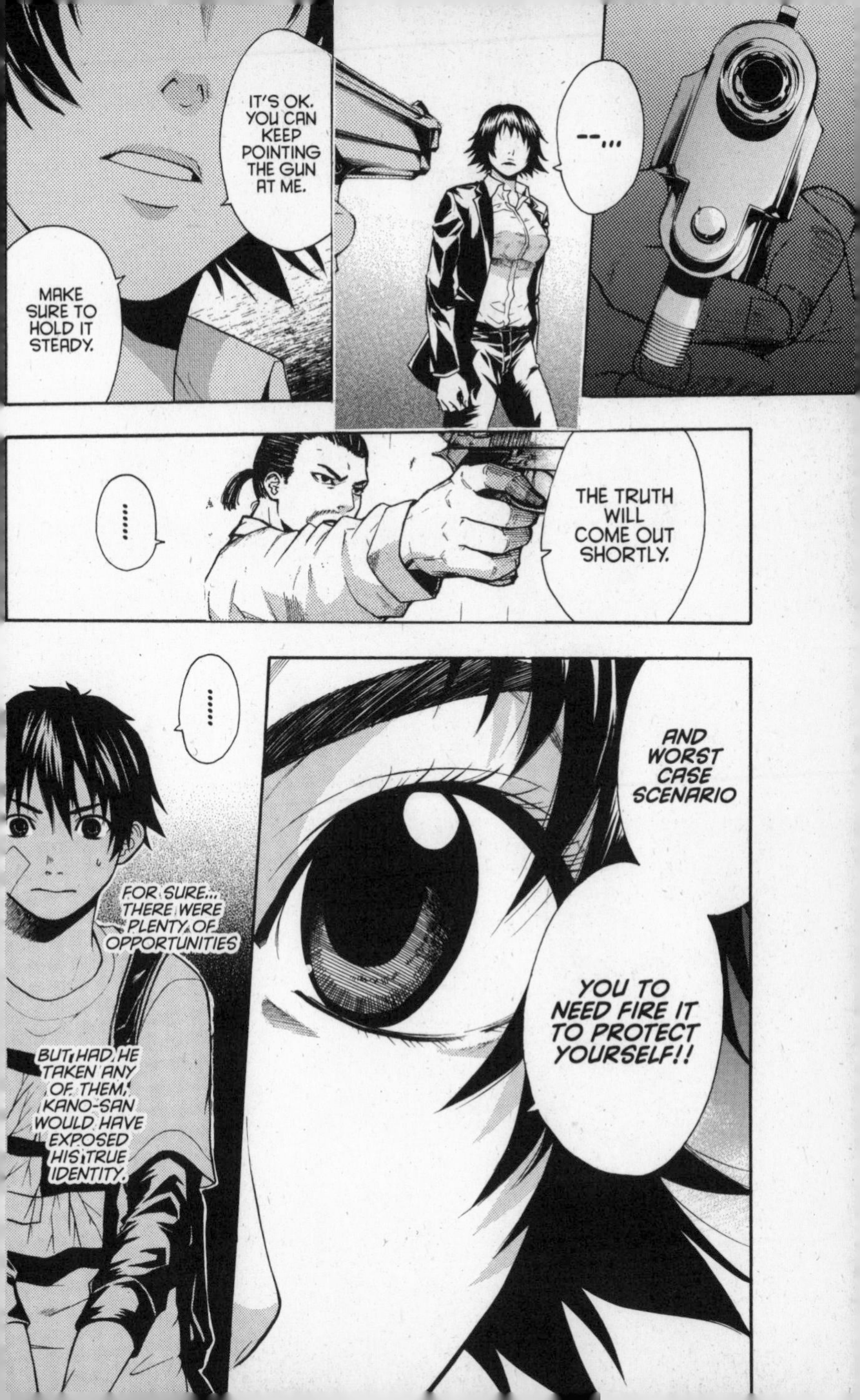
--...
IT'S OK. YOU CAN KEEP POINTING THE GUN AT ME.
MAKE SURE TO HOLD IT STEADY.
THE TRUTH WILL COME OUT SHORTLY.
......
AND WORST CASE SCENARIO
YOU TO NEED FIRE IT TO PROTECT YOURSELF!!
......
FOR SURE... THERE WERE PLENTY OF OPPORTUNITIES
BUT, HAD HE TAKEN ANY OF THEM, KANO-SAN WOULD HAVE EXPOSED HIS TRUE IDENTITY.

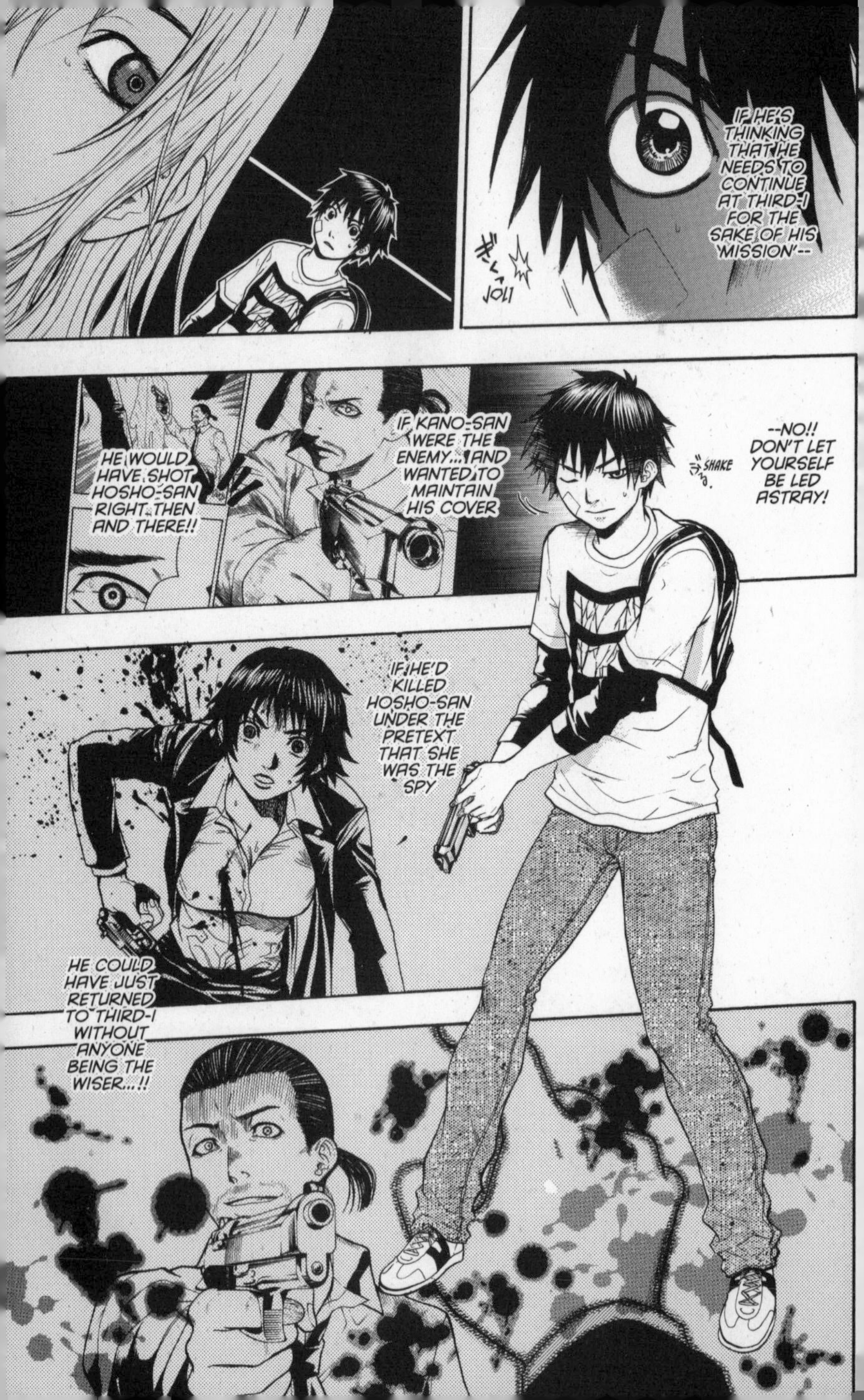
IF HE'S THINKING THAT HE NEEDS TO CONTINUE AT THIRD-I FOR THE SAKE OF HIS MISSION'--
JOLT
--NO!! DON'T LET YOURSELF BE LED ASTRAY!
SHAKE
IF KANO-SAN WERE THE ENEMY... AND WANTED TO MAINTAIN HIS COVER
HE WOULD HAVE SHOT HOSHO-SAN RIGHT THEN AND THERE!!
IF HE'D KILLED HOSHO-SAN UNDER THE PRETEXT THAT SHE WAS THE SPY
HE COULD HAVE JUST RETURNED TO THIRD-I WITHOUT ANYONE BEING THE WISER...!!

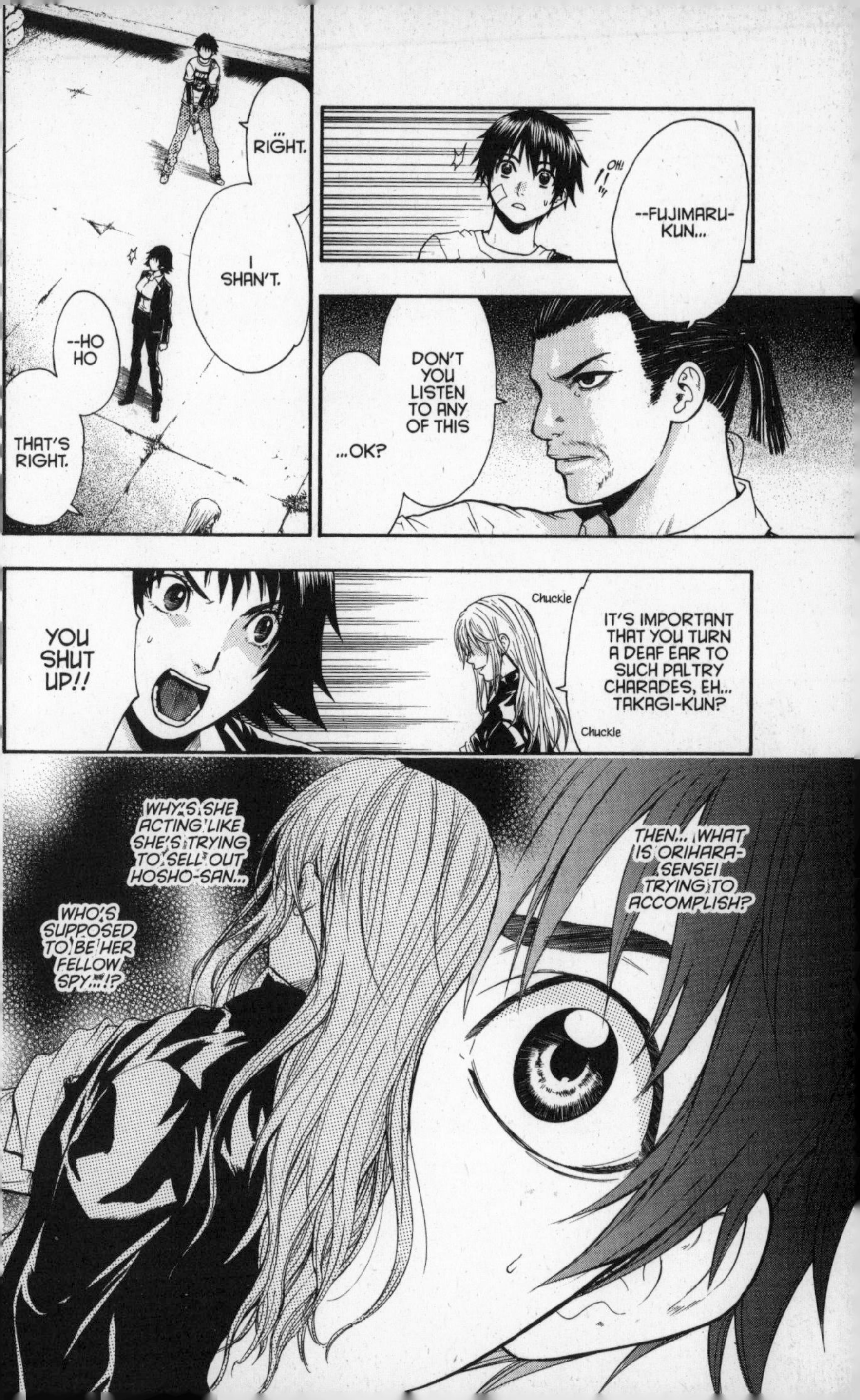
--FUJIMARU-KUN...
OH!
DON'T YOU LISTEN TO ANY OF THIS
...OK?
...RIGHT.
I SHAN'T.
--HO HO
THAT'S RIGHT.
Chuckle
IT'S IMPORTANT THAT YOU TURN A DEAF EAR TO SUCH PALTRY CHARADES, EH... TAKAGI-KUN?
Chuckle
YOU SHUT UP!!
THEN... WHAT IS ORIHARA-SENSEI TRYING TO ACCOMPLISH?
WHY'S SHE ACTING LIKE SHE'S TRYING TO SELL OUT HOSHO-SAN...
WHO'S SUPPOSED TO BE HER FELLOW SPY...!?

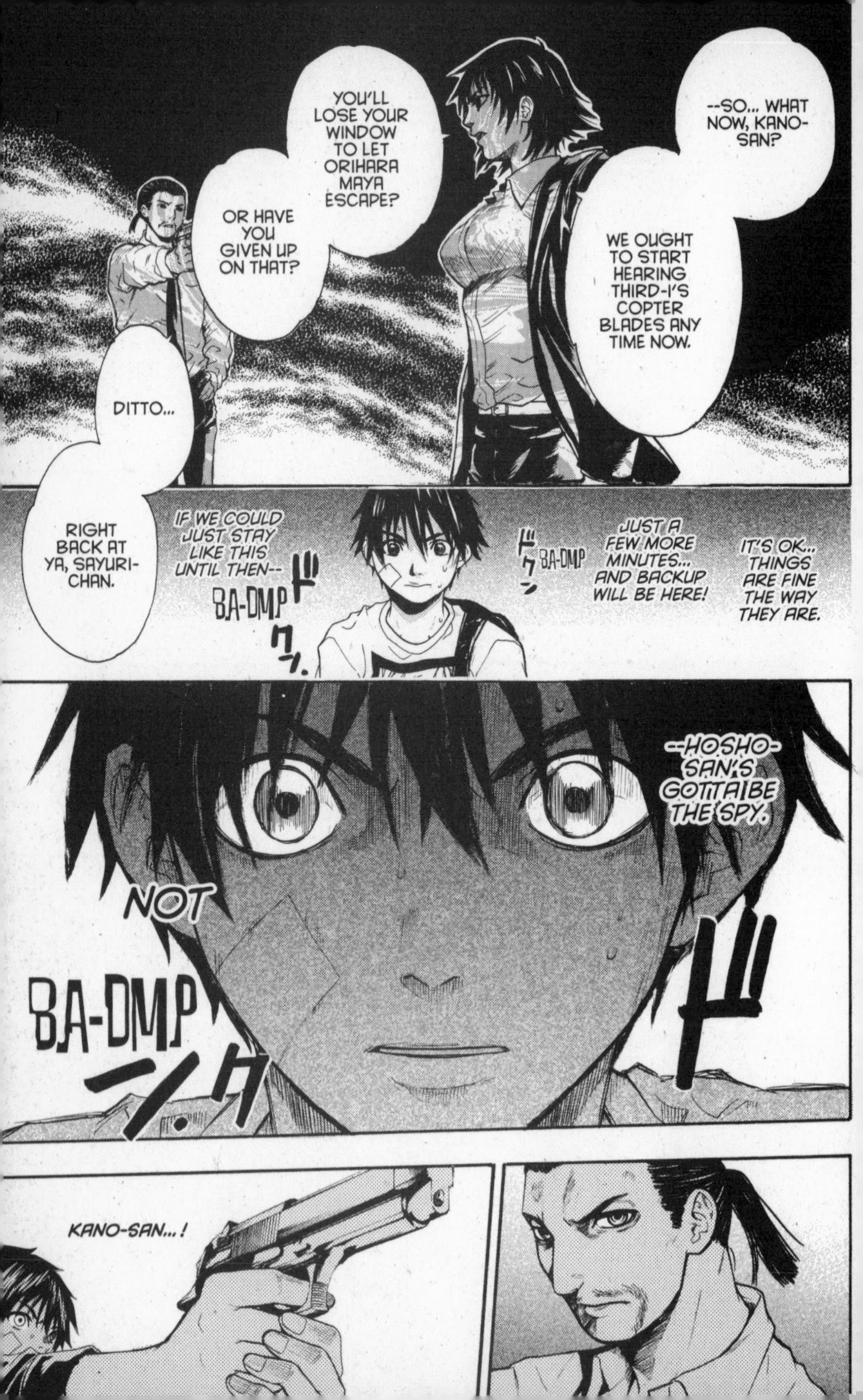
--SO... WHAT NOW, KANO-SAN?
WE OUGHT TO START HEARING THIRD-I'S COPTER BLADES ANY TIME NOW.
YOU'LL LOSE YOUR WINDOW TO LET ORIHARA MAYA ESCAPE?
OR HAVE YOU GIVEN UP ON THAT?
DITTO...
RIGHT BACK AT YA, SAYURI-CHAN.
IT'S OK... THINGS ARE FINE THE WAY THEY ARE.
JUST A FEW MORE MINUTES... AND BACKUP WILL BE HERE!
BA-DMP
IF WE COULD JUST STAY LIKE THIS UNTIL THEN--
BA-DMP
--HOSHO-SAN'S GOTTA BE THE SPY.
NOT
BA-DMP
KANO-SAN...!

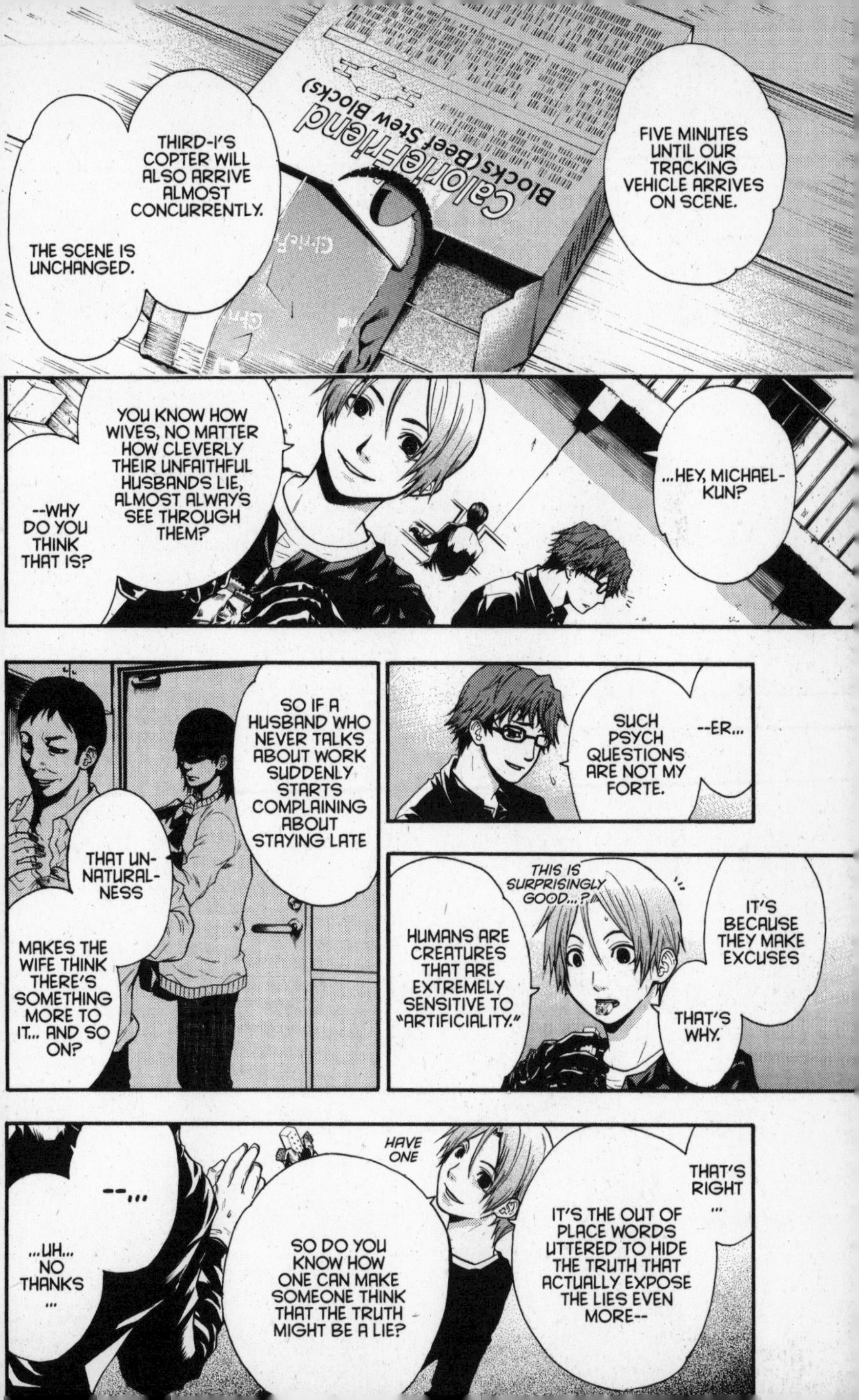
FIVE MINUTES UNTIL OUR TRACKING VEHICLE ARRIVES ON SCENE.
Calorie Friend Blocks (Beef Stew Blocks)
THIRD-I'S COPTER WILL ALSO ARRIVE ALMOST CONCURRENTLY.
THE SCENE IS UNCHANGED.
...HEY, MICHAEL-KUN?
YOU KNOW HOW WIVES, NO MATTER HOW CLEVERLY THEIR UNFAITHFUL HUSBANDS LIE, ALMOST ALWAYS SEE THROUGH THEM?
--WHY DO YOU THINK THAT IS?
--ER...
SUCH PSYCH QUESTIONS ARE NOT MY FORTE.
IT'S BECAUSE THEY MAKE EXCUSES
THAT'S WHY.
THIS IS SURPRISINGLY GOOD...?
HUMANS ARE CREATURES THAT ARE EXTREMELY SENSITIVE TO "ARTIFICIALITY."
SO IF A HUSBAND WHO NEVER TALKS ABOUT WORK SUDDENLY STARTS COMPLAINING ABOUT STAYING LATE
THAT UN-NATURAL-NESS
MAKES THE WIFE THINK THERE'S SOMETHING MORE TO IT... AND SO ON?
THAT'S RIGHT ...
IT'S THE OUT OF PLACE WORDS UTTERED TO HIDE THE TRUTH THAT ACTUALLY EXPOSE THE LIES EVEN MORE--
HAVE ONE
SO DO YOU KNOW HOW ONE CAN MAKE SOMEONE THINK THAT THE TRUTH MIGHT BE A LIE?
--,...
...UH... NO THANKS ...

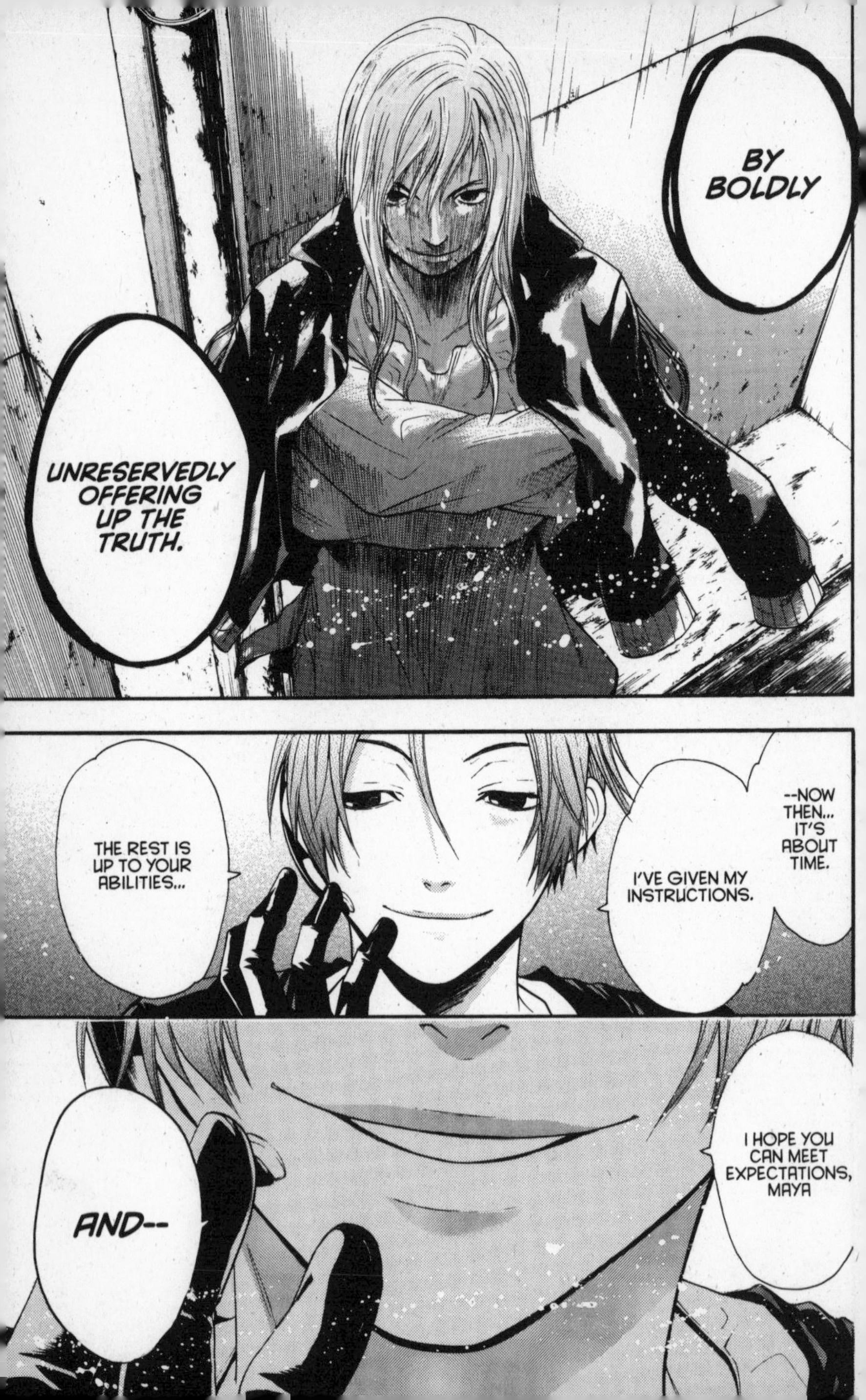
BY BOLDLY
UNRESERVEDLY OFFERING UP THE TRUTH.
--NOW THEN... IT'S ABOUT TIME.
I'VE GIVEN MY INSTRUCTIONS.
THE REST IS UP TO YOUR ABILITIES...
I HOPE YOU CAN MEET EXPECTATIONS, MAYA
AND--

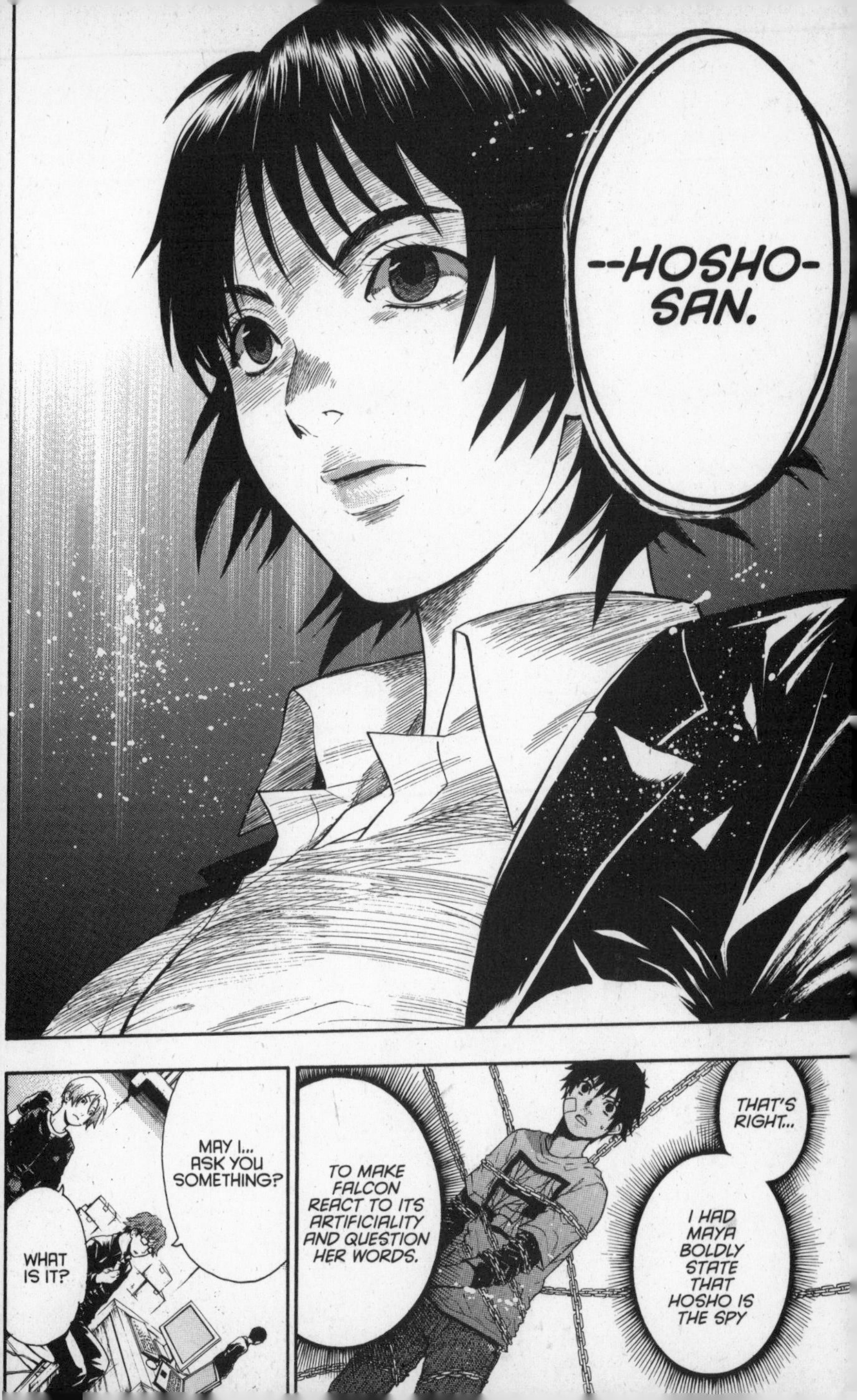
--HOSHO-SAN.
THAT'S RIGHT...
I HAD MAYA BOLDLY STATE THAT HOSHO IS THE SPY
TO MAKE FALCON REACT TO ITS ARTIFICIALITY AND QUESTION HER WORDS.
MAY I... ASK YOU SOMETHING?
WHAT IS IT?

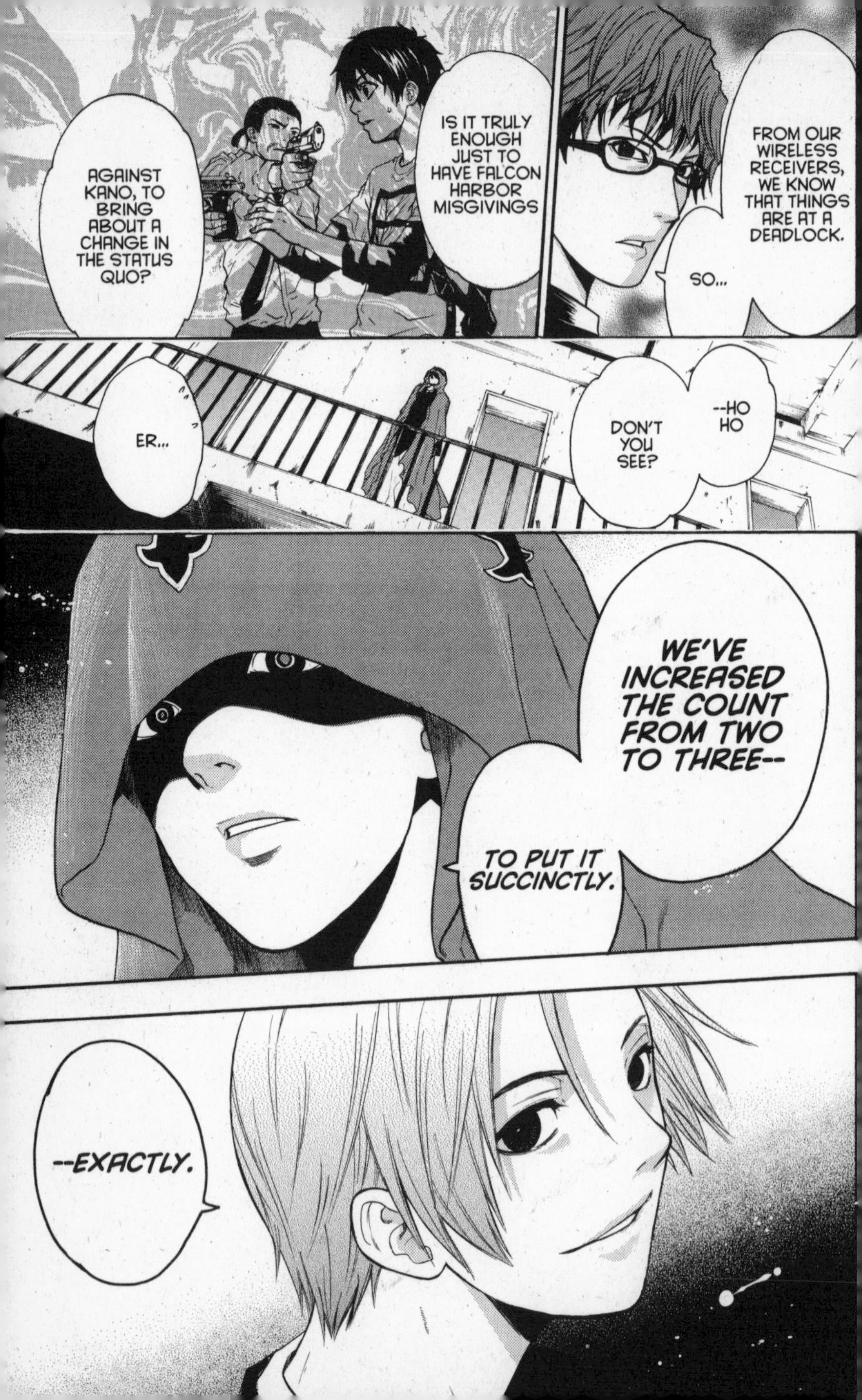
FROM OUR WIRELESS RECEIVERS, WE KNOW THAT THINGS ARE AT A DEADLOCK.
SO...
IS IT TRULY ENOUGH JUST TO HAVE FALCON HARBOR MISGIVINGS
AGAINST KANO, TO BRING ABOUT A CHANGE IN THE STATUS QUO?
--HO HO
DON'T YOU SEE?
ER...
WE'VE INCREASED THE COUNT FROM TWO TO THREE--
TO PUT IT SUCCINCTLY.
--EXACTLY.

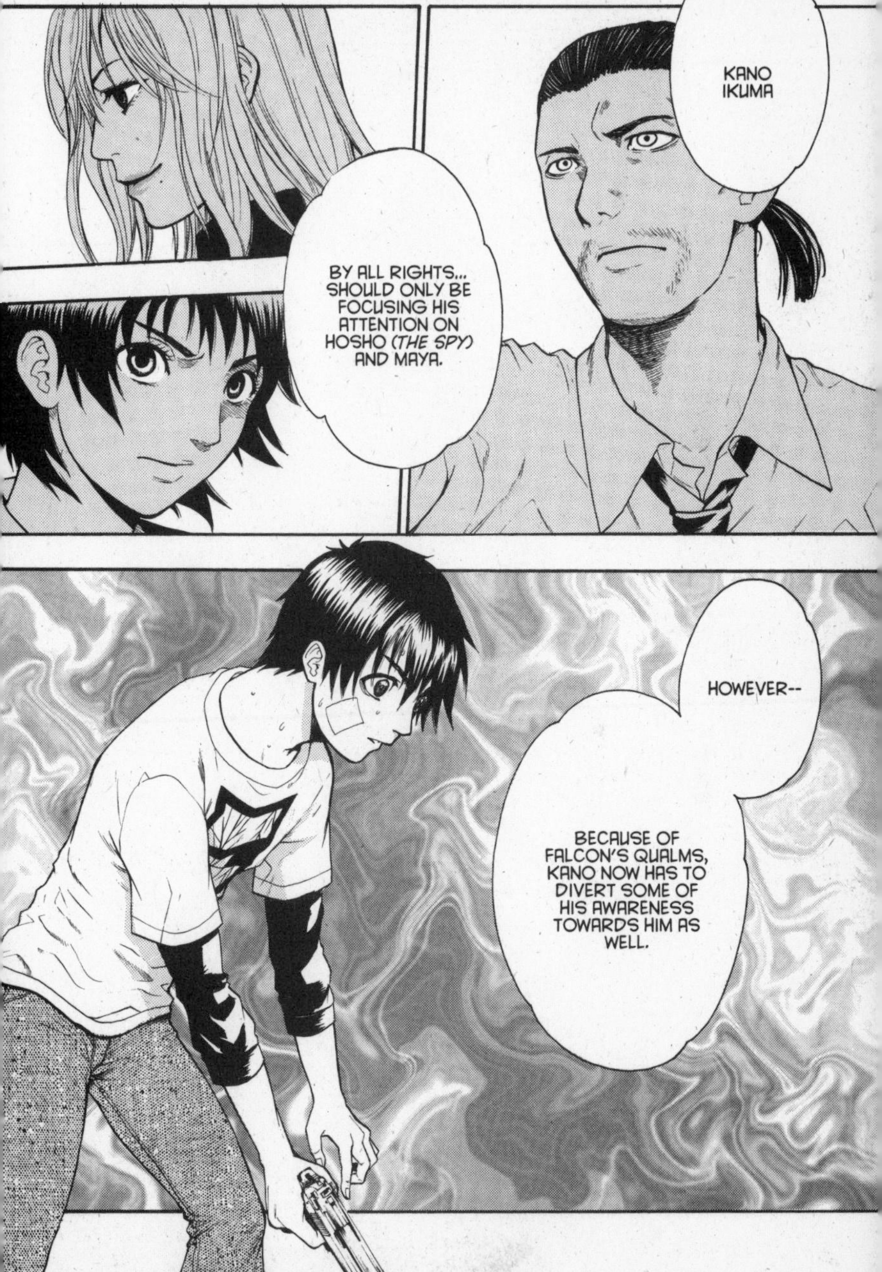
KANO IKUMA
BY ALL RIGHTS... SHOULD ONLY BE FOCUSING HIS ATTENTION ON HOSHO (*THE SPY*) AND MAYA.
HOWEVER--
BECAUSE OF FALCON'S QUALMS, KANO NOW HAS TO DIVERT SOME OF HIS AWARENESS TOWARDS HIM AS WELL.

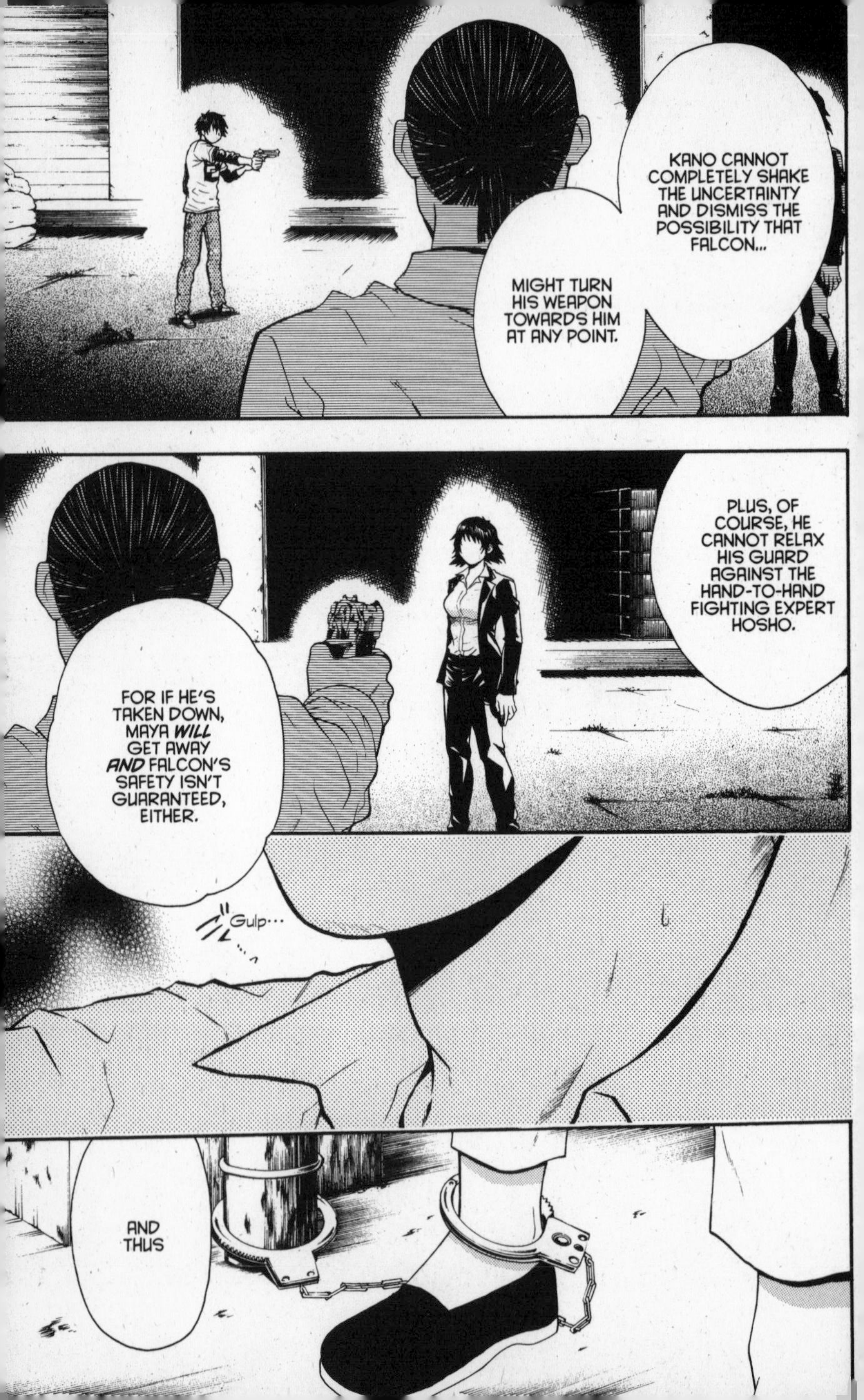

KANO CANNOT COMPLETELY SHAKE THE UNCERTAINTY AND DISMISS THE POSSIBILITY THAT FALCON...
MIGHT TURN HIS WEAPON TOWARDS HIM AT ANY POINT.
PLUS, OF COURSE, HE CANNOT RELAX HIS GUARD AGAINST THE HAND-TO-HAND FIGHTING EXPERT HOSHO.
FOR IF HE'S TAKEN DOWN, MAYA *WILL* GET AWAY *AND* FALCON'S SAFETY ISN'T GUARANTEED, EITHER.
Gulp...
AND THUS

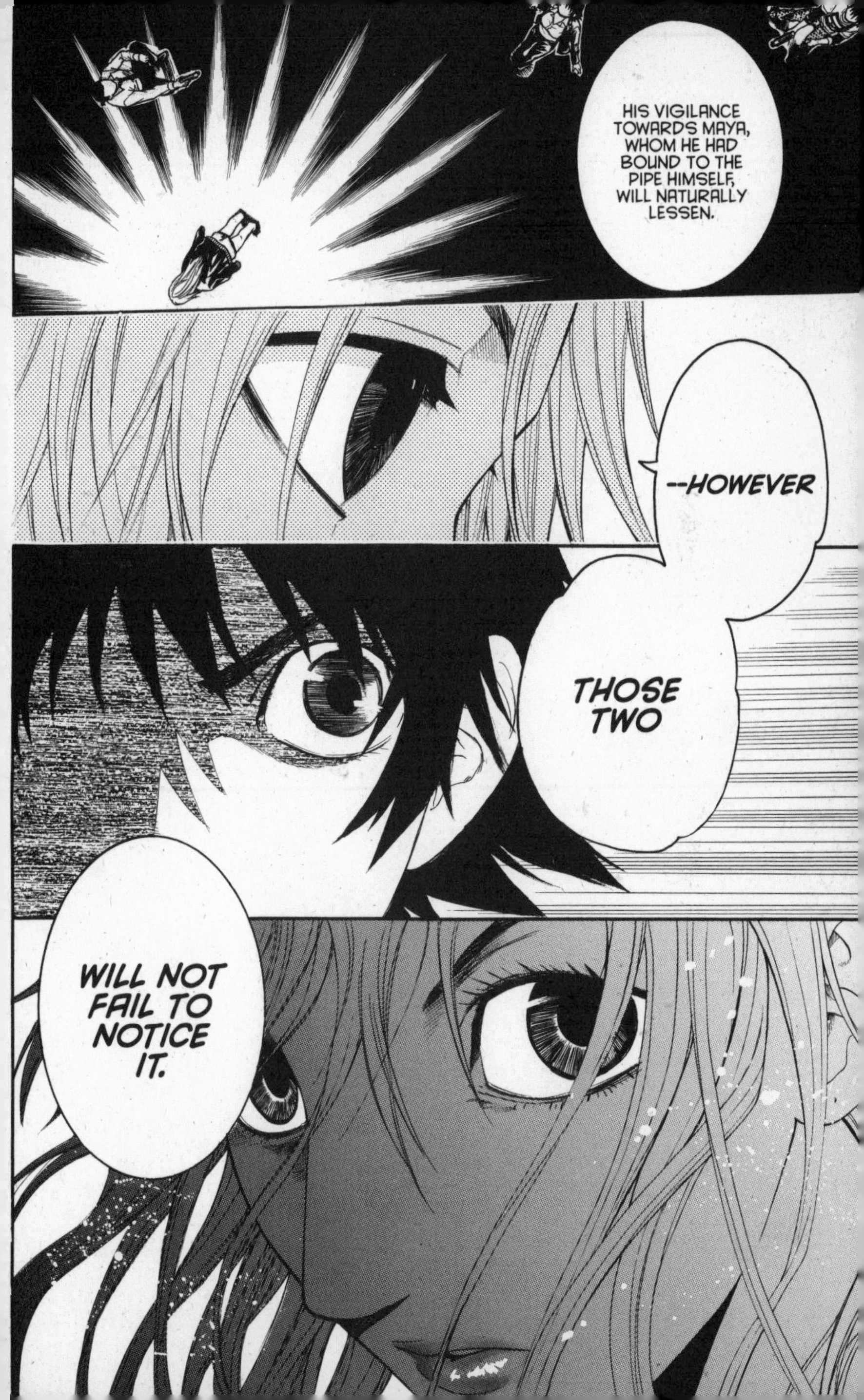
HIS VIGILANCE TOWARDS MAYA, WHOM HE HAD BOUND TO THE PIPE HIMSELF, WILL NATURALLY LESSEN.
--HOWEVER
THOSE TWO
WILL NOT FAIL TO NOTICE IT.

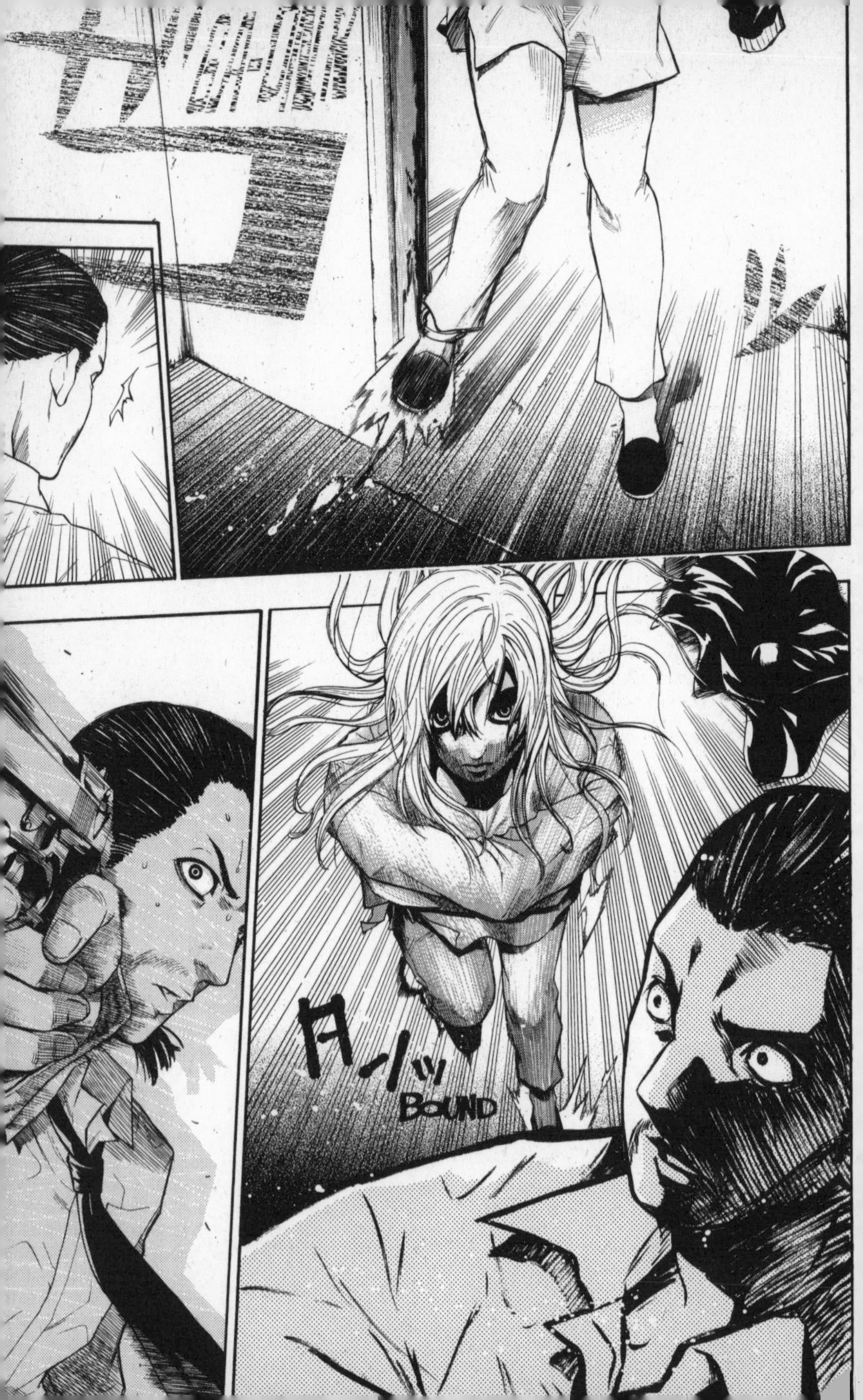
BOUND

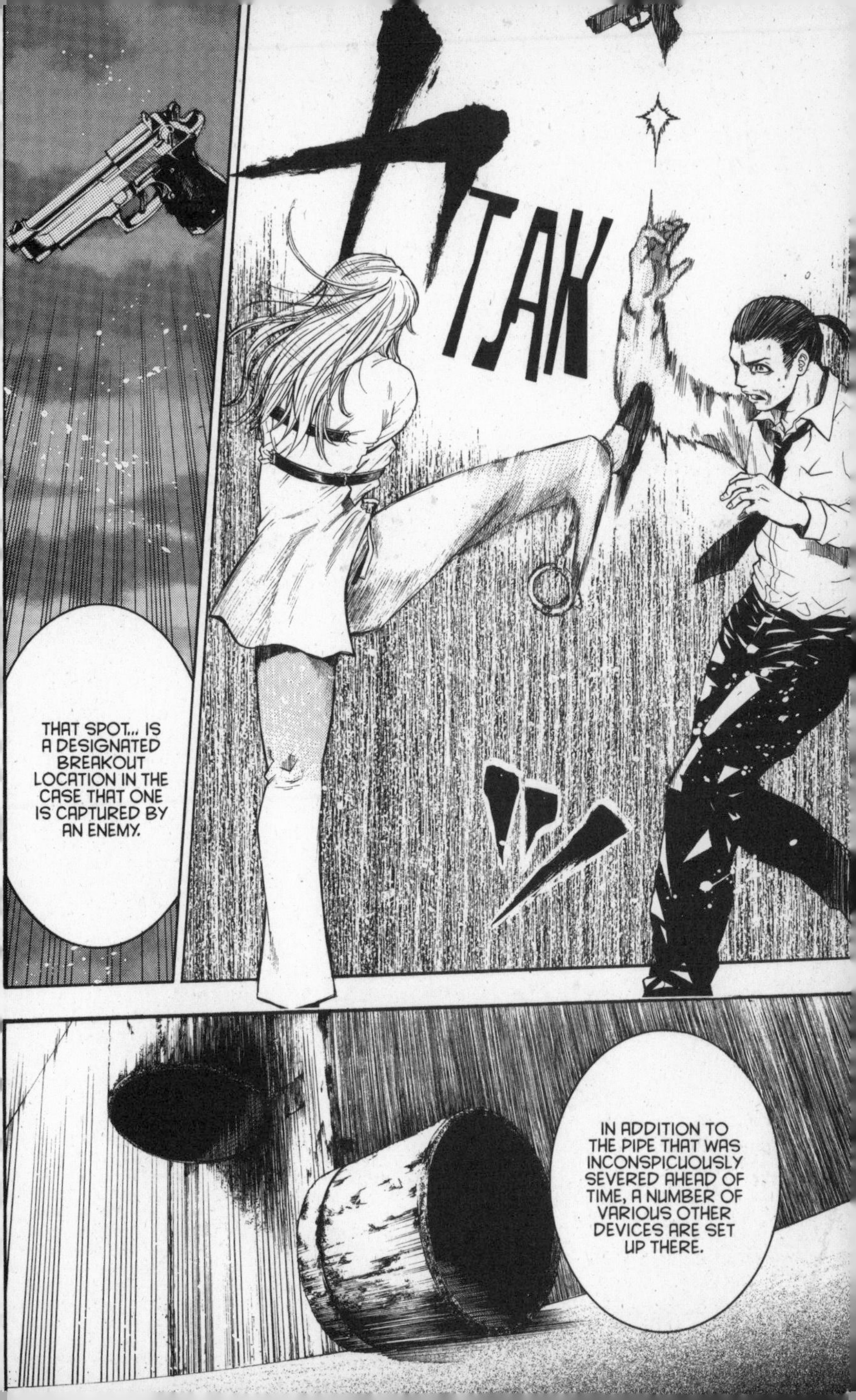
TAK
THAT SPOT... IS A DESIGNATED BREAKOUT LOCATION IN THE CASE THAT ONE IS CAPTURED BY AN ENEMY.
IN ADDITION TO THE PIPE THAT WAS INCONSPICUOUSLY SEVERED AHEAD OF TIME, A NUMBER OF VARIOUS OTHER DEVICES ARE SET UP THERE.

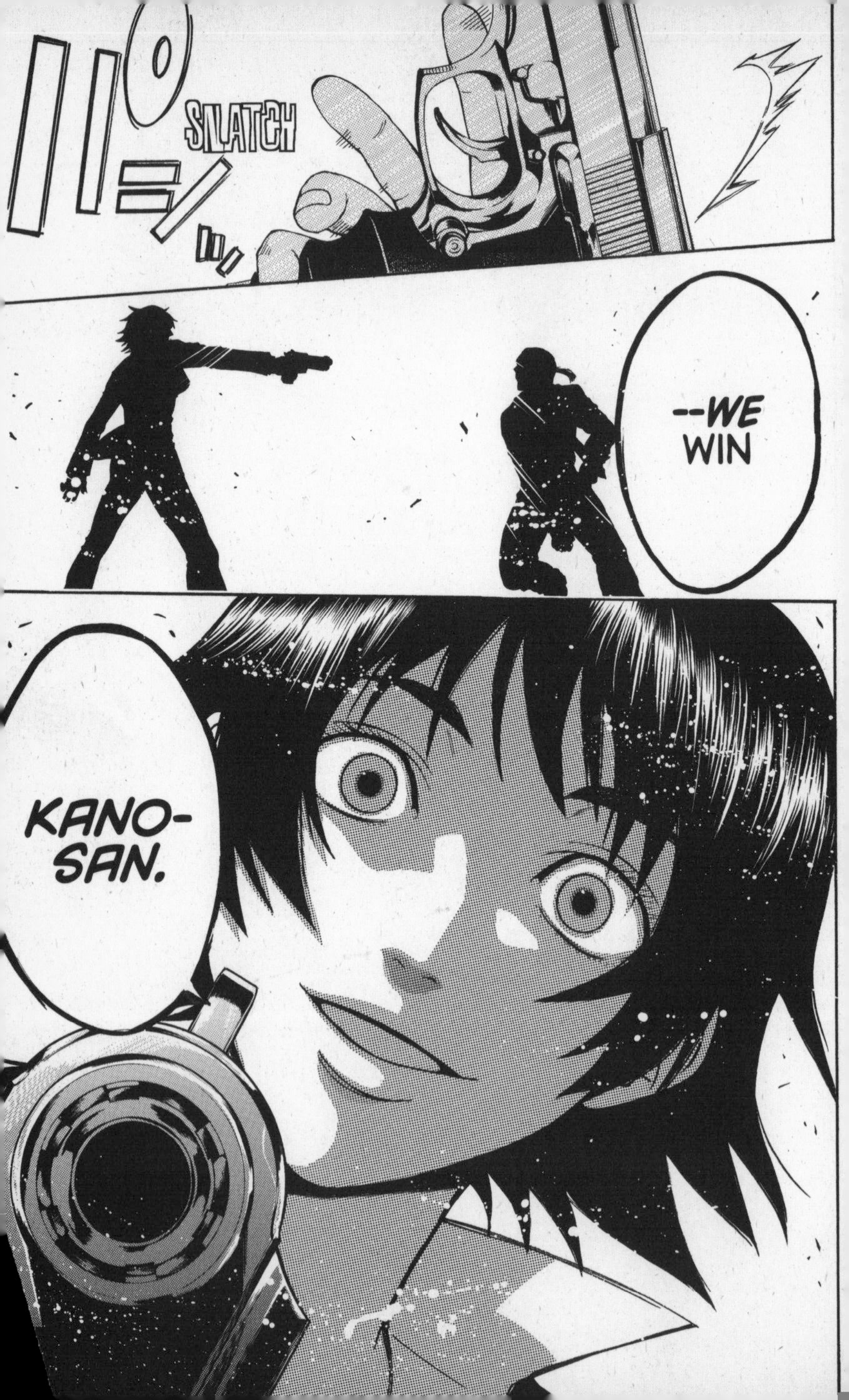
SNLATCH
--WE WIN
KANO-SAN.

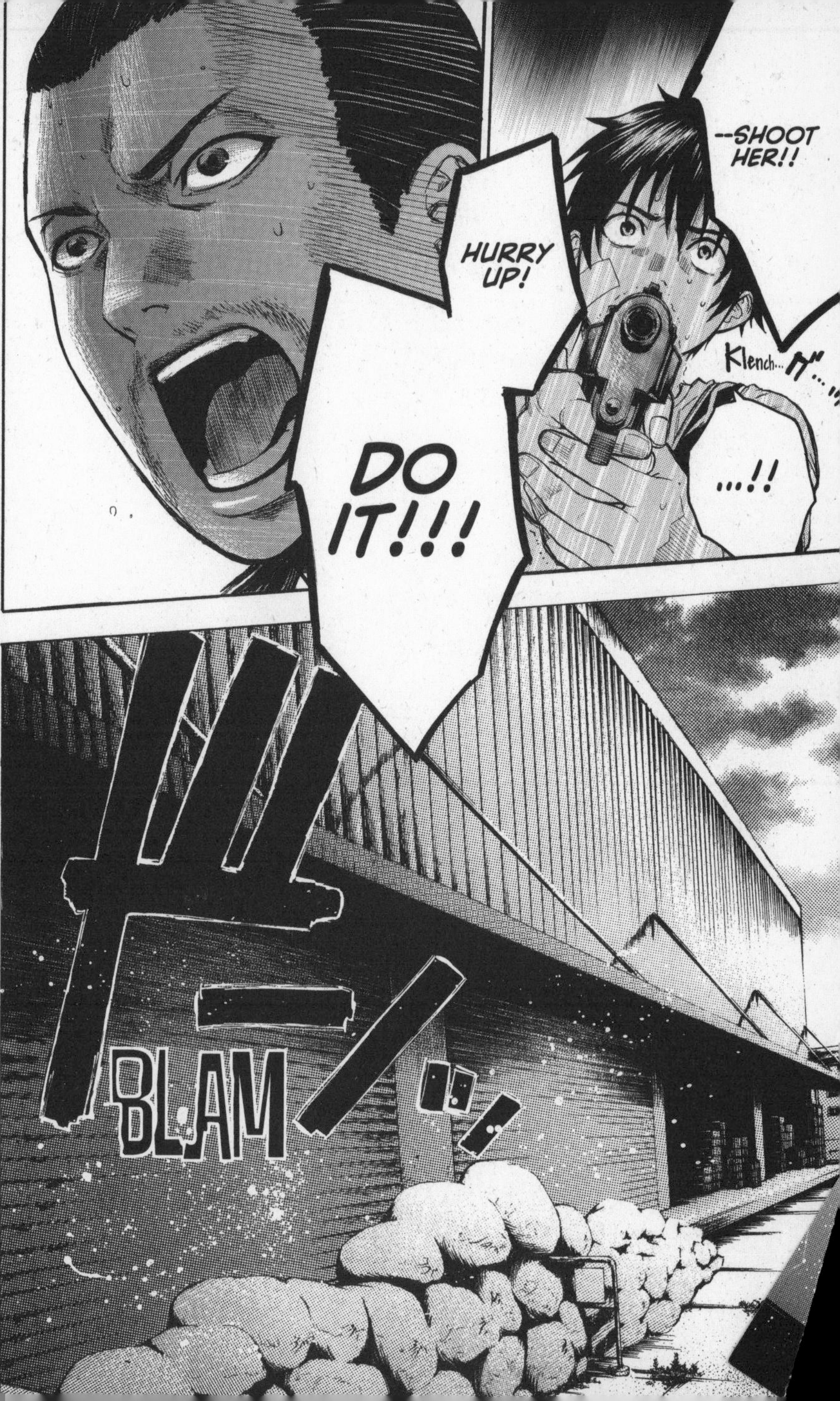
--SHOOT HER!!
Klench...
...!!
HURRY UP!
DO IT!!!
BLAM

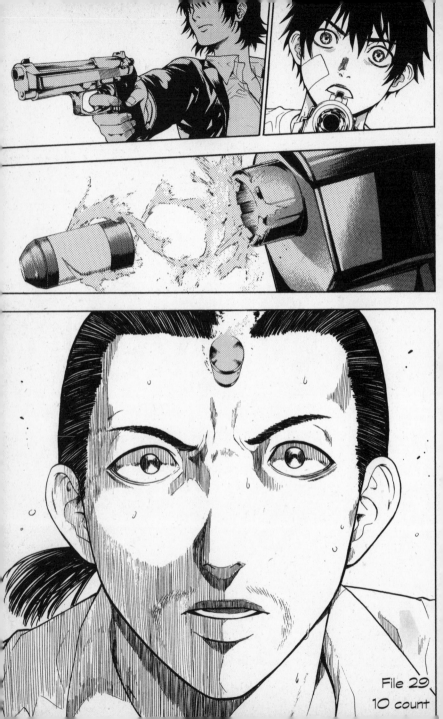

File 29
10 count

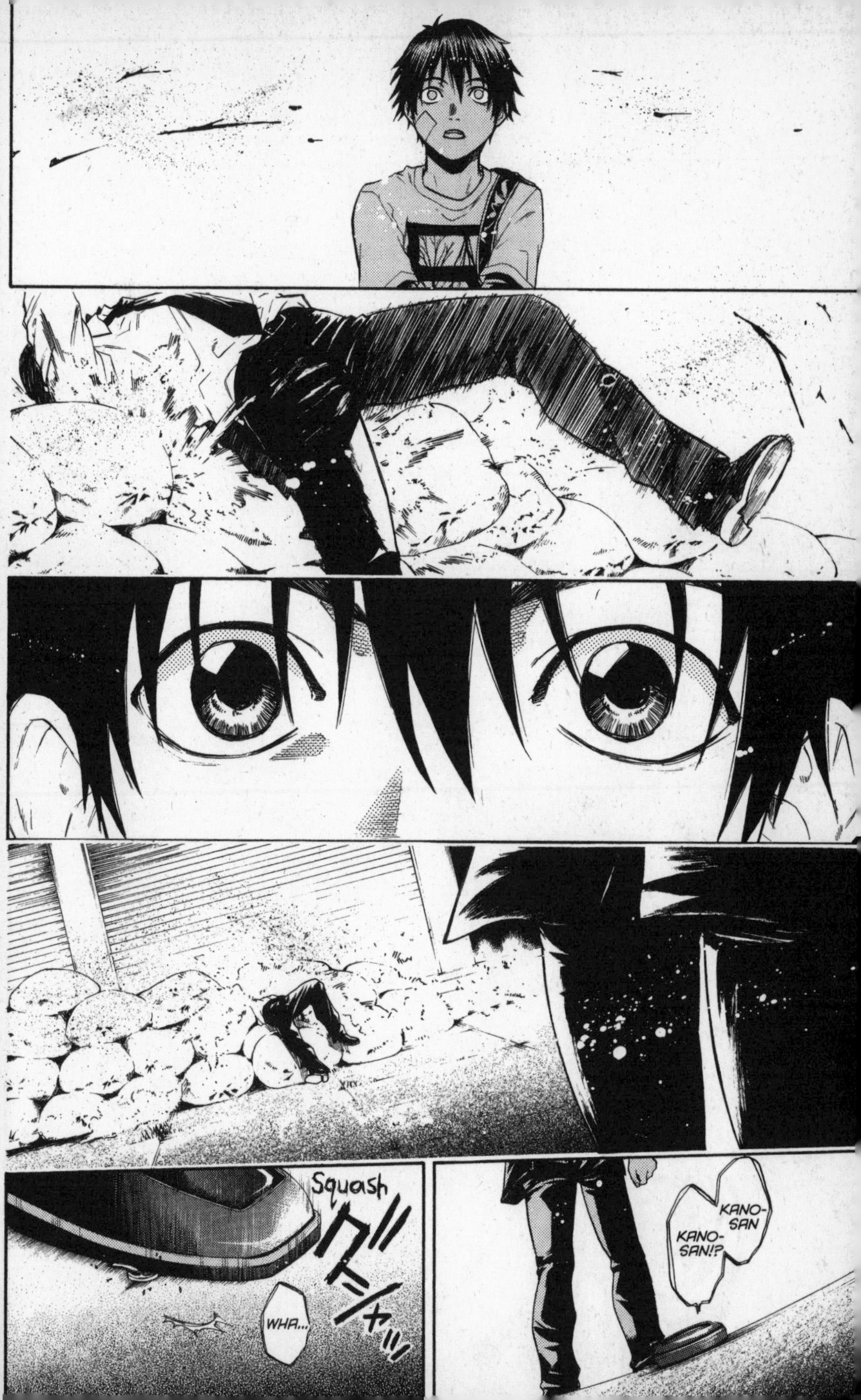
KANO-SAN
KANO-SAN!?
Squash
WHA...

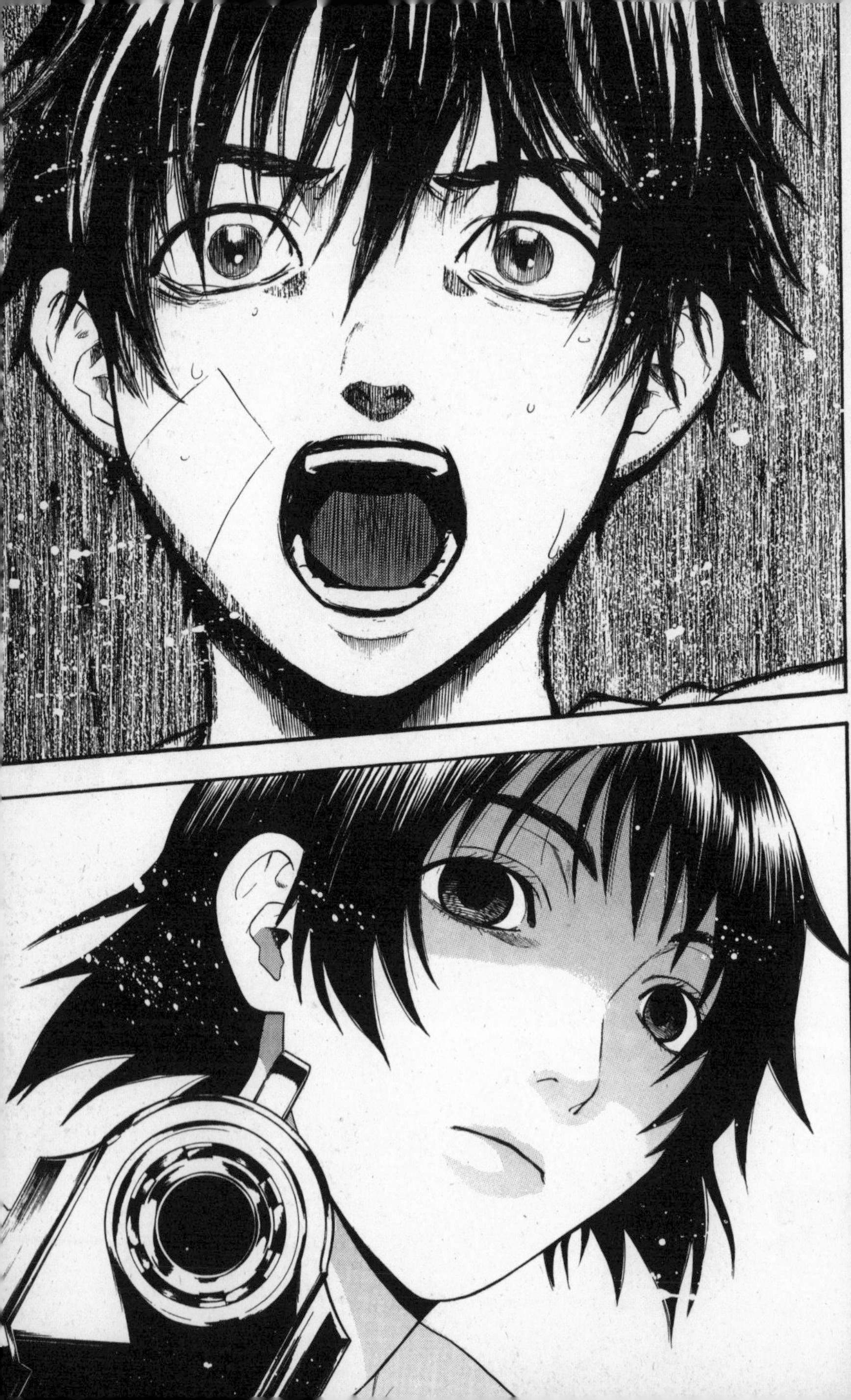

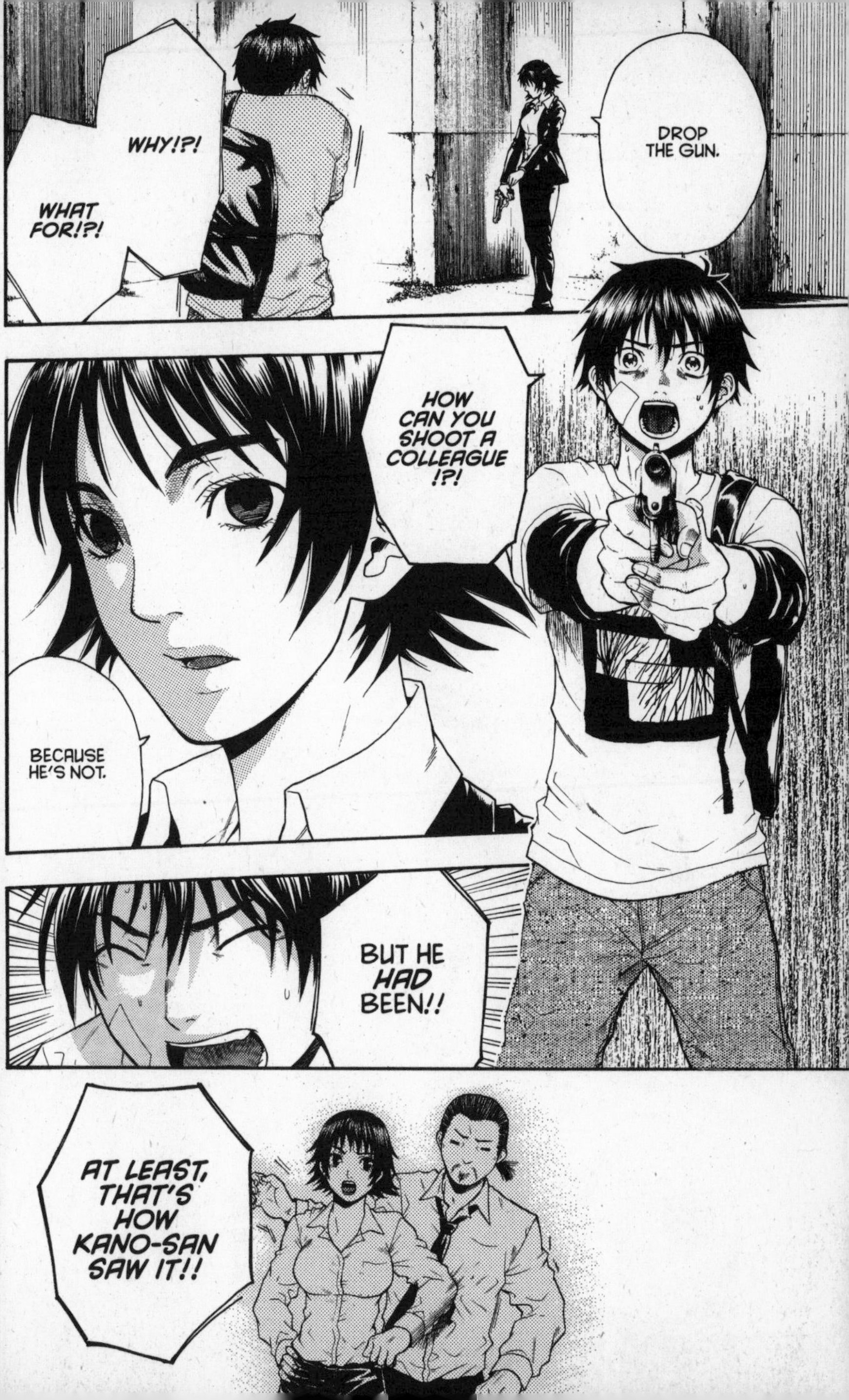
DROP THE GUN.
WHY!?!
WHAT FOR!?!
HOW CAN YOU SHOOT A COLLEAGUE !?!
BECAUSE HE'S NOT.
BUT HE HAD BEEN!!
AT LEAST, THAT'S HOW KANO-SAN SAW IT!!

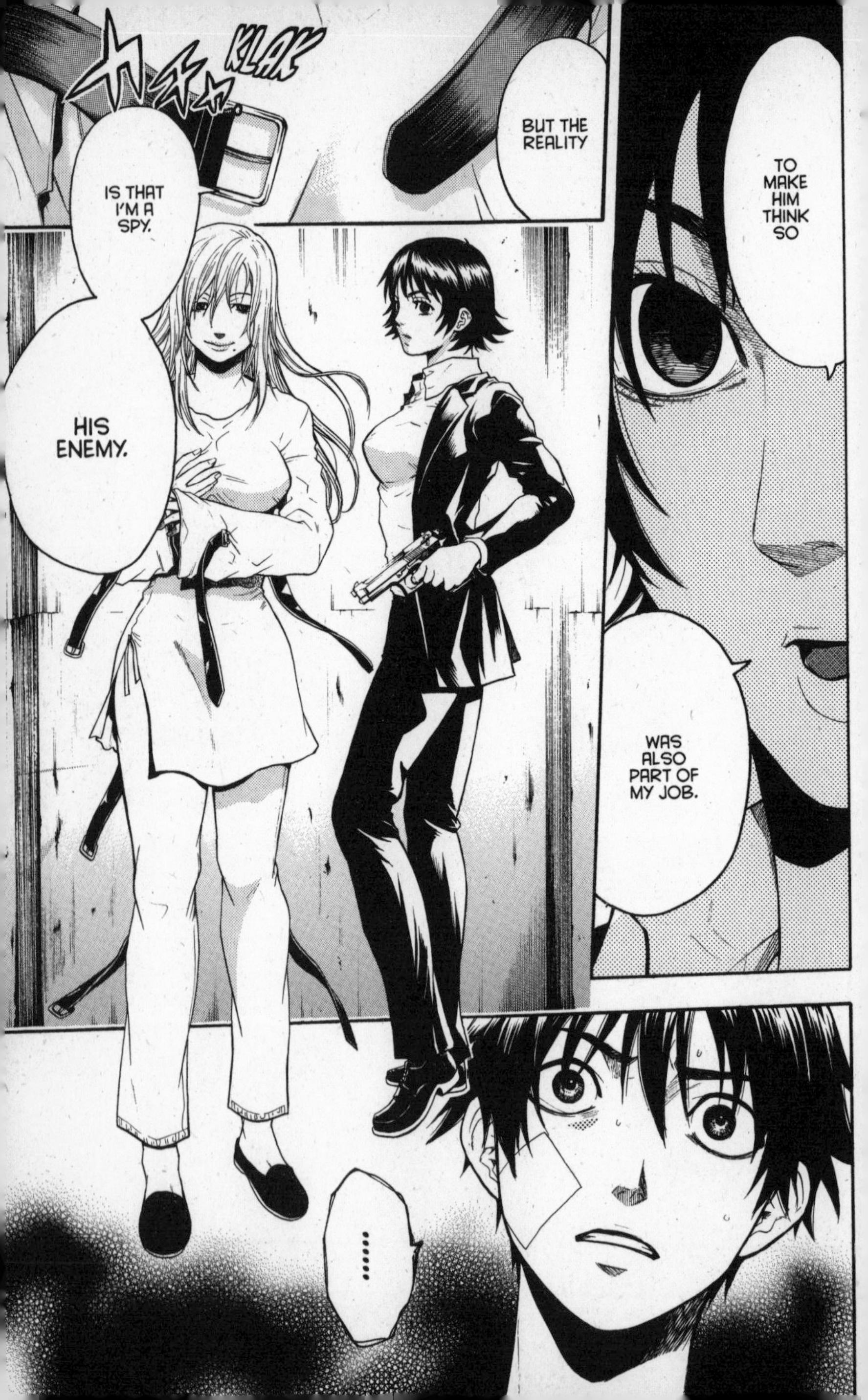
TO MAKE HIM THINK SO
WAS ALSO PART OF MY JOB.
KLAK
BUT THE REALITY
IS THAT I'M A SPY.
HIS ENEMY.
……

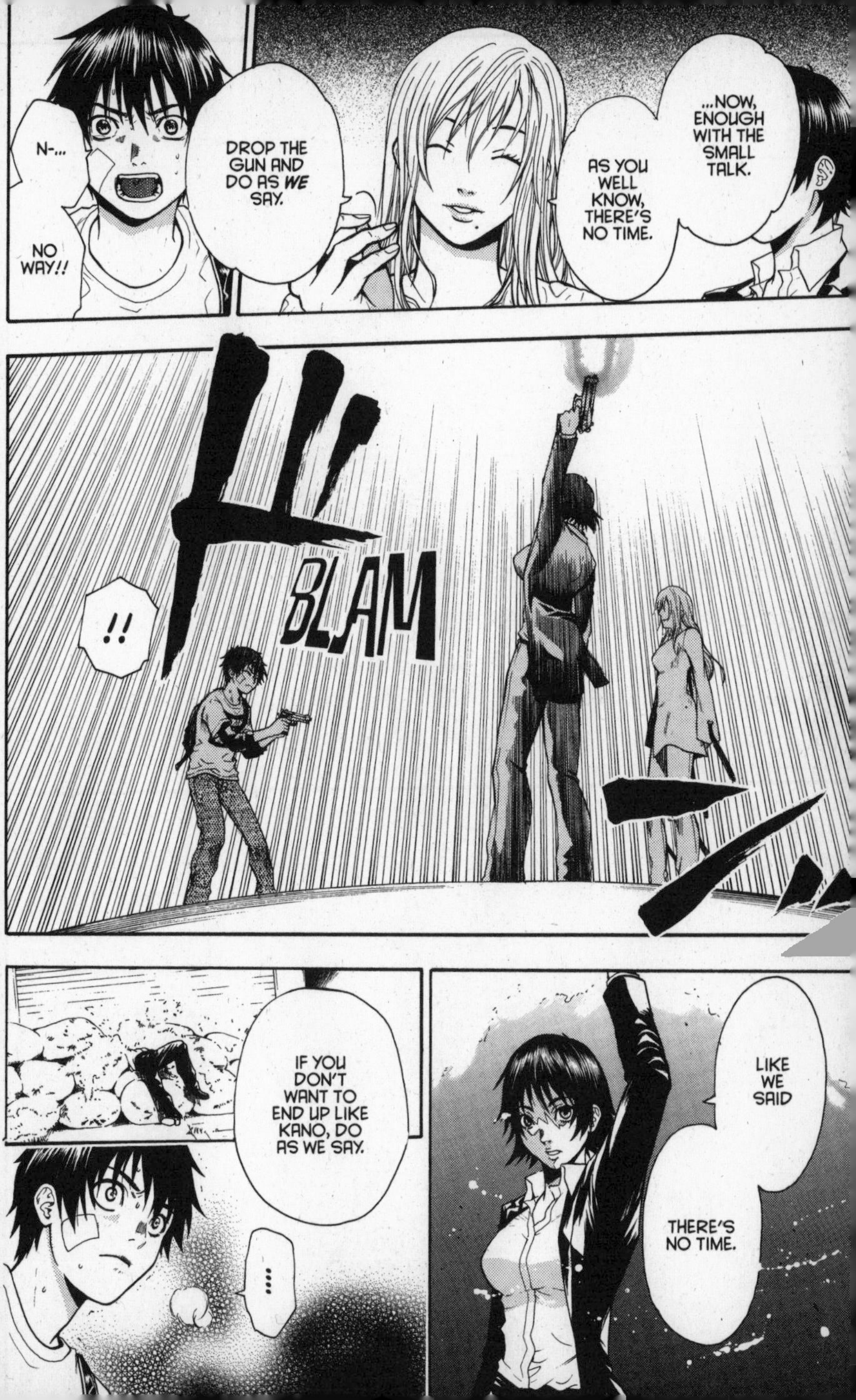
...NOW, ENOUGH WITH THE SMALL TALK.
AS YOU WELL KNOW, THERE'S NO TIME.
DROP THE GUN AND DO AS *WE* SAY.
N-...
NO WAY!!
BLAM
!!
LIKE WE SAID
THERE'S NO TIME.
IF YOU DON'T WANT TO END UP LIKE KANO, DO AS WE SAY.
....

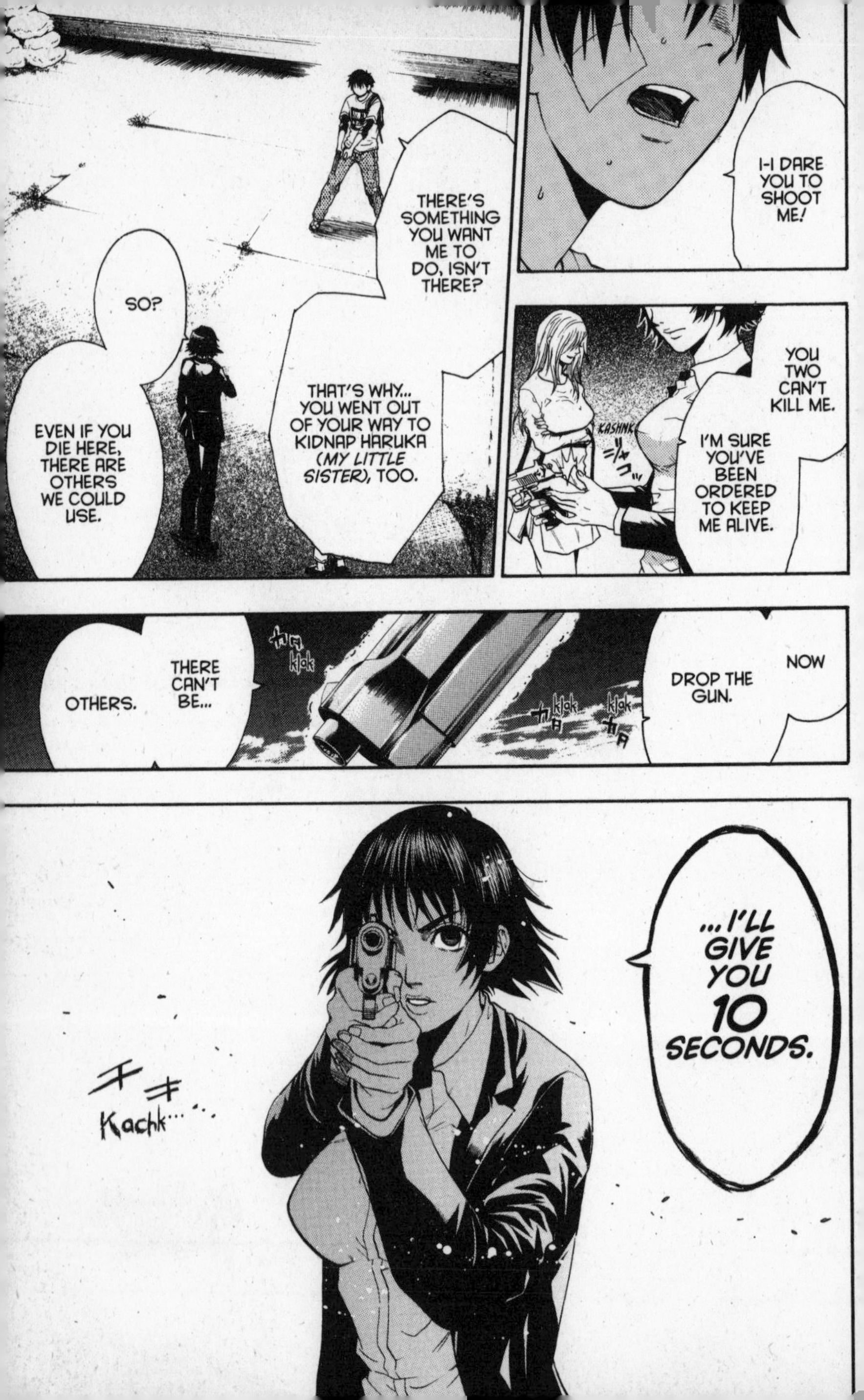
I-I DARE YOU TO SHOOT ME!
YOU TWO CAN'T KILL ME.
KASHNK
I'M SURE YOU'VE BEEN ORDERED TO KEEP ME ALIVE.
THERE'S SOMETHING YOU WANT ME TO DO, ISN'T THERE?
THAT'S WHY... YOU WENT OUT OF YOUR WAY TO KIDNAP HARUKA (MY LITTLE SISTER), TOO.
SO?
EVEN IF YOU DIE HERE, THERE ARE OTHERS WE COULD USE.
NOW
DROP THE GUN.
klak
klak
klak
THERE CAN'T BE...
OTHERS.
...I'LL GIVE YOU 10 SECONDS.
Kachk...

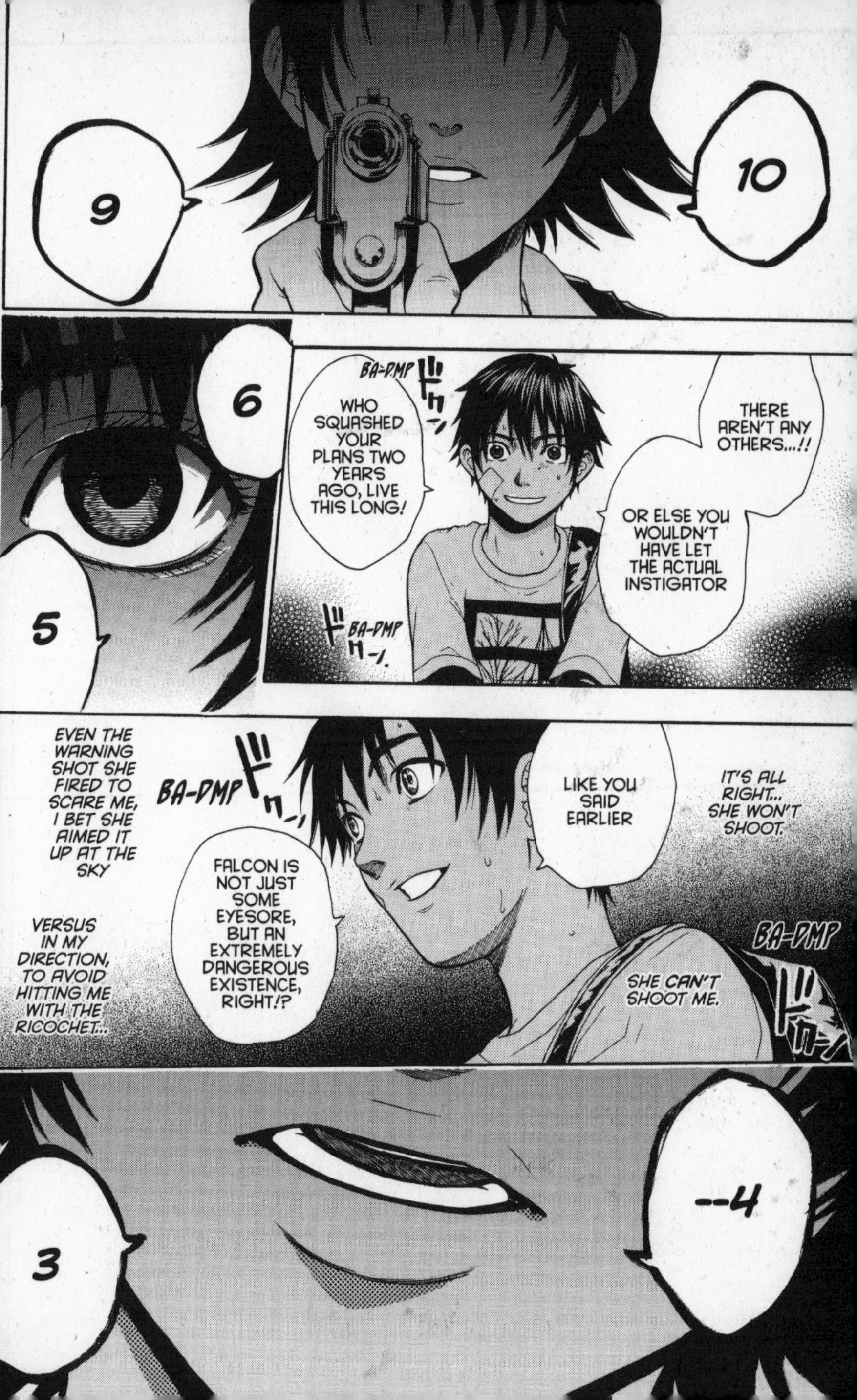
10
9
THERE AREN'T ANY OTHERS...!!
OR ELSE YOU WOULDN'T HAVE LET THE ACTUAL INSTIGATOR
BA-DMP
WHO SQUASHED YOUR PLANS TWO YEARS AGO, LIVE THIS LONG!
BA-DMP
6
5
IT'S ALL RIGHT... SHE WON'T SHOOT.
LIKE YOU SAID EARLIER
BA-DMP
SHE CAN'T SHOOT ME.
FALCON IS NOT JUST SOME EYESORE, BUT AN EXTREMELY DANGEROUS EXISTENCE, RIGHT!?
BA-DMP
EVEN THE WARNING SHOT SHE FIRED TO SCARE ME, I BET SHE AIMED IT UP AT THE SKY
VERSUS IN MY DIRECTION, TO AVOID HITTING ME WITH THE RICOCHET...
--4
3

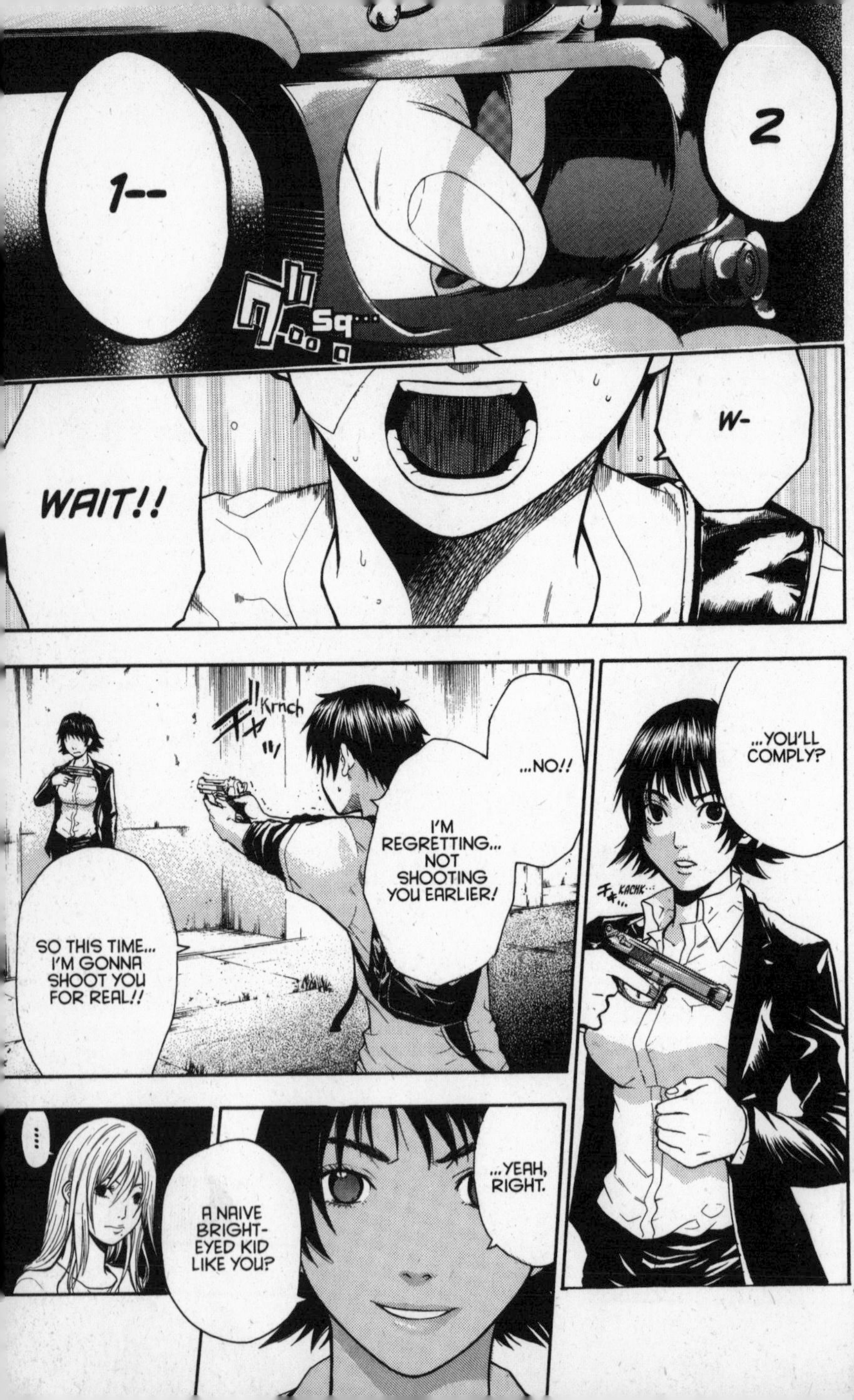
2
1--
Sq...
W-
WAIT!!
...YOU'LL COMPLY?
KACHK...
...NO!!
I'M REGRETTING... NOT SHOOTING YOU EARLIER!
Krnch
SO THIS TIME... I'M GONNA SHOOT YOU FOR REAL!!
...YEAH, RIGHT.
A NAIVE BRIGHT-EYED KID LIKE YOU?
....

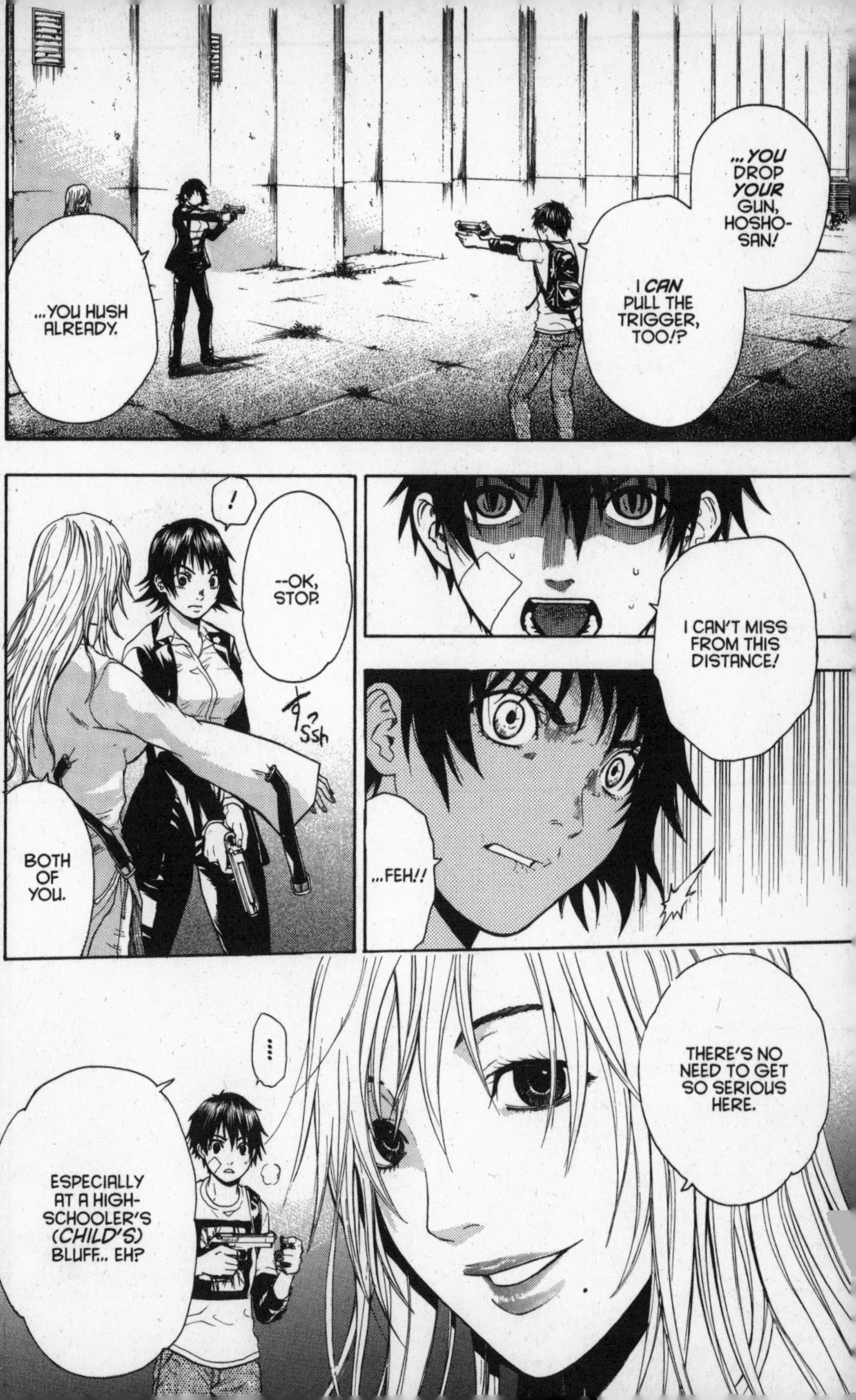
...YOU DROP YOUR GUN, HOSHO-SAN!
I CAN PULL THE TRIGGER, TOO!?
...YOU HUSH ALREADY.
I CAN'T MISS FROM THIS DISTANCE!
...FEH!!
!
--OK, STOP.
Ssh
BOTH OF YOU.
THERE'S NO NEED TO GET SO SERIOUS HERE.
....
ESPECIALLY AT A HIGH-SCHOOLER'S (CHILD'S) BLUFF... EH?

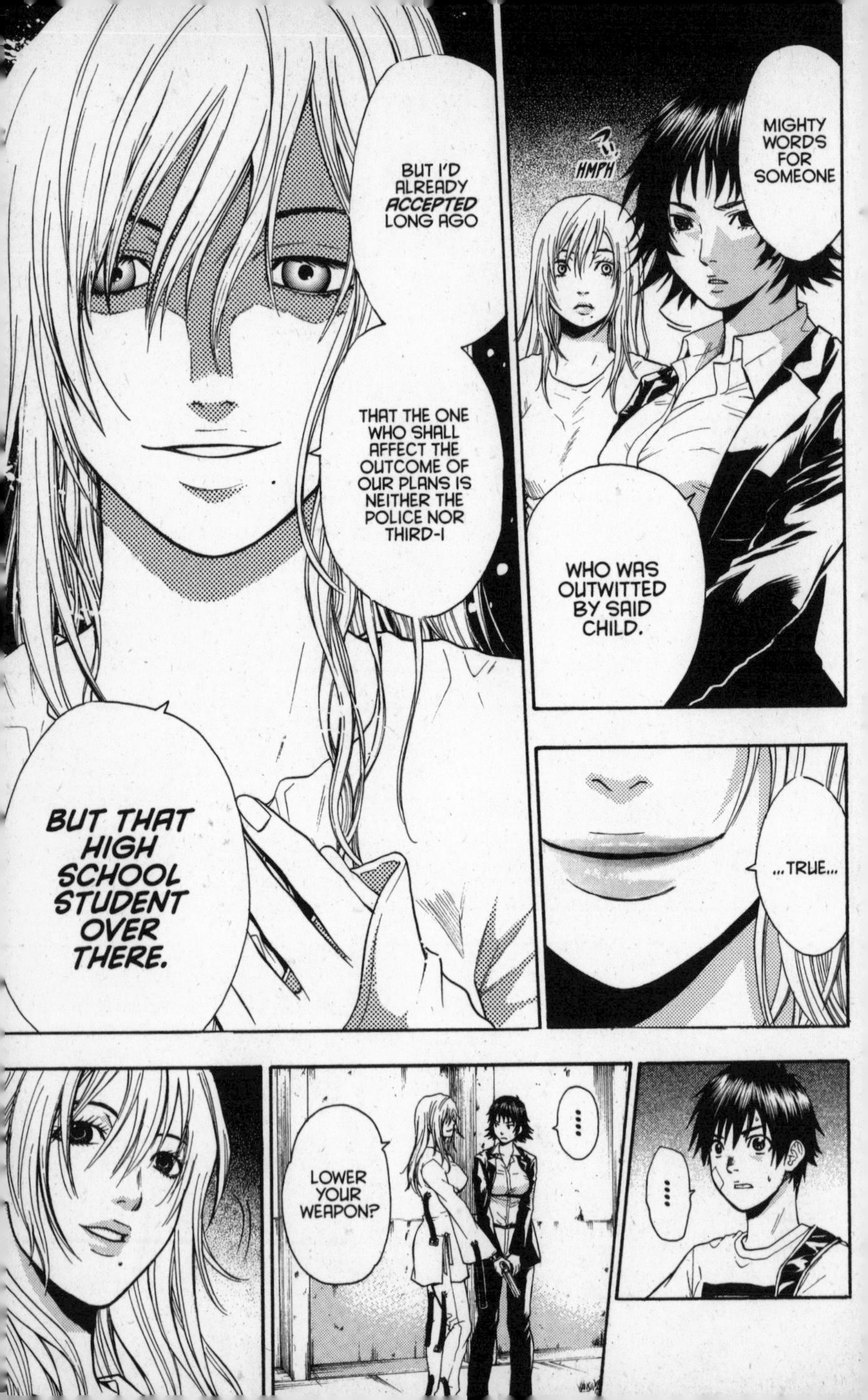
HMPH
MIGHTY WORDS FOR SOMEONE
WHO WAS OUTWITTED BY SAID CHILD.
...TRUE...
BUT I'D ALREADY *ACCEPTED* LONG AGO
THAT THE ONE WHO SHALL AFFECT THE OUTCOME OF OUR PLANS IS NEITHER THE POLICE NOR THIRD-I
BUT THAT HIGH SCHOOL STUDENT OVER THERE.
....
....
LOWER YOUR WEAPON?

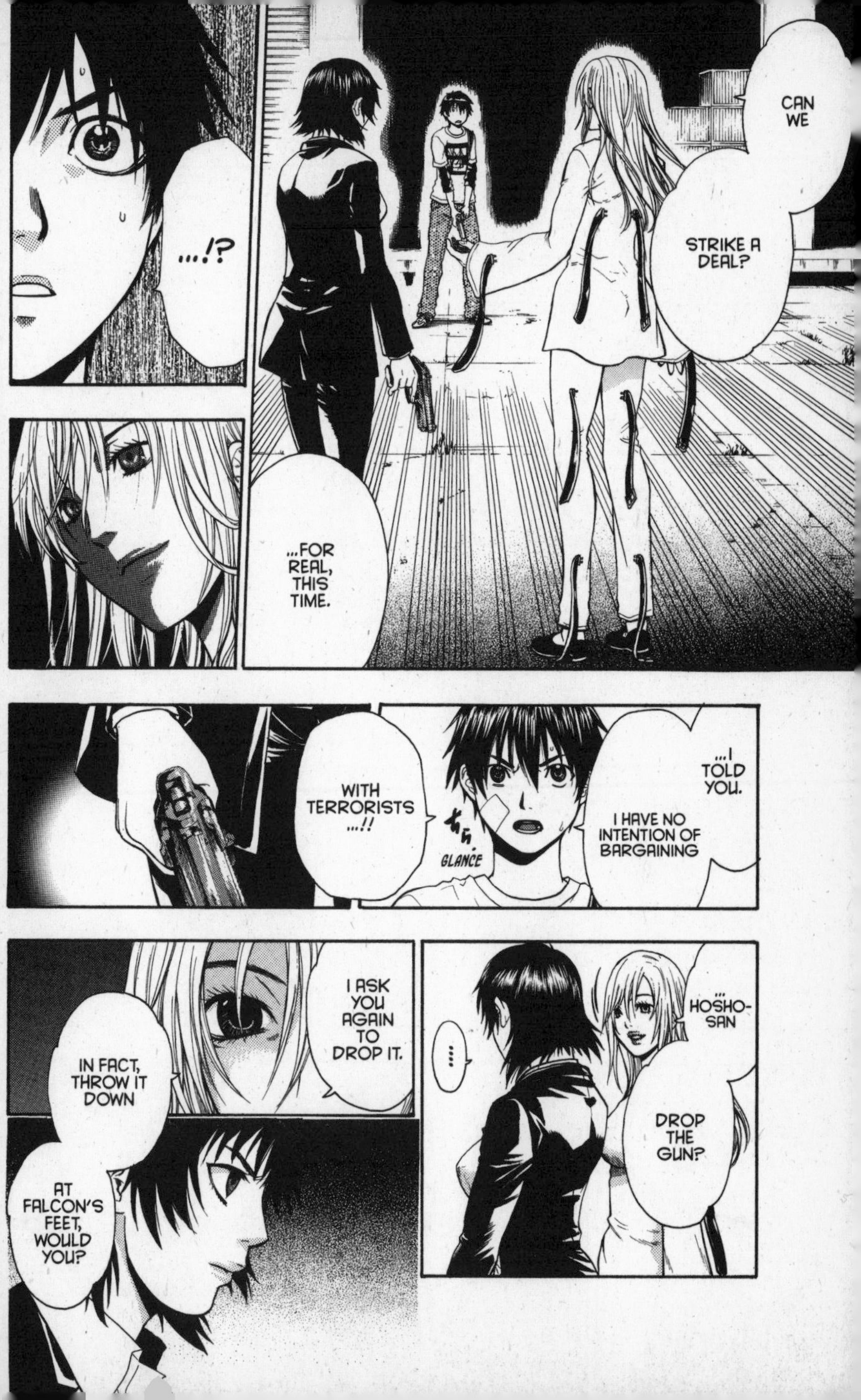
CAN WE
STRIKE A DEAL?
...FOR REAL, THIS TIME.
...!?
...I TOLD YOU.
I HAVE NO INTENTION OF BARGAINING
GLANCE
WITH TERRORISTS ...!!
... HOSHO-SAN
DROP THE GUN?
....
I ASK YOU AGAIN TO DROP IT.
IN FACT, THROW IT DOWN
AT FALCON'S FEET, WOULD YOU?

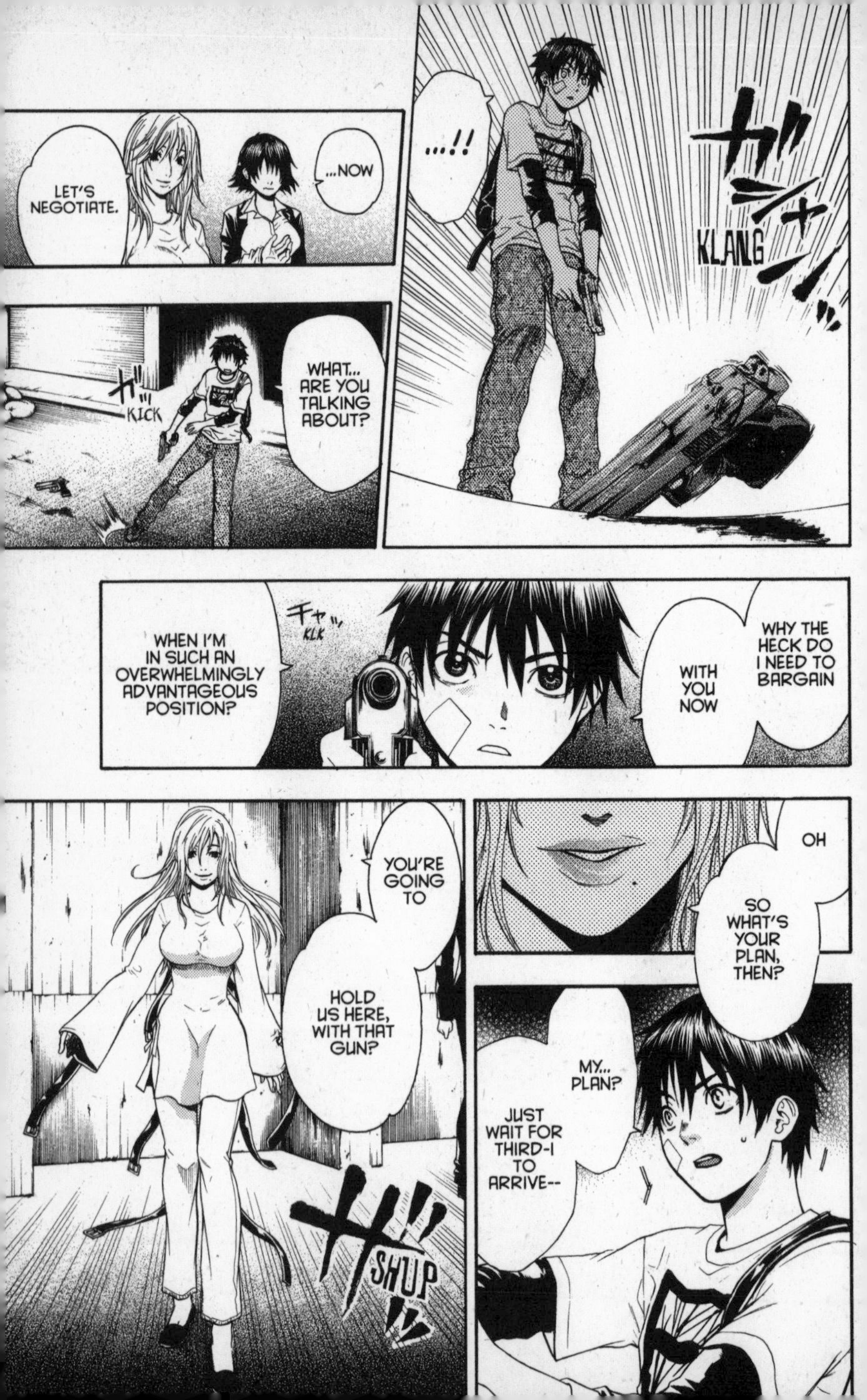
...!!
KLANG
...NOW
LET'S NEGOTIATE.
KICK
WHAT... ARE YOU TALKING ABOUT?
WHY THE HECK DO I NEED TO BARGAIN
WITH YOU NOW
KLK
WHEN I'M IN SUCH AN OVERWHELMINGLY ADVANTAGEOUS POSITION?
OH
SO WHAT'S YOUR PLAN, THEN?
MY... PLAN?
JUST WAIT FOR THIRD-I TO ARRIVE--
YOU'RE GOING TO
HOLD US HERE, WITH THAT GUN?
SHUP

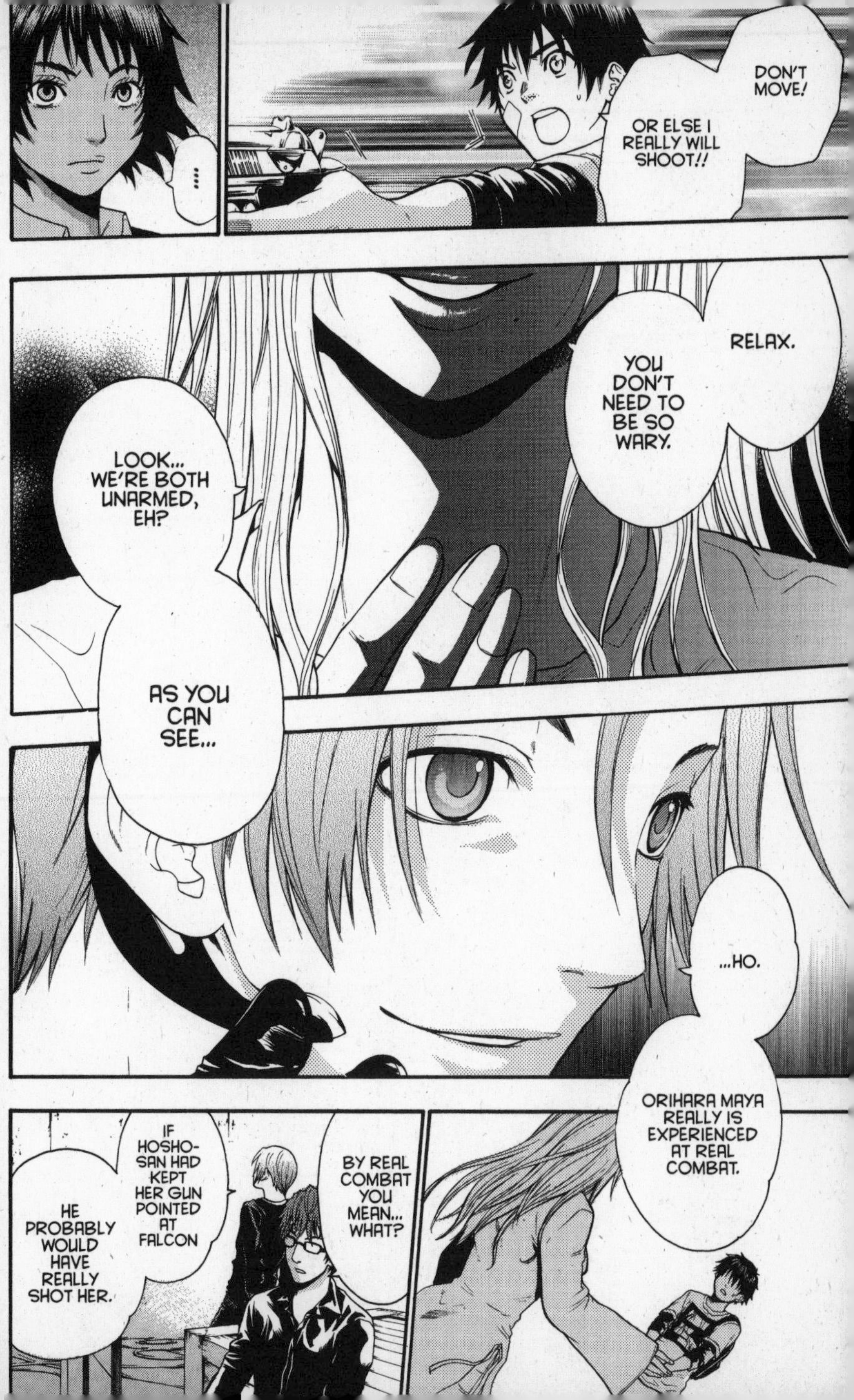
DON'T MOVE!
OR ELSE I REALLY WILL SHOOT!!
....
RELAX.
YOU DON'T NEED TO BE SO WARY.
LOOK... WE'RE BOTH UNARMED, EH?
AS YOU CAN SEE...
...HO.
ORIHARA MAYA REALLY IS EXPERIENCED AT REAL COMBAT.
BY REAL COMBAT YOU MEAN... WHAT?
IF HOSHO-SAN HAD KEPT HER GUN POINTED AT FALCON
HE PROBABLY WOULD HAVE REALLY SHOT HER.

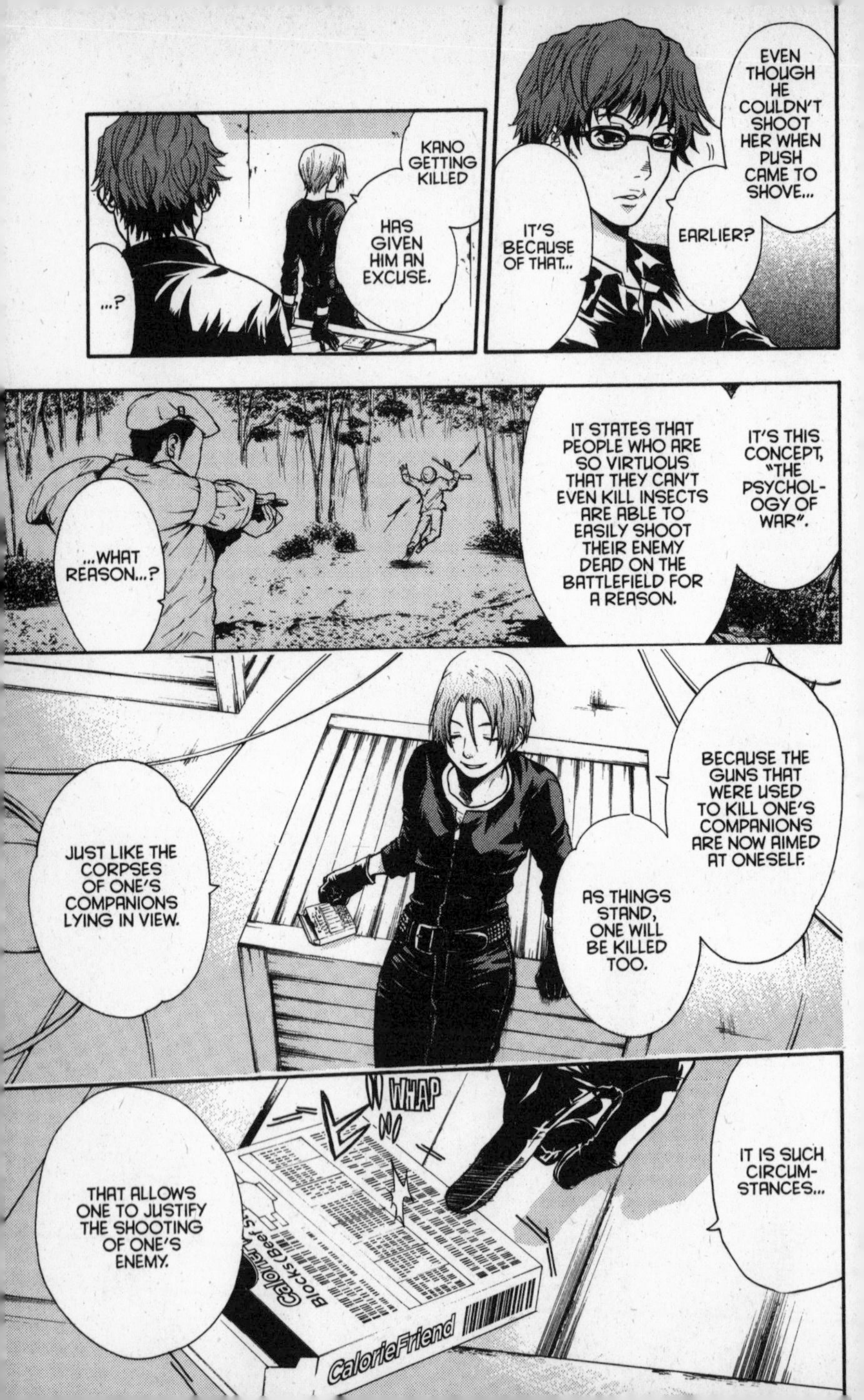
EVEN THOUGH HE COULDN'T SHOOT HER WHEN PUSH CAME TO SHOVE...
EARLIER?
IT'S BECAUSE OF THAT...
KANO GETTING KILLED
HAS GIVEN HIM AN EXCUSE.
...?
IT'S THIS CONCEPT, "THE PSYCHOLOGY OF WAR".
IT STATES THAT PEOPLE WHO ARE SO VIRTUOUS THAT THEY CAN'T EVEN KILL INSECTS ARE ABLE TO EASILY SHOOT THEIR ENEMY DEAD ON THE BATTLEFIELD FOR A REASON.
...WHAT REASON...?
BECAUSE THE GUNS THAT WERE USED TO KILL ONE'S COMPANIONS ARE NOW AIMED AT ONESELF.
AS THINGS STAND, ONE WILL BE KILLED TOO.
JUST LIKE THE CORPSES OF ONE'S COMPANIONS LYING IN VIEW.
WHAP
IT IS SUCH CIRCUMSTANCES...
THAT ALLOWS ONE TO JUSTIFY THE SHOOTING OF ONE'S ENEMY.
CalorieFriend

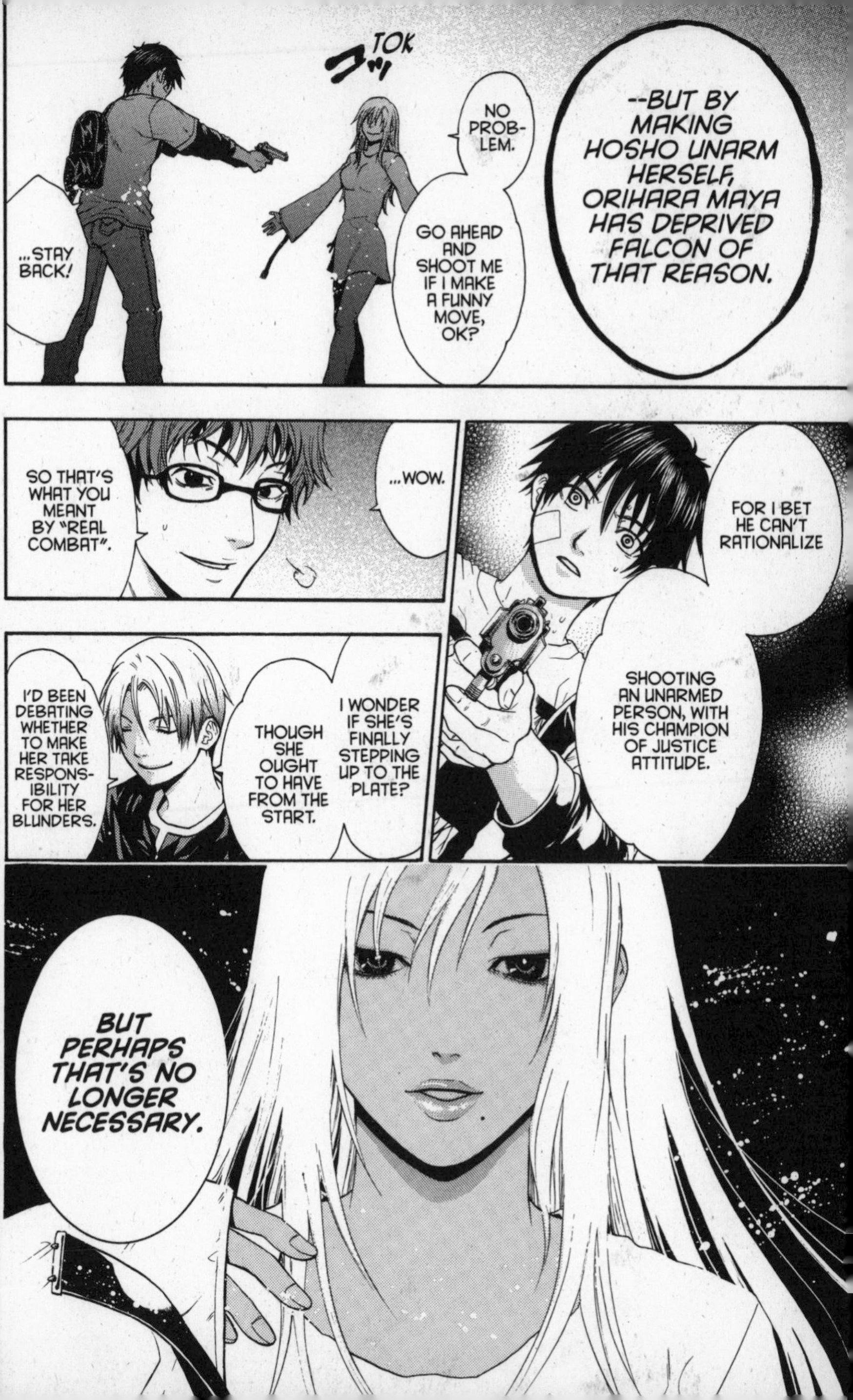
--BUT BY MAKING HOSHO UNARM HERSELF, ORIHARA MAYA HAS DEPRIVED FALCON OF THAT REASON.
TOK
NO PROB-LEM.
GO AHEAD AND SHOOT ME IF I MAKE A FUNNY MOVE, OK?
...STAY BACK!
FOR I BET HE CAN'T RATIONALIZE
SHOOTING AN UNARMED PERSON, WITH HIS CHAMPION OF JUSTICE ATTITUDE.
...WOW.
SO THAT'S WHAT YOU MEANT BY "REAL COMBAT".
I WONDER IF SHE'S FINALLY STEPPING UP TO THE PLATE?
THOUGH SHE OUGHT TO HAVE FROM THE START.
I'D BEEN DEBATING WHETHER TO MAKE HER TAKE RESPONS-IBILITY FOR HER BLUNDERS.
BUT PERHAPS THAT'S NO LONGER NECESSARY.

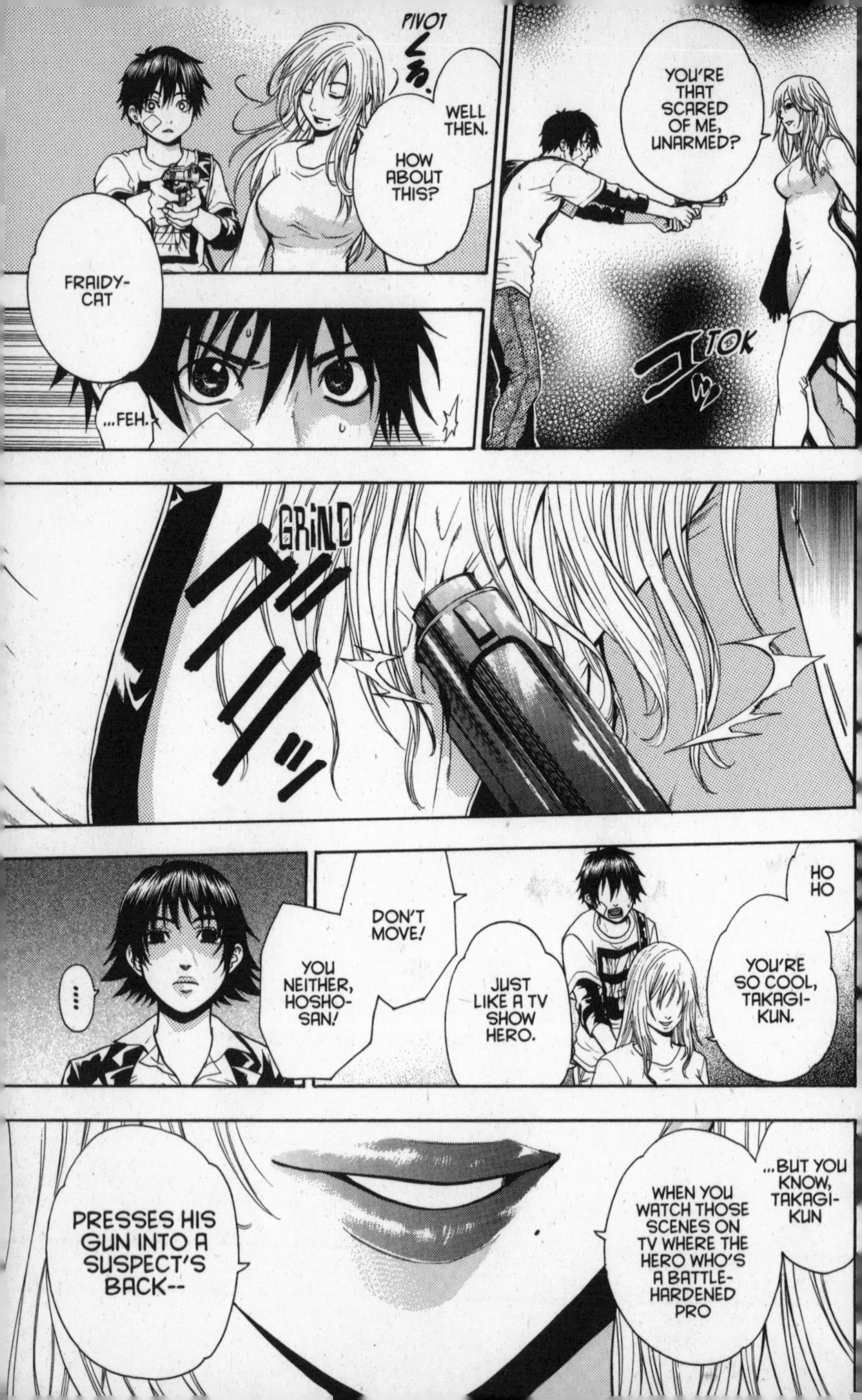
YOU'RE THAT SCARED OF ME, UNARMED?
TOK
PIVOT
WELL THEN.
HOW ABOUT THIS?
FRAIDY-CAT
...FEH.
GRIND
HO HO
YOU'RE SO COOL, TAKAGI-KUN.
JUST LIKE A TV SHOW HERO.
DON'T MOVE!
YOU NEITHER, HOSHO-SAN!
....
...BUT YOU KNOW, TAKAGI-KUN
WHEN YOU WATCH THOSE SCENES ON TV WHERE THE HERO WHO'S A BATTLE-HARDENED PRO
PRESSES HIS GUN INTO A SUSPECT'S BACK--

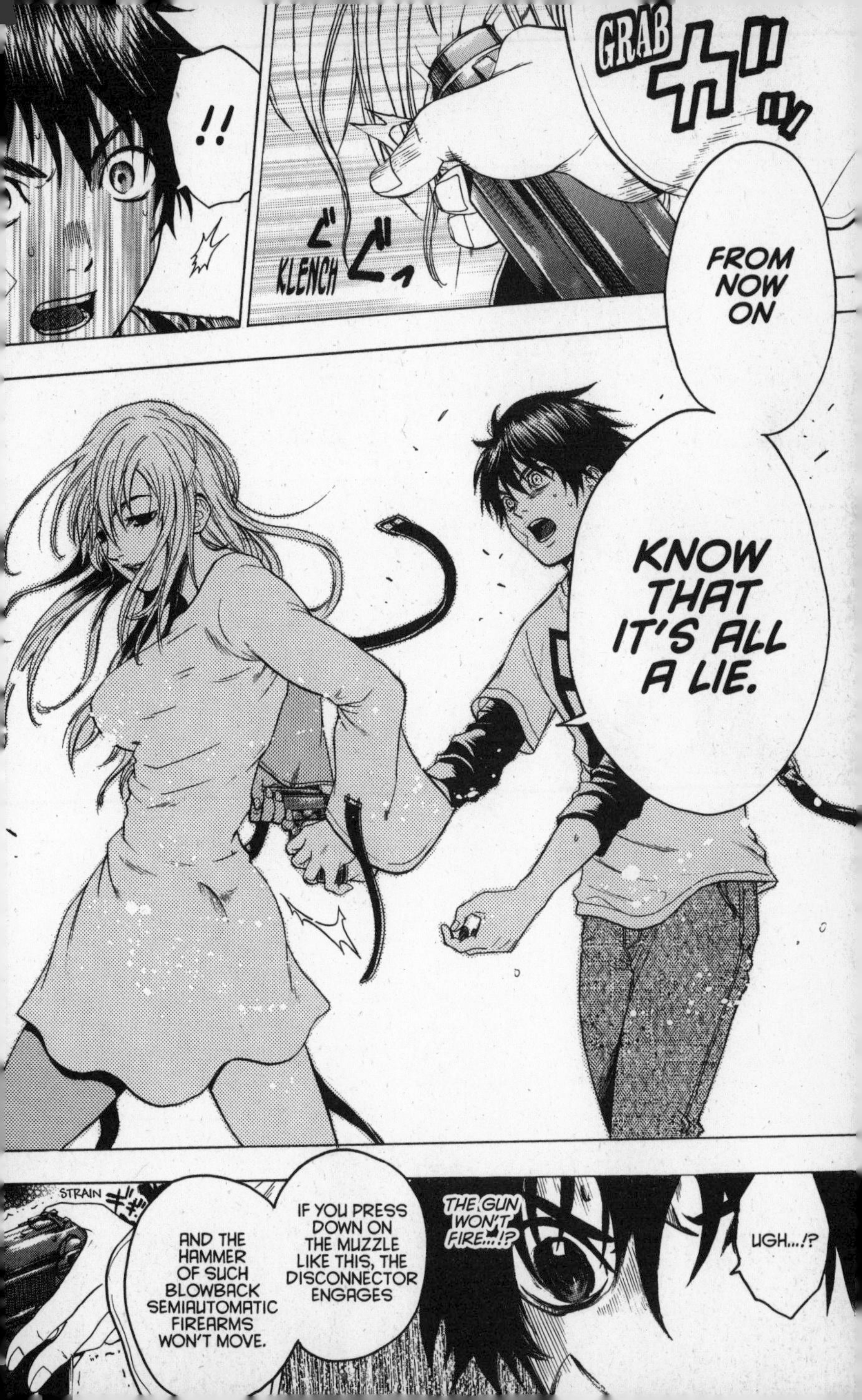
GRAB
FROM NOW ON
KLENCH
!!
KNOW THAT IT'S ALL A LIE.
UGH...!?
THE GUN WON'T FIRE...!?
IF YOU PRESS DOWN ON THE MUZZLE LIKE THIS, THE DISCONNECTOR ENGAGES
AND THE HAMMER OF SUCH BLOWBACK SEMIAUTOMATIC FIREARMS WON'T MOVE.
STRAIN

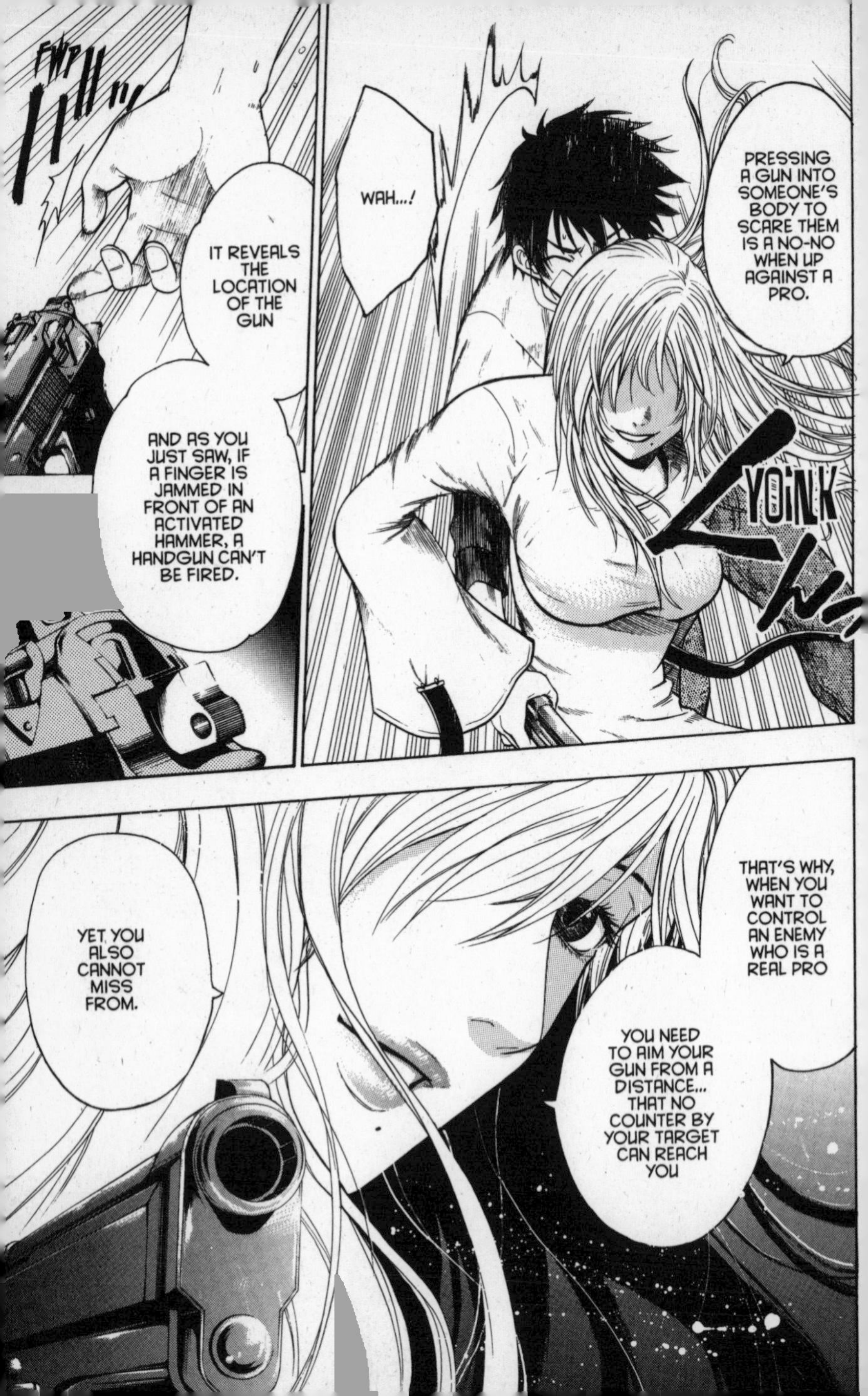
PRESSING A GUN INTO SOMEONE'S BODY TO SCARE THEM IS A NO-NO WHEN UP AGAINST A PRO.
WAH...!
YOINK
FWIP
IT REVEALS THE LOCATION OF THE GUN
AND AS YOU JUST SAW, IF A FINGER IS JAMMED IN FRONT OF AN ACTIVATED HAMMER, A HANDGUN CAN'T BE FIRED.
THAT'S WHY, WHEN YOU WANT TO CONTROL AN ENEMY WHO IS A REAL PRO
YOU NEED TO AIM YOUR GUN FROM A DISTANCE... THAT NO COUNTER BY YOUR TARGET CAN REACH YOU
YET YOU ALSO CANNOT MISS FROM.

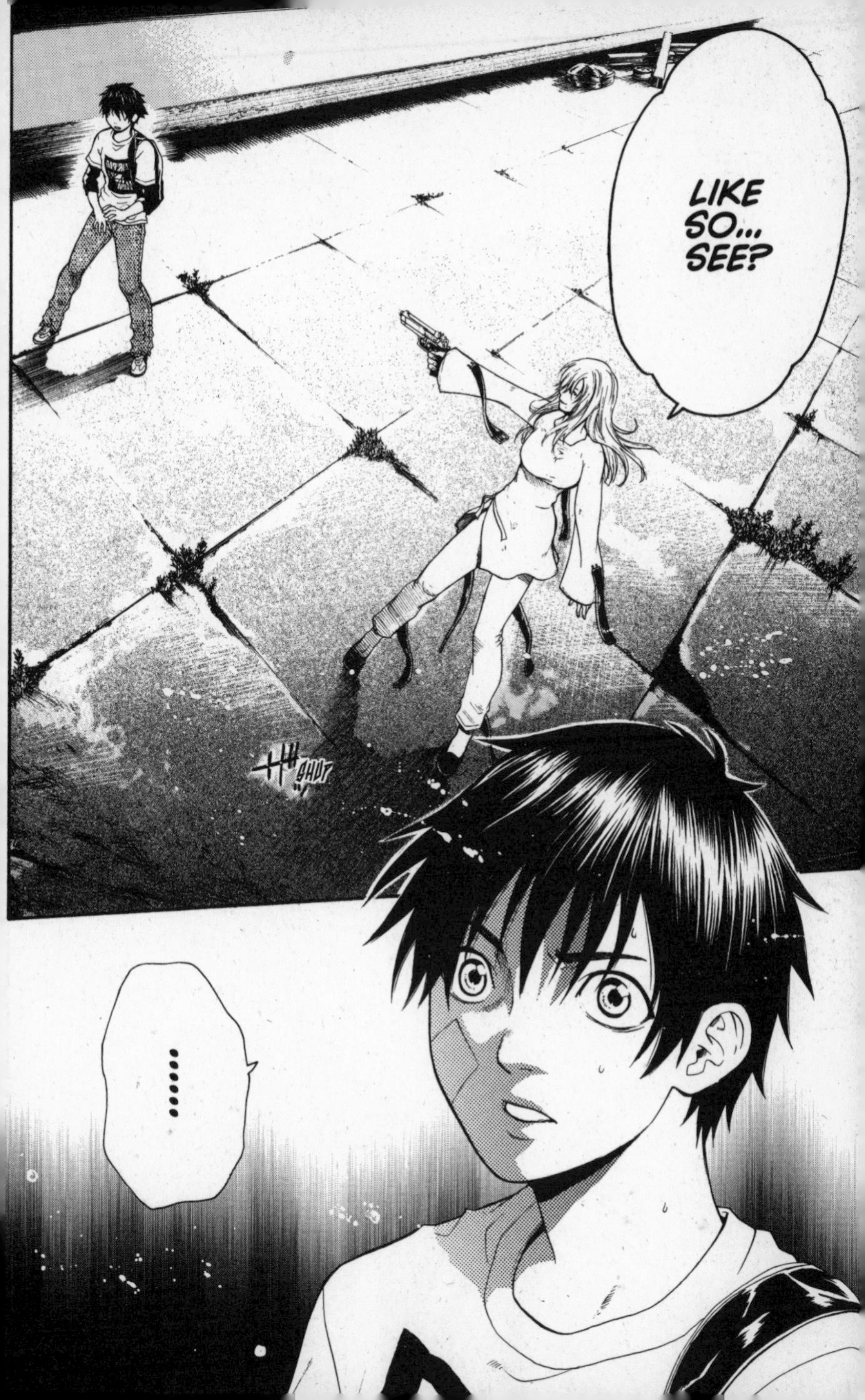
LIKE SO... SEE?
SHUT
......

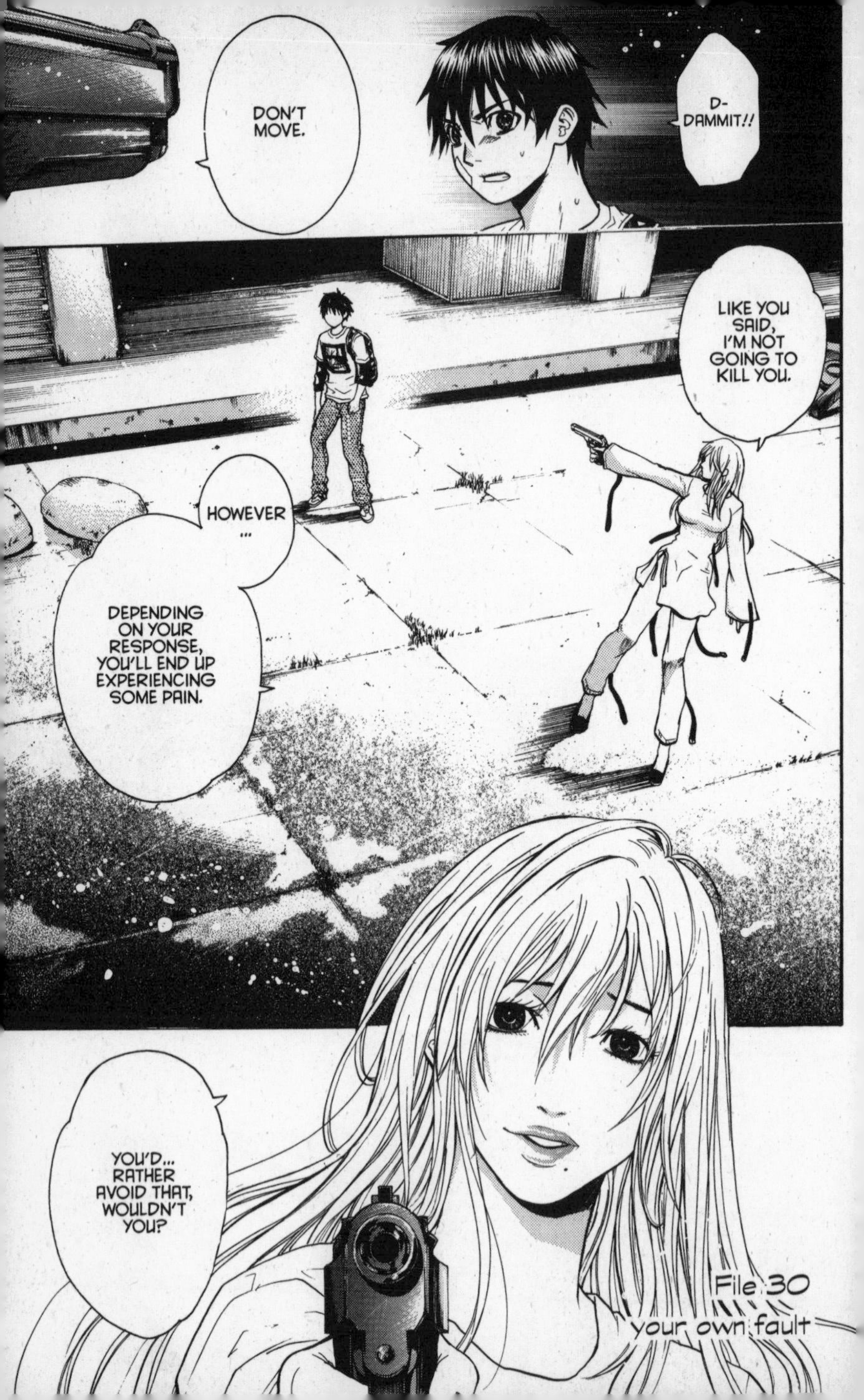
D-DAMMIT!!
DON'T MOVE.
LIKE YOU SAID, I'M NOT GOING TO KILL YOU.
HOWEVER ...
DEPENDING ON YOUR RESPONSE, YOU'LL END UP EXPERIENCING SOME PAIN.
YOU'D... RATHER AVOID THAT, WOULDN'T YOU?
File 30
your own fault

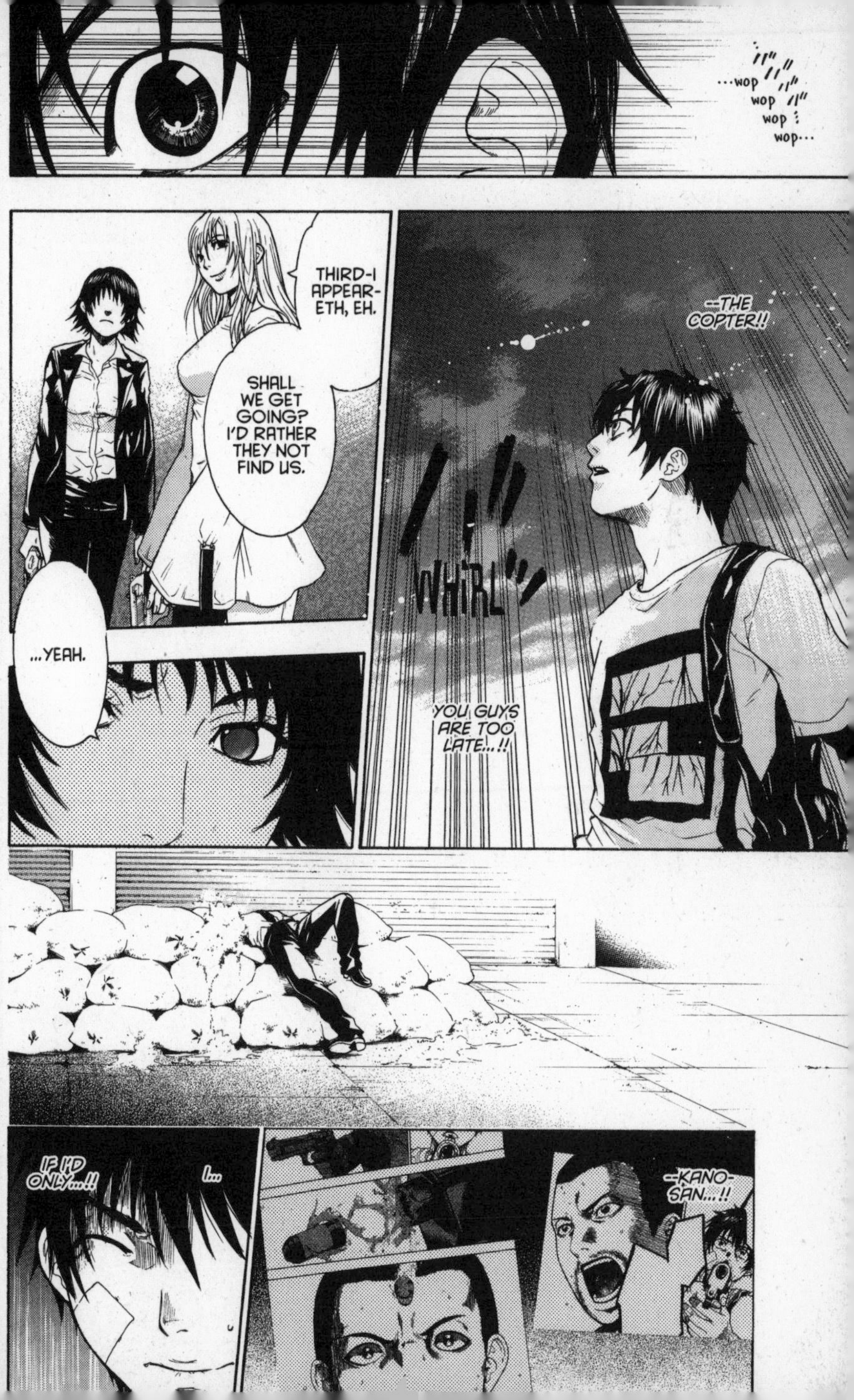
...wop wop wop wop...
--THE COPTER!!
WHIRL
YOU GUYS ARE TOO LATE...!!
THIRD-I APPEAR-ETH, EH.
SHALL WE GET GOING? I'D RATHER THEY NOT FIND US.
...YEAH.
--KANO-SAN...!!
I...
IF I'D ONLY...!!

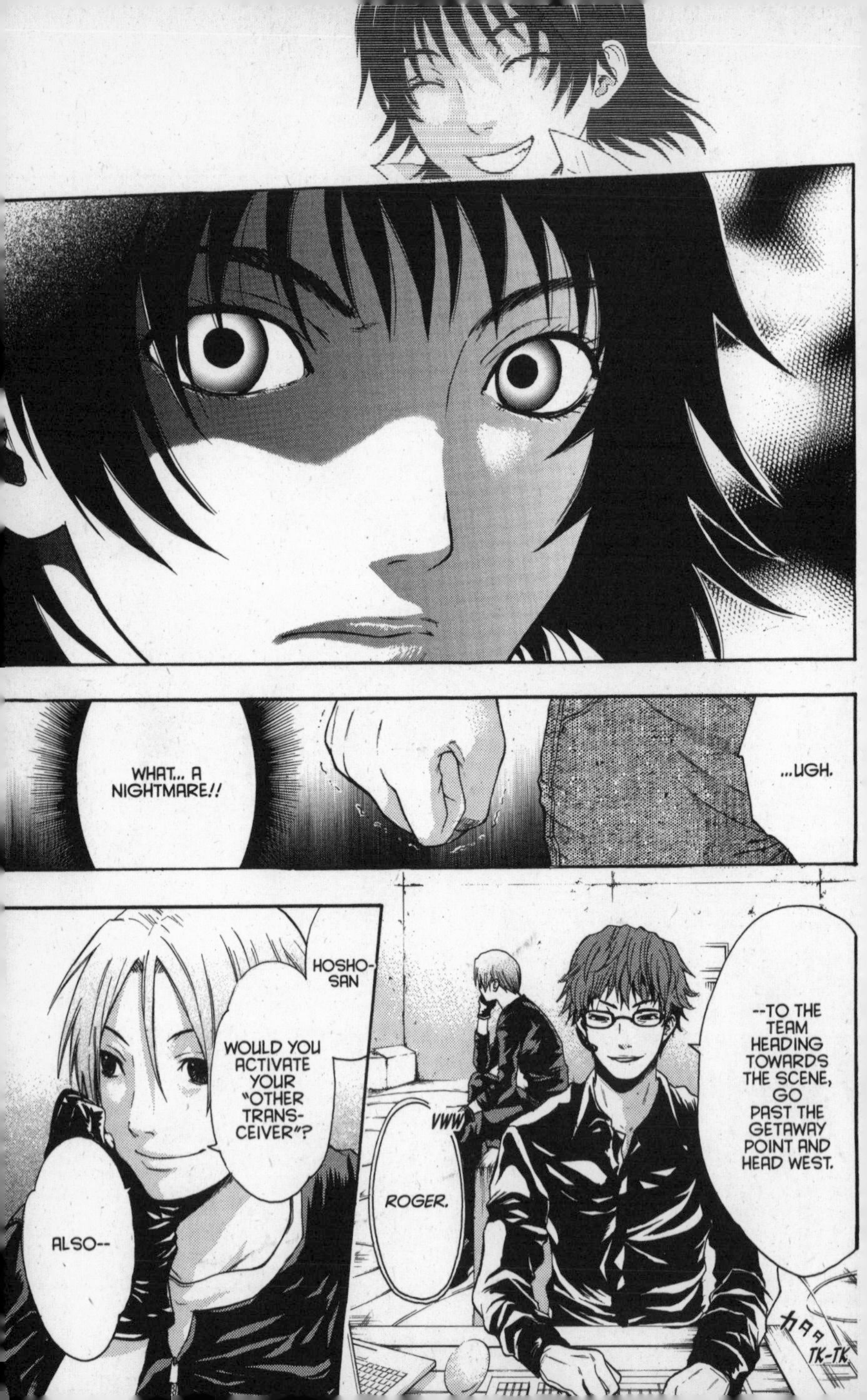
...UGH.
WHAT... A NIGHTMARE!!
--TO THE TEAM HEADING TOWARDS THE SCENE, GO PAST THE GETAWAY POINT AND HEAD WEST.
カタタ TK-TK
VWW
ROGER.
HOSHO-SAN
WOULD YOU ACTIVATE YOUR "OTHER TRANSCEIVER"?
ALSO--

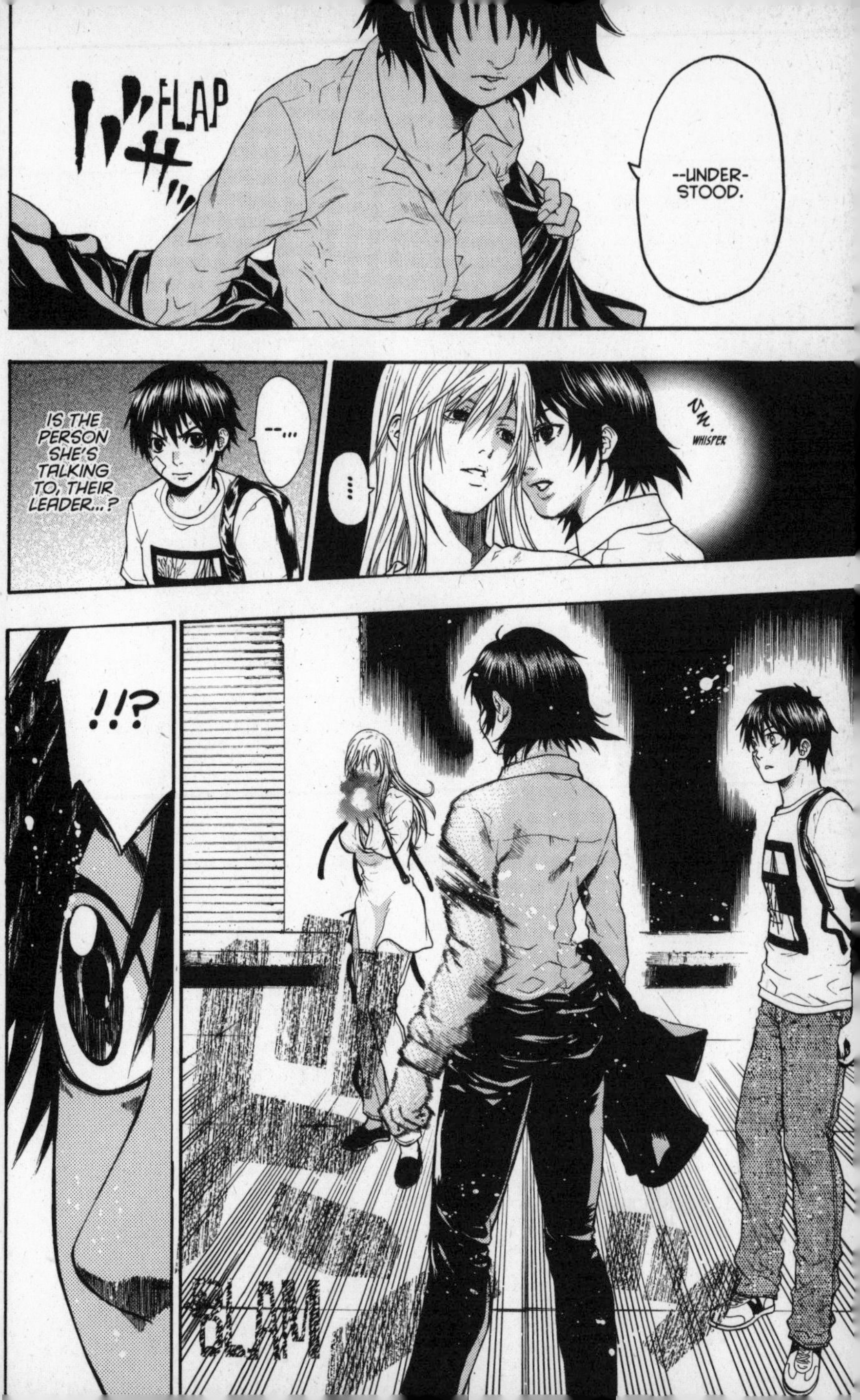
--UNDER-STOOD.
FLAP
WHISPER
...
--...
IS THE PERSON SHE'S TALKING TO, THEIR LEADER...?
SLAM
!!?

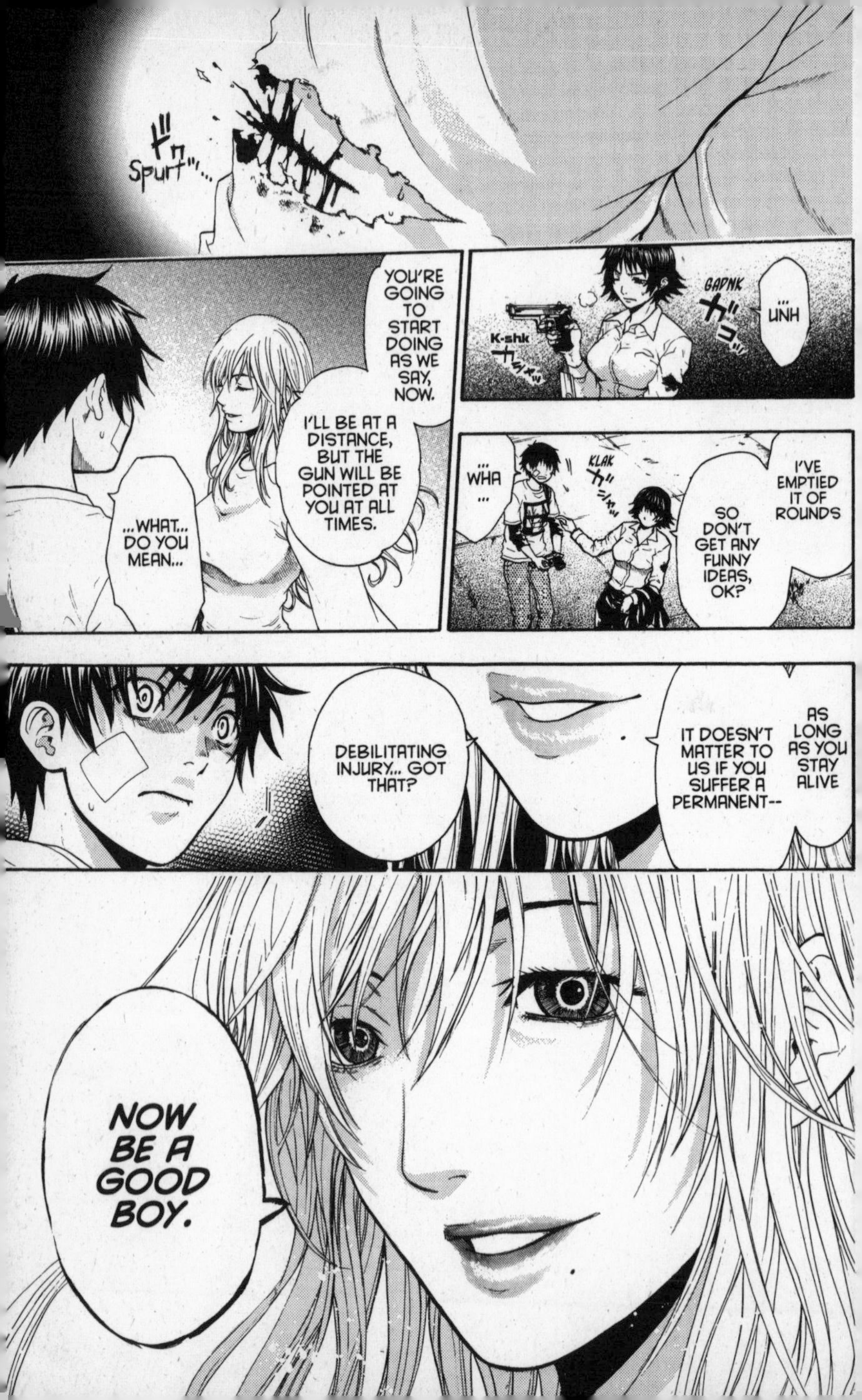

Spurt'''...
... UNH
GADNK
K-shk
I'VE EMPTIED IT OF ROUNDS
SO DON'T GET ANY FUNNY IDEAS, OK?
KLAK
... WHA ...
YOU'RE GOING TO START DOING AS WE SAY, NOW.
I'LL BE AT A DISTANCE, BUT THE GUN WILL BE POINTED AT YOU AT ALL TIMES.
...WHAT... DO YOU MEAN...
AS LONG AS YOU STAY ALIVE
IT DOESN'T MATTER TO US IF YOU SUFFER A PERMANENT--
DEBILITATING INJURY... GOT THAT?
NOW BE A GOOD BOY.

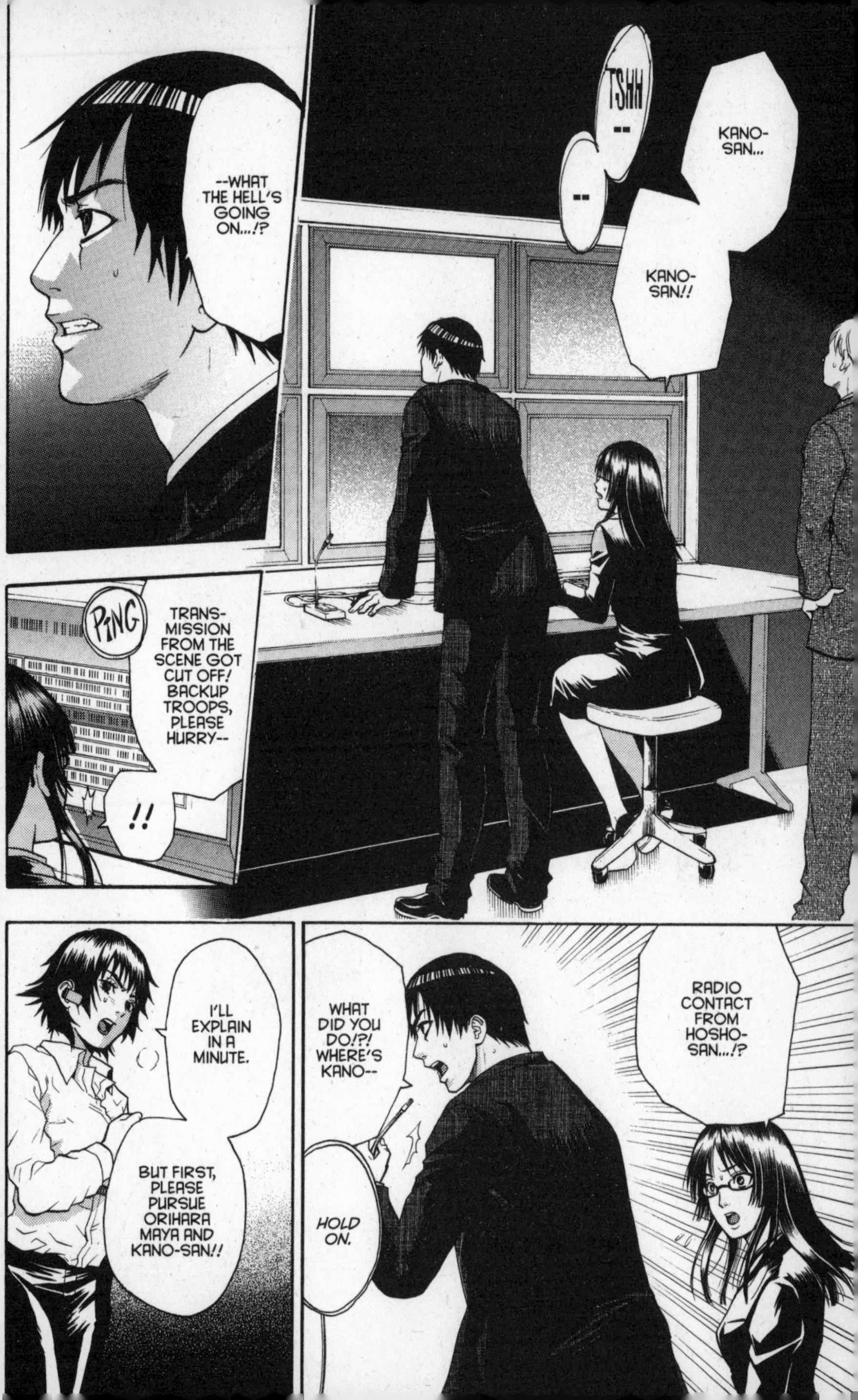
KANO-SAN...
TSHH --
--
KANO-SAN!!
--WHAT THE HELL'S GOING ON...!?
PING
TRANS-MISSION FROM THE SCENE GOT CUT OFF! BACKUP TROOPS, PLEASE HURRY--
!!
RADIO CONTACT FROM HOSHO-SAN...!?
WHAT DID YOU DO!?! WHERE'S KANO--
HOLD ON.
I'LL EXPLAIN IN A MINUTE.
BUT FIRST, PLEASE PURSUE ORIHARA MAYA AND KANO-SAN!!

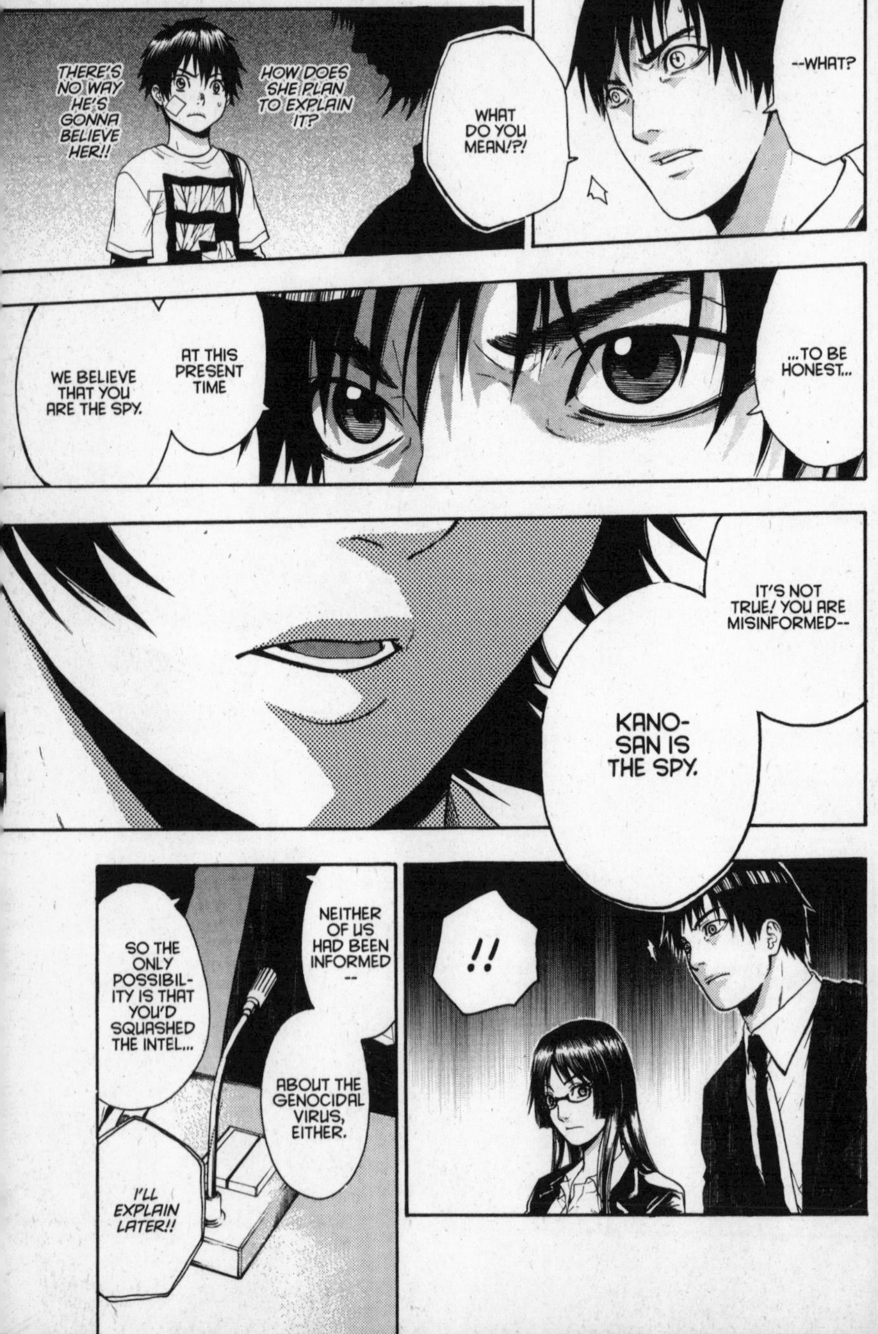
--WHAT?
WHAT DO YOU MEAN!?!
HOW DOES SHE PLAN TO EXPLAIN IT?
THERE'S NO WAY HE'S GONNA BELIEVE HER!!
...TO BE HONEST...
AT THIS PRESENT TIME
WE BELIEVE THAT YOU ARE THE SPY.
IT'S NOT TRUE! YOU ARE MISINFORMED--
KANO-SAN IS THE SPY.
!!
NEITHER OF US HAD BEEN INFORMED --
ABOUT THE GENOCIDAL VIRUS, EITHER.
SO THE ONLY POSSIBILITY IS THAT YOU'D SQUASHED THE INTEL...
I'LL EXPLAIN LATER!!

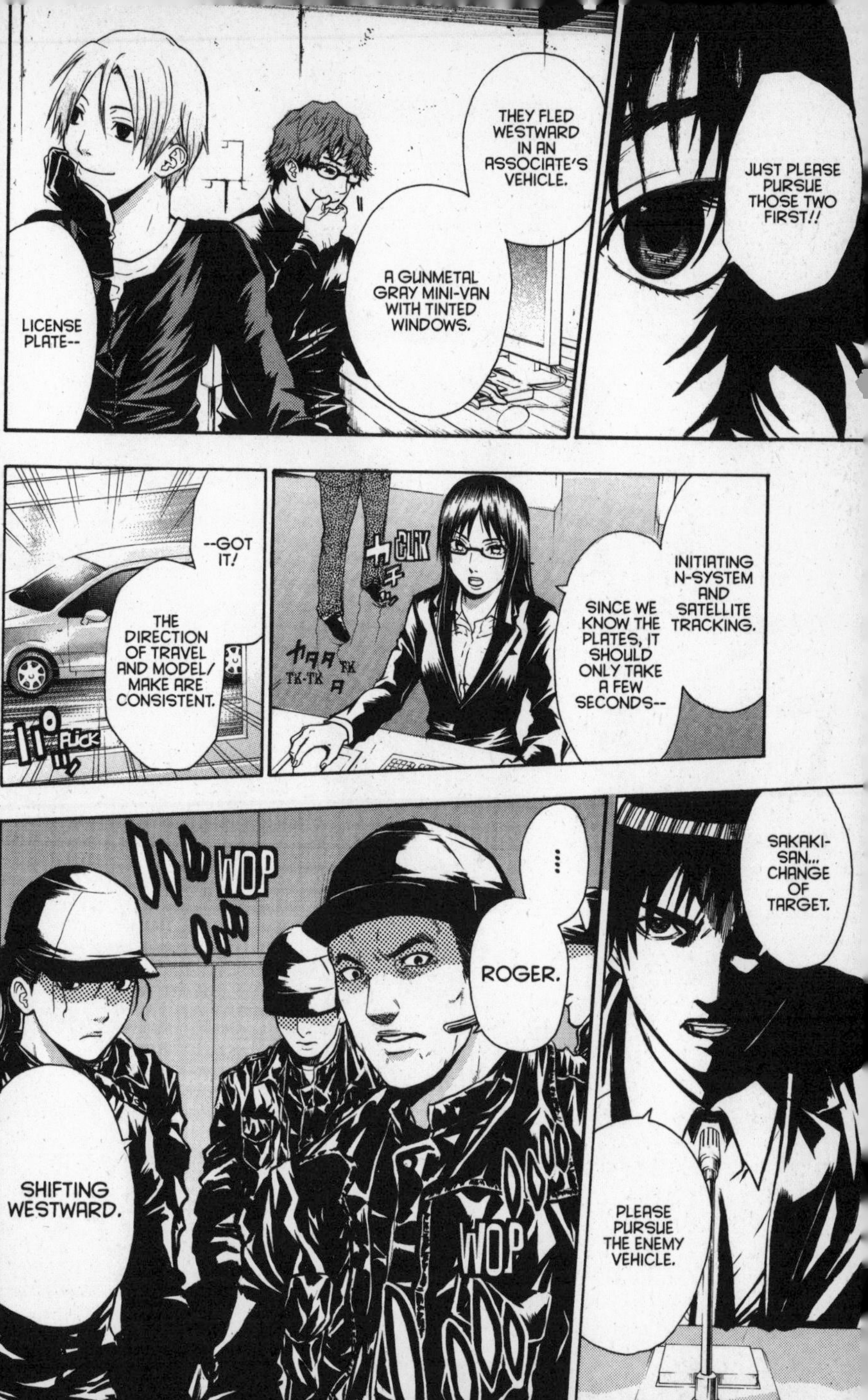
JUST PLEASE PURSUE THOSE TWO FIRST!!
THEY FLED WESTWARD IN AN ASSOCIATE'S VEHICLE.
A GUNMETAL GRAY MINI-VAN WITH TINTED WINDOWS.
LICENSE PLATE--
INITIATING N-SYSTEM AND SATELLITE TRACKING.
SINCE WE KNOW THE PLATES, IT SHOULD ONLY TAKE A FEW SECONDS--
CLIK
TK-TK TK
--GOT IT!
THE DIRECTION OF TRAVEL AND MODEL/MAKE ARE CONSISTENT.
FLICK
SAKAKI-SAN... CHANGE OF TARGET.
PLEASE PURSUE THE ENEMY VEHICLE.
...
ROGER.
WOP
SHIFTING WESTWARD.
WOP

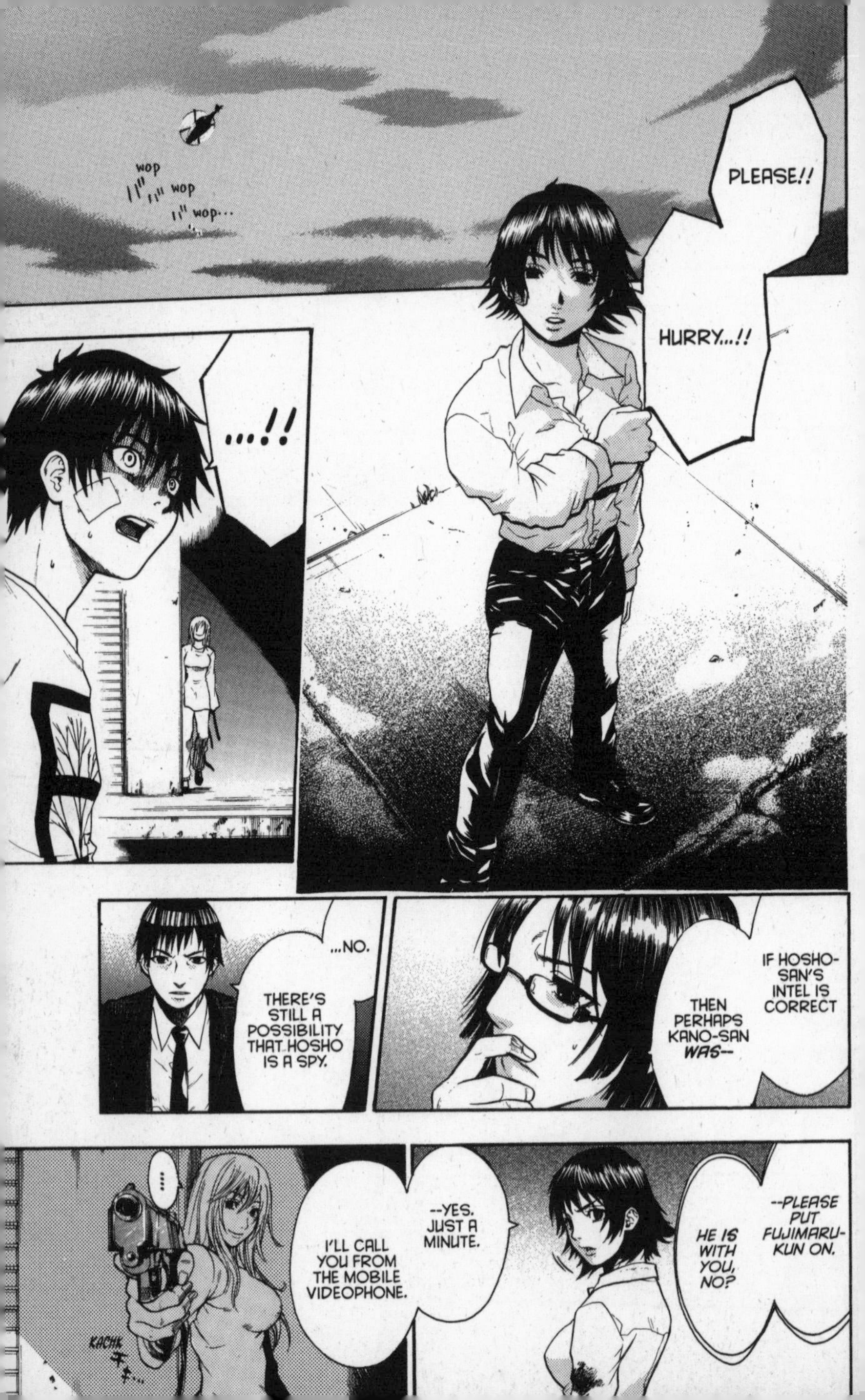
PLEASE!!
wop wop wop...
HURRY...!!
...!!
IF HOSHO-SAN'S INTEL IS CORRECT
THEN PERHAPS KANO-SAN *WAS*--
...NO.
THERE'S STILL A POSSIBILITY THAT HOSHO IS A SPY.
--PLEASE PUT FUJIMARU-KUN ON.
HE IS WITH YOU, NO?
--YES. JUST A MINUTE.
I'LL CALL YOU FROM THE MOBILE VIDEOPHONE.
...
KACHK

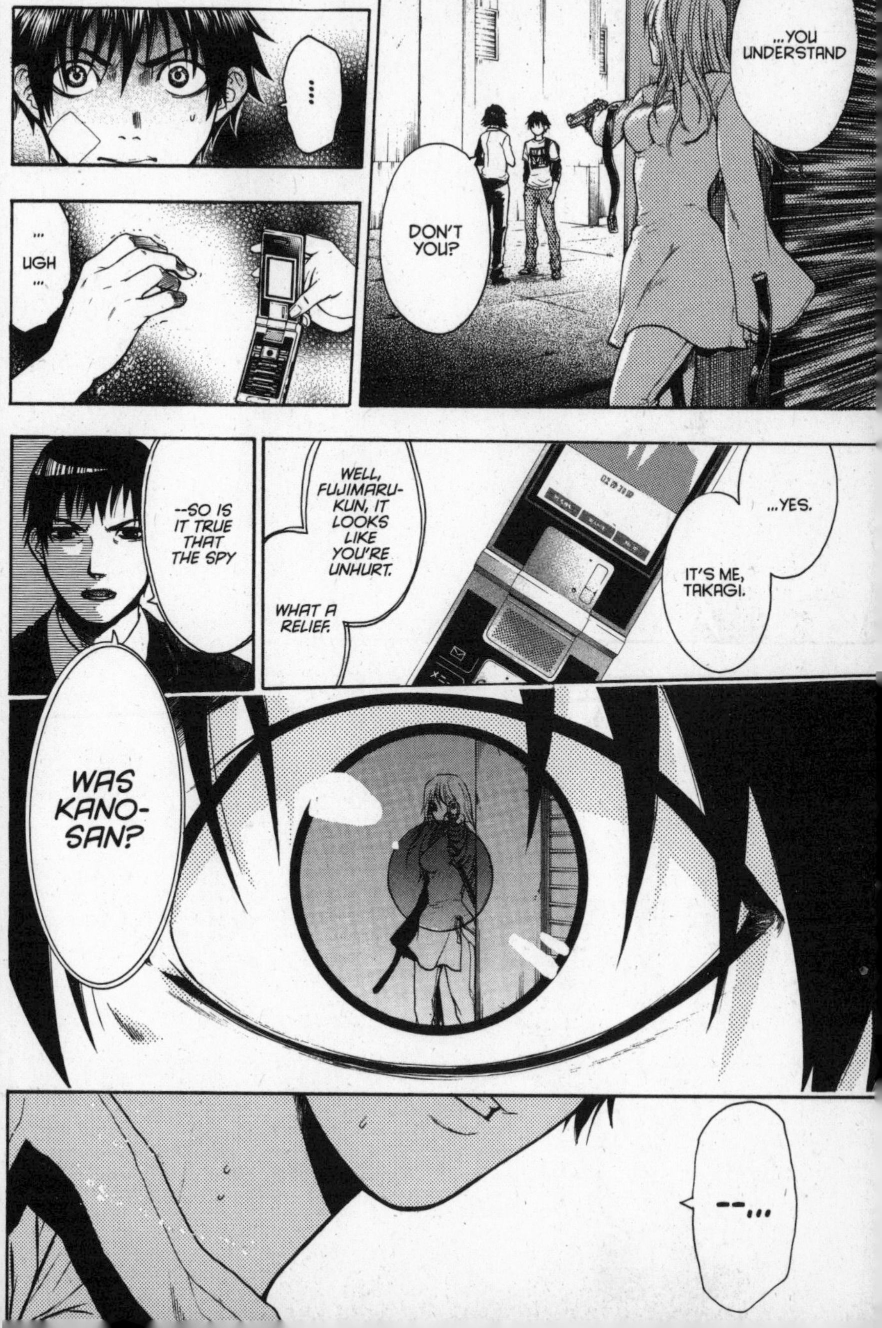
...YOU UNDERSTAND
DON'T YOU?
....
... UGH ...
...YES.
IT'S ME, TAKAGI.
WELL, FUJIMARU-KUN, IT LOOKS LIKE YOU'RE UNHURT.
WHAT A RELIEF.
--SO IS IT TRUE THAT THE SPY
WAS KANO-SAN?
--...

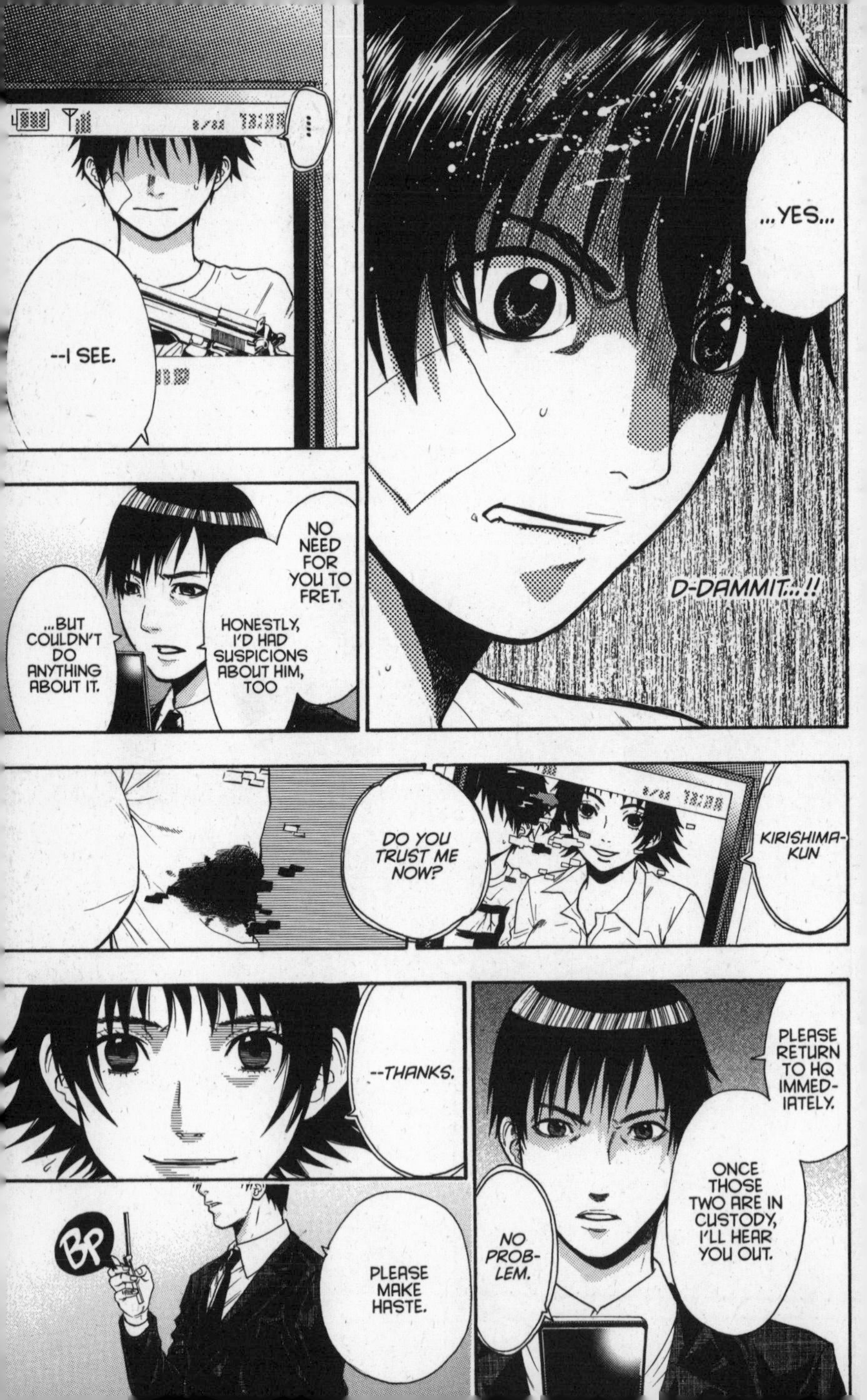
...YES...
D-DAMMIT...!!
...
--I SEE.
NO NEED FOR YOU TO FRET.
HONESTLY, I'D HAD SUSPICIONS ABOUT HIM, TOO
...BUT COULDN'T DO ANYTHING ABOUT IT.
KIRISHIMA-KUN
DO YOU TRUST ME NOW?
PLEASE RETURN TO HQ IMMEDIATELY.
ONCE THOSE TWO ARE IN CUSTODY, I'LL HEAR YOU OUT.
NO PROBLEM.
--THANKS.
PLEASE MAKE HASTE.
BP

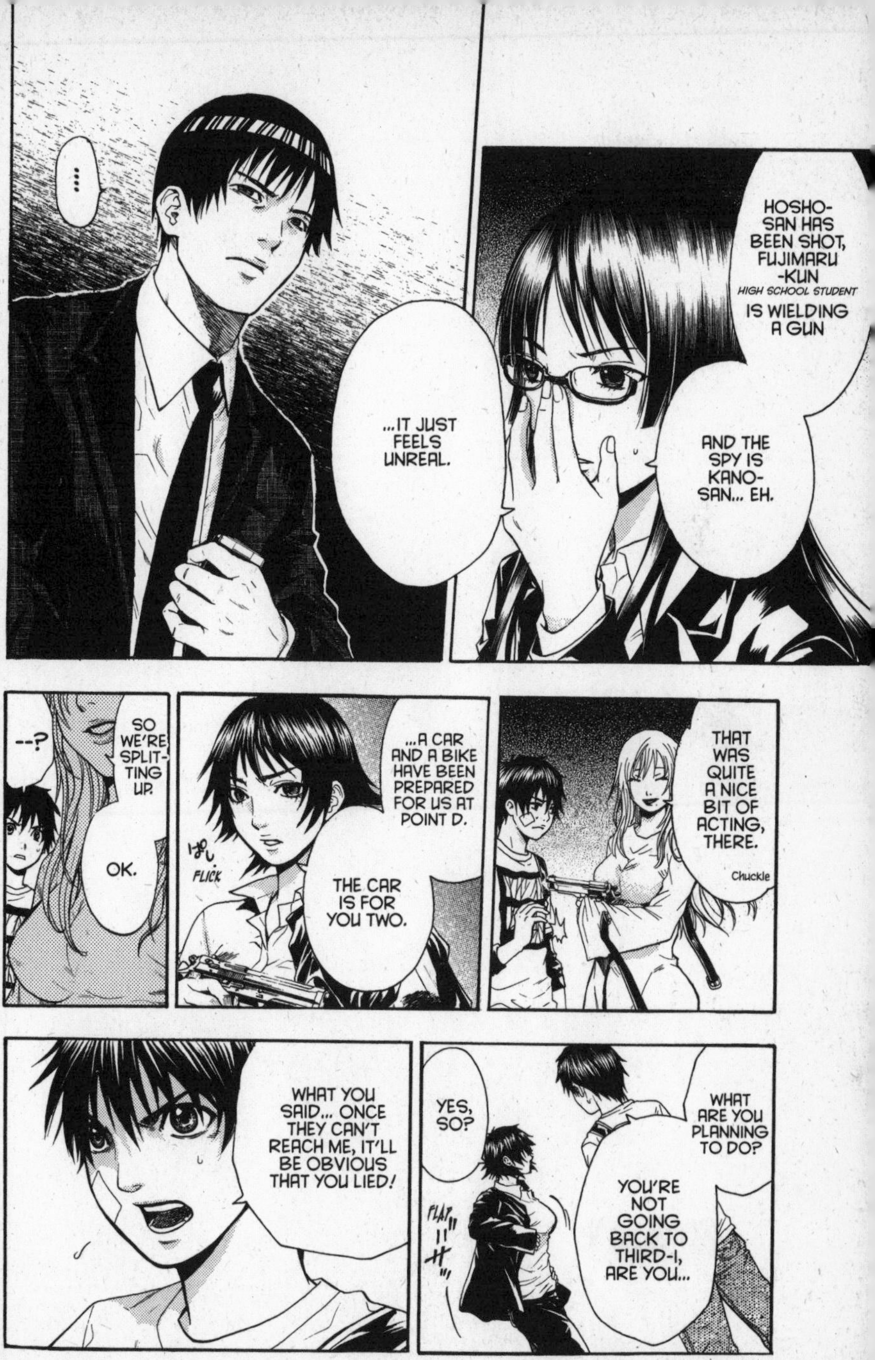
HOSHO-SAN HAS BEEN SHOT, FUJIMARU-KUN
HIGH SCHOOL STUDENT
IS WIELDING A GUN
AND THE SPY IS KANO-SAN... EH.
...IT JUST FEELS UNREAL.
......
THAT WAS QUITE A NICE BIT OF ACTING, THERE.
Chuckle
...A CAR AND A BIKE HAVE BEEN PREPARED FOR US AT POINT D.
THE CAR IS FOR YOU TWO.
FLICK
SO WE'RE SPLIT-TING UP.
OK.
--?
WHAT ARE YOU PLANNING TO DO?
YOU'RE NOT GOING BACK TO THIRD-I, ARE YOU...
YES, SO?
FLAP
WHAT YOU SAID... ONCE THEY CAN'T REACH ME, IT'LL BE OBVIOUS THAT YOU LIED!

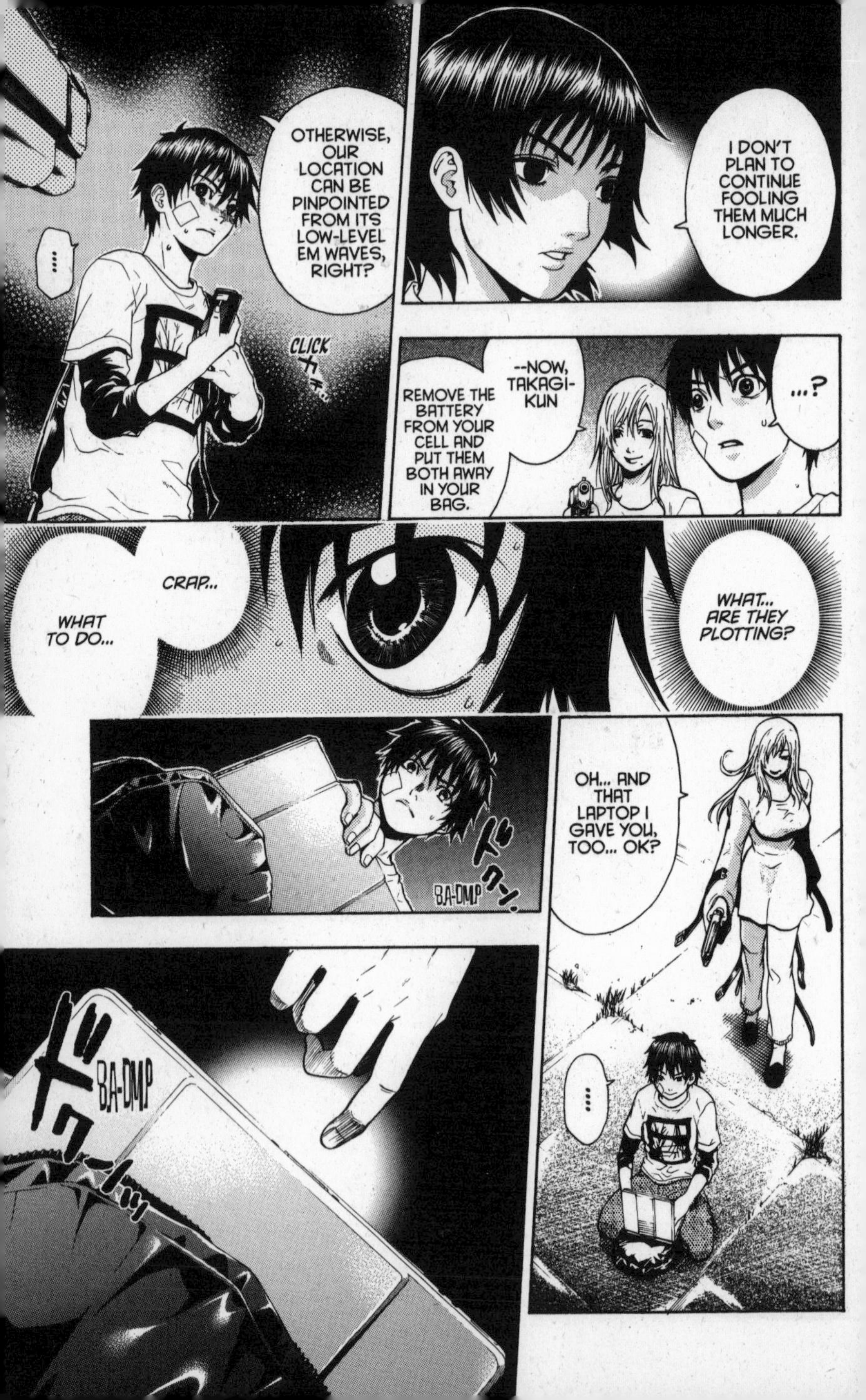
I DON'T PLAN TO CONTINUE FOOLING THEM MUCH LONGER.
...?
--NOW, TAKAGI-KUN
REMOVE THE BATTERY FROM YOUR CELL AND PUT THEM BOTH AWAY IN YOUR BAG.
OTHERWISE, OUR LOCATION CAN BE PINPOINTED FROM ITS LOW-LEVEL EM WAVES, RIGHT?
....
CLICK
WHAT... ARE THEY PLOTTING?
CRAP...
WHAT TO DO...
OH... AND THAT LAPTOP I GAVE YOU, TOO... OK?
....
BA-DMP
BA-DMP

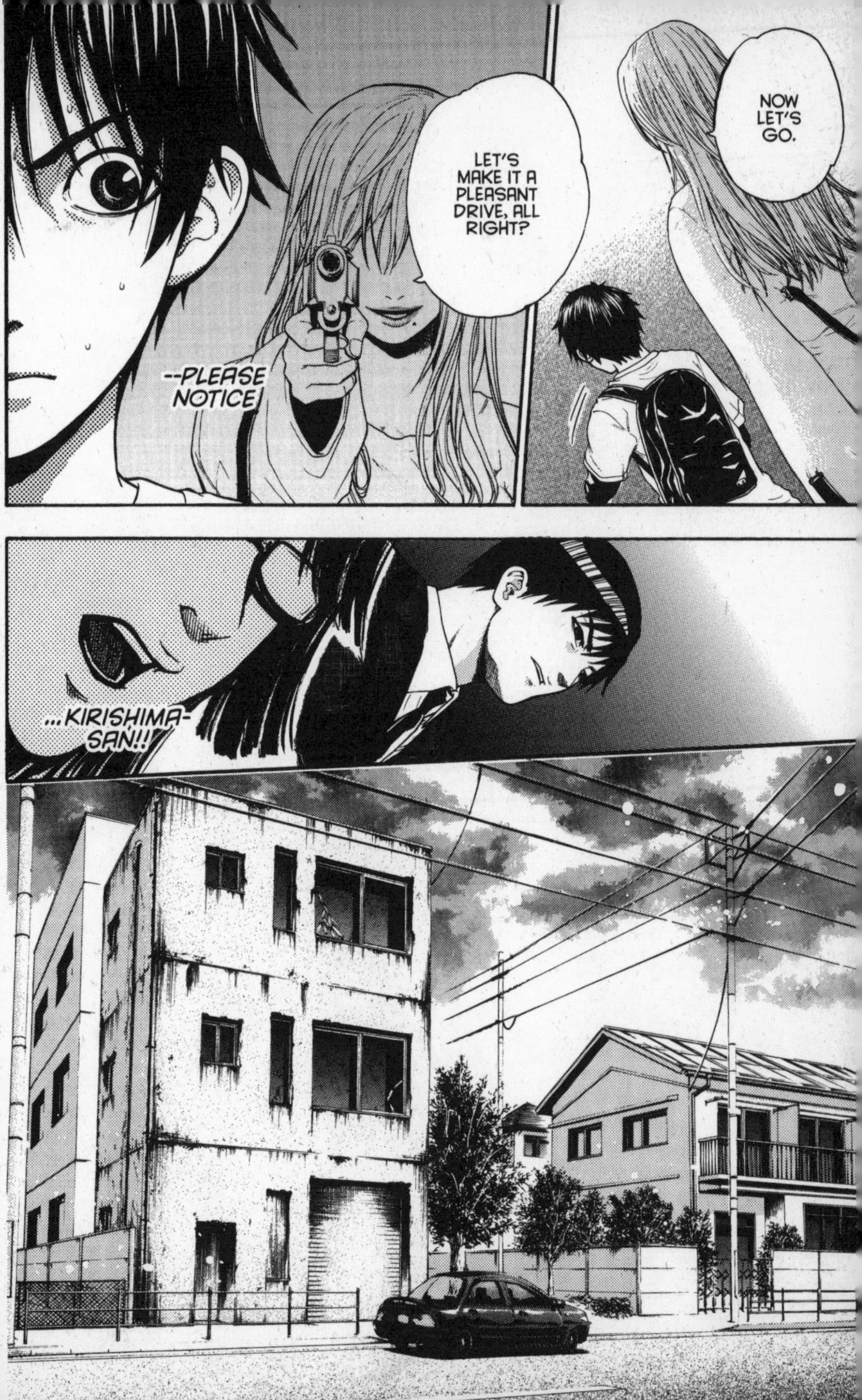
NOW LET'S GO.
LET'S MAKE IT A PLEASANT DRIVE, ALL RIGHT?
--PLEASE NOTICE
...KIRISHIMA-SAN!!

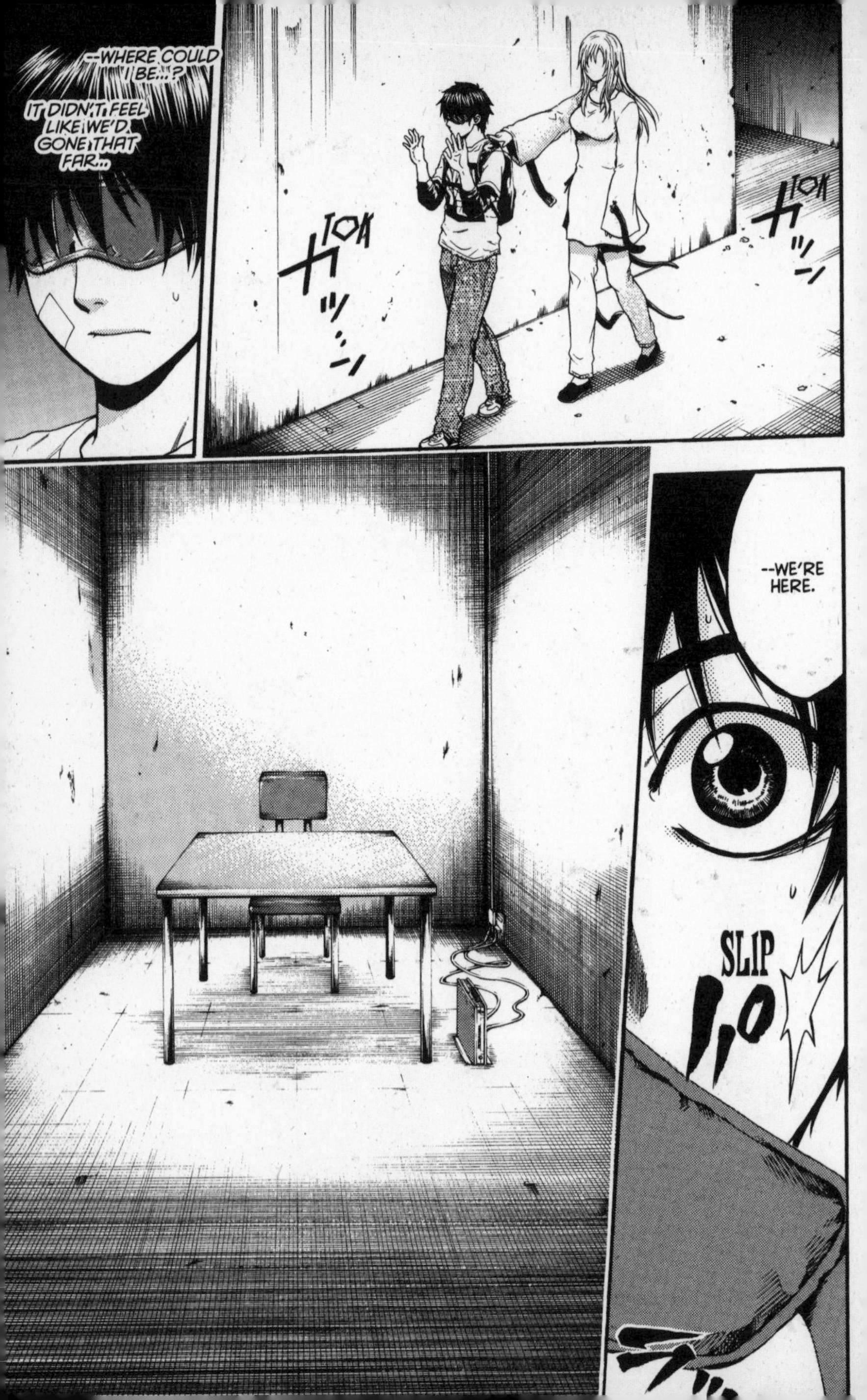
TOK
TOK
--WHERE COULD I BE...?
IT DIDN'T FEEL LIKE WE'D GONE THAT FAR...
--WE'RE HERE.
SLIP

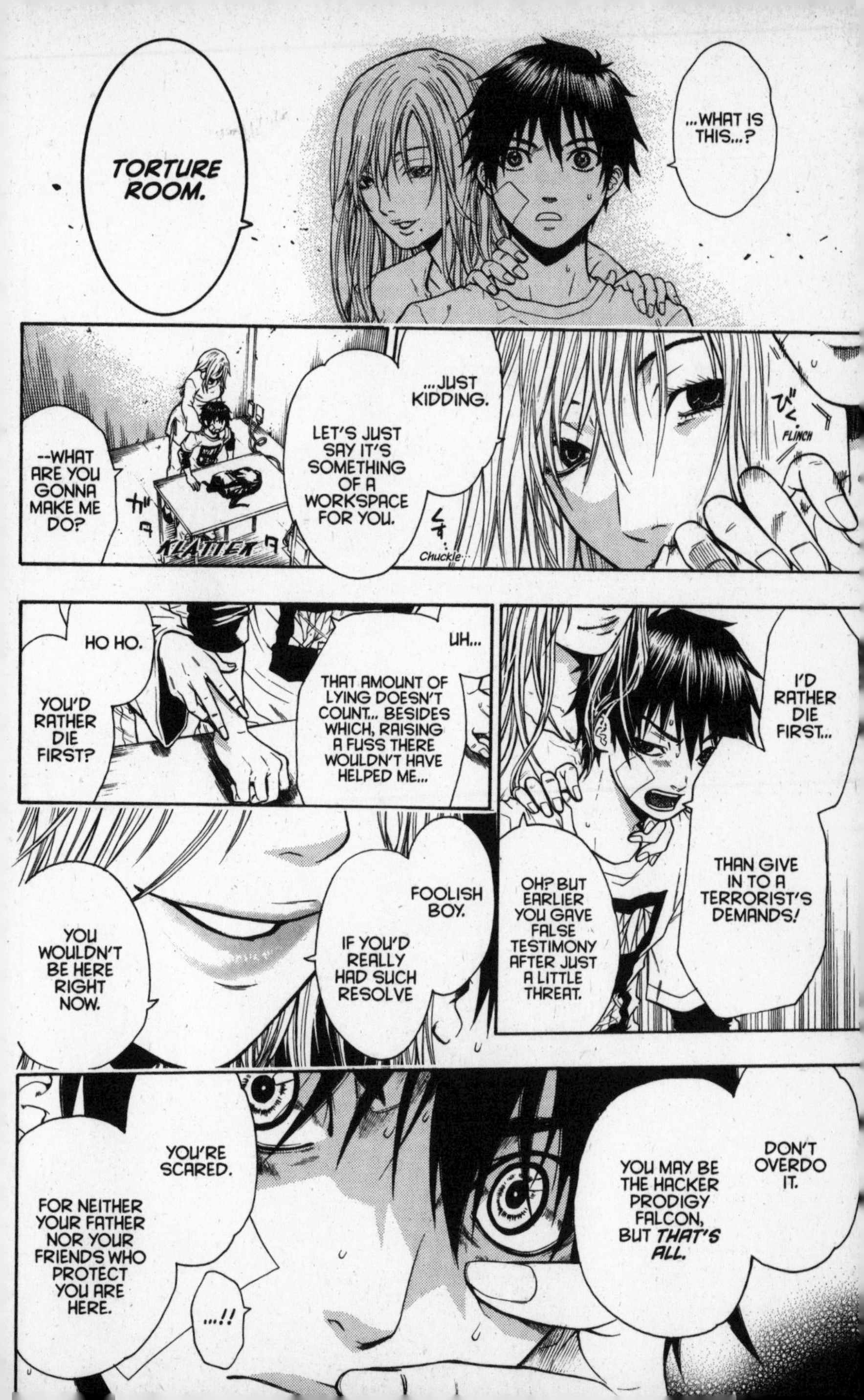
...WHAT IS THIS...?
TORTURE ROOM.
FLINCH
...JUST KIDDING.
LET'S JUST SAY IT'S SOMETHING OF A WORKSPACE FOR YOU.
Chuckle...
--WHAT ARE YOU GONNA MAKE ME DO?
KLATTER
I'D RATHER DIE FIRST...
THAN GIVE IN TO A TERRORIST'S DEMANDS!
OH? BUT EARLIER YOU GAVE FALSE TESTIMONY AFTER JUST A LITTLE THREAT.
UH...
THAT AMOUNT OF LYING DOESN'T COUNT... BESIDES WHICH, RAISING A FUSS THERE WOULDN'T HAVE HELPED ME...
HO HO.
YOU'D RATHER DIE FIRST?
FOOLISH BOY.
IF YOU'D REALLY HAD SUCH RESOLVE
YOU WOULDN'T BE HERE RIGHT NOW.
DON'T OVERDO IT.
YOU MAY BE THE HACKER PRODIGY FALCON, BUT *THAT'S ALL.*
YOU'RE SCARED.
FOR NEITHER YOUR FATHER NOR YOUR FRIENDS WHO PROTECT YOU ARE HERE.
...!!

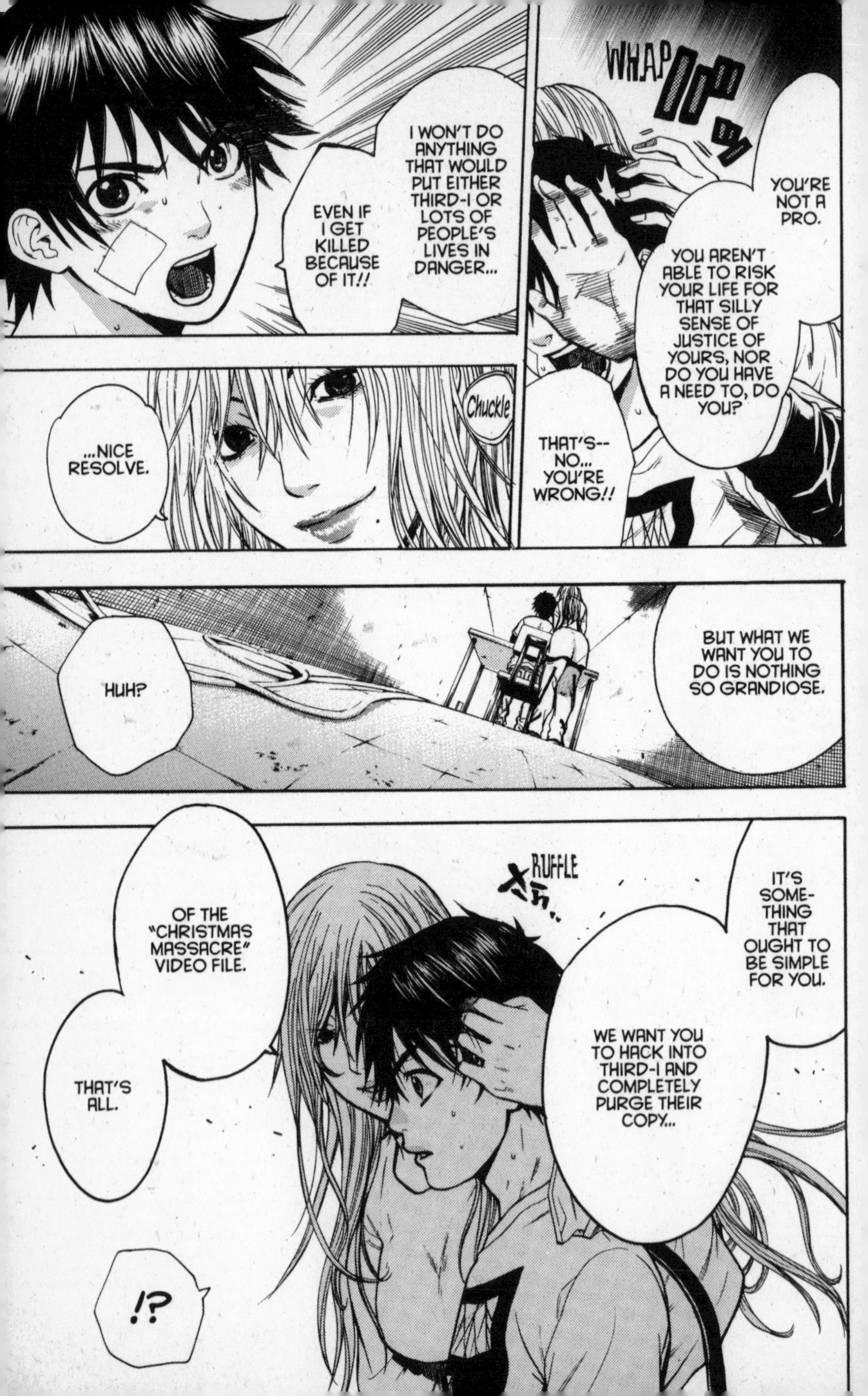
WHAP
YOU'RE NOT A PRO.
YOU AREN'T ABLE TO RISK YOUR LIFE FOR THAT SILLY SENSE OF JUSTICE OF YOURS, NOR DO YOU HAVE A NEED TO, DO YOU?
THAT'S-- NO... YOU'RE WRONG!!
I WON'T DO ANYTHING THAT WOULD PUT EITHER THIRD-I OR LOTS OF PEOPLE'S LIVES IN DANGER...
EVEN IF I GET KILLED BECAUSE OF IT!!
Chuckle
...NICE RESOLVE.
BUT WHAT WE WANT YOU TO DO IS NOTHING SO GRANDIOSE.
HUH?
RUFFLE
IT'S SOME-THING THAT OUGHT TO BE SIMPLE FOR YOU.
WE WANT YOU TO HACK INTO THIRD-I AND COMPLETELY PURGE THEIR COPY...
OF THE "CHRISTMAS MASSACRE" VIDEO FILE.
THAT'S ALL.
!?

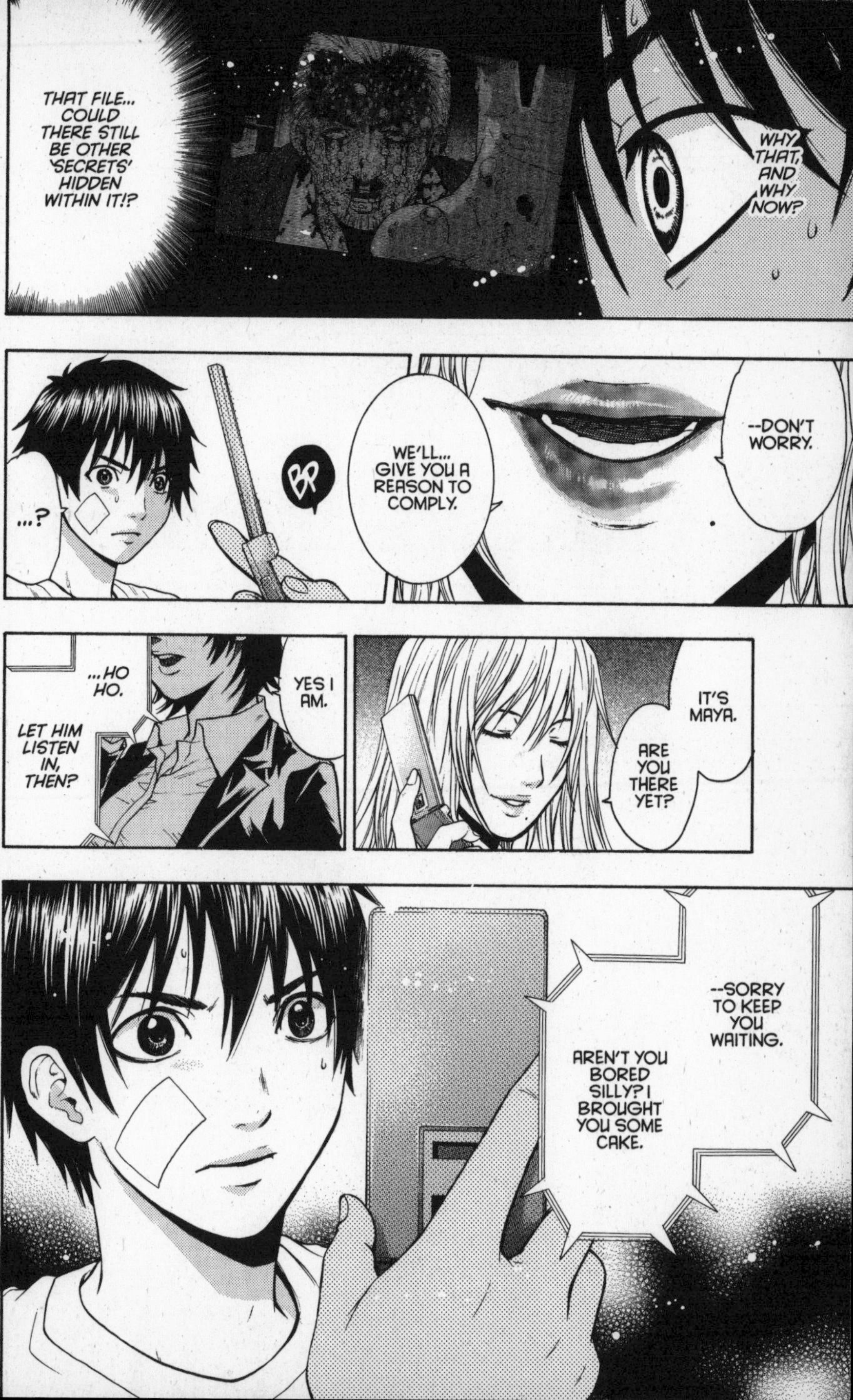
WHY THAT, AND WHY NOW?
THAT FILE... COULD THERE STILL BE OTHER 'SECRETS' HIDDEN WITHIN IT!?
--DON'T WORRY.
WE'LL... GIVE YOU A REASON TO COMPLY.
BP
...?
IT'S MAYA.
ARE YOU THERE YET?
YES I AM.
...HO HO.
LET HIM LISTEN IN, THEN?
--SORRY TO KEEP YOU WAITING.
AREN'T YOU BORED SILLY? I BROUGHT YOU SOME CAKE.

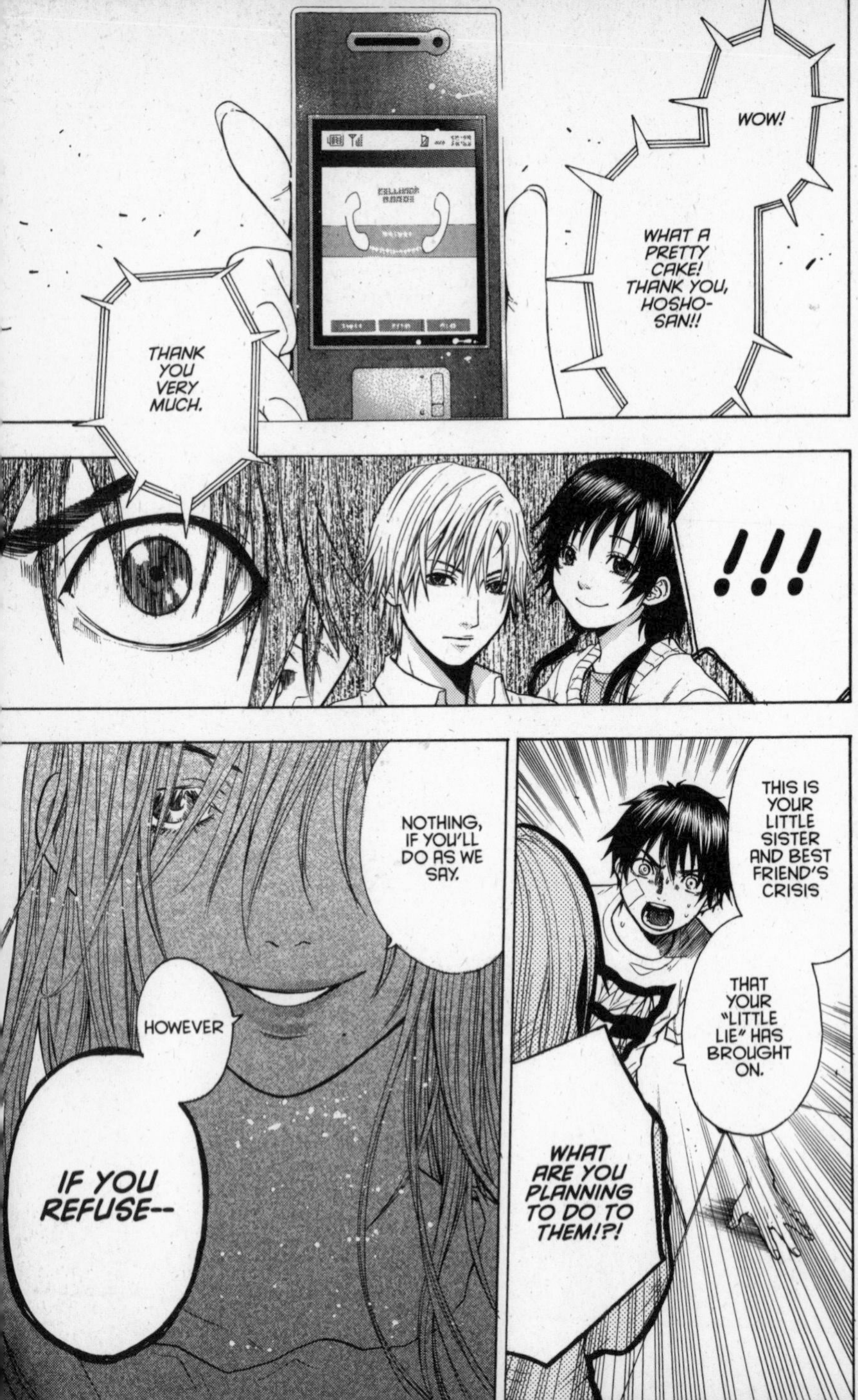
WOW!
WHAT A PRETTY CAKE! THANK YOU, HOSHO-SAN!!
THANK YOU VERY MUCH.
!!!
THIS IS YOUR LITTLE SISTER AND BEST FRIEND'S CRISIS
THAT YOUR "LITTLE LIE" HAS BROUGHT ON.
WHAT ARE YOU PLANNING TO DO TO THEM!?!
NOTHING, IF YOU'LL DO AS WE SAY.
HOWEVER
IF YOU REFUSE--

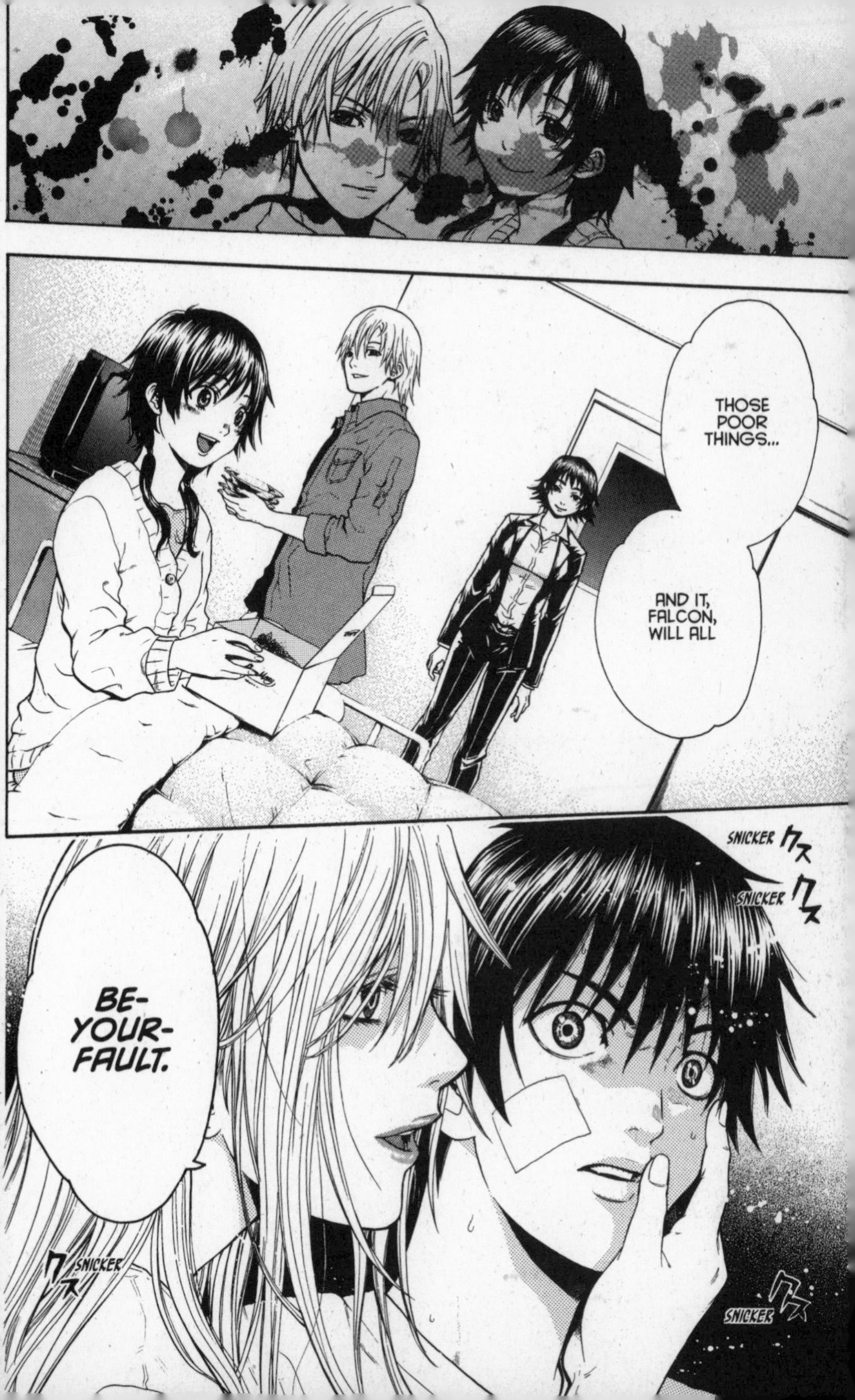
THOSE POOR THINGS...
AND IT, FALCON, WILL ALL
SNICKER クス
SNICKER クス
BE- YOUR- FAULT.
クス SNICKER
SNICKER クス

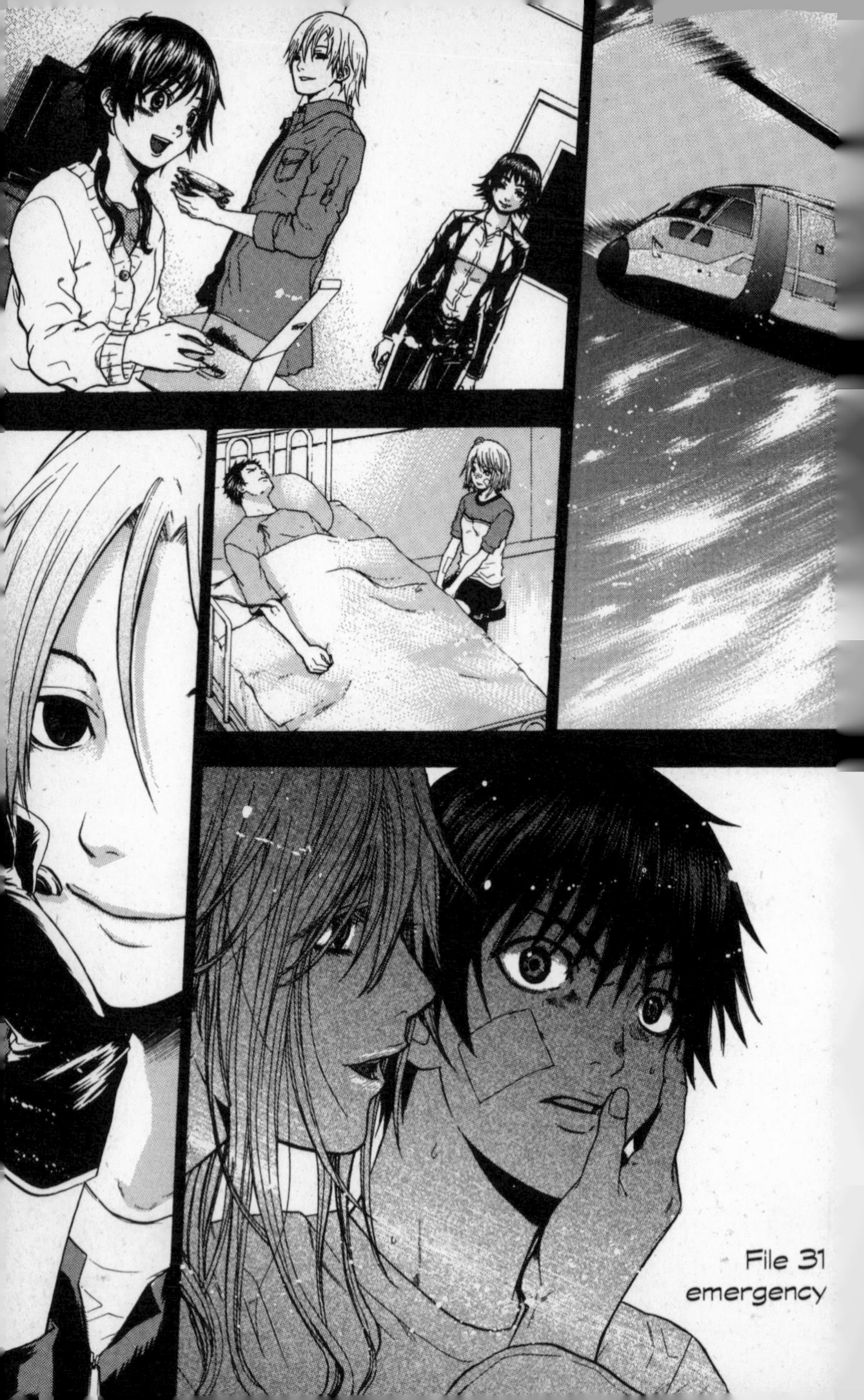
File 31
emergency

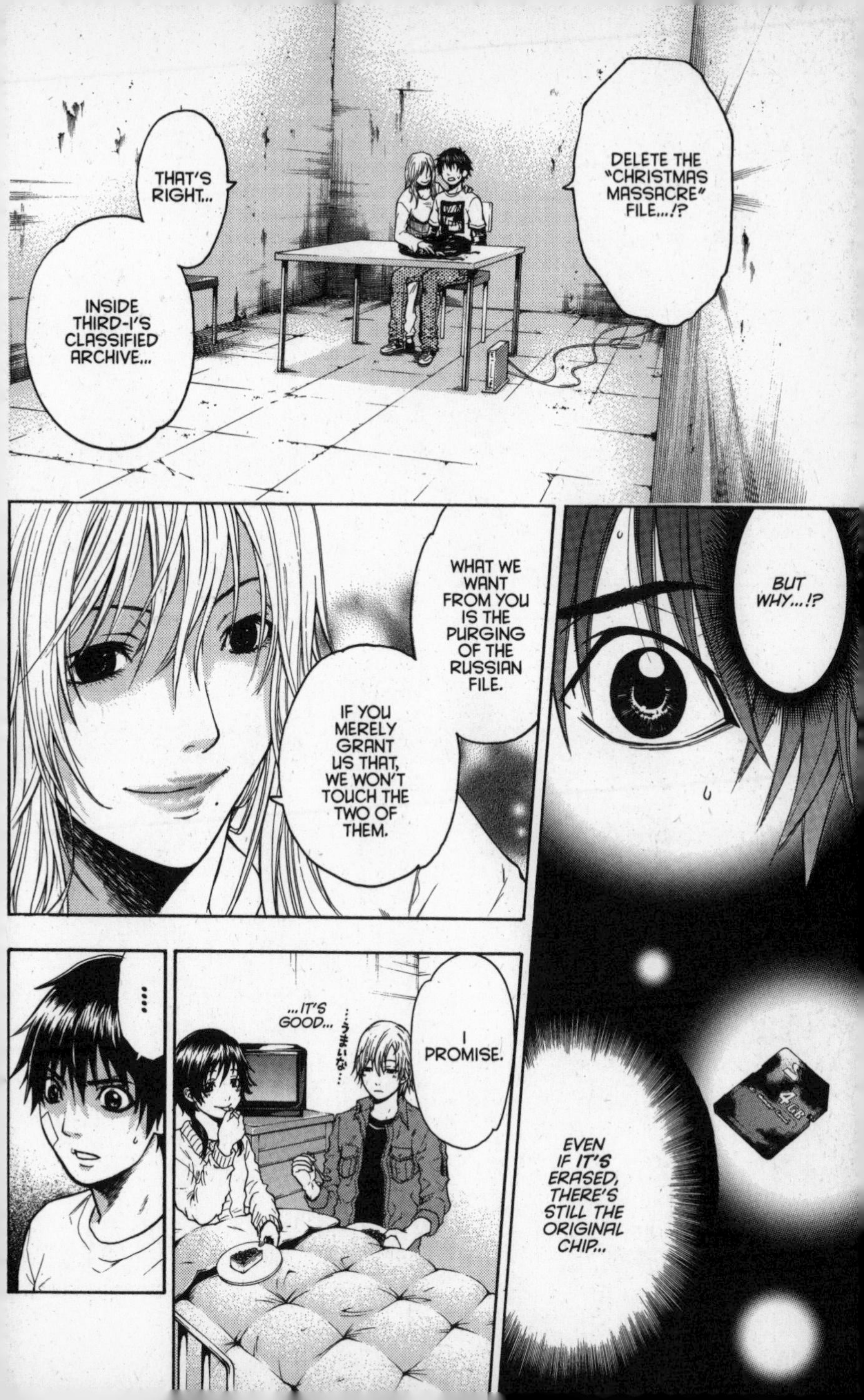
DELETE THE "CHRISTMAS MASSACRE" FILE...!?
THAT'S RIGHT...
INSIDE THIRD-I'S CLASSIFIED ARCHIVE...
BUT WHY...!?
EVEN IF IT'S ERASED, THERE'S STILL THE ORIGINAL CHIP...
WHAT WE WANT FROM YOU IS THE PURGING OF THE RUSSIAN FILE.
IF YOU MERELY GRANT US THAT, WE WON'T TOUCH THE TWO OF THEM.
I PROMISE.
...うまいな...
...IT'S GOOD...
....

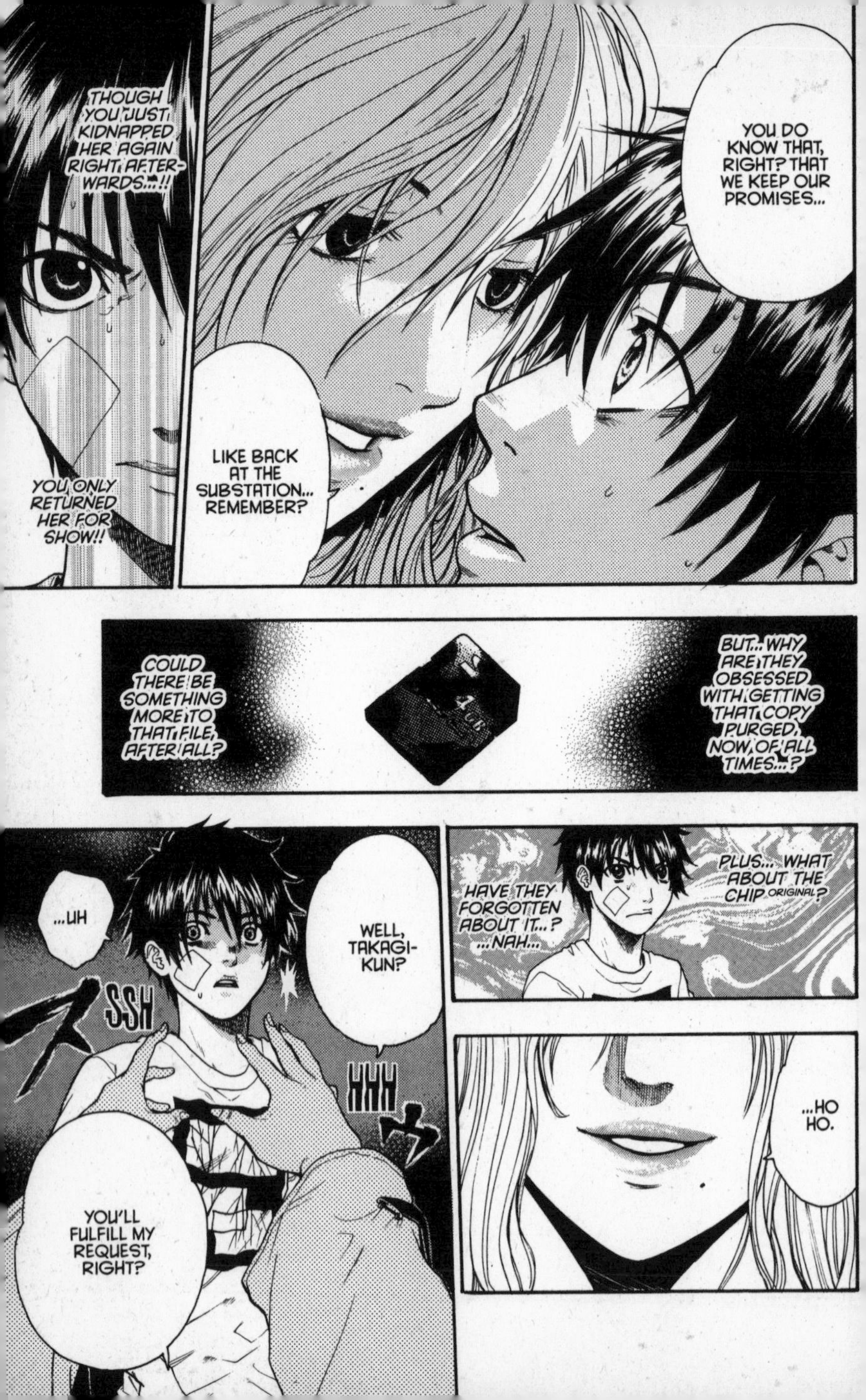
YOU DO KNOW THAT, RIGHT? THAT WE KEEP OUR PROMISES...
LIKE BACK AT THE SUBSTATION... REMEMBER?
THOUGH YOU JUST KIDNAPPED HER AGAIN RIGHT AFTER-WARDS...!!
YOU ONLY RETURNED HER FOR SHOW!!
BUT... WHY ARE THEY OBSESSED WITH GETTING THAT COPY PURGED, NOW OF ALL TIMES...?
COULD THERE BE SOMETHING MORE TO THAT FILE, AFTER ALL?
PLUS... WHAT ABOUT THE CHIP ORIGINAL?
HAVE THEY FORGOTTEN ABOUT IT...? ...NAH...
...HO HO.
WELL, TAKAGI-KUN?
HHH
SSH
...UH
YOU'LL FULFILL MY REQUEST, RIGHT?

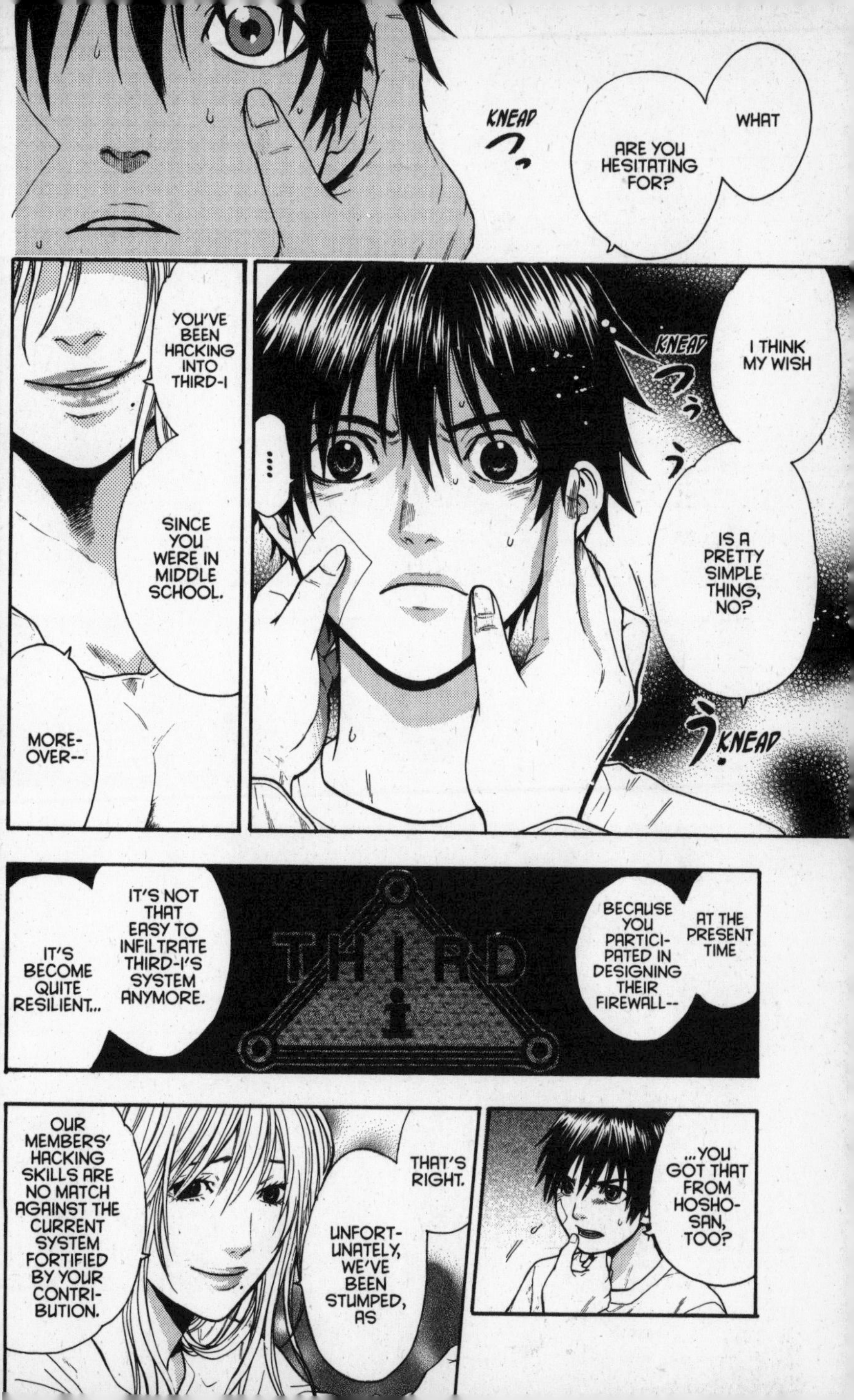
WHAT ARE YOU HESITATING FOR?
KNEAD
I THINK MY WISH
KNEAD
IS A PRETTY SIMPLE THING, NO?
....
KNEAD
YOU'VE BEEN HACKING INTO THIRD-I
SINCE YOU WERE IN MIDDLE SCHOOL.
MORE-OVER--
AT THE PRESENT TIME
BECAUSE YOU PARTICI-PATED IN DESIGNING THEIR FIREWALL--
THIRD i
IT'S NOT THAT EASY TO INFILTRATE THIRD-I'S SYSTEM ANYMORE.
IT'S BECOME QUITE RESILIENT...
...YOU GOT THAT FROM HOSHO-SAN, TOO?
THAT'S RIGHT.
UNFORT-UNATELY, WE'VE BEEN STUMPED, AS
OUR MEMBERS' HACKING SKILLS ARE NO MATCH AGAINST THE CURRENT SYSTEM FORTIFIED BY YOUR CONTRI-BUTION.

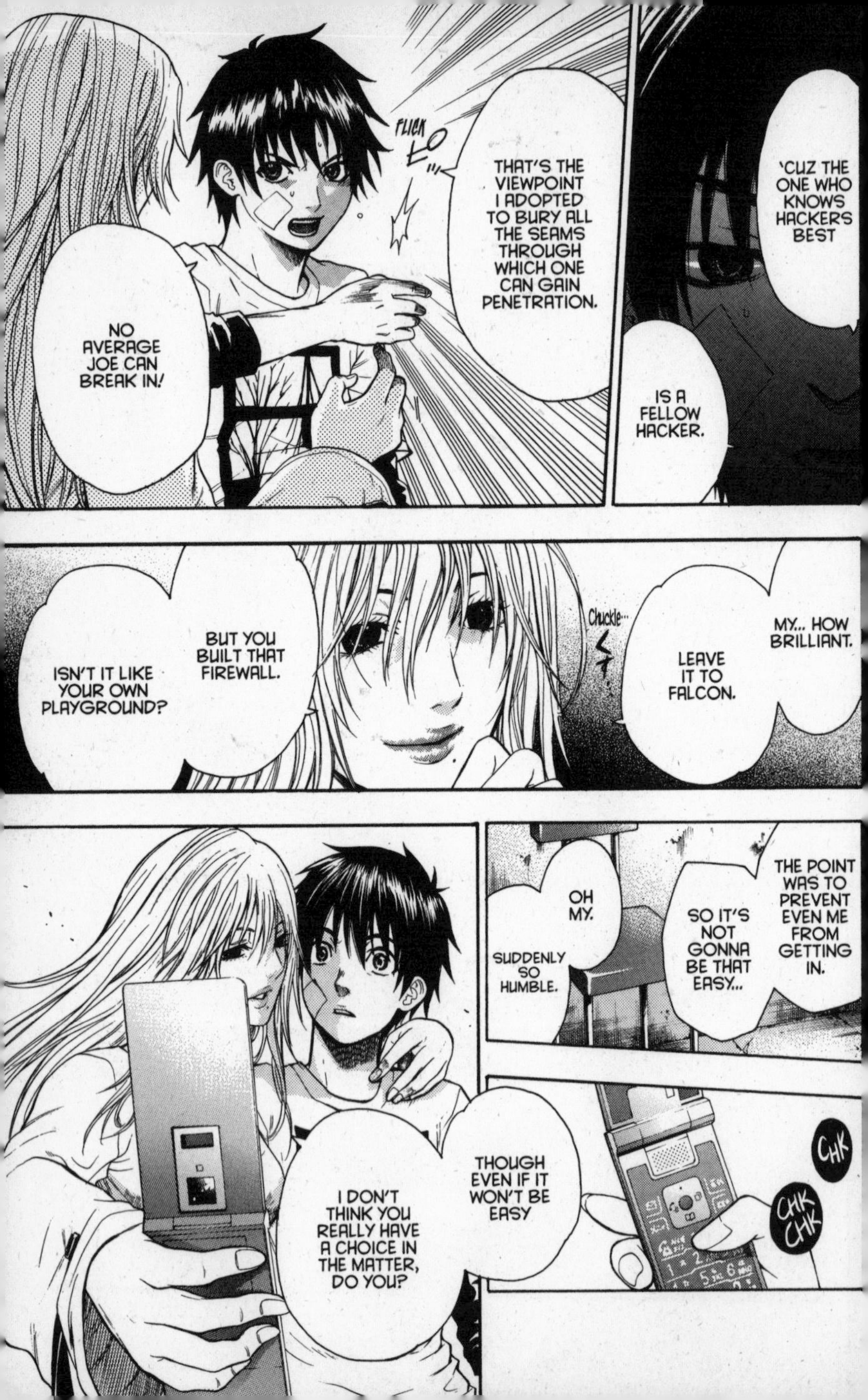
'CUZ THE ONE WHO KNOWS HACKERS BEST
IS A FELLOW HACKER.
THAT'S THE VIEWPOINT I ADOPTED TO BURY ALL THE SEAMS THROUGH WHICH ONE CAN GAIN PENETRATION.
FLICK
NO AVERAGE JOE CAN BREAK IN!
MY... HOW BRILLIANT.
LEAVE IT TO FALCON.
Chuckle...
BUT YOU BUILT THAT FIREWALL.
ISN'T IT LIKE YOUR OWN PLAYGROUND?
THE POINT WAS TO PREVENT EVEN ME FROM GETTING IN.
SO IT'S NOT GONNA BE THAT EASY...
OH MY.
SUDDENLY SO HUMBLE.
CHK
CHK CHK
THOUGH EVEN IF IT WON'T BE EASY
I DON'T THINK YOU REALLY HAVE A CHOICE IN THE MATTER, DO YOU?

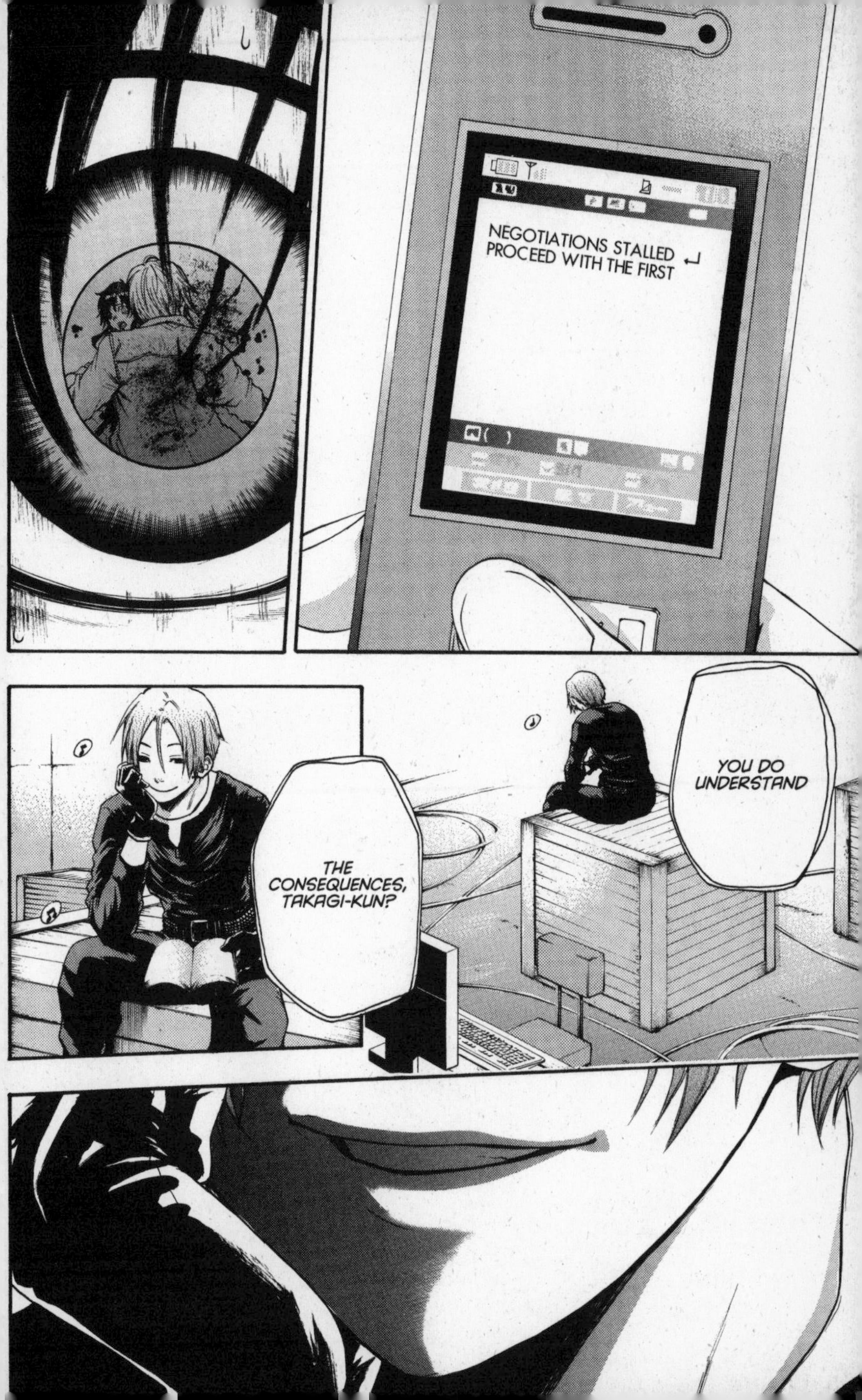
NEGOTIATIONS STALLED
PROCEED WITH THE FIRST
YOU DO UNDERSTAND
THE CONSEQUENCES, TAKAGI-KUN?

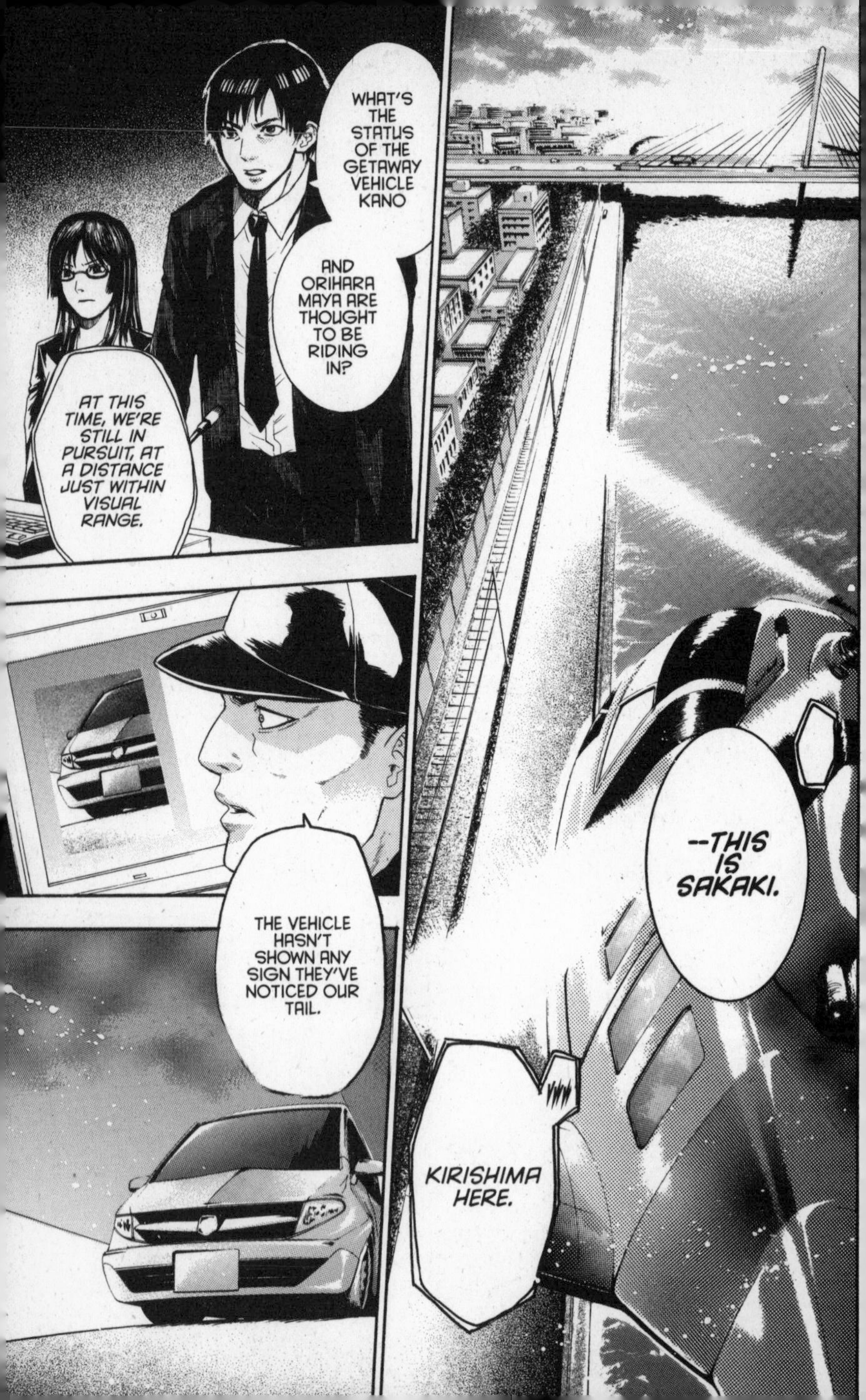
--THIS IS SAKAKI.
KIRISHIMA HERE.
WHAT'S THE STATUS OF THE GETAWAY VEHICLE KANO
AND ORIHARA MAYA ARE THOUGHT TO BE RIDING IN?
AT THIS TIME, WE'RE STILL IN PURSUIT, AT A DISTANCE JUST WITHIN VISUAL RANGE.
THE VEHICLE HASN'T SHOWN ANY SIGN THEY'VE NOTICED OUR TAIL.

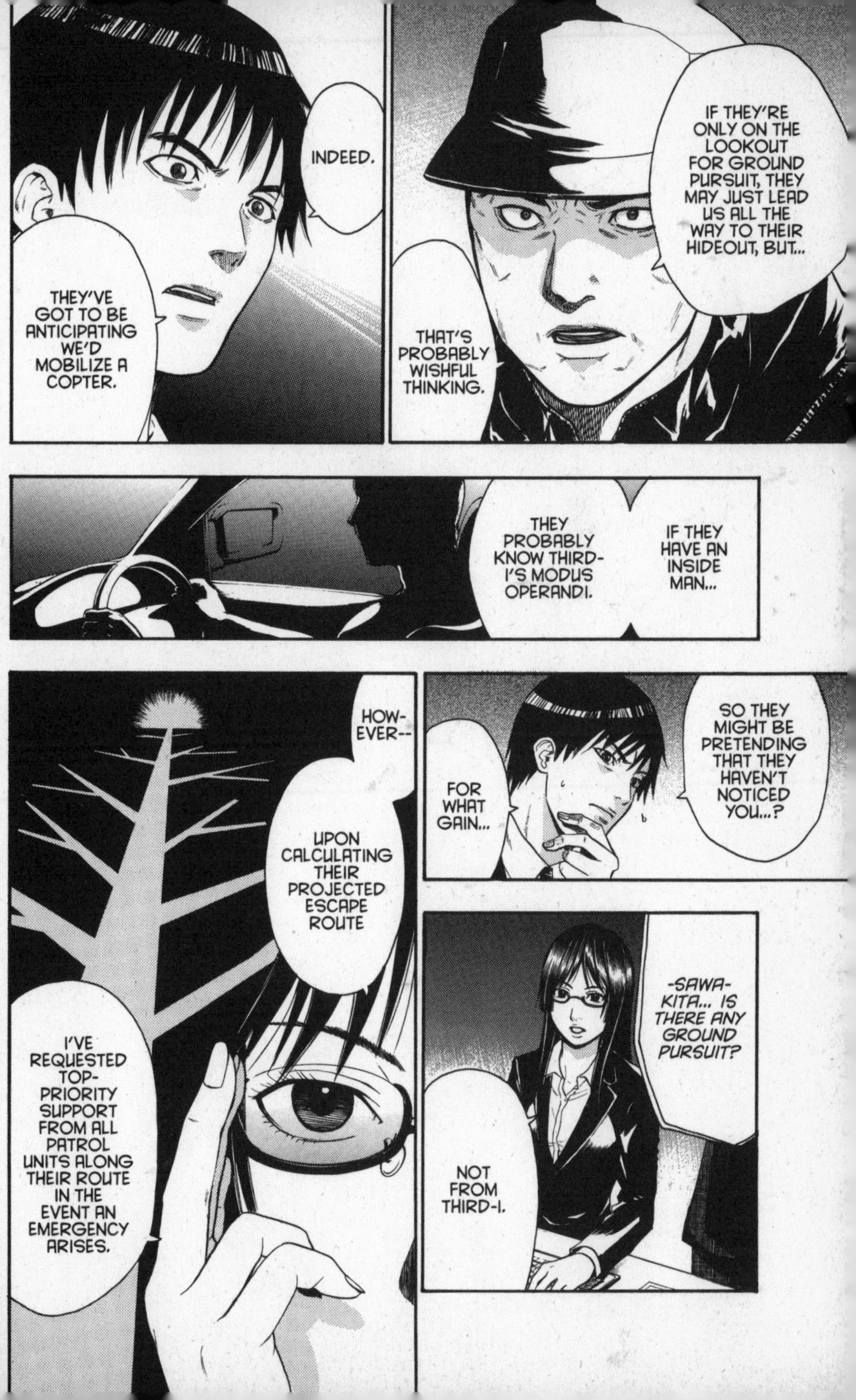
IF THEY'RE ONLY ON THE LOOKOUT FOR GROUND PURSUIT, THEY MAY JUST LEAD US ALL THE WAY TO THEIR HIDEOUT, BUT...
THAT'S PROBABLY WISHFUL THINKING.
INDEED.
THEY'VE GOT TO BE ANTICIPATING WE'D MOBILIZE A COPTER.
IF THEY HAVE AN INSIDE MAN...
THEY PROBABLY KNOW THIRD-I'S MODUS OPERANDI.
SO THEY MIGHT BE PRETENDING THAT THEY HAVEN'T NOTICED YOU...?
FOR WHAT GAIN...
-SAWA-KITA... IS THERE ANY GROUND PURSUIT?
NOT FROM THIRD-I.
HOW-EVER--
UPON CALCULATING THEIR PROJECTED ESCAPE ROUTE
I'VE REQUESTED TOP-PRIORITY SUPPORT FROM ALL PATROL UNITS ALONG THEIR ROUTE IN THE EVENT AN EMERGENCY ARISES.

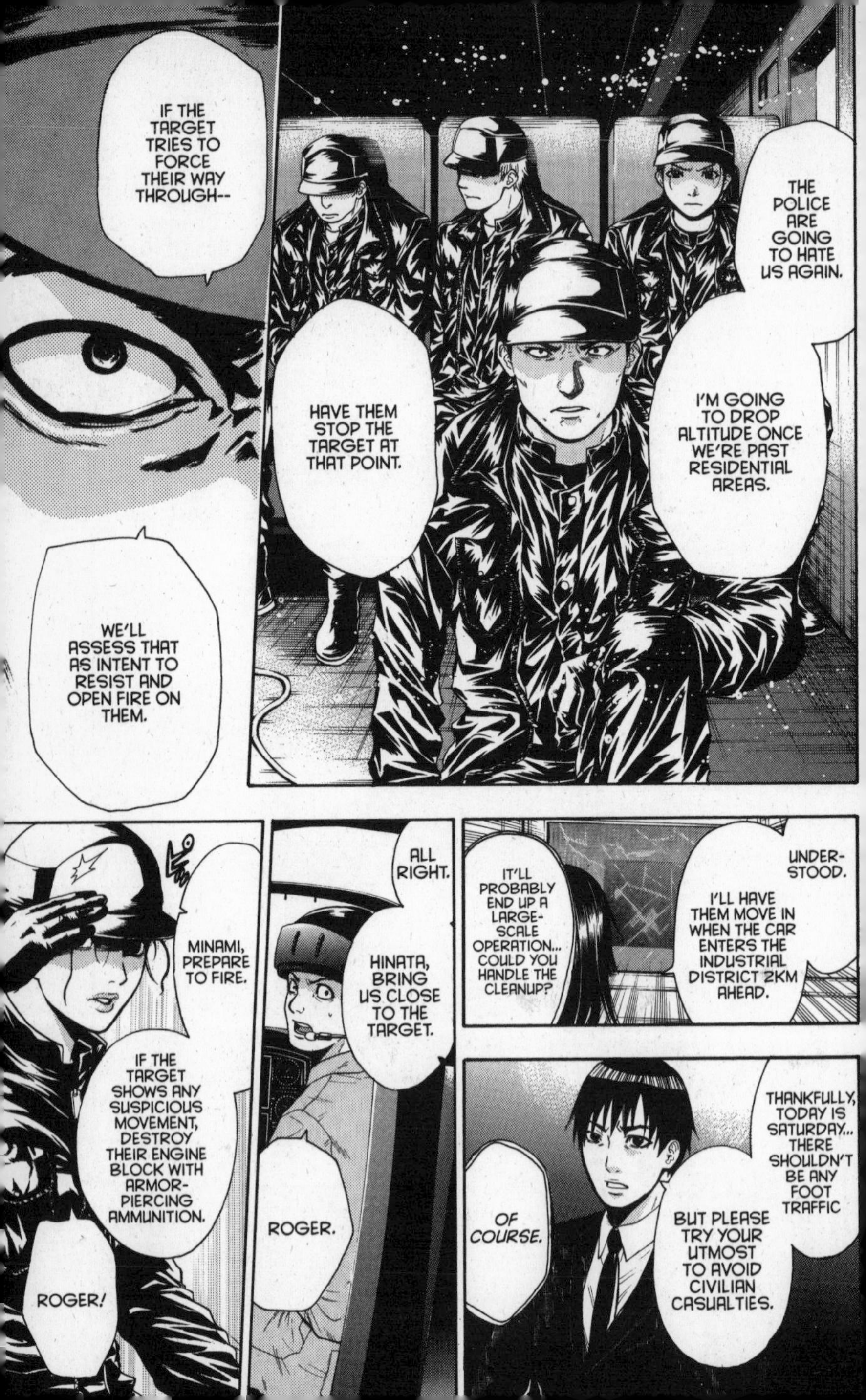
THE POLICE ARE GOING TO HATE US AGAIN.
I'M GOING TO DROP ALTITUDE ONCE WE'RE PAST RESIDENTIAL AREAS.
HAVE THEM STOP THE TARGET AT THAT POINT.
IF THE TARGET TRIES TO FORCE THEIR WAY THROUGH--
WE'LL ASSESS THAT AS INTENT TO RESIST AND OPEN FIRE ON THEM.
UNDER-STOOD.
I'LL HAVE THEM MOVE IN WHEN THE CAR ENTERS THE INDUSTRIAL DISTRICT 2KM AHEAD.
IT'LL PROBABLY END UP A LARGE-SCALE OPERATION... COULD YOU HANDLE THE CLEANUP?
THANKFULLY, TODAY IS SATURDAY... THERE SHOULDN'T BE ANY FOOT TRAFFIC
BUT PLEASE TRY YOUR UTMOST TO AVOID CIVILIAN CASUALTIES.
OF COURSE.
ALL RIGHT.
HINATA, BRING US CLOSE TO THE TARGET.
ROGER.
MINAMI, PREPARE TO FIRE.
IF THE TARGET SHOWS ANY SUSPICIOUS MOVEMENT, DESTROY THEIR ENGINE BLOCK WITH ARMOR-PIERCING AMMUNITION.
ROGER!

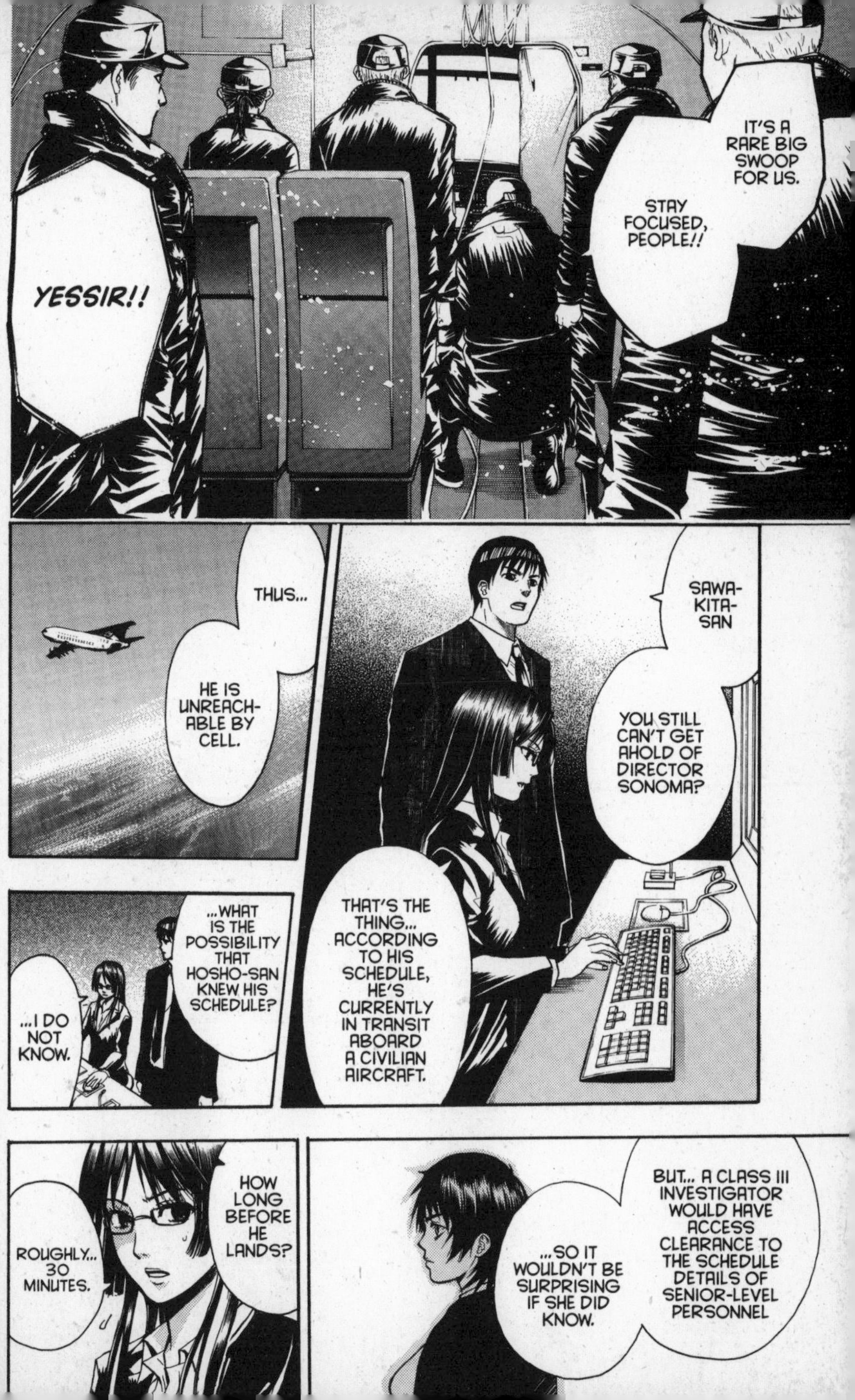
IT'S A RARE BIG SWOOP FOR US.
STAY FOCUSED, PEOPLE!!
YESSIR!!
SAWA-KITA-SAN
YOU STILL CAN'T GET AHOLD OF DIRECTOR SONOMA?
THAT'S THE THING... ACCORDING TO HIS SCHEDULE, HE'S CURRENTLY IN TRANSIT ABOARD A CIVILIAN AIRCRAFT.
THUS...
HE IS UNREACHABLE BY CELL.
...WHAT IS THE POSSIBILITY THAT HOSHO-SAN KNEW HIS SCHEDULE?
...I DO NOT KNOW.
BUT... A CLASS III INVESTIGATOR WOULD HAVE ACCESS CLEARANCE TO THE SCHEDULE DETAILS OF SENIOR-LEVEL PERSONNEL
...SO IT WOULDN'T BE SURPRISING IF SHE DID KNOW.
HOW LONG BEFORE HE LANDS?
ROUGHLY... 30 MINUTES.

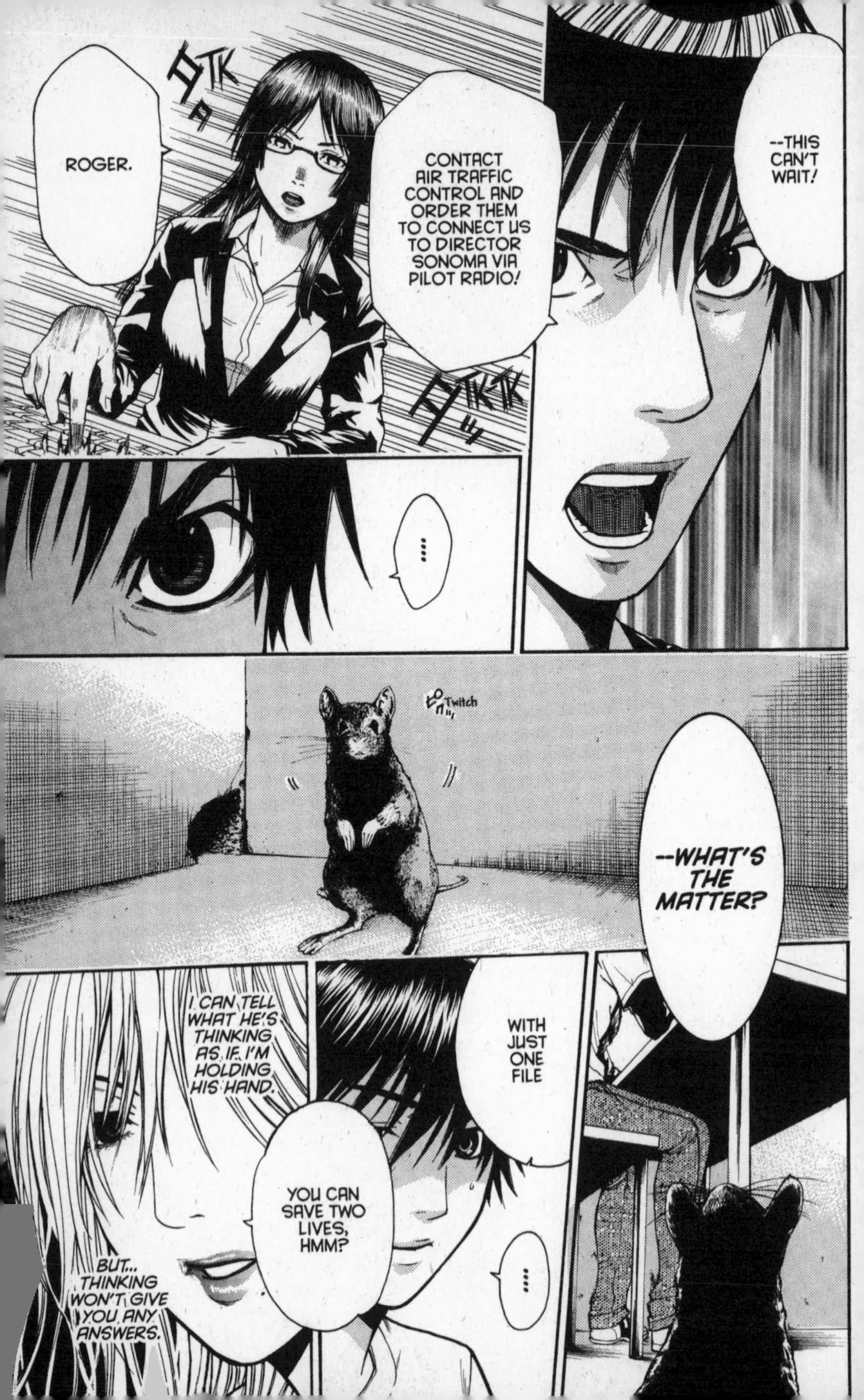
--THIS CAN'T WAIT!
CONTACT AIR TRAFFIC CONTROL AND ORDER THEM TO CONNECT US TO DIRECTOR SONOMA VIA PILOT RADIO!
TK
ROGER.
TK-TK
...
Twitch
--WHAT'S THE MATTER?
WITH JUST ONE FILE
YOU CAN SAVE TWO LIVES, HMM?
...
I CAN TELL WHAT HE'S THINKING AS IF I'M HOLDING HIS HAND.
BUT... THINKING WON'T GIVE YOU ANY ANSWERS.

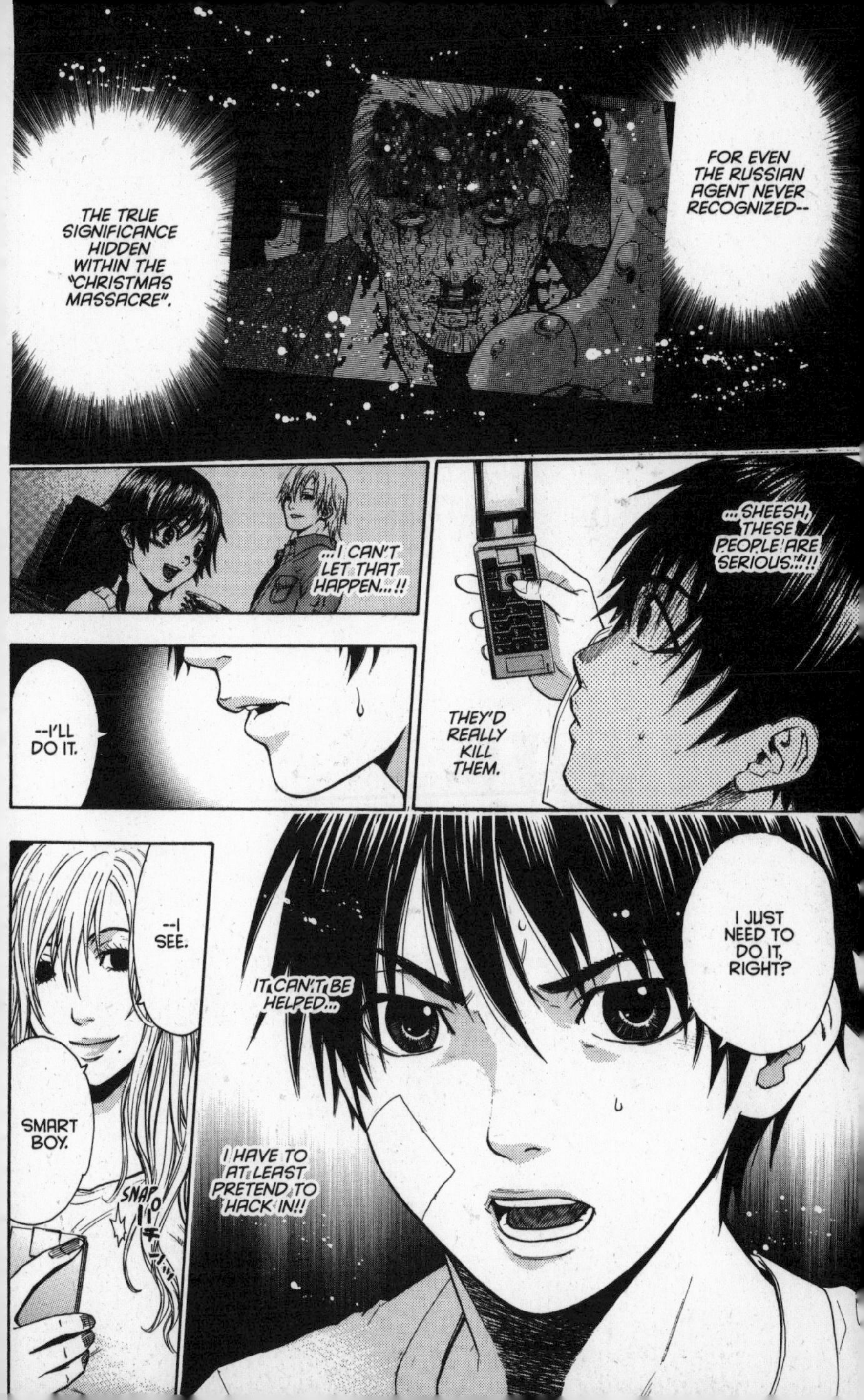
FOR EVEN THE RUSSIAN AGENT NEVER RECOGNIZED--
THE TRUE SIGNIFICANCE HIDDEN WITHIN THE "CHRISTMAS MASSACRE".
...SHEESH, THESE PEOPLE ARE SERIOUS...!!
THEY'D REALLY KILL THEM.
...I CAN'T LET THAT HAPPEN...!!
--I'LL DO IT.
I JUST NEED TO DO IT, RIGHT?
IT CAN'T BE HELPED...
I HAVE TO AT LEAST PRETEND TO HACK IN!!
--I SEE.
SMART BOY.
SNAP

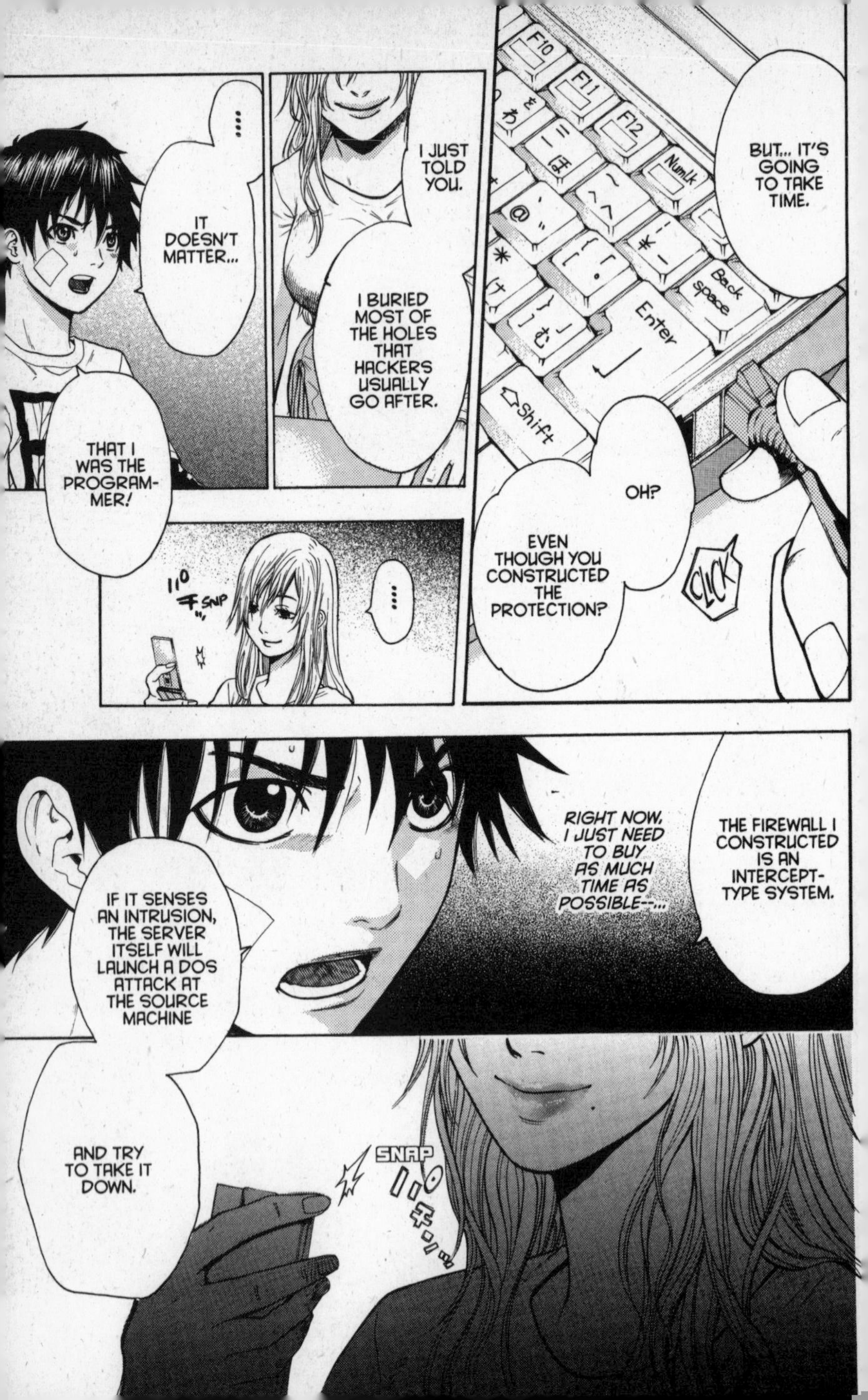
BUT... IT'S GOING TO TAKE TIME.
OH?
EVEN THOUGH YOU CONSTRUCTED THE PROTECTION?
CLICK
I JUST TOLD YOU.
I BURIED MOST OF THE HOLES THAT HACKERS USUALLY GO AFTER.
...
IT DOESN'T MATTER...
THAT I WAS THE PROGRAMMER!
...
SNP
THE FIREWALL I CONSTRUCTED IS AN INTERCEPT-TYPE SYSTEM.
RIGHT NOW, I JUST NEED TO BUY AS MUCH TIME AS POSSIBLE--...
IF IT SENSES AN INTRUSION, THE SERVER ITSELF WILL LAUNCH A DOS ATTACK AT THE SOURCE MACHINE
AND TRY TO TAKE IT DOWN.
SNAP

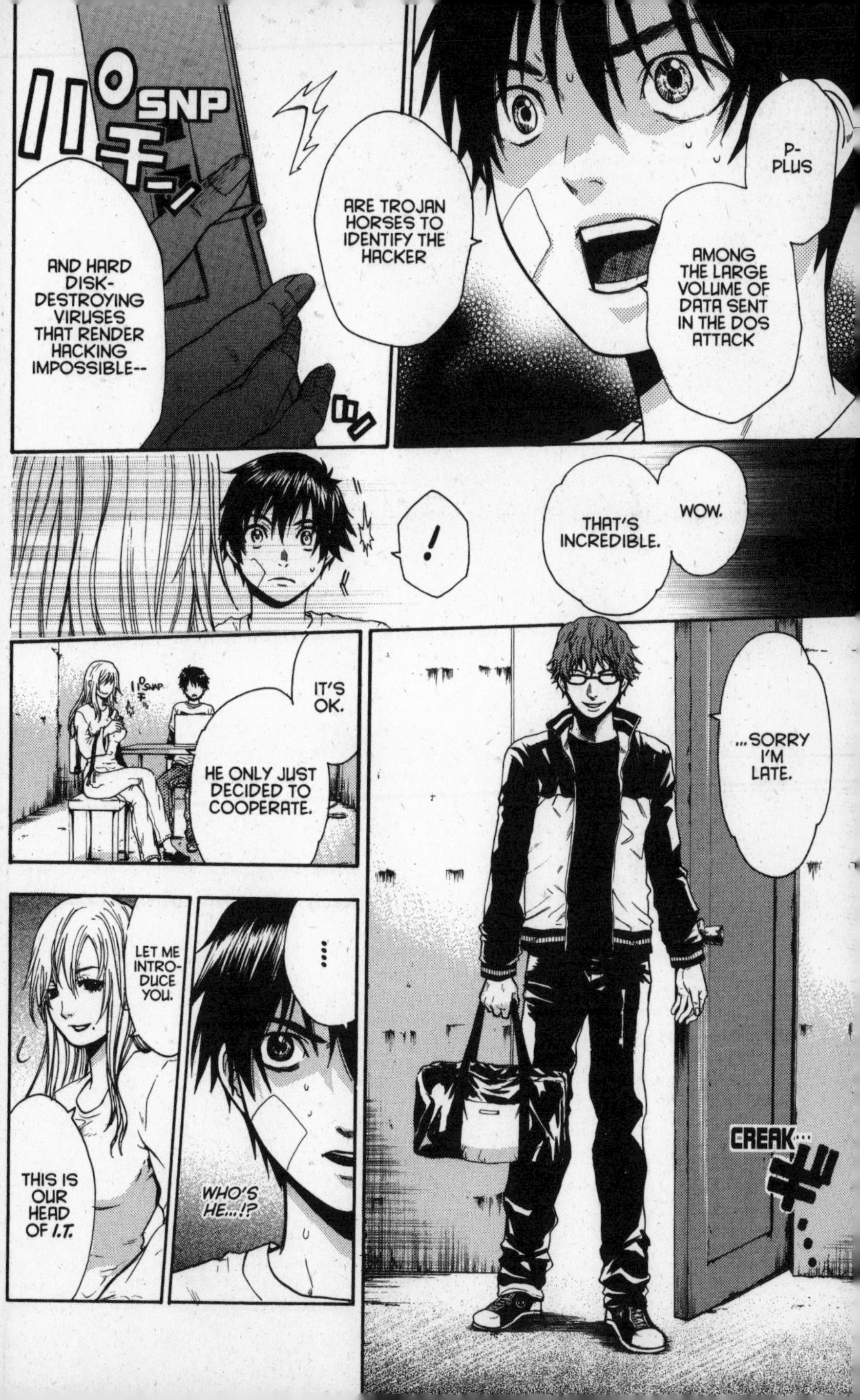
P-
PLUS
AMONG THE LARGE VOLUME OF DATA SENT IN THE DOS ATTACK
ARE TROJAN HORSES TO IDENTIFY THE HACKER
SNP
AND HARD DISK-DESTROYING VIRUSES THAT RENDER HACKING IMPOSSIBLE--
WOW.
THAT'S INCREDIBLE.
!
...SORRY I'M LATE.
CREAK...
SNAP
IT'S OK.
HE ONLY JUST DECIDED TO COOPERATE.
....
WHO'S HE...!?
LET ME INTRODUCE YOU.
THIS IS OUR HEAD OF *I.T.*

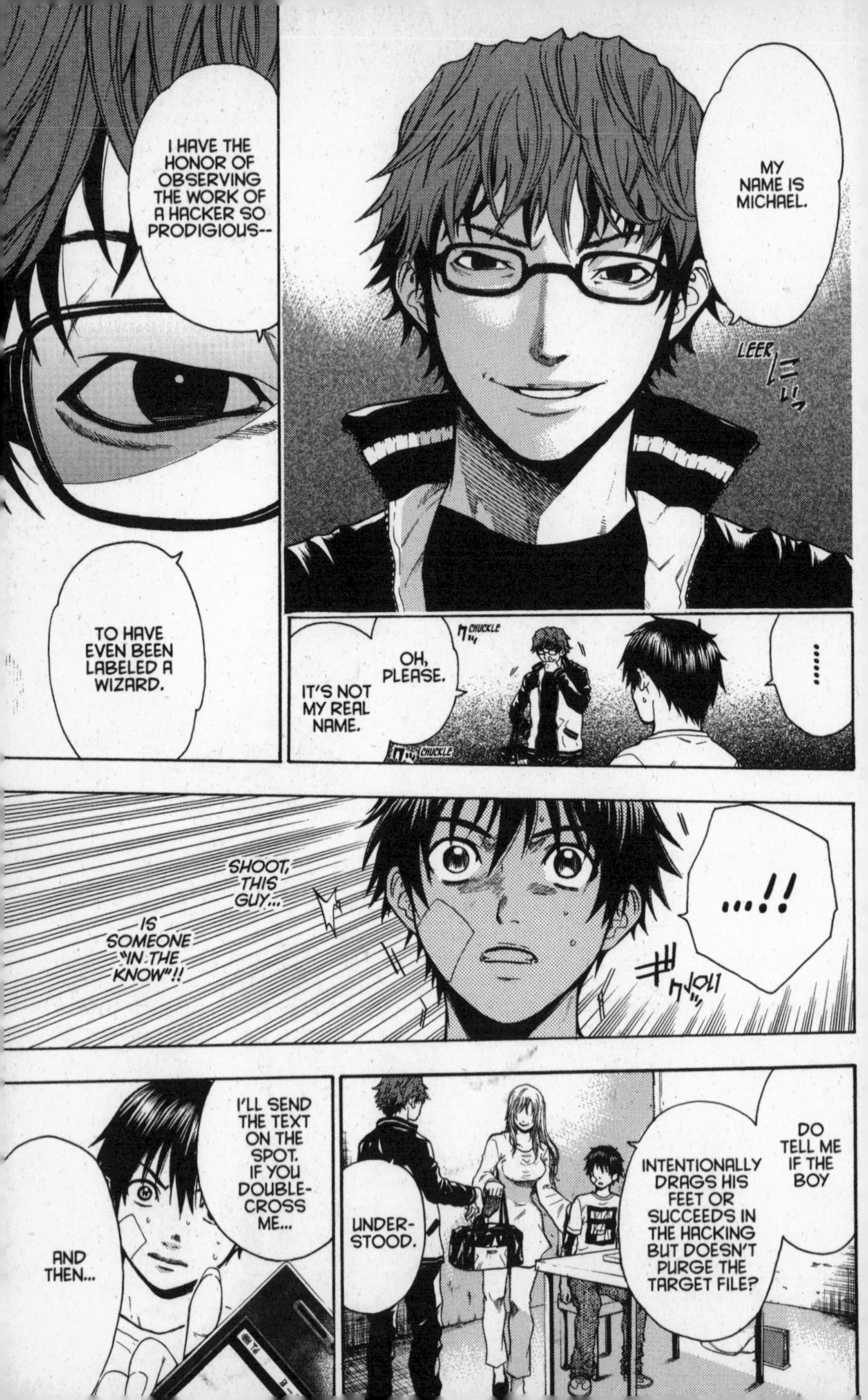
MY NAME IS MICHAEL.
LEER
.....
OH, PLEASE.
IT'S NOT MY REAL NAME.
CHUCKLE
CHUCKLE
I HAVE THE HONOR OF OBSERVING THE WORK OF A HACKER SO PRODIGIOUS--
TO HAVE EVEN BEEN LABELED A WIZARD.
...!!
SHOOT, THIS GUY...
IS SOMEONE "IN THE KNOW"!!
DO TELL ME IF THE BOY
INTENTIONALLY DRAGS HIS FEET OR SUCCEEDS IN THE HACKING BUT DOESN'T PURGE THE TARGET FILE?
UNDER-STOOD.
I'LL SEND THE TEXT ON THE SPOT. IF YOU DOUBLE-CROSS ME...
AND THEN...

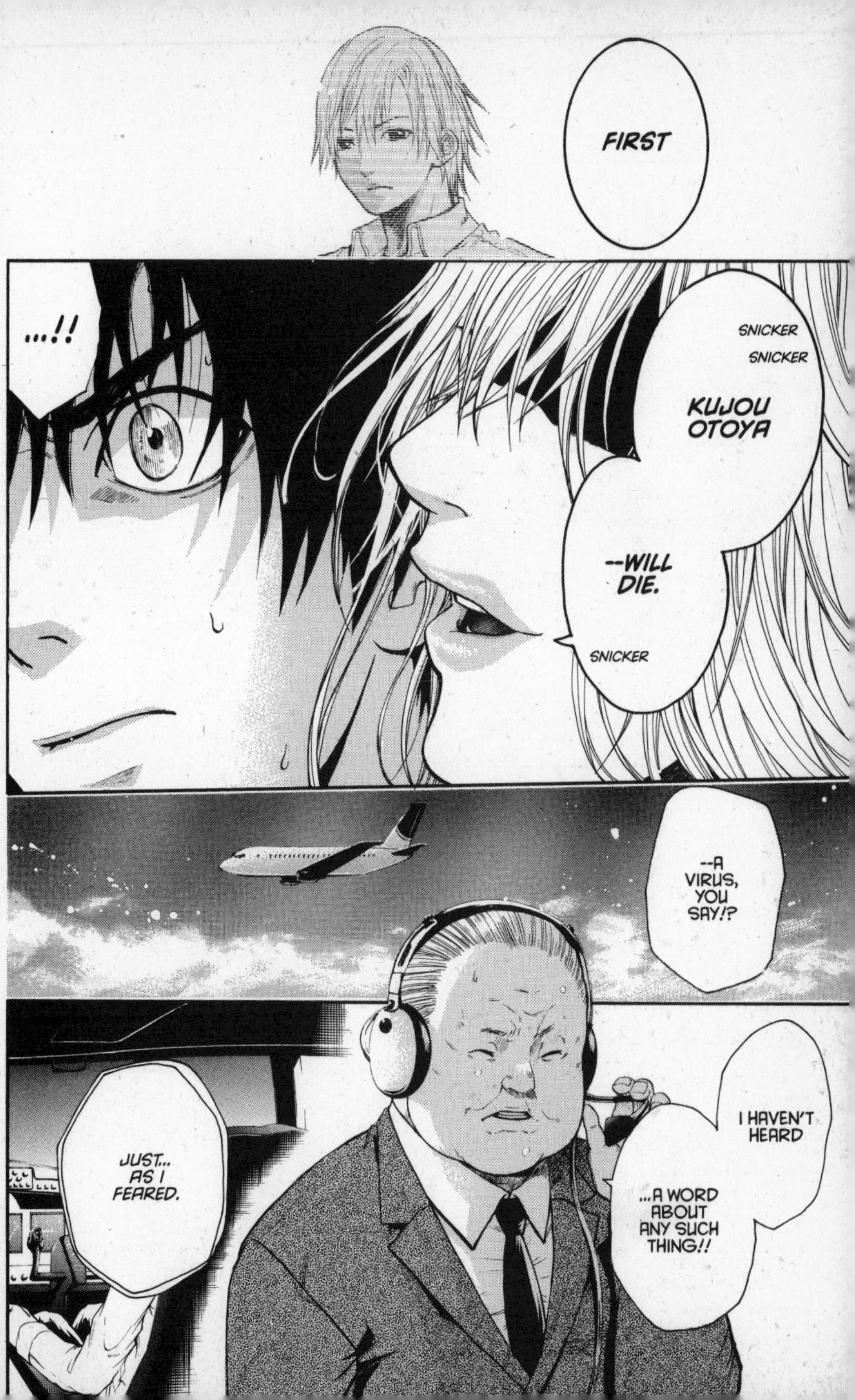
FIRST
SNICKER SNICKER
KUJOU OTOYA
--WILL DIE.
SNICKER
...!!
--A VIRUS, YOU SAY!?
I HAVEN'T HEARD
...A WORD ABOUT ANY SUCH THING!!
JUST... AS I FEARED.

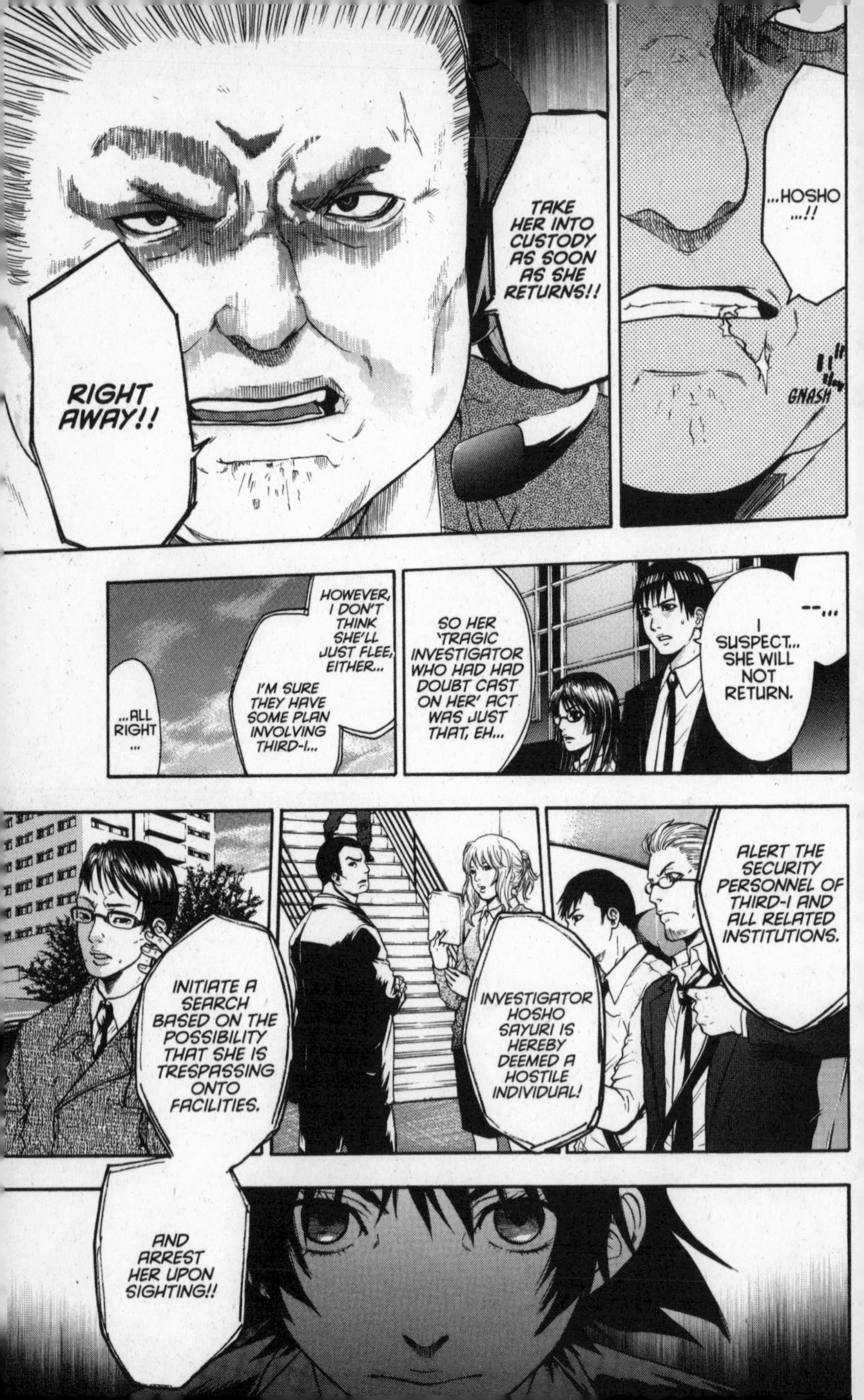
...HOSHO ...!!
GNASH
TAKE HER INTO CUSTODY AS SOON AS SHE RETURNS!!
RIGHT AWAY!!
--...
I SUSPECT... SHE WILL NOT RETURN.
SO HER 'TRAGIC INVESTIGATOR WHO HAD HAD DOUBT CAST ON HER' ACT WAS JUST THAT, EH...
HOWEVER, I DON'T THINK SHE'LL JUST FLEE, EITHER...
I'M SURE THEY HAVE SOME PLAN INVOLVING THIRD-I...
...ALL RIGHT ...
ALERT THE SECURITY PERSONNEL OF THIRD-I AND ALL RELATED INSTITUTIONS.
INVESTIGATOR HOSHO SAYURI IS HEREBY DEEMED A HOSTILE INDIVIDUAL!
INITIATE A SEARCH BASED ON THE POSSIBILITY THAT SHE IS TRESPASSING ONTO FACILITIES.
AND ARREST HER UPON SIGHTING!!

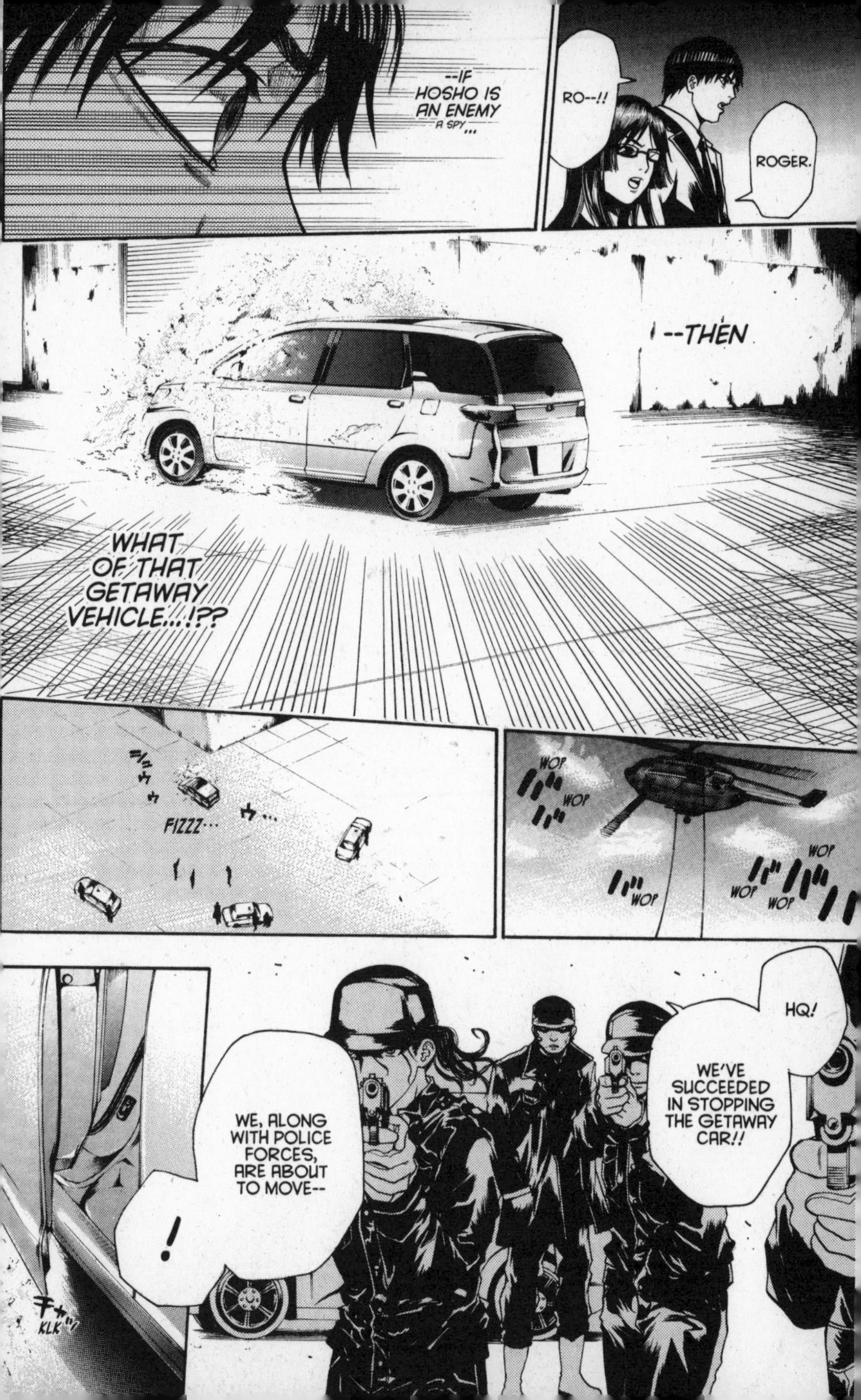
RO--!!
ROGER.
--IF HOSHO IS AN ENEMY A SPY...
--THEN
WHAT OF THAT GETAWAY VEHICLE...!??
WOP
WOP
WOP
WOP
WOP
WOP
FIZZZ...
HQ!
WE'VE SUCCEEDED IN STOPPING THE GETAWAY CAR!!
WE, ALONG WITH POLICE FORCES, ARE ABOUT TO MOVE--
!
KLK

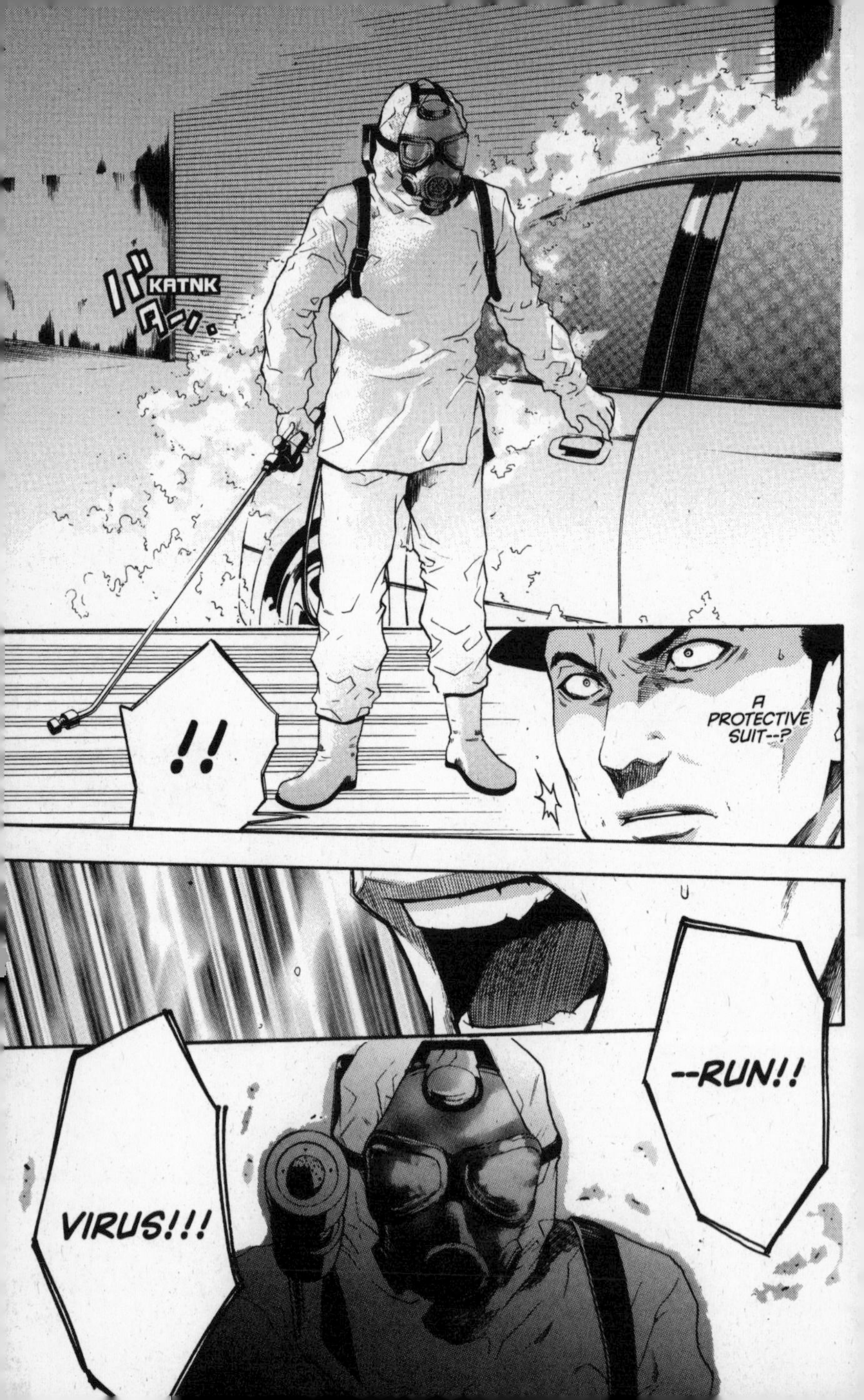
KATNK
A PROTECTIVE SUIT--?
!!
--RUN!!
VIRUS!!!

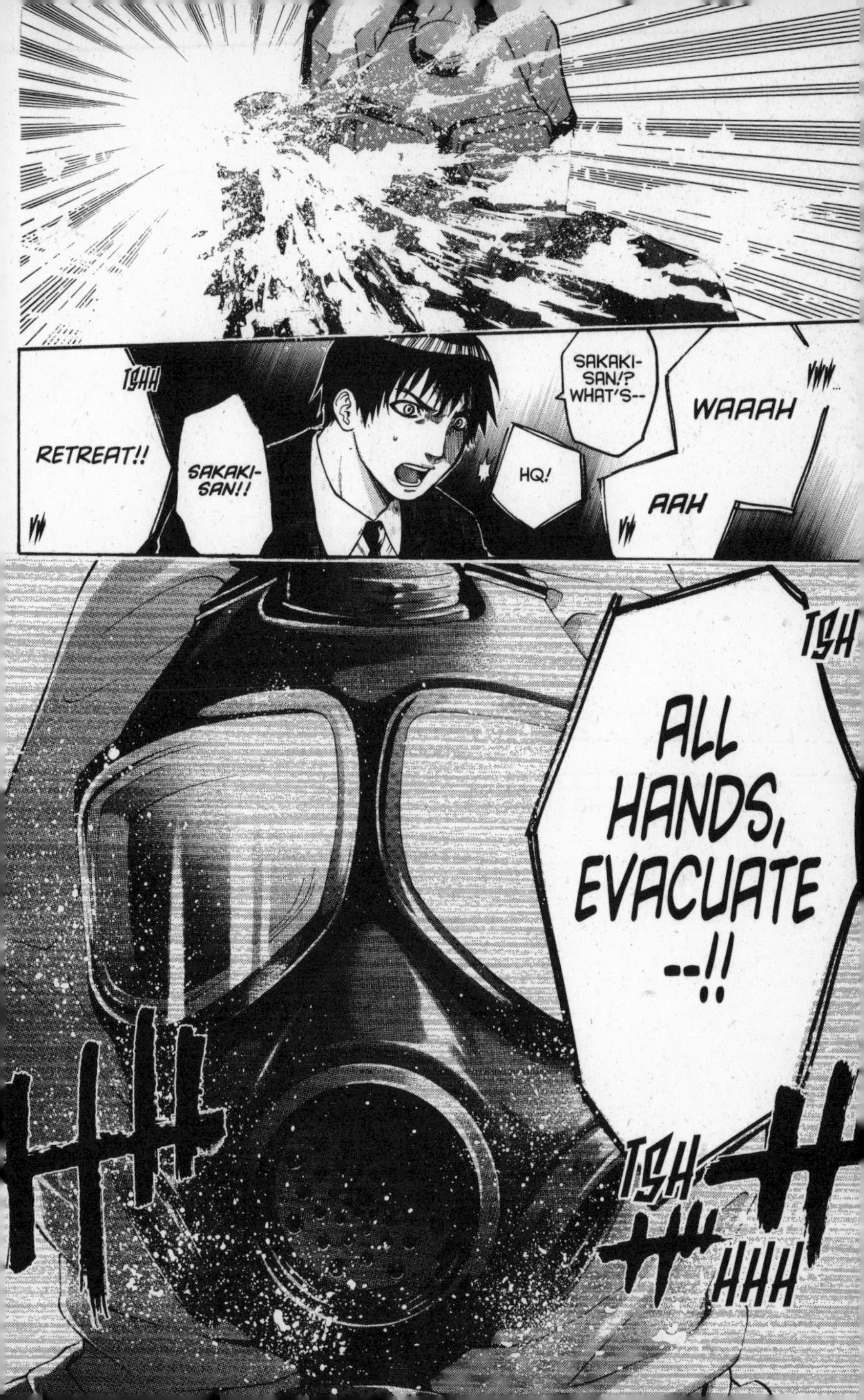
VVV...
WAAAH
AAH
VV
SAKAKI-SAN!? WHAT'S--
HQ!
SAKAKI-SAN!!
TSHH
RETREAT!!
VV
TSH
ALL HANDS, EVACUATE --!!
TSH
HHH

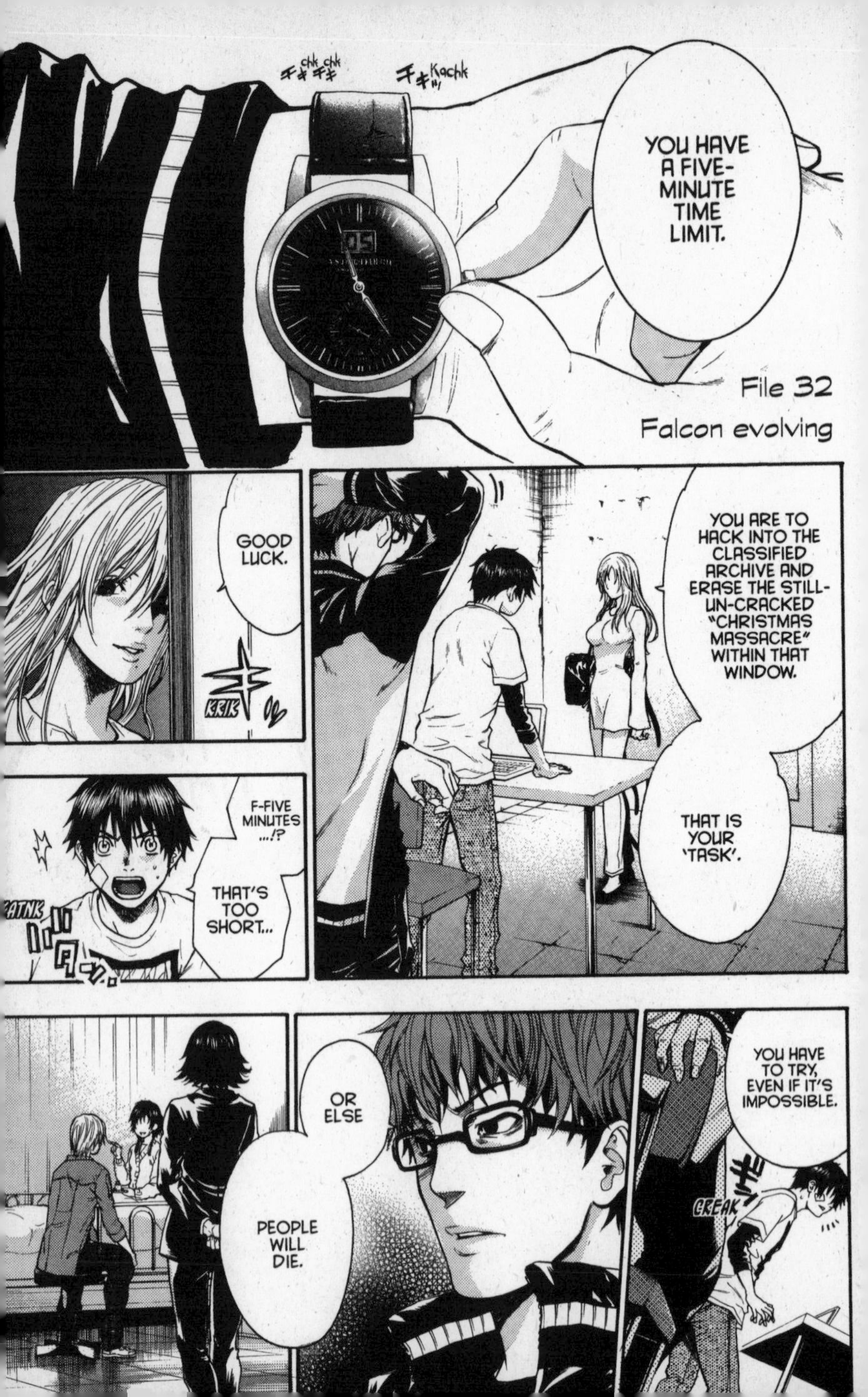
chk chk
Kachk
YOU HAVE A FIVE-MINUTE TIME LIMIT.
File 32
Falcon evolving
YOU ARE TO HACK INTO THE CLASSIFIED ARCHIVE AND ERASE THE STILL-UN-CRACKED "CHRISTMAS MASSACRE" WITHIN THAT WINDOW.
THAT IS YOUR 'TASK'.
GOOD LUCK.
KRIK
F-FIVE MINUTES ...!?
THAT'S TOO SHORT...
YOU HAVE TO TRY, EVEN IF IT'S IMPOSSIBLE.
CREAK
OR ELSE
PEOPLE WILL DIE.

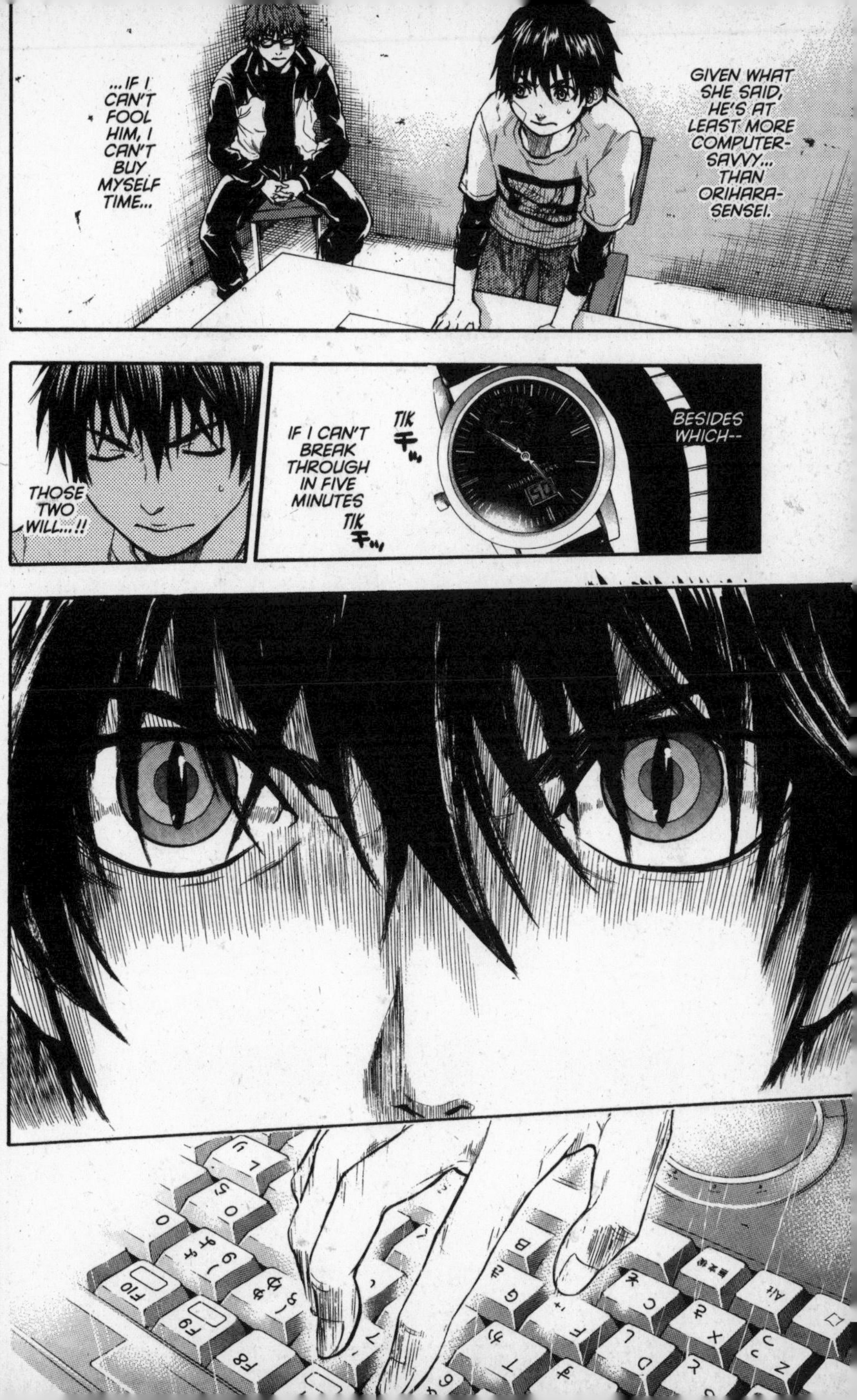
GIVEN WHAT SHE SAID, HE'S AT LEAST MORE COMPUTER-SAVVY... THAN ORIHARA-SENSEI.
...IF I CAN'T FOOL HIM, I CAN'T BUY MYSELF TIME...
BESIDES WHICH--
TIK
IF I CAN'T BREAK THROUGH IN FIVE MINUTES
TIK
THOSE TWO WILL...!!

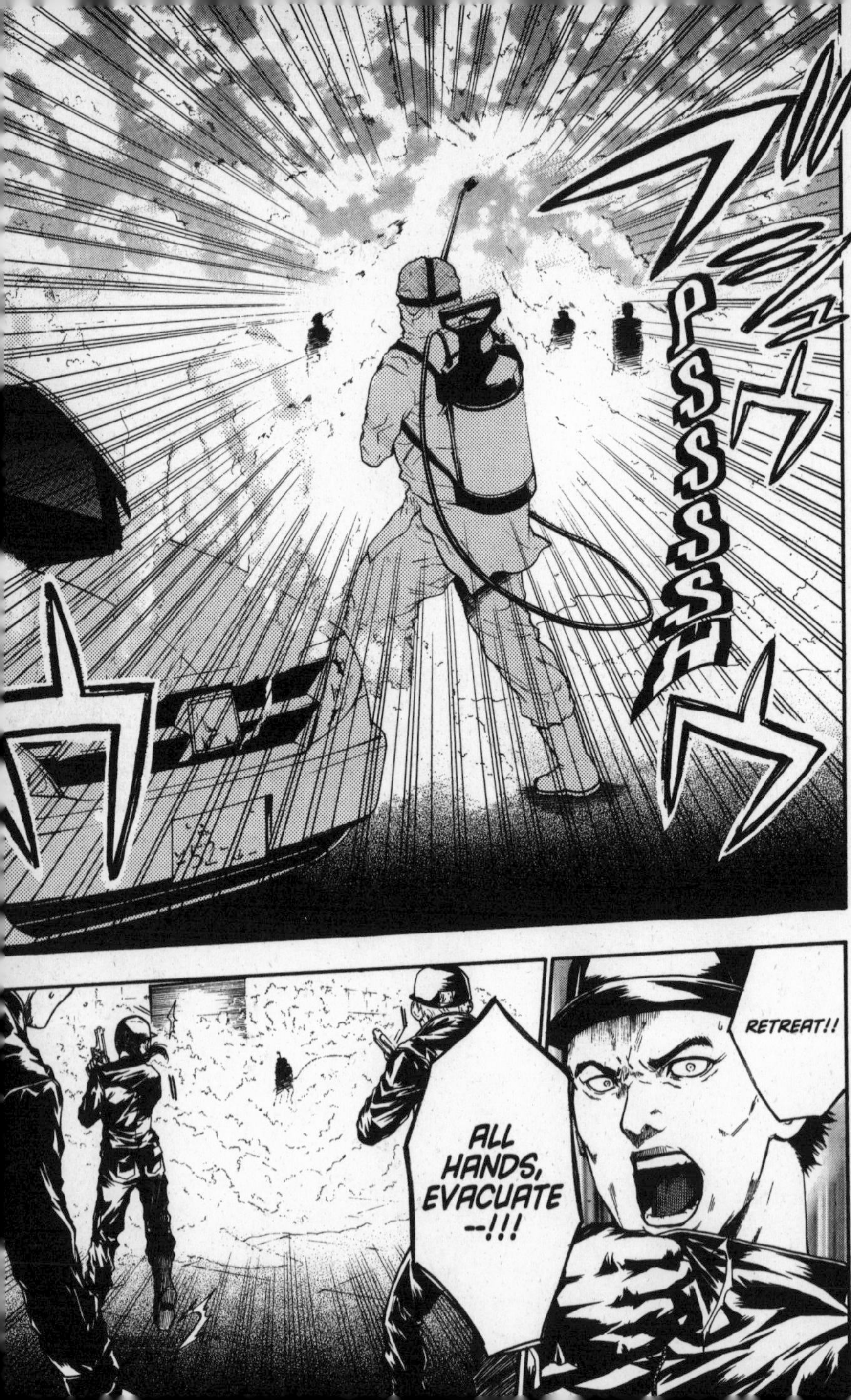
PSSSSH
RETREAT!!
ALL HANDS, EVACUATE --!!!

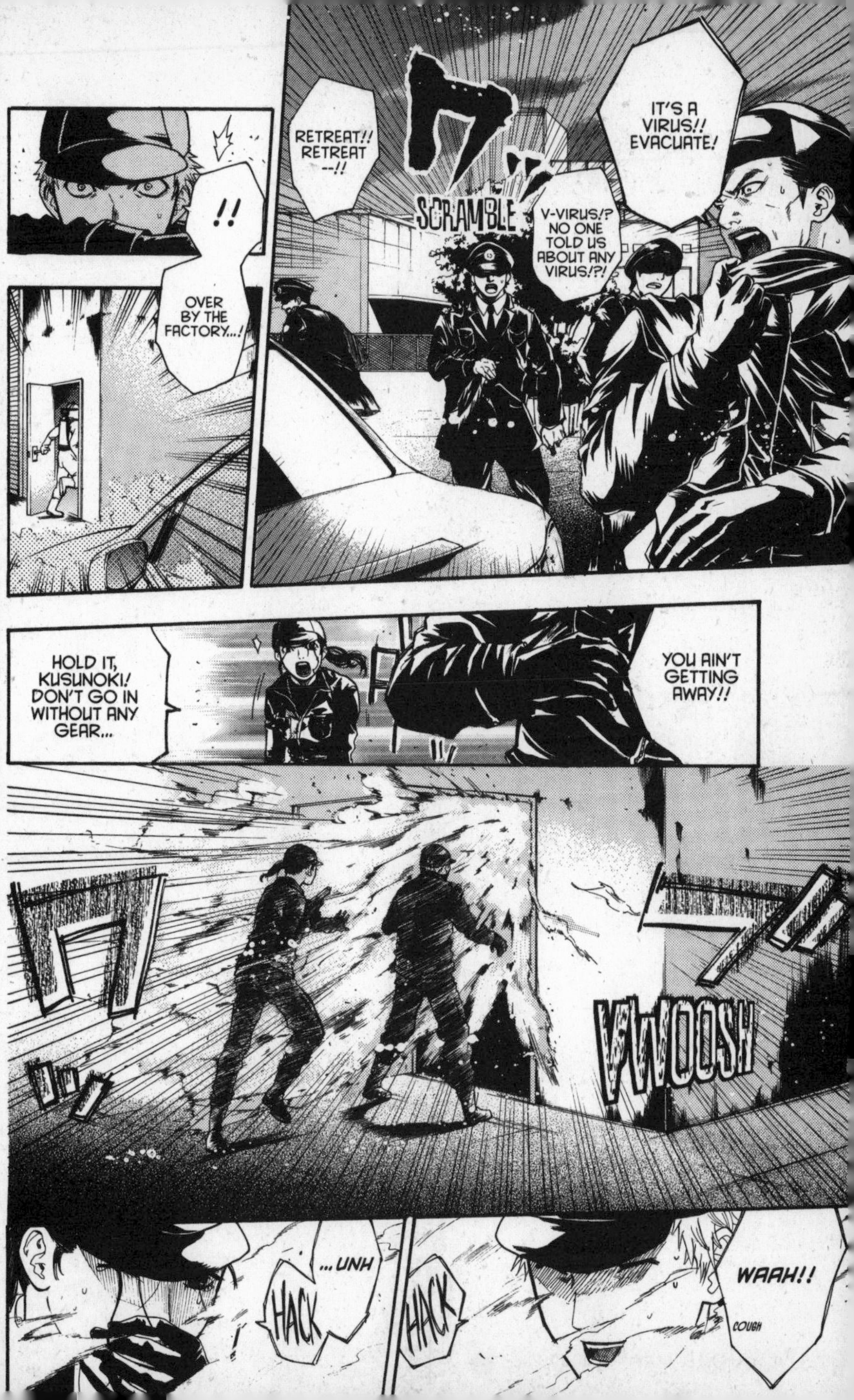
IT'S A VIRUS!! EVACUATE!
V-VIRUS!? NO ONE TOLD US ABOUT ANY VIRUS!?!
RETREAT!! RETREAT --!!
SCRAMBLE
!!
OVER BY THE FACTORY...!
YOU AIN'T GETTING AWAY!!
HOLD IT, KUSUNOKI! DON'T GO IN WITHOUT ANY GEAR...
VWOOSH
WAAH!!
COUGH
HACK
...UNH
HACK

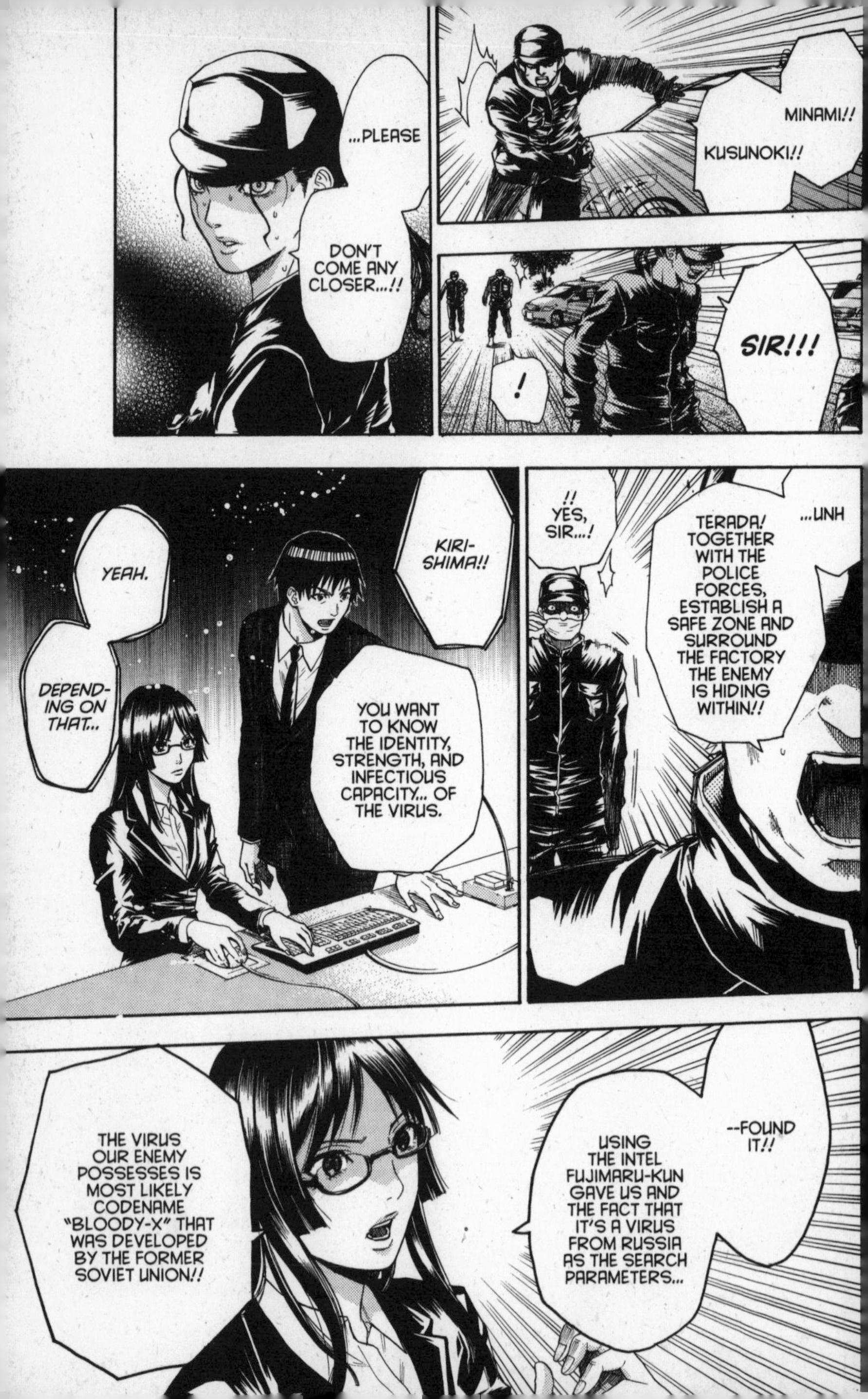
MINAMI!!
KUSUNOKI!!
SIR!!!
!
...PLEASE
DON'T COME ANY CLOSER...!!
...UNH
TERADA! TOGETHER WITH THE POLICE FORCES, ESTABLISH A SAFE ZONE AND SURROUND THE FACTORY THE ENEMY IS HIDING WITHIN!!
!! YES, SIR...!
KIRI-SHIMA!!
YOU WANT TO KNOW THE IDENTITY, STRENGTH, AND INFECTIOUS CAPACITY... OF THE VIRUS.
YEAH.
DEPEND-ING ON THAT...
--FOUND IT!!
USING THE INTEL FUJIMARU-KUN GAVE US AND THE FACT THAT IT'S A VIRUS FROM RUSSIA AS THE SEARCH PARAMETERS...
THE VIRUS OUR ENEMY POSSESSES IS MOST LIKELY CODENAME "BLOODY-X" THAT WAS DEVELOPED BY THE FORMER SOVIET UNION!!

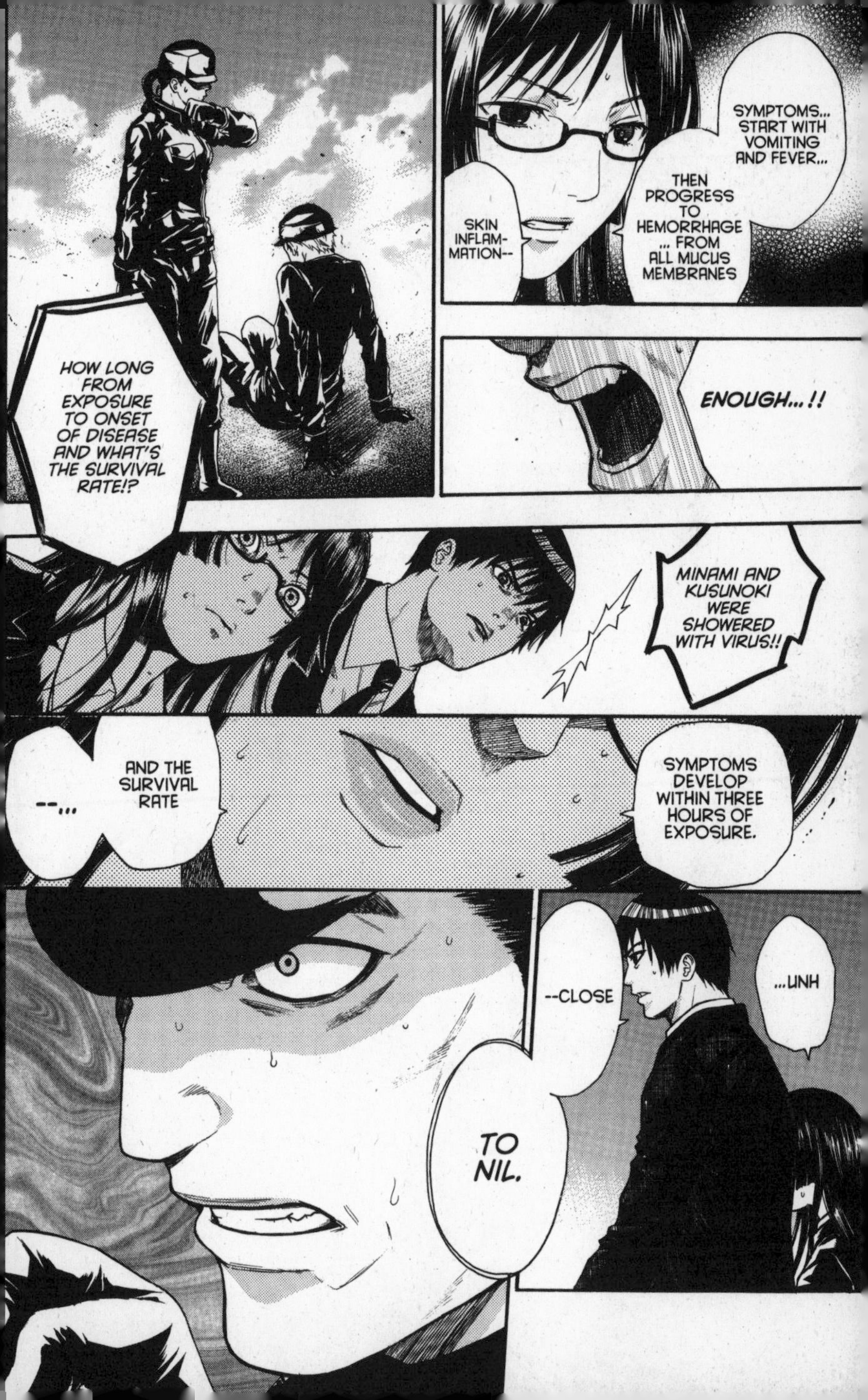
SYMPTOMS... START WITH VOMITING AND FEVER...
THEN PROGRESS TO HEMORRHAGE ... FROM ALL MUCUS MEMBRANES
SKIN INFLAMMATION--
ENOUGH...!!
HOW LONG FROM EXPOSURE TO ONSET OF DISEASE AND WHAT'S THE SURVIVAL RATE!?
MINAMI AND KUSUNOKI WERE SHOWERED WITH VIRUS!!
SYMPTOMS DEVELOP WITHIN THREE HOURS OF EXPOSURE.
AND THE SURVIVAL RATE
--...
...UNH
--CLOSE
TO NIL.

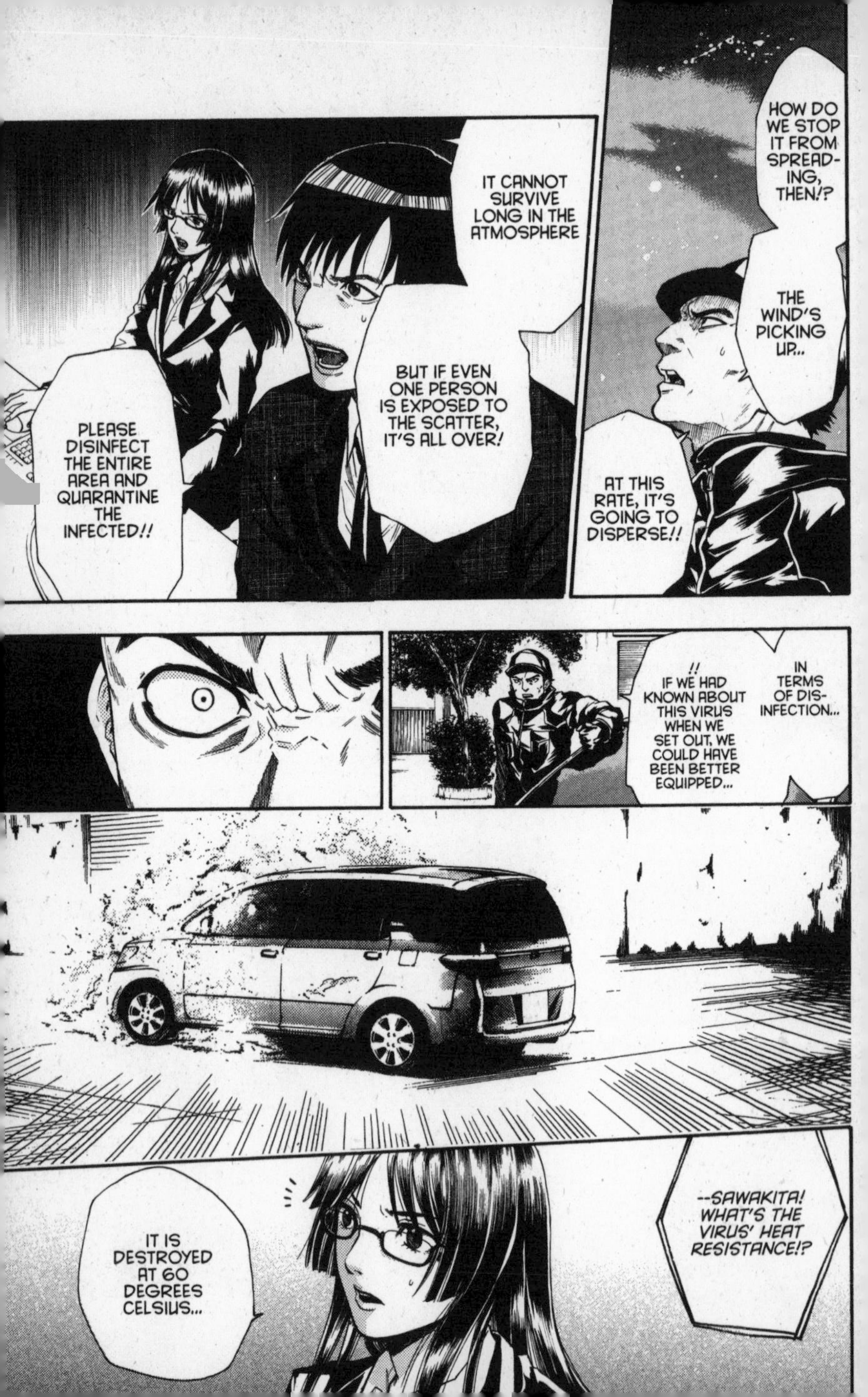
HOW DO WE STOP IT FROM SPREADING, THEN!?
THE WIND'S PICKING UP...
AT THIS RATE, IT'S GOING TO DISPERSE!!
IT CANNOT SURVIVE LONG IN THE ATMOSPHERE
BUT IF EVEN ONE PERSON IS EXPOSED TO THE SCATTER, IT'S ALL OVER!
PLEASE DISINFECT THE ENTIRE AREA AND QUARANTINE THE INFECTED!!
IN TERMS OF DISINFECTION...
!! IF WE HAD KNOWN ABOUT THIS VIRUS WHEN WE SET OUT, WE COULD HAVE BEEN BETTER EQUIPPED...
--SAWAKITA! WHAT'S THE VIRUS' HEAT RESISTANCE!?
IT IS DESTROYED AT 60 DEGREES CELSIUS...

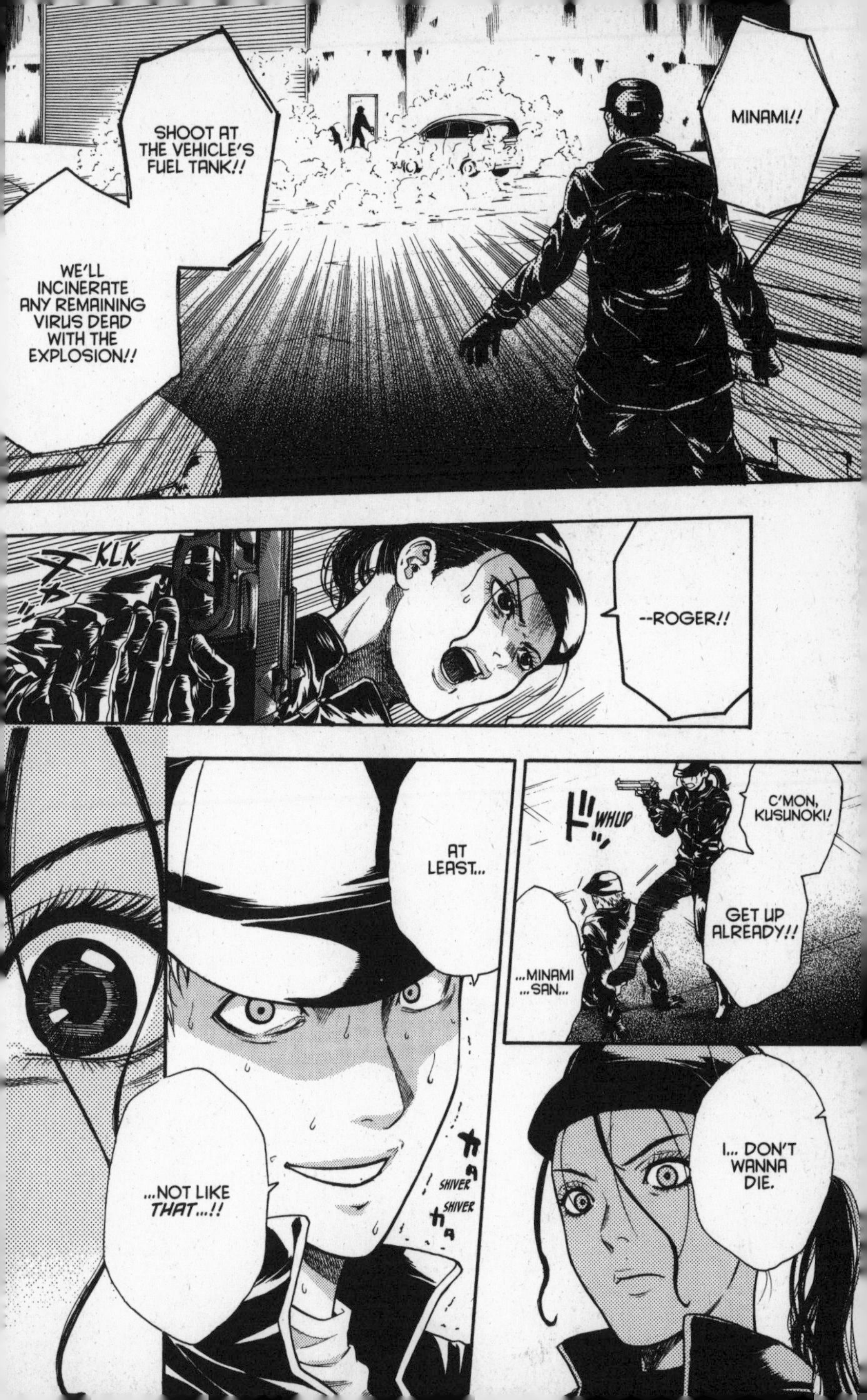
MINAMI!!
SHOOT AT THE VEHICLE'S FUEL TANK!!
WE'LL INCINERATE ANY REMAINING VIRUS DEAD WITH THE EXPLOSION!!
--ROGER!!
KLK
C'MON, KUSUNOKI!
WHUP
GET UP ALREADY!!
...MINAMI ...SAN...
I... DON'T WANNA DIE.
AT LEAST...
SHIVER
SHIVER
...NOT LIKE *THAT*...!!

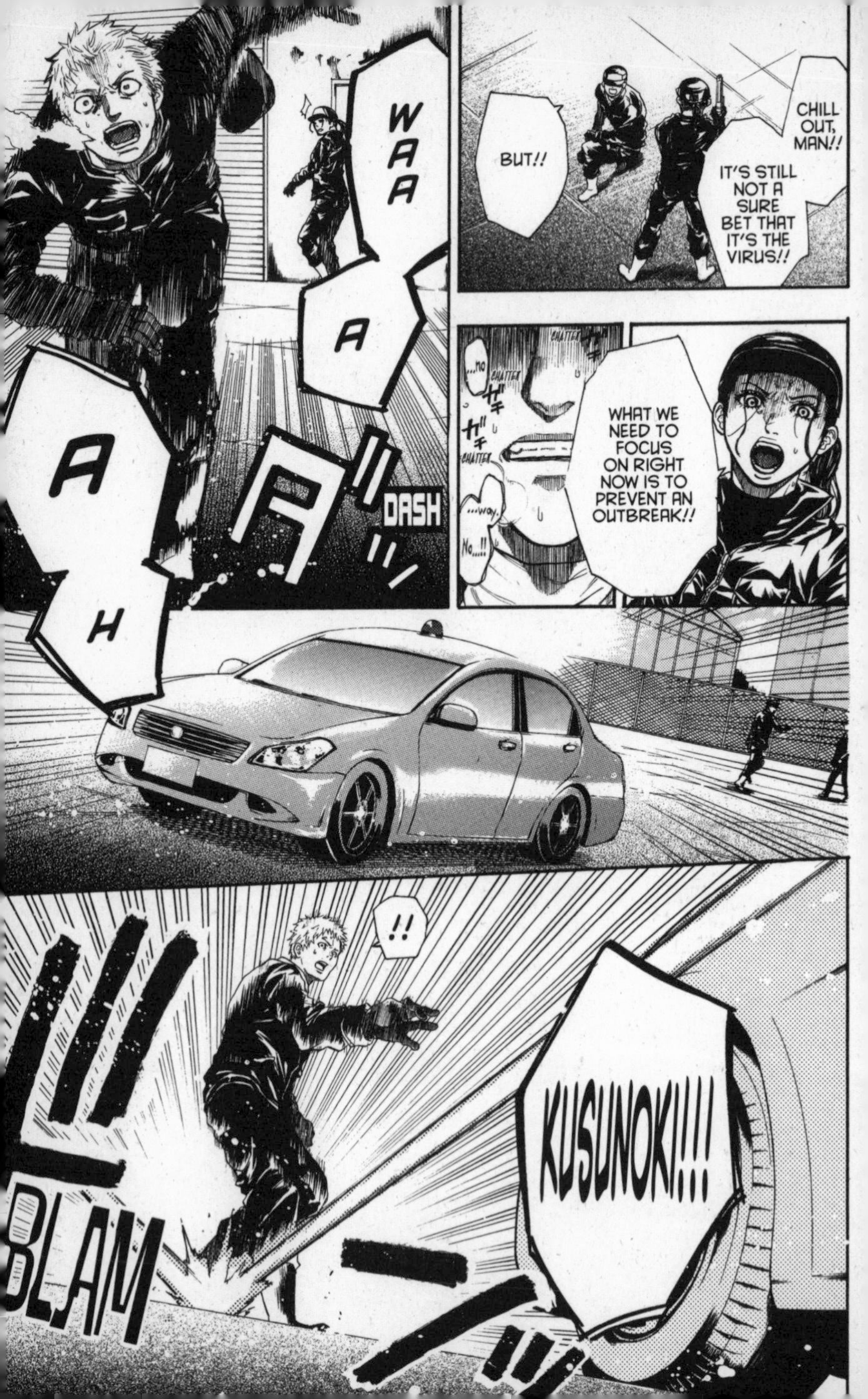
CHILL OUT, MAN!!
IT'S STILL NOT A SURE BET THAT IT'S THE VIRUS!!
BUT!!
WHAT WE NEED TO FOCUS ON RIGHT NOW IS TO PREVENT AN OUTBREAK!!
...no
CHATTER
CHATTER
...way.
No...!!
WAA
A
A
H
DASH
!!
KUSUNOKI!!!
BLAM

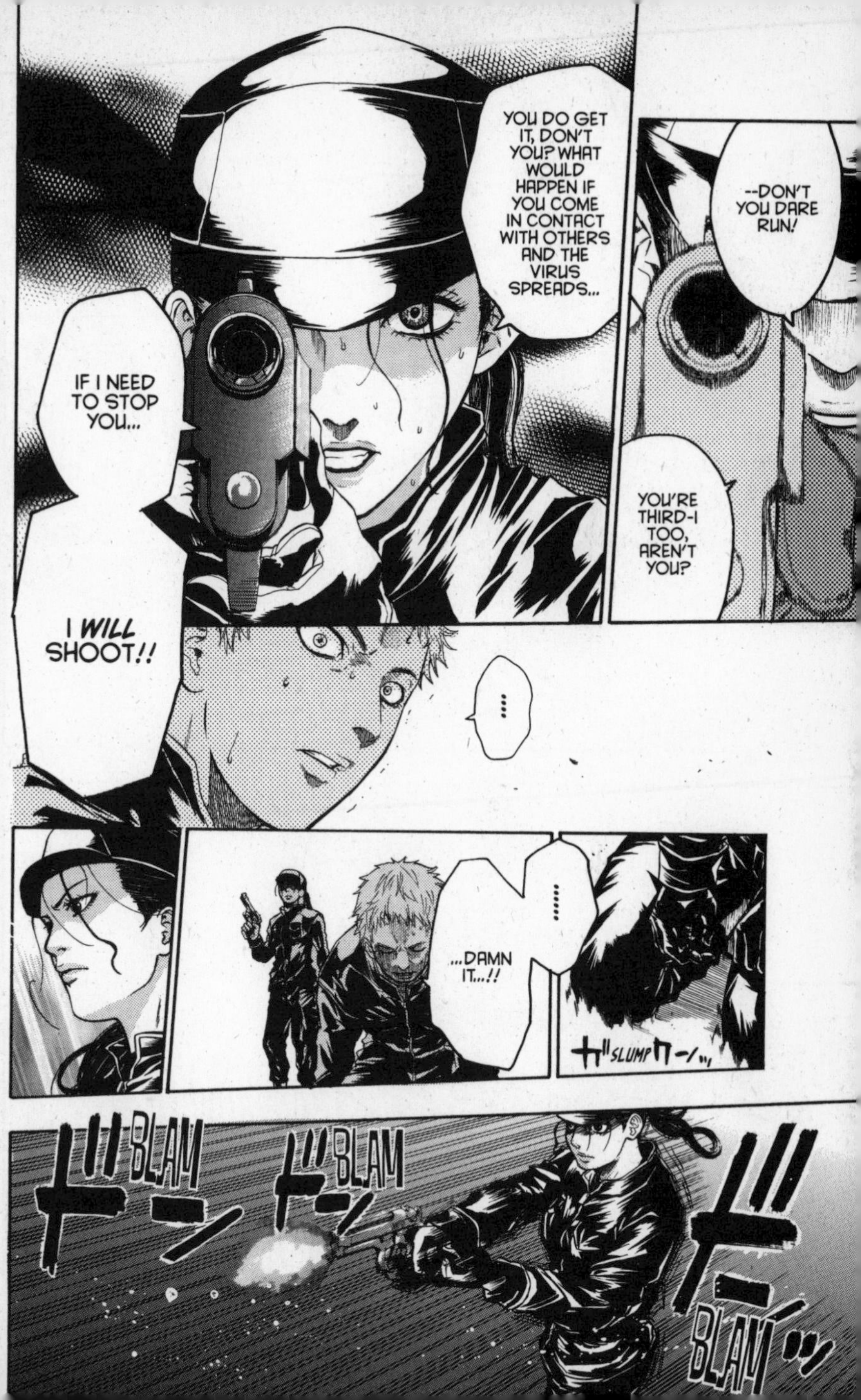
--DON'T YOU DARE RUN!
YOU'RE THIRD-I TOO, AREN'T YOU?
YOU DO GET IT, DON'T YOU? WHAT WOULD HAPPEN IF YOU COME IN CONTACT WITH OTHERS AND THE VIRUS SPREADS...
IF I NEED TO STOP YOU...
I *WILL* SHOOT!!
....
SLUMP
......
...DAMN IT...!!
BLAM
BLAM
BLAM

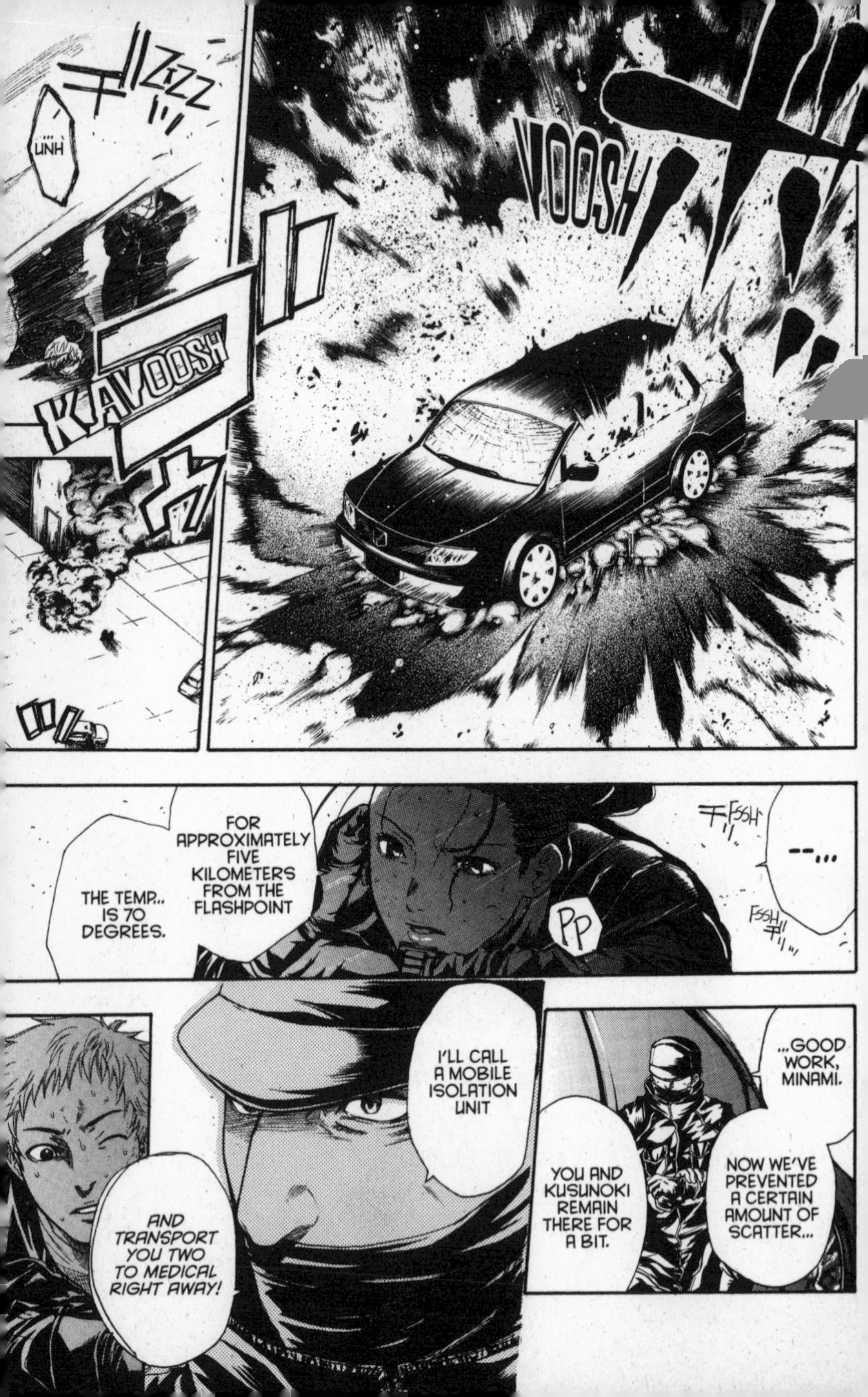
VOOSH
...UNH
ZIZZ
KAVOOSH
--...
FSSH
FSSH
PP
FOR APPROXIMATELY FIVE KILOMETERS FROM THE FLASHPOINT
THE TEMP... IS 70 DEGREES.
...GOOD WORK, MINAMI.
NOW WE'VE PREVENTED A CERTAIN AMOUNT OF SCATTER...
YOU AND KUSUNOKI REMAIN THERE FOR A BIT.
I'LL CALL A MOBILE ISOLATION UNIT
AND TRANSPORT YOU TWO TO MEDICAL RIGHT AWAY!

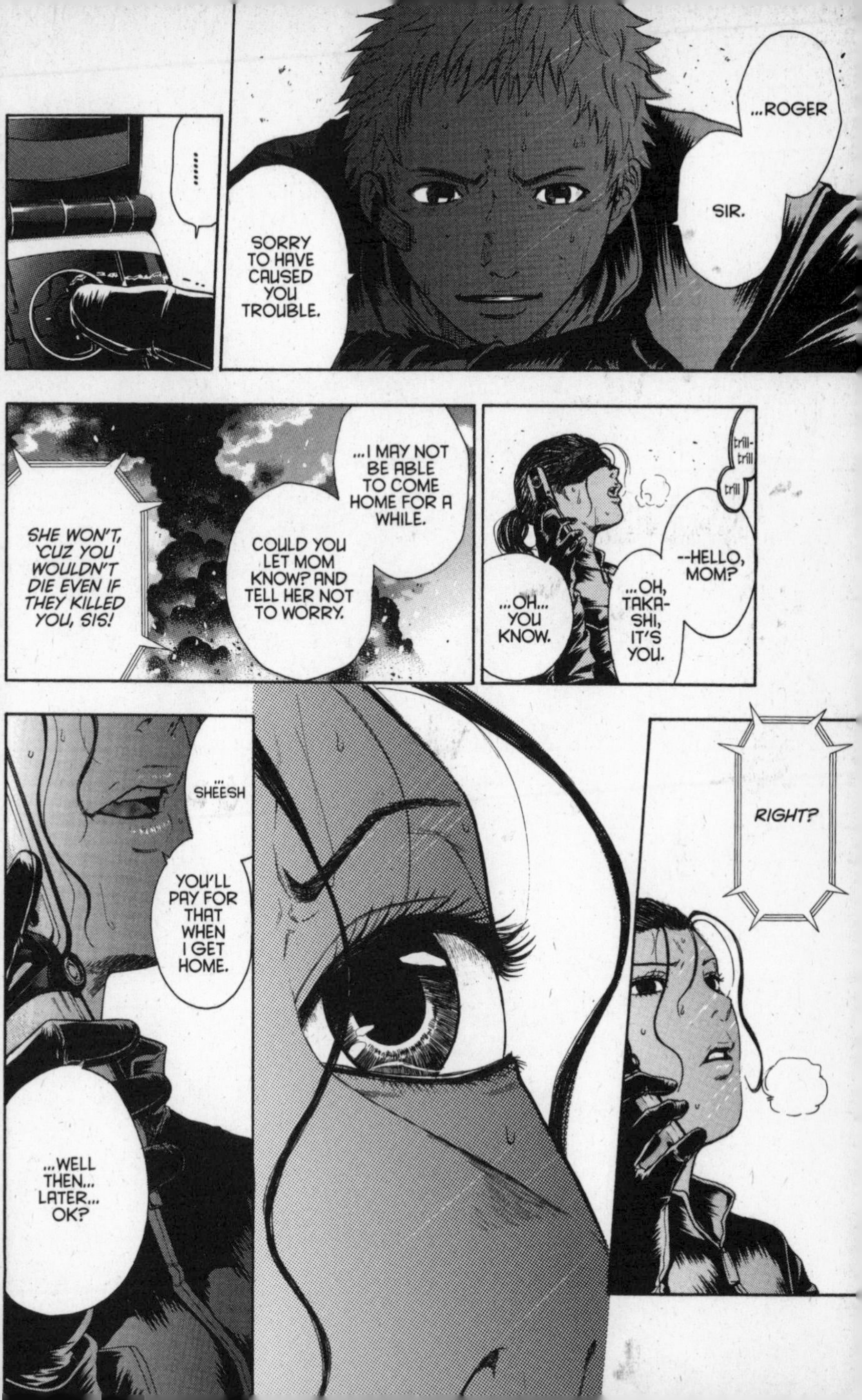
...ROGER
SIR.
SORRY TO HAVE CAUSED YOU TROUBLE.
......
trill-trill
trill
--HELLO, MOM?
...OH, TAKASHI, IT'S YOU.
...OH... YOU KNOW.
...I MAY NOT BE ABLE TO COME HOME FOR A WHILE.
COULD YOU LET MOM KNOW? AND TELL HER NOT TO WORRY.
SHE WON'T, 'CUZ YOU WOULDN'T DIE EVEN IF THEY KILLED YOU, SIS!
RIGHT?
...SHEESH
YOU'LL PAY FOR THAT WHEN I GET HOME.
...WELL THEN... LATER... OK?

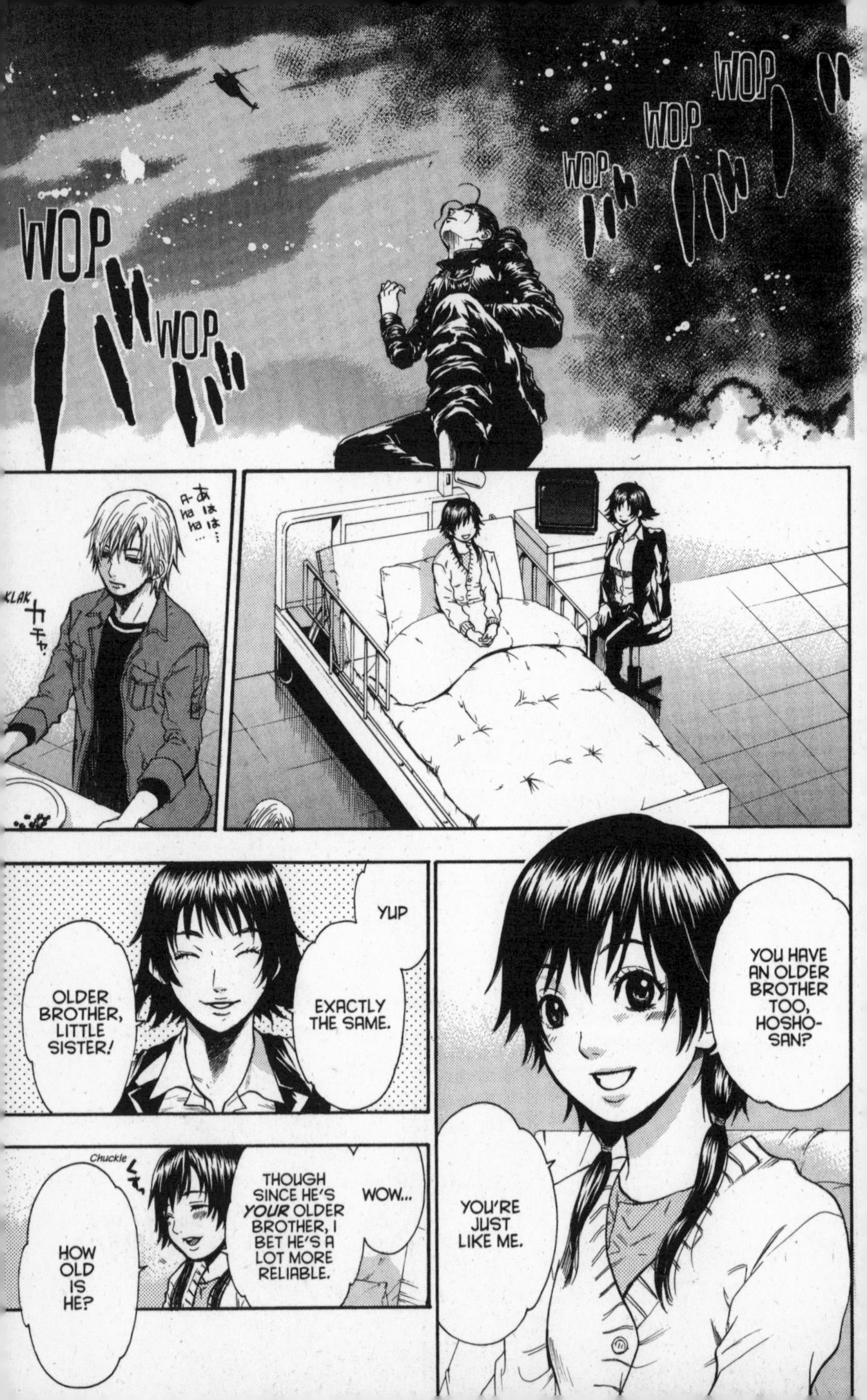
WOP
WOP
WOP
WOP
WOP
A-ha ha ha...
あはは…
KLAK
カチャ
YOU HAVE AN OLDER BROTHER TOO, HOSHO-SAN?
YOU'RE JUST LIKE ME.
YUP
EXACTLY THE SAME.
OLDER BROTHER, LITTLE SISTER!
WOW...
THOUGH SINCE HE'S *YOUR* OLDER BROTHER, I BET HE'S A LOT MORE RELIABLE.
Chuckle
HOW OLD IS HE?

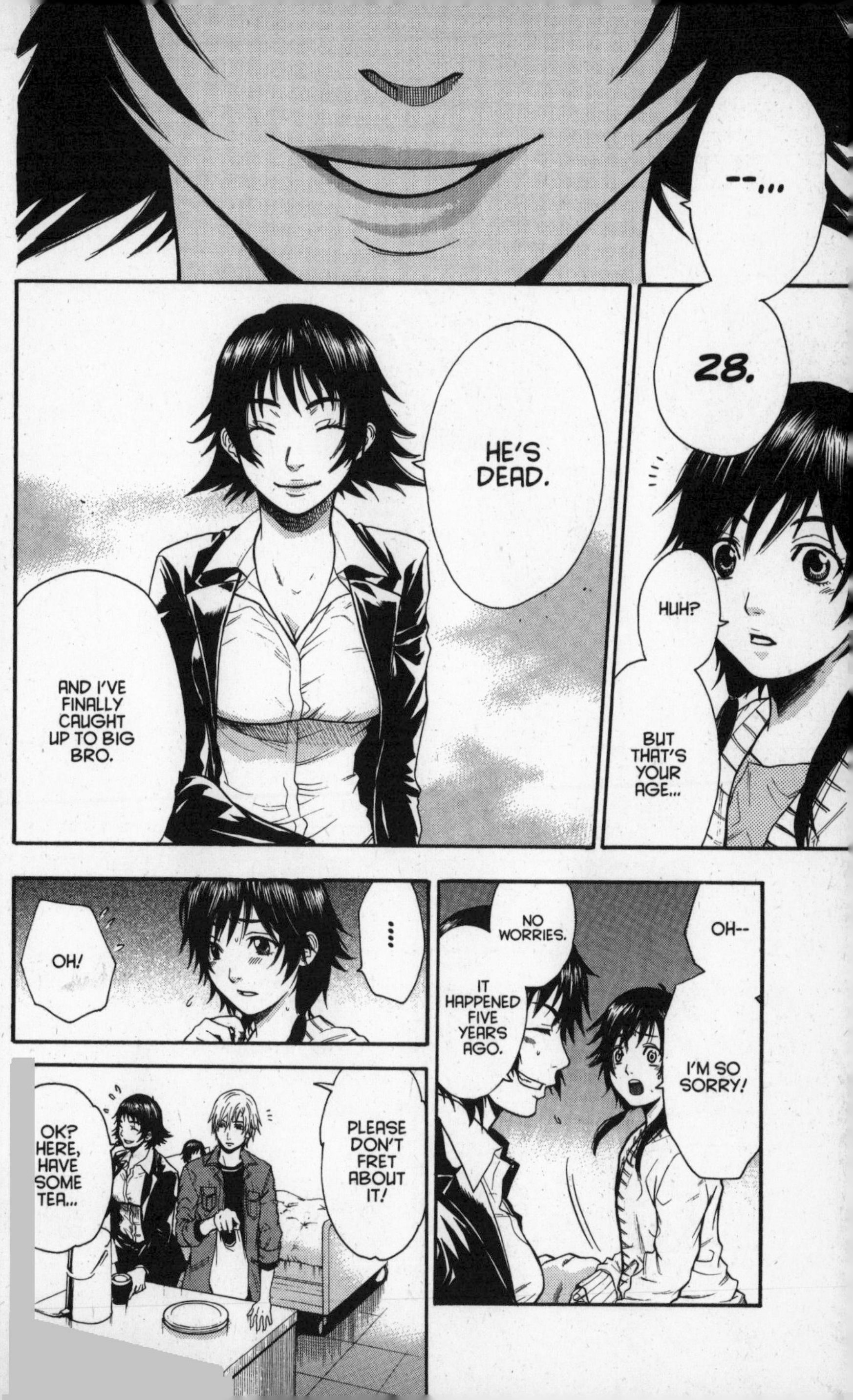
--...
28.
HUH?
BUT THAT'S YOUR AGE...
HE'S DEAD.
AND I'VE FINALLY CAUGHT UP TO BIG BRO.
OH--
I'M SO SORRY!
NO WORRIES.
IT HAPPENED FIVE YEARS AGO.
....
OH!
PLEASE DON'T FRET ABOUT IT!
OK? HERE, HAVE SOME TEA...

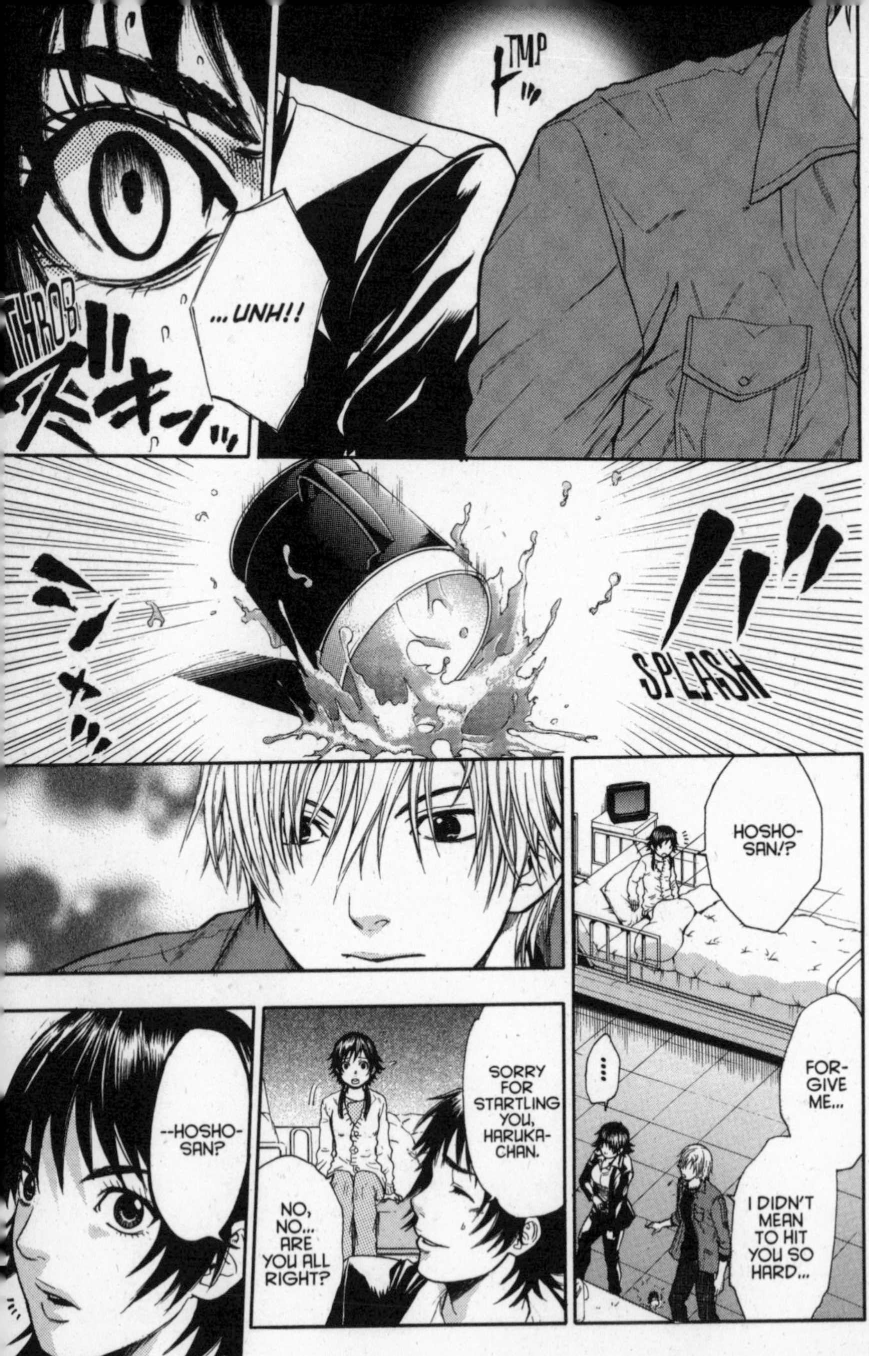
TMP
...UNH!!
THROB
SPLASH
HOSHO-SAN!?
FOR-GIVE ME...
I DIDN'T MEAN TO HIT YOU SO HARD...
....
SORRY FOR STARTLING YOU, HARUKA-CHAN.
NO, NO... ARE YOU ALL RIGHT?
--HOSHO-SAN?

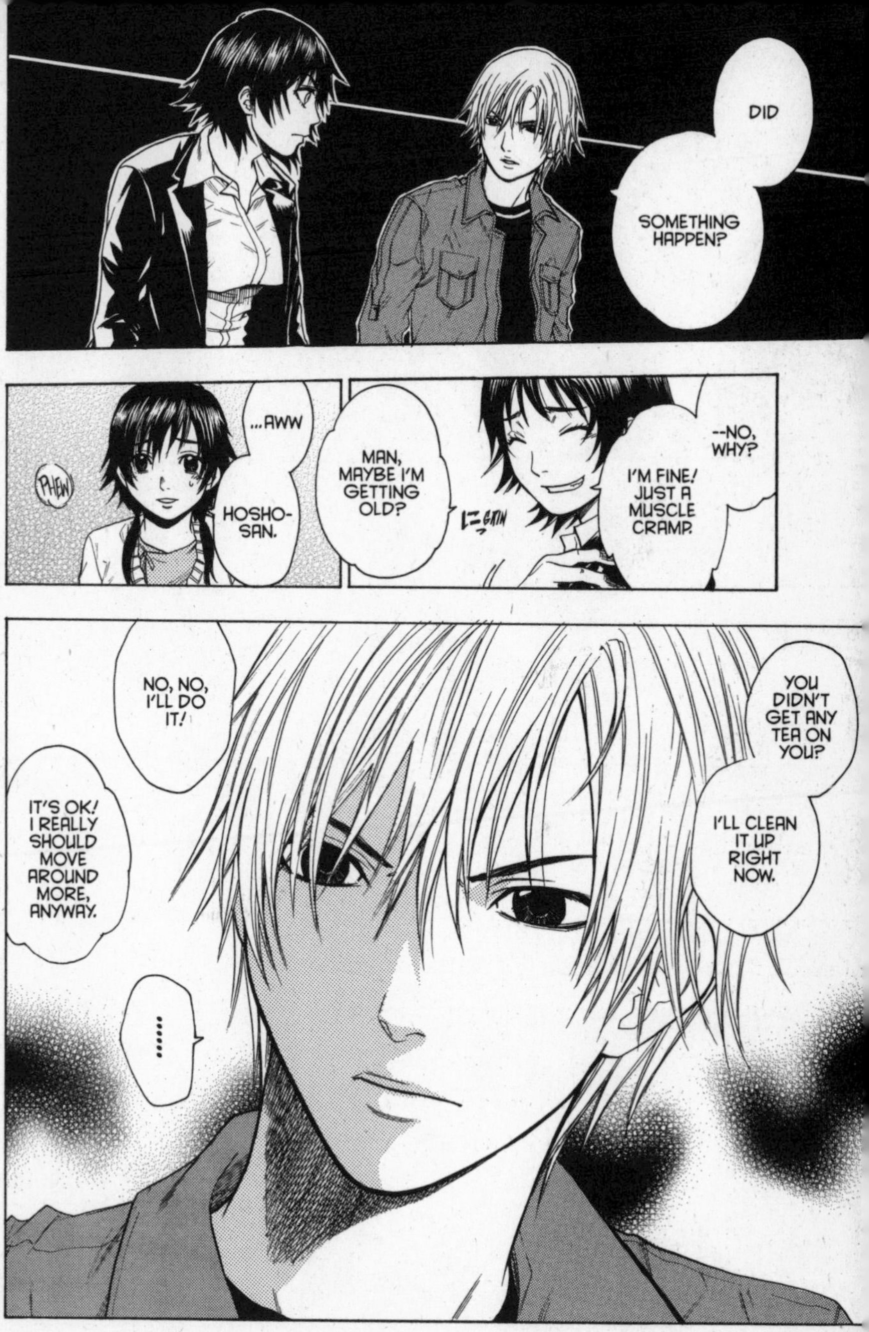
DID
SOMETHING HAPPEN?
--NO, WHY?
I'M FINE! JUST A MUSCLE CRAMP.
GRIN
MAN, MAYBE I'M GETTING OLD?
...AWW
HOSHO-SAN.
PHEW
YOU DIDN'T GET ANY TEA ON YOU?
I'LL CLEAN IT UP RIGHT NOW.
NO, NO, I'LL DO IT!
IT'S OK! I REALLY SHOULD MOVE AROUND MORE, ANYWAY.
......

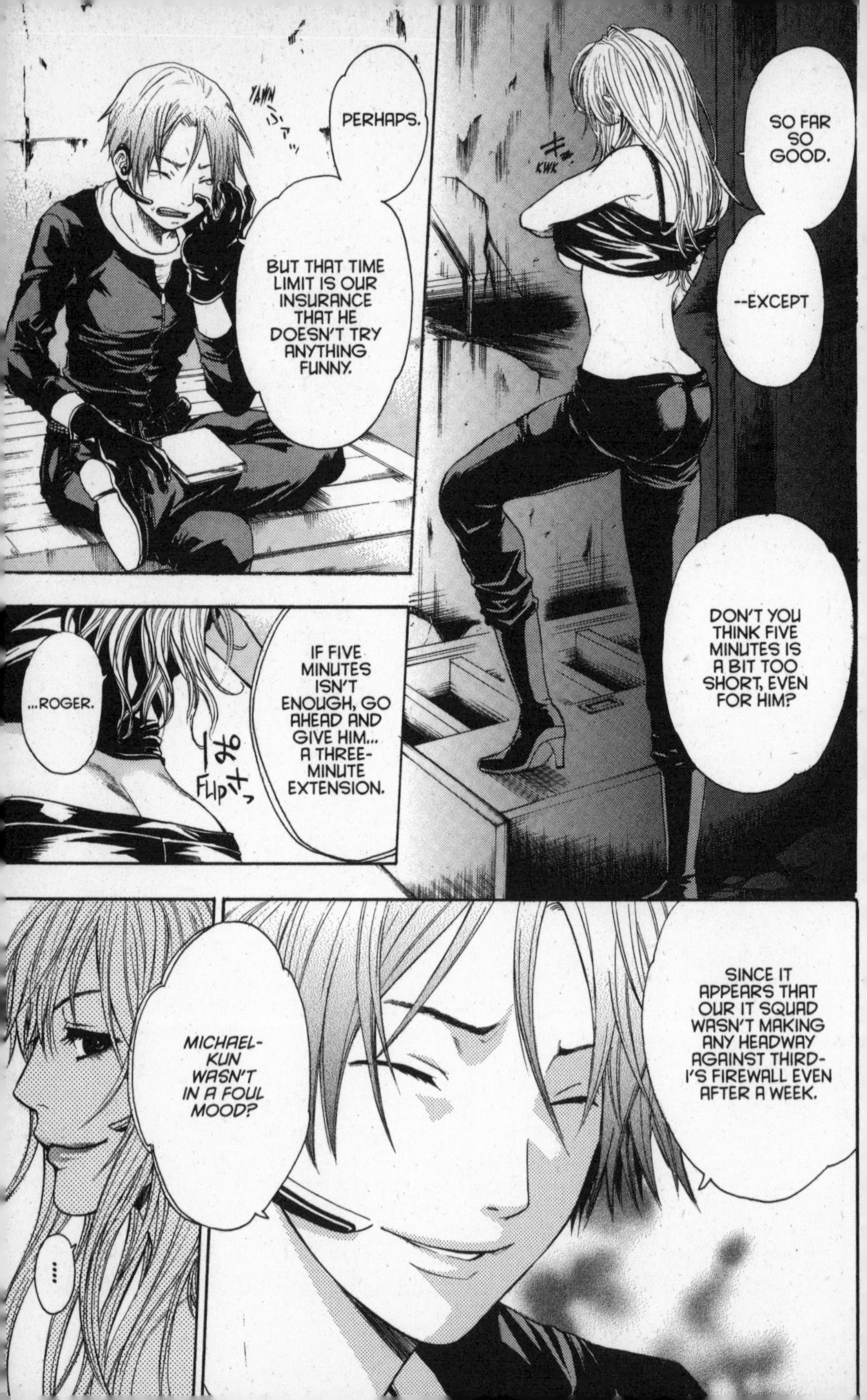
SO FAR SO GOOD.
--EXCEPT
KWK
DON'T YOU THINK FIVE MINUTES IS A BIT TOO SHORT, EVEN FOR HIM?
YAWN
PERHAPS.
BUT THAT TIME LIMIT IS OUR INSURANCE THAT HE DOESN'T TRY ANYTHING FUNNY.
IF FIVE MINUTES ISN'T ENOUGH, GO AHEAD AND GIVE HIM... A THREE-MINUTE EXTENSION.
...ROGER.
FLIP
SINCE IT APPEARS THAT OUR IT SQUAD WASN'T MAKING ANY HEADWAY AGAINST THIRD-I'S FIREWALL EVEN AFTER A WEEK.
MICHAEL-KUN WASN'T IN A FOUL MOOD?
....

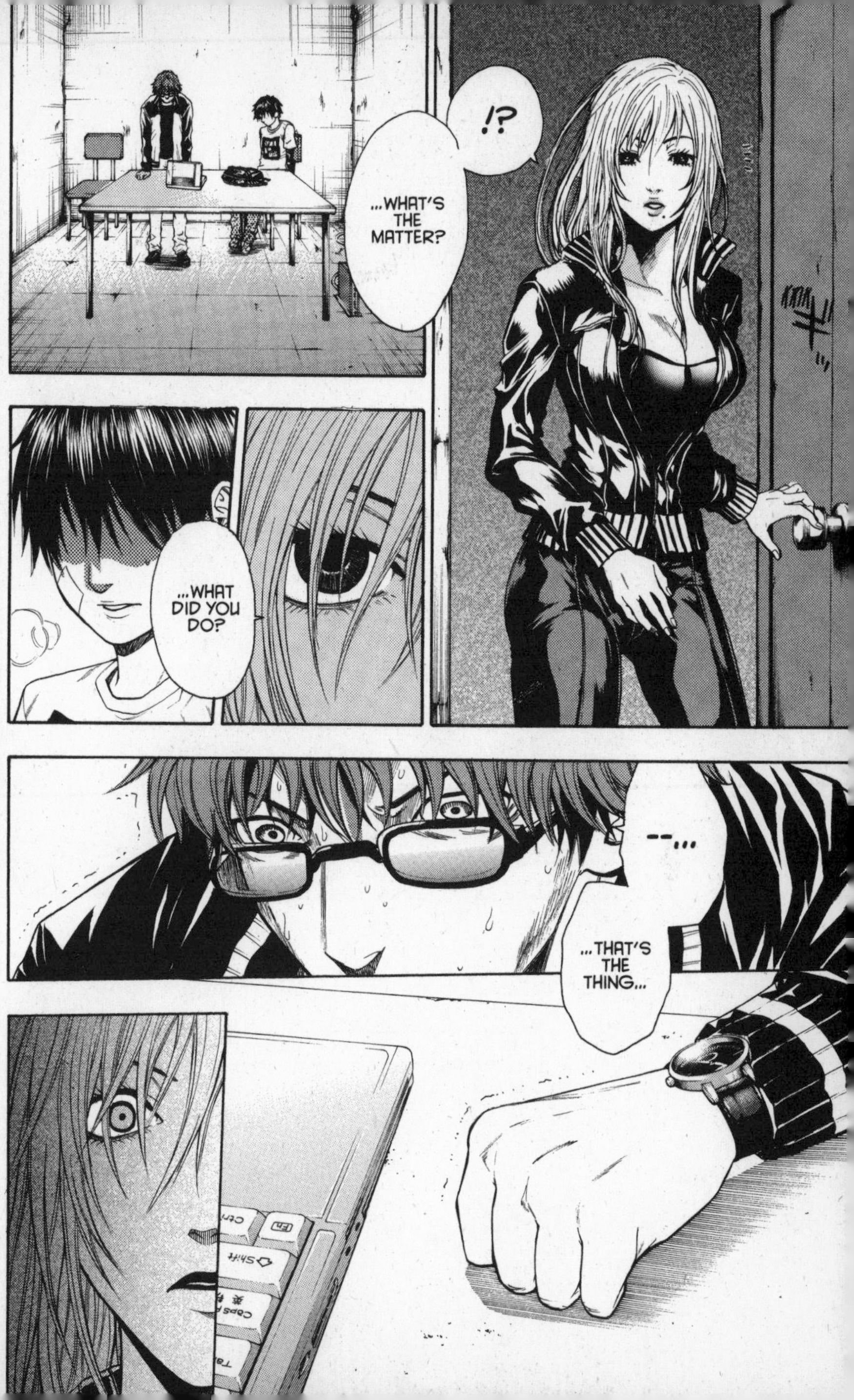
!?
...WHAT'S THE MATTER?
...WHAT DID YOU DO?
--...
...THAT'S THE THING...

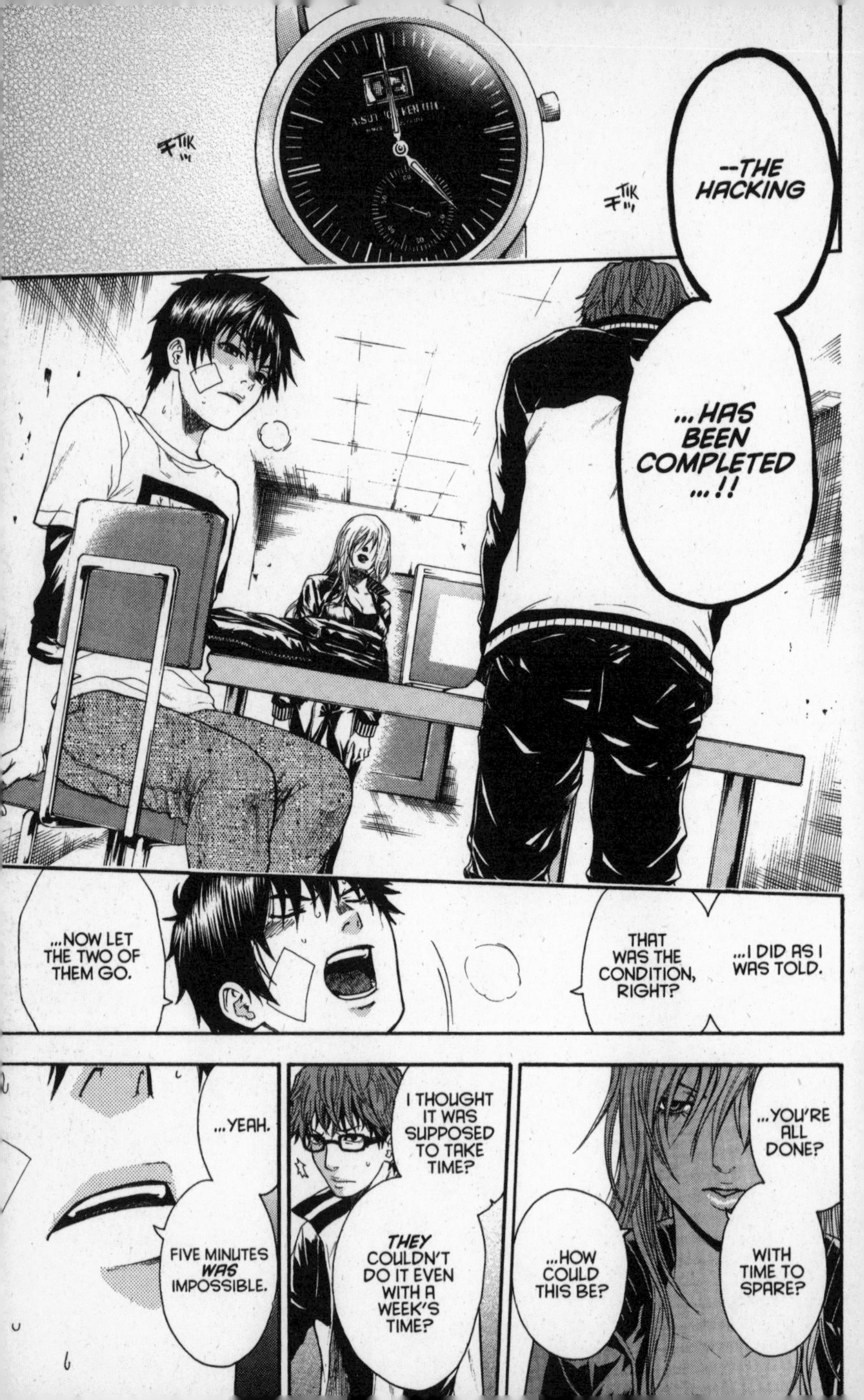
TIK
TIK
--THE HACKING
...HAS BEEN COMPLETED...!!
...I DID AS I WAS TOLD.
THAT WAS THE CONDITION, RIGHT?
...NOW LET THE TWO OF THEM GO.
...YOU'RE ALL DONE?
WITH TIME TO SPARE?
...HOW COULD THIS BE?
I THOUGHT IT WAS SUPPOSED TO TAKE TIME?
THEY COULDN'T DO IT EVEN WITH A WEEK'S TIME?
...YEAH.
FIVE MINUTES *WAS* IMPOSSIBLE.

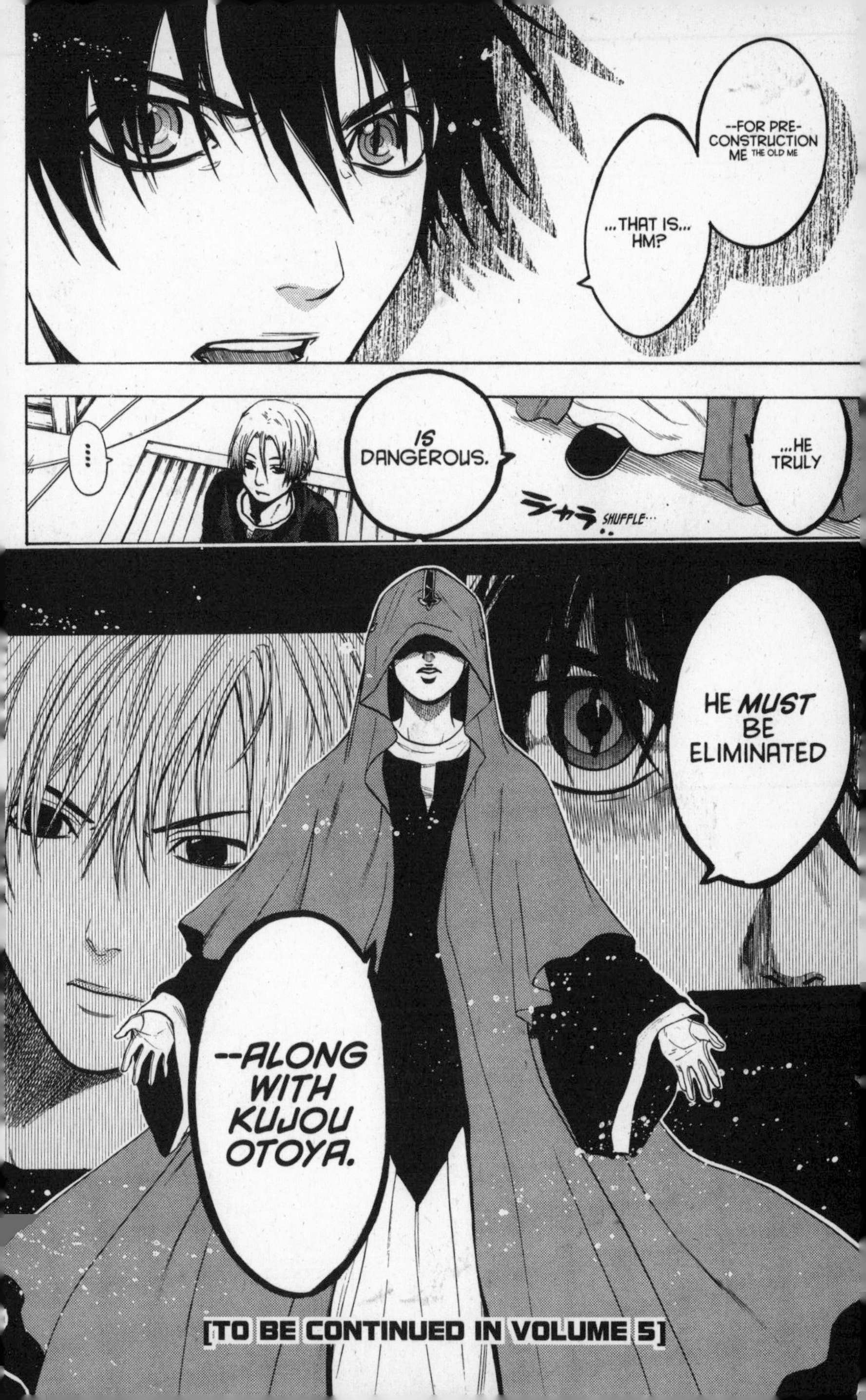
--FOR PRE-CONSTRUCTION ME THE OLD ME
...THAT IS... HM?
...HE TRULY
IS DANGEROUS.
シャラ SHUFFLE...
...
HE MUST BE ELIMINATED
--ALONG WITH KUJOU OTOYA.
[TO BE CONTINUED IN VOLUME 5]

✦ BLOODY MONDAY ✦ 4 ✦

- Many thanks
  Daiwa Mitsu   Kawabata Kunihiro   Takeda Manabu   Sasaki Keiko

- Editorial
  Sugawara-san   Sato-san   Kawakubo-san

- Manga
  Ryumon Ryou X Megumi Kouji

- THANK YOU FOR READING! •

TRANSLATION NOTES

Japanese is a tricky language for most Westerners, and translation is often more art than science. For your edification and reading pleasure, here are notes on some of the places where we could have gone in a different direction with our translation of the work, or where a Japanese cultural reference is used.

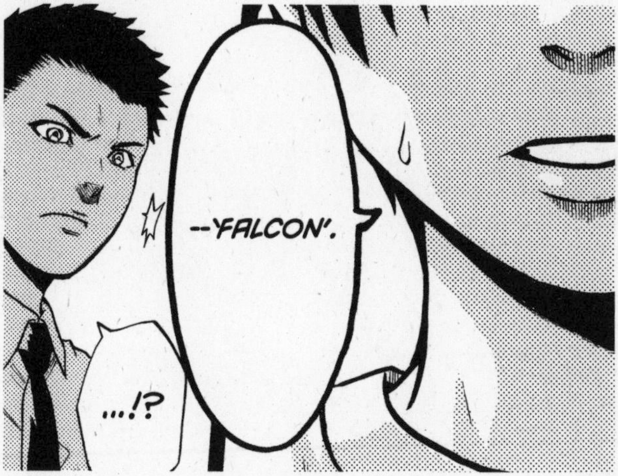
--'FALCON'.
...!?

"Falcon", page 7

Fujimaru's alter ego and hacker name. A phonetic pun, derived from the first part of his last name "Takagi"… it is only phonetic because his name uses a different kanji than that of the "taka" that means "hawk" or "falcon".

Japan Self-Defense Forces, page 9

The unified military forces of Japan established after the end of World War II and the post-war Allied Occupation. Following the ban of (offensive) rearmament as written into the post-war Japanese constitution, these military forces were originally restricted to defensive actions domestically only, although this has been relaxed in recent times to permit deployment abroad for peace-keeping and humanitarian operations.

Travel Authorization Police Certificate, page 9

Also known as a "Certificate of Criminal Record", a registered resident of Tokyo would go to the Police Clearance Certificate Office of the Tokyo Metropolitan Department if this document is requested by a foreign authority, such as an embassy or immigration agency.

MPD, page 11

MPD is short for Metropolitan Police Department, the police force that serves the entire city of Tokyo and is the largest municipal law enforcement agency in the world.

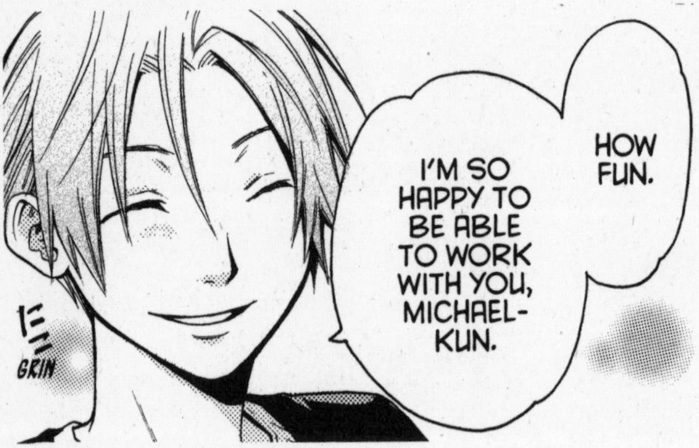
HOW FUN.
I'M SO HAPPY TO BE ABLE TO WORK WITH YOU, MICHAEL-KUN.
GRIN

Michael, page 43

While the author has indicated the Romanized spelling "Michael" for this character, the *katakana* used spell out "Mi-ha-e-ru", indicating a pronunciation that renders the "c" silent.

Vertical reading, page 69

As an addendum to Fujimaru's explanation on page 69, vertical reading as a type of word play or code has existed long before the digital age, potentially as far back as the *iroha* poem thought to have been written during the Heian period (AD 794-1179), where the *last* syllable or letter of each line revealed a distinct sentence.

CalorieFriend, page 100

A parody of or homage to Otsuka Pharmaceutical's CalorieMate brand of energy-supplement foods. The actual products come in three forms: boxed cookie- or bar-like blocks (as does CalorieFriend here), jelly foil packs, and drink cans.

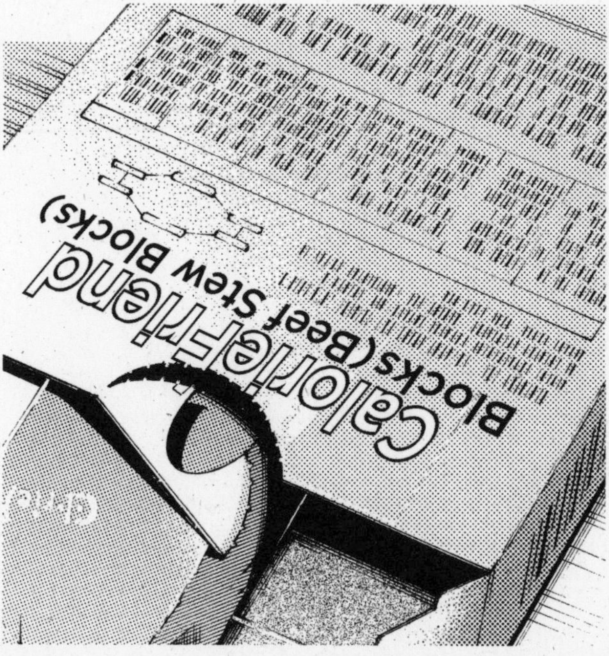
Blocks (Beef Stew Blocks)
CalorieFriend
(Blocks)

Preview of

BLOODY
MONDAY

VOLUME 5

We're pleased to present you an unlettered preview
from *Bloody Monday*, volume 5.
Please check our website
(www.kodanshacomics.com)
to see when this volume will be available.

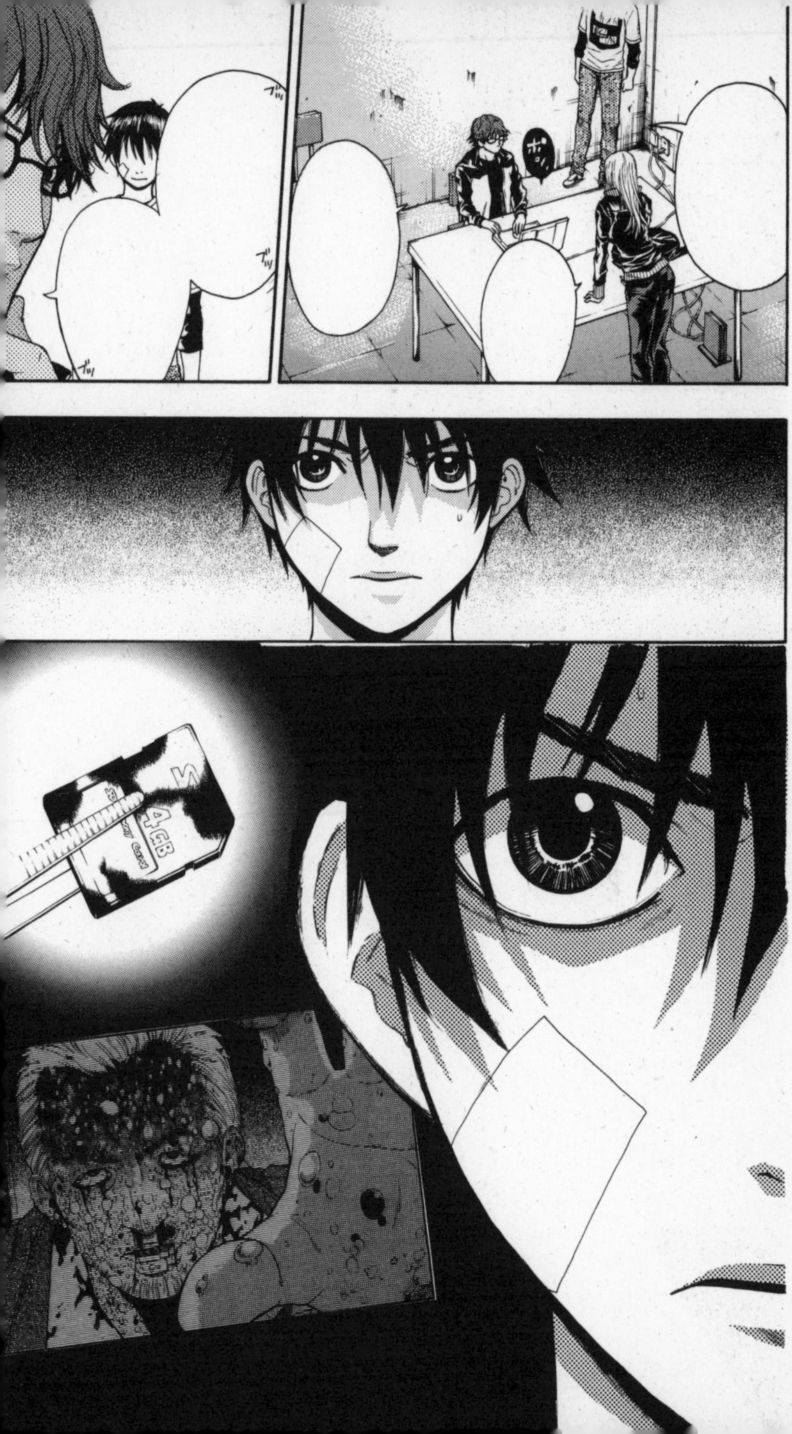
ポン
ブツ
ブツ
ブツ
4GB

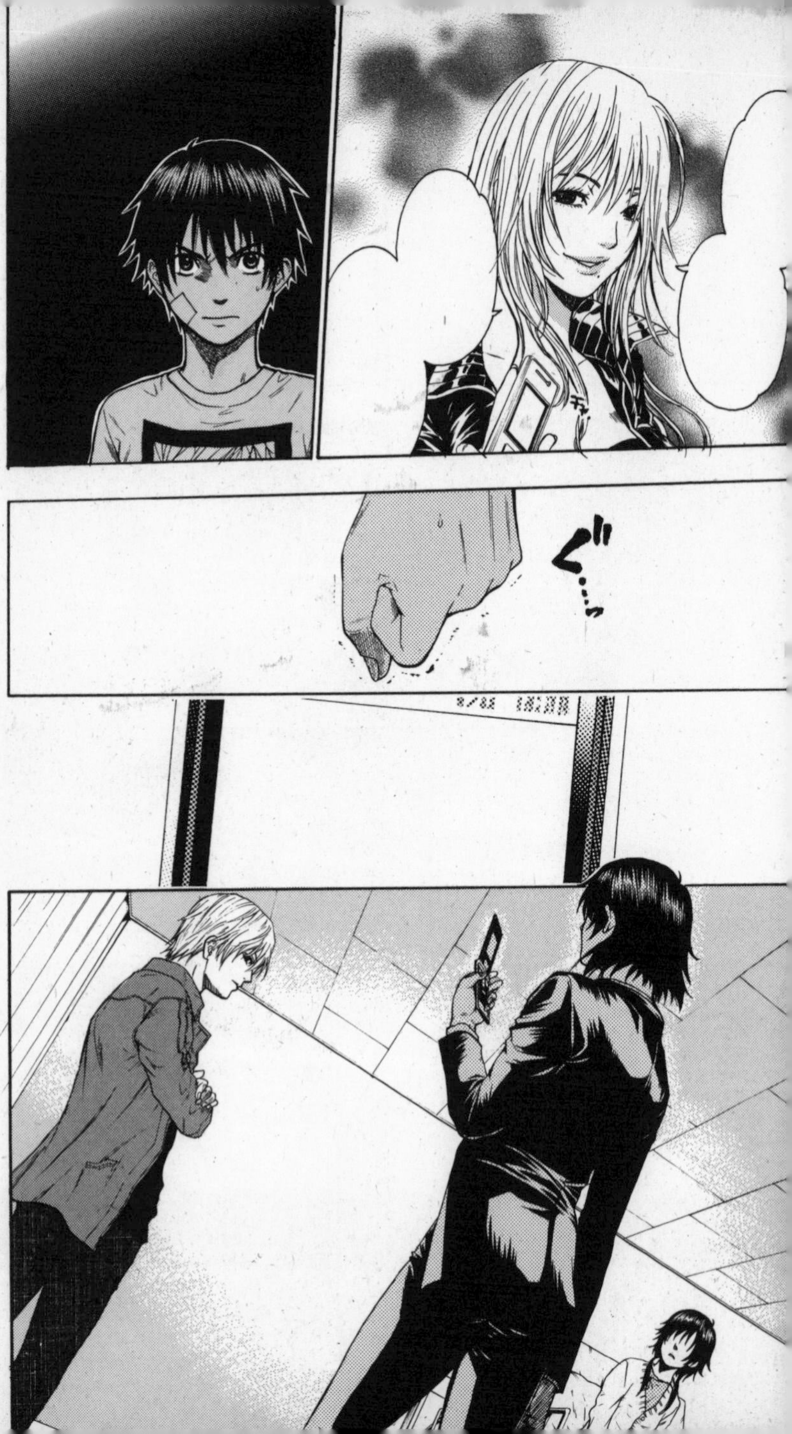
チャ
ぐ…っ

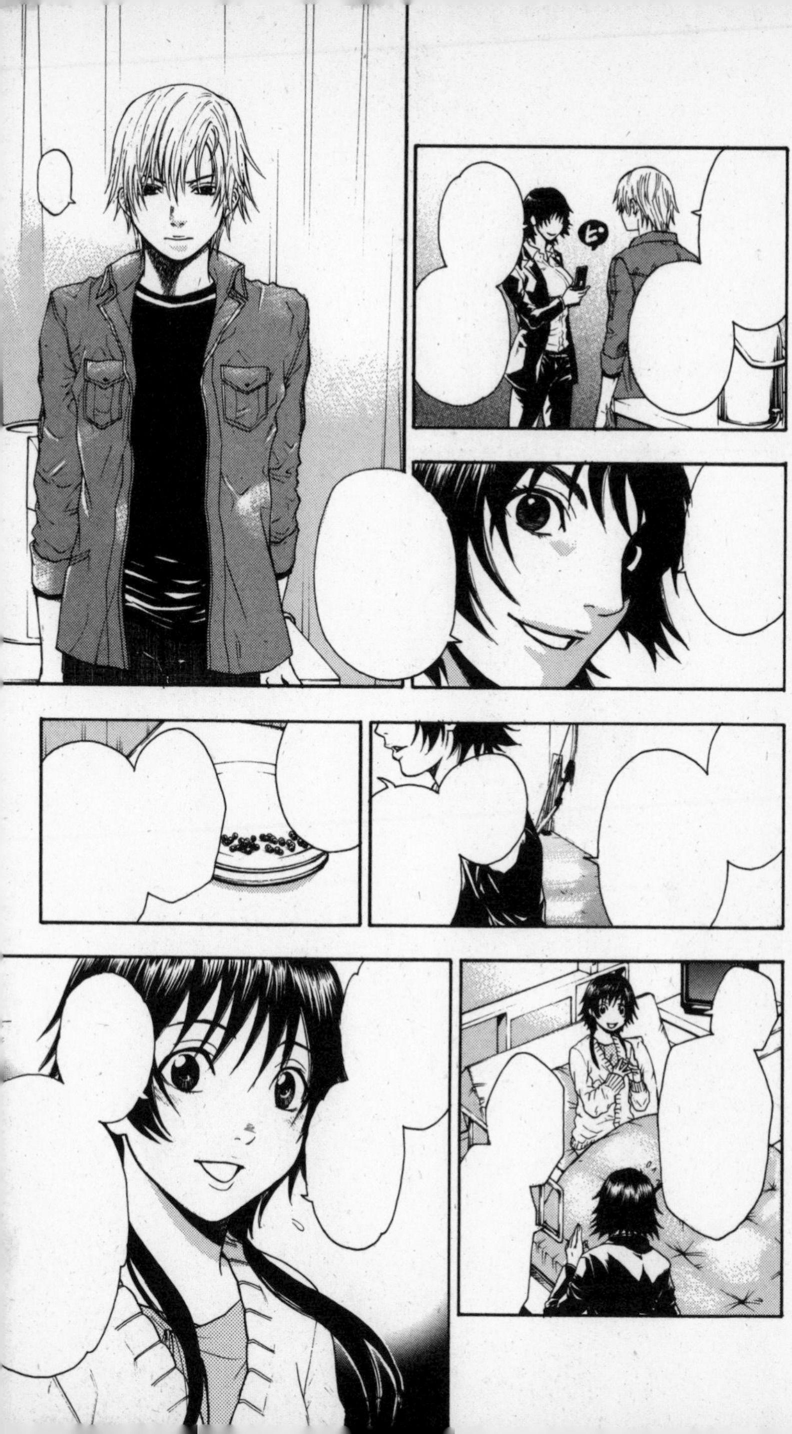
ピ

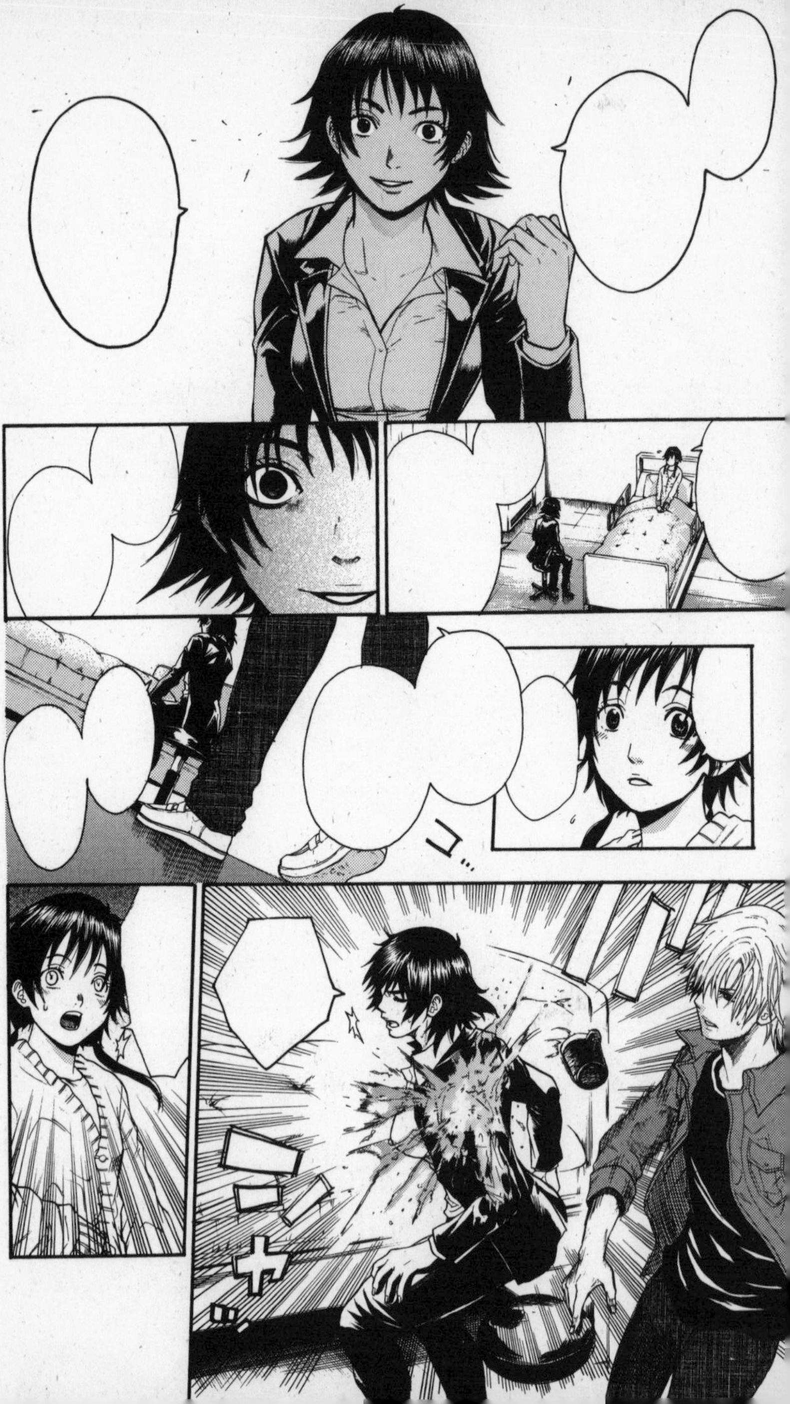

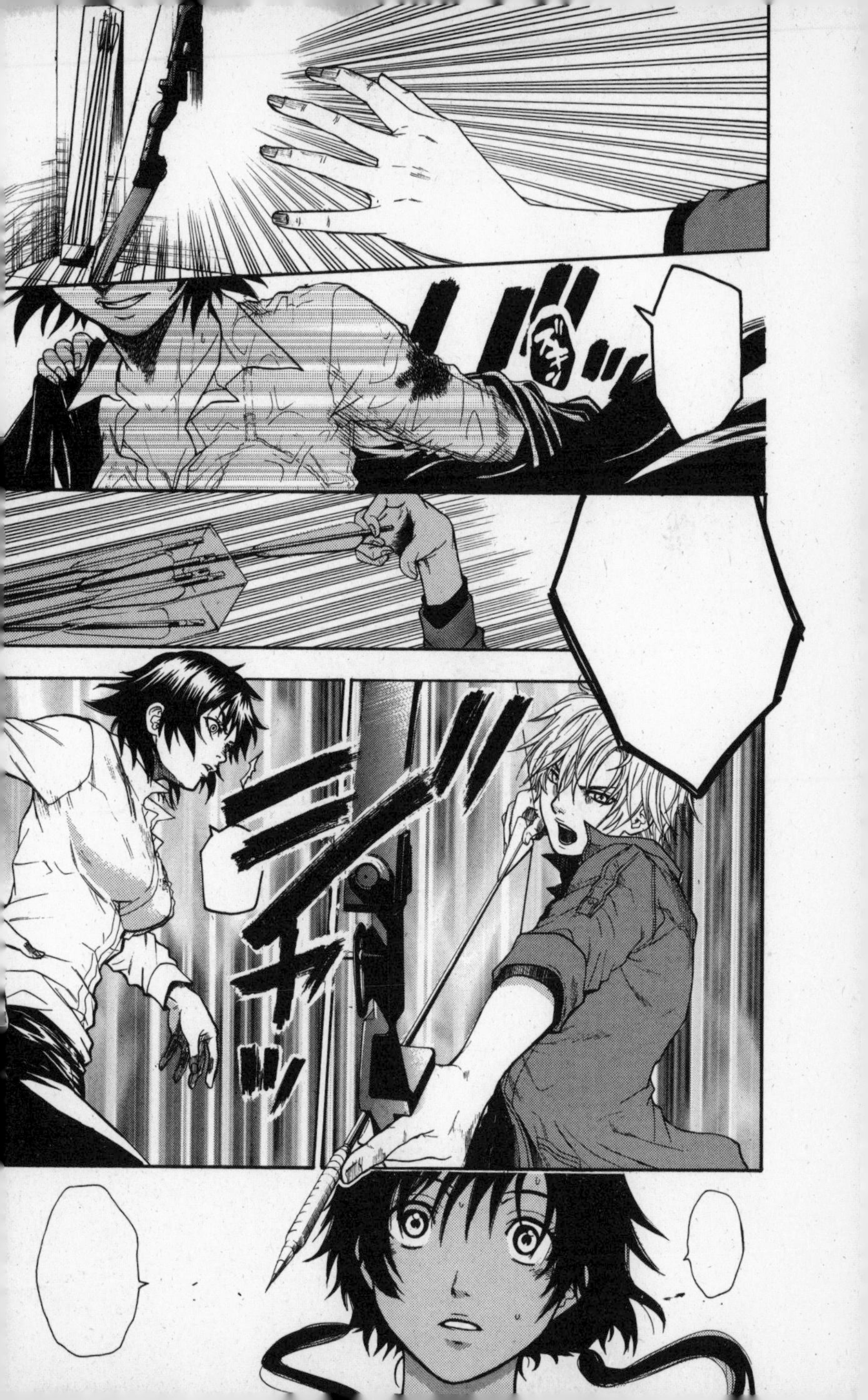
ズキッ

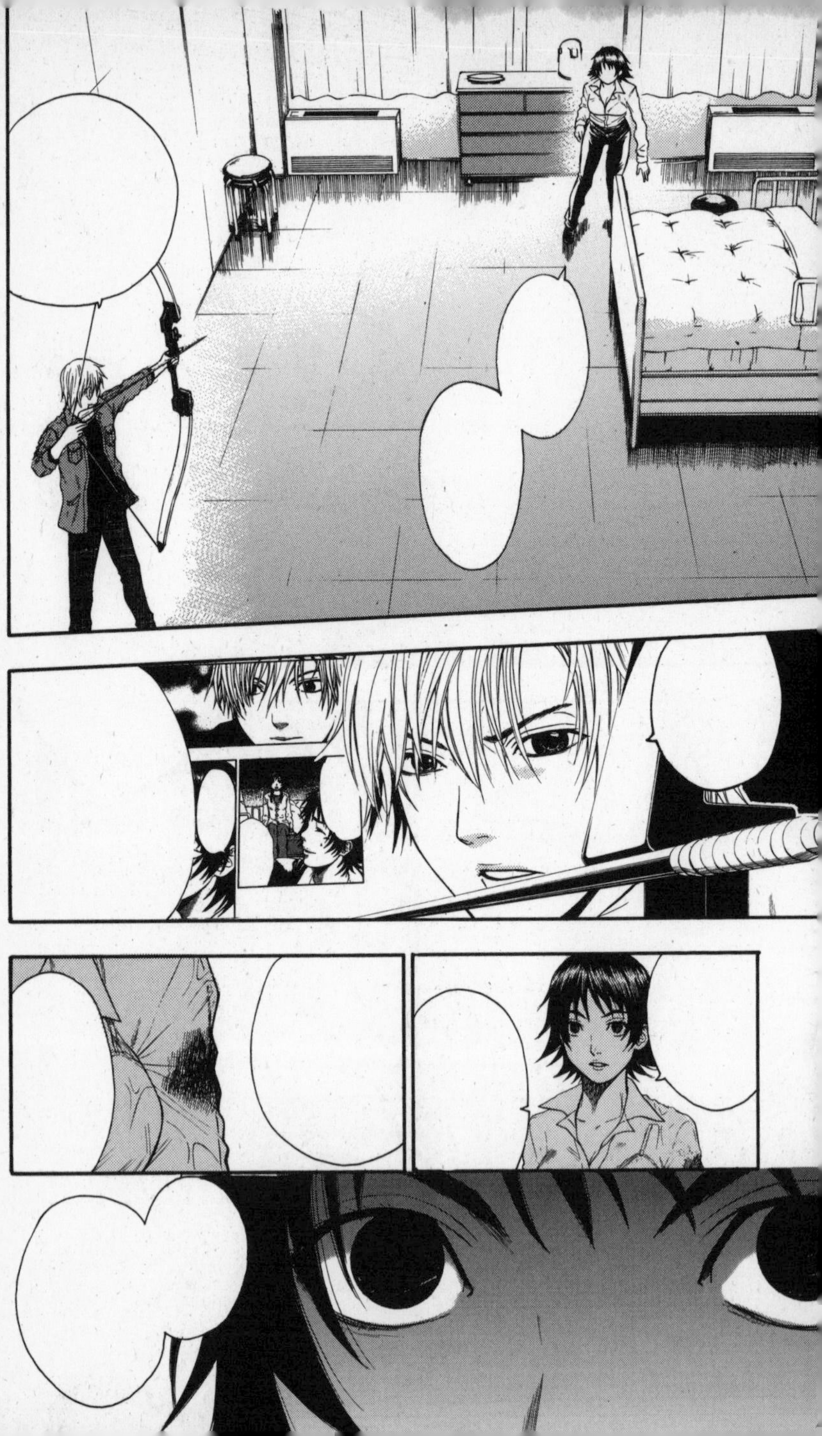

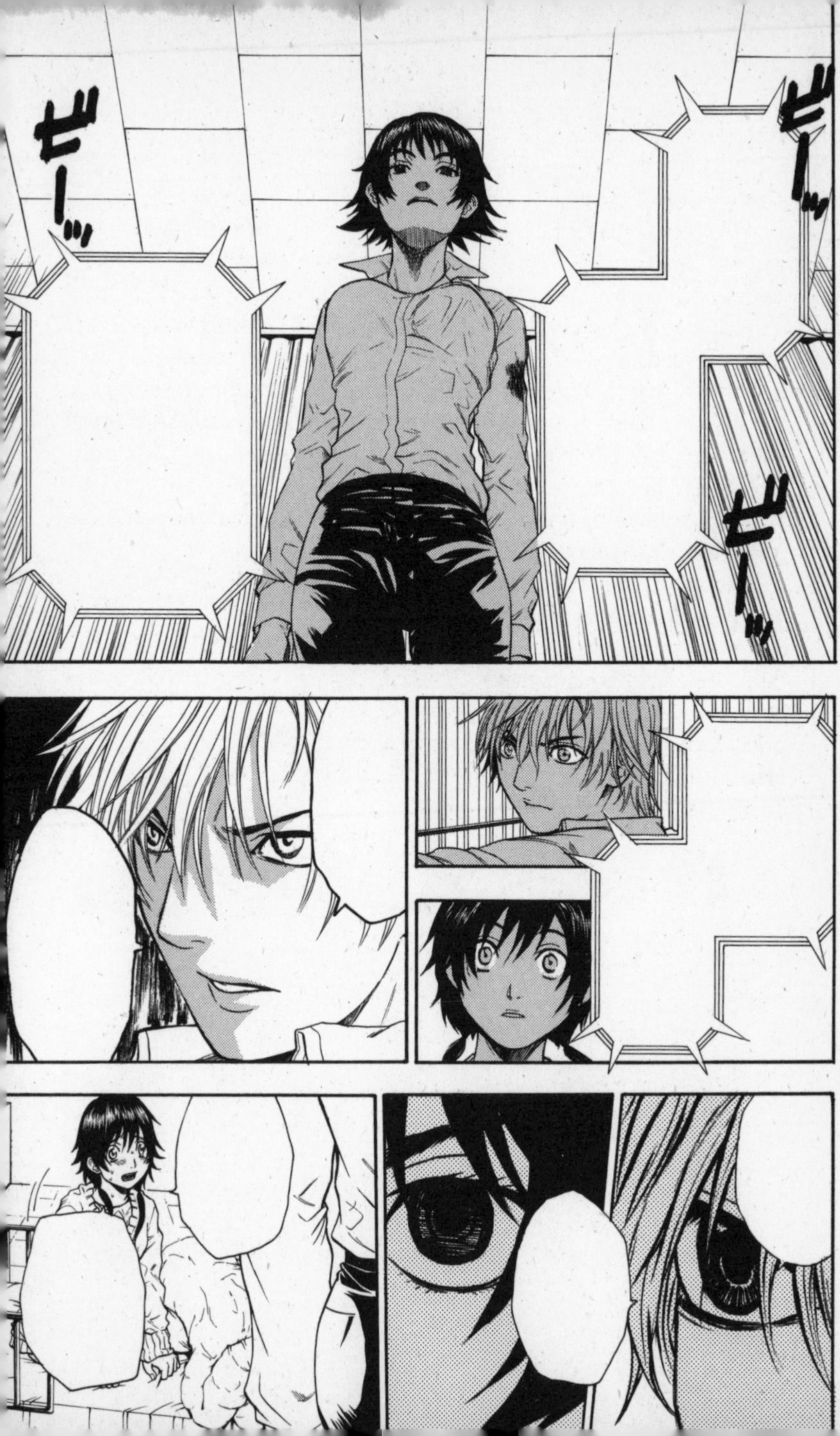
ゼーッ
ゼーッ
ゼーッ

HONORIFICS EXPLAINED

Throughout the Kodansha Comics books, you will find Japanese honorifics left intact in the translations. For those not familiar with how the Japanese use honorifics and, more important, how they differ from American honorifics, we present this brief overview.

Politeness has always been a critical facet of Japanese culture. Ever since the feudal era, when Japan was a highly stratified society, use of honorifics—which can be defined as polite speech that indicates relationship or status—has played an essential role in the Japanese language. When addressing someone in Japanese, an honorific usually takes the form of a suffix attached to one's name (example: "Asuna-san"), is used as a title at the end of one's name, or appears in place of the name itself (example: "Negi-sensei," or simply "Sensei!").

Honorifics can be expressions of respect or endearment. In the context of manga and anime, honorifics give insight into the nature of the relationship between characters. Many English translations leave out these important honorifics and therefore distort the feel of the original Japanese. Because Japanese honorifics contain nuances that English honorifics lack, it is our policy at Kodansha Comics not to translate them. Here, instead, is a guide to some of the honorifics you may encounter in Kodansha Comics.

-san: This is the most common honorific and is equivalent to Mr., Miss, Ms., or Mrs. It is the all-purpose honorific and can be used in any situation where politeness is required.

-sama: This is one level higher than "-san" and is used to confer great respect.

-dono: This comes from the word "tono," which means "lord." It is an even higher level than "-sama" and confers utmost respect.

-kun: This suffix is used at the end of boys' names to express familiarity or endearment. It is also sometimes used by men among friends, or when addressing someone younger or of a lower station.

-chan: This is used to express endearment, mostly toward girls. It is also used for little boys, pets, and even among lovers. It gives a sense of childish cuteness.

Bozu: This is an informal way to refer to a boy, similar to the English terms "kid" and "squirt."

Sempai/
Senpai: This title suggests that the addressee is one's senior in a group or organization. It is most often used in a school setting, where underclassmen refer to their upperclassmen as "sempai." It can also be used in the workplace, such as when a newer employee addresses an employee who has seniority in the company.

Kohai: This is the opposite of "sempai" and is used toward underclassmen in school or newcomers in the workplace. It connotes that the addressee is of a lower station.

Sensei: Literally meaning "one who has come before," this title is used for teachers, doctors, or masters of any profession or art.

-[blank]: This is usually forgotten in these lists, but it is perhaps the most significant difference between Japanese and English. The lack of honorific means that the speaker has permission to address the person in a very intimate way. Usually, only family, spouses, or very close friends have this kind of permission. Known as *yobisute*, it can be gratifying when someone who has earned the intimacy starts to call one by one's name without an honorific. But when that intimacy hasn't been earned, it can be very insulting.

Bloody Monday volume 4 is a work of fiction. Names, characters, places, and incidents are the products of the author's imagination or are used fictitiously. Any resemblance to actual events, locales, or persons, living or dead, is entirely coincidental.

A Kodansha Comics Trade Paperback Original

Published in the United States by Kodansha Comics,
an imprint of Kodansha USA Publishing, LLC, New York.

Publication rights for this English edition arranged through Kodansha Ltd, Tokyo.

First published in Japan in 2008 by Kodansha Ltd., Tokyo.

ISBN 978-1-61262-040-4
Original cover design by Takashi Shimoyama (Red Rooster)

Printed in the United States of America.

www.kodanshacomics.com

9 8 7 6 5 4 3 2 1

Translator: Mari Morimoto
Lettering: Karl Felton

TOMARE!

[STOP!]

You are going the wrong way!

Manga is a completely different type of reading experience.

To start at the *beginning,* go to the *end*!

That's right! Authentic manga is read the traditional Japanese way—from right to left, exactly the opposite of how American books are read. It's easy to follow: Just go to the other end of the book, and read each page—and each panel—from the right side to the left side, starting at the top right. Now you're experiencing manga as it was meant to be.